the
classic
1000
student
recipes

Everyday Eating made more exciting

		QUANTITY	AMOUNT
New Classic 1000 Recipes	0-572-02868-7	£6.99	
Classic 1000 Chinese Recipes	0-572-02849-0	£6.99	
Classic 1000 Indian Recipes	0-572-02807-5	£6.99	
Classic 1000 Italian Recipes	0-572-02848-2	£6.99	
Classic 1000 Pasta & Rice Recipes	0-572-02867-9	£6.99	
Classic 1000 Vegetarian Recipes	0-572-02808-3	£6.99	
Classic 1000 Quick and Easy Recipes	0-572-02909-8	£6.99	
Classic 1000 Cake & Bake Recipes	0-572-02803-2	£6.99	
Classic 1000 Calorie-counted Recipes	0-572-02405-3	£5.99	
Classic 1000 Microwave Recipes	0-572-01945-9	£5.99	
Classic 1000 Dessert Recipes	0-572-02542-4	£6.99	
Classic 1000 Low-Fat Recipes	0-572-02804-0	£6.99	
Classic 1000 Chicken Recipes	0-572-02646-3	£5.99	
Classic 1000 Seafood Recipes	0-572-02696-X	£6.99	
Classic 1000 Beginners' Recipes	0-572-02967-5	£6.99	

Please allow 75p per book for post & packing in UK *POST & PACKING
Overseas customers £1 per book. **TOTAL**

Foulsham books are available from local bookshops. Should you have any difficulty obtaining supplies please send Cheque/Eurocheque/Postal Order (£ sterling only) made out to BSBP or debit my credit card:

☐ ACCESS ☐ VISA ☐ MASTER CARD ☐☐☐☐☐☐☐☐☐☐☐☐☐☐☐☐

EXPIRY DATE   SIGNATURE

ALL ORDERS TO:
Foulsham Books, PO Box 29, Douglas, Isle of Man IM99 1BQ
Telephone 01624 836000, Fax 01624 837033, Internet http://www.bookpost.co.uk

NAME

ADDRESS

Please allow 28 days for delivery.
Please tick box if you do not wish to receive any additional information ☐
Prices and availability subject to change without notice.

the classic 1000 student recipes

carolyn humphries

foulsham

LONDON • NEW YORK • TORONTO • SYDNEY

foulsham

The Publishing House, Bennetts Close, Cippenham, Slough, Berkshire, SL1 5AP, England

ISBN 0-572-02981-0

Cover photograph © Anthony Blake picture library

A CIP record for this book is available from the British Library

Printed in Great Britain by Creative Print & Design (Wales), Ebbw Vale

contents

InTRODUCTiON

You're starting to fend for yourself for the first time. You've probably never had to cook in your life and the chances are you are used to some pretty good food at home, so you don't want to live on just cold baked beans! Worse than that, not only do you have to make your own meals, but you're probably also finding you don't have much money to spend on them.

In my experience, not many students are very keen on cooking. However, there are three things they do want: tasty, healthy food (well, mostly healthy) that they can prepare quickly and easily in a basic kitchen; plenty of different ideas to suit everyone's taste; and as much money as possible left for books and beer. I cover all of that in this book. And I don't assume you are a culinary genius – everything is explained in plain, straightforward language.

There are lots of recipe books for students, but this one is unique in the way the recipes are organised. For the first batch of recipes, all you need is a knife and a chopping board (and, preferably, a plate to eat from) to make tasty meals with little or no effort at all. Then, from chapters full of brilliant ideas using the most basic utensils – nothing more than a kettle and a toaster – we work right through to slap-up meals to impress your friends.

Also, because kitchens in student accommodation are notoriously badly equipped, I've designed the recipes so you don't have to have any proper measuring spoons or scales – all you need are ordinary spoons and a mug. I've included plenty of recipes for vegetarians, too, and they are all clearly marked with a **V** – so non-meat-eating students needn't plough through every recipe wondering if they can eat it or not!

So this is the only student cookery book you'll need. It'll help you eat well when you've practically no equipment, no ideas or inclination, and very little money. Enjoy it – and recommend it to your friends!

useful equipment

Your student accommodation may have a ready-equipped kitchen, but it's more likely you're putting together a few items 'borrowed' from home and then buying others for yourself. The lists in this chapter provide a rough guide to what you do need – and what you don't. You don't want to waste money for beer – sorry, for books – on smart utensils and fancy ingredients that you will almost certainly never use. So I suggest that you start with the bare minimum, then add to your stock as and when you need things.

You can often pick up utensils at car boot sales – they may look a bit grubby, but they probably only need a good scrub.

If you are really into cooking, however, you may want to ask for a gadget or two as a going-away or Christmas gift. For example, I haven't included an electric steamer on this list (because you can just use a colander over a saucepan) but many students have them as they do save a lot of fuel.

You can't really do without

Bottle opener

Can opener (although many cans have ring-pull tops)

Chopping boards: It's a good idea to have several different ones, each with a specific use. I have one for raw meat; one for strong-smelling foods like onions; one for fruit and vegetables; and one for bread

Corkscrew

Fish slice

Frying pan (skillet)

Grater: A round or square one with a top handle is easier to use than a flat one

Kettle

Kitchen scissors

Potato peeler

Saucepans: Ideally 1 small, 1 medium and 1 large, all with lids

Sharp knives: At least 1 small (for vegetables etc.) and 1 large (for cutting up meat etc.), plus a bread knife with a serrated edge

Wooden spoons

You'll probably need

Baking (cookie) sheet: For everything from pizza to oven chips (fries)

Baking tins (pans): Square or rectangular, various sizes

Colander: For straining cooked vegetables etc. A metal one is best because you can use it for steaming as well

Draining spoon (long-handled, with holes in the bowl)

Hand blender

Measuring jug (useful but not necessary for this book!)

Potato masher

Sandwich maker

Toaster

Whisk: A balloon one is ideal for making sauces etc.

You'll only need if you are keen on cooking

Casserole dishes (Dutch ovens): Various sizes, including a flameproof one for use on the hob (although you can use a saucepan)

Omelette pan (non-stick is a good idea)

Ovenproof dishes: Various sizes, oval or round and rectangular or square

Rolling pin (not vital as a clean bottle will do)

Sieve (strainer): Metal or plastic with a fine mesh for making purées and straining foods

Wok

Stocking Up Before You Start

Most students persuade their parents to do a big shop for them before they start term. The following list contains all the basics but, obviously, it's up to you and what you are likely to need, so use it as a guide only.

Ingredients to keep in the cupboard

Baking powder

Bicarbonate of soda (baking soda)

Breakfast cereal

Bulghar (cracked wheat)

Cocoa (unsweetened chocolate) powder

Couscous

Dried herbs: Mixed, basil, chives, oregano, thyme, mint, sage, parsley

Dried milk (non-fat dry milk)

Dried minced (ground) onion and **dried red and green (bell) peppers:** Not vital but great for brightening up rice or pasta and they keep for ages

Drinking (sweetened) chocolate powder: An instant chocolate drink powder, with added milk powder is good

Flour: Plain (all-purpose) and self-raising (self-rising)

Garlic purée (paste): Great if you can't be bothered to crush whole cloves. Use ½–1 tsp per garlic clove

Honey, clear

Horseradish relish

Instant coffee

Lemon juice: Not vital but a bottle will keep in the fridge for ages and is often better than vinegar

Marmalade

Marmite or other yeast extract

Mayonnaise

Mustard: Made English and Dijon

Oil: Sunflower and, perhaps, olive

Passata (sieved tomatoes) or jars of tomato pasta sauce

Pasta: Quick-cook macaroni and/or other shapes, spaghetti, lasagne sheets, stuffed tortellini, Chinese egg noodles, flavoured 'instant' noodles

Pepper: Black (peppercorns in a mill, preferably) and ground white

Rice: Long-grain, risotto and round-grain (pudding)

Salt

Sugar: If you're only buying one sort, use caster (superfine) for everything. But you could have granulated, icing (confectioners'), light and dark brown as well

Spices: Ground cayenne and/or chilli powder, cinnamon, mixed (apple-pie) spice, ginger, cumin, coriander (cilantro), curry powder or paste, grated nutmeg

Stock cubes: Vegetable, chicken, beef

Table sauces: Ketchup (catsup), brown, soy, Worcestershire, Tabasco or other chilli

Tomato purée (paste): Tubes keep best

Vinegar: Red or white wine or cider

Cans for convenience

Baked beans: Be wary of economy brands – too much liquid and not many beans!

Corned beef and/or ham

Custard

Fish: Mackerel, pilchards or sardines, tuna (check the label for 'dolphin friendly')

Fruits: Any you like. Pineapple is very useful in cooking

Minced (ground) beef: Great with pasta

Pulses: Red kidney beans, butter (lima) beans, cannellini beans, etc. Economy brands are okay here

Rice pudding

Soup: Condensed mushroom, chicken and tomato are all ideal for sauces

Tomatoes: Ready-chopped varieties are good for quick sauces but may be more expensive. If using whole canned tomatoes instead, break them up with a wooden spoon. Economy brands are fine

Vegetables: Sweetcorn (corn), peas, carrots, green beans, mixed diced

Perishables

Bread/rolls/pitta breads: Store in the freezer if you have one, and take out when required. You can toast slices of bread from frozen

Butter/margarine: Margarine is cheaper than butter although the flavour isn't as good in some recipes. If you are going to cook with it, check on the label that it is suitable – some low-fat varieties turn into a watery slush when heated

Cheese: Cheddar and grated Parmesan, plus others as you need

Eggs, medium

Fresh fruit: Apples, oranges, lemons, bananas

Milk: Keep a carton in the freezer so you won't run out but remember, it takes ages to thaw and will need a good shake once defrosted

Yoghurt: Plain is good for sauces and dressings as well as for breakfast with cereal or with honey or fruit for dessert

Fresh vegetables: Potatoes, onions, carrots, mushrooms, (bell) peppers, green veg and salad stuffs

Frozen foods: Peas, beans, fish, minced (ground) beef, lamb, chicken or pork. Beware of 'economy' mince, which may be very fatty, so is not the bargain it seems

Health and Hygiene

Food hygiene isn't complicated. Most of it is just common sense. However, it is important, as it will stop you giving yourself – or your friends – food poisoning.

Preparation and storage

- Always wash your hands before preparing food.

- Always wash and dry fresh fruit and vegetables before use.

- Don't keep tasting and stirring with the same spoon, and don't put your fingers in the food, then lick them. Use a clean spoon every time you taste the food.

- Never use a cloth to wipe down a chopping board you have been using for cutting up meat, for instance, then use the same one to wipe down your work surfaces – you will simply spread germs. Always wash your cloth well in hot, soapy water and, ideally, use an anti-bacterial kitchen cleaner on all surfaces too.

- Always transfer leftovers to a clean container and cover with a lid, clingfilm (plastic wrap) or foil. Leave until completely cold, then store in the fridge. Never put any warm food in the fridge.

- Don't store raw and cooked meat together in the fridge – keep them separate, preferably on different shelves. Raw meat is best kept on the bottom shelf, so it can't drip over other foods.

- Keep all perishable foods wrapped separately. Don't overfill the fridge or it will remain too warm.

- When reheating food, always make sure it is piping hot throughout. If you just warm it, you will simply wake up any bugs lurking inside, without actually killing them off (see Reheating, pages 17–18).

- Never reheat previously cooked food more than once.

- Don't re-freeze raw foods that have defrosted unless you cook them first.

Eat well, stay well

To enjoy college to the full, you want to remain fit and healthy. You also want your brain to function with optimum efficiency! To achieve this, you do need to eat a properly balanced diet. There's nothing fancy about this and it doesn't mean you have to eat expensive food or cranky stuff. Just try to include the following in your meals every day.

- **At least five portions of fruit and vegetables.** That can include a glass of fruit juice, and canned and frozen stuff as well as fresh. These help maintain your body and mind, supplying vital vitamins and minerals.

- **Plenty of starchy carbohydrates.** These come from bread, cereals, potatoes, pasta, rice, etc., and should form at least half of your daily food. They will help your body to produce energy and keep you warm.

- **At least two portions of protein.** Protein is contained in meat, poultry, fish, eggs, dairy products like cheese, milk and yoghurt, pulses (dried peas, lentils and beans – including baked beans), tofu, Quorn and soya products.

- **Lots of fibre.** This is contained in fruit and veg (especially in any edible skin on potatoes and apples), dried fruits, breakfast cereals and bread (especially the whole grain varieties), seeds and nuts. It will help to keep your digestive system functioning well, which in turn will help you to feel brighter and more energetic.

- **A very little fat.** Your body needs some fat for warmth and to keep your organs functioning properly. However, you get plenty naturally in foods, especially dairy products, meat, poultry, fish, nuts, seeds and cereals, and too much fat is not good for you, so try not to slap butter on bread with a trowel, or deep-fry loads of foods.

CHilleD anD FRoZen FooDs

If you're not sure about your culinary skills, the first thing you are most likely to do when you want a hot meal is to head for the fridge or freezer and heat up something ready-made. The worst thing about that is that it's very expensive; however, it is quick and easy and an ideal solution when you're tired and hungry. So, if we accept that you're bound to do it sometimes, there are just a few things you need to know to get the best results.

Cooking from frozen

Lots of foods and dishes can be cooked straight from the freezer – and some can't. Here's how to turn that rock-hard lump of frozen dinner into something edible, whether it's a frozen ready-meal or something you've banged in the freezer for use another day.

Fruit, vegetables and fish: These cook very well from frozen. They can be cooked exactly like fresh produce, but you must remember that they will take a few minutes longer to allow for thawing as they cook – especially thick pieces of fish. If you're cooking commercially prepared frozen foods, always cook according to the packet directions.

Ready-prepared meals and convenience foods: Ready-prepared pizzas, sausages and burgers often say 'best cooked from frozen'. If so, follow the manufacturer's instructions.

Home-frozen dishes: These are best thawed first, ideally in the fridge overnight, otherwise, covered, at room temperature. If thawing at room temperature, cook as soon as possible after thawing.

Chops and steaks: It is possible to cook chops or steaks from frozen. After quickly browning, cook at a more gentle heat than when thawed, to ensure that the meat is cooked in the middle before you've cremated the outside, and allow longer cooking time too. You must make sure they are cooked right through before serving, so it is always preferable to defrost them first.

Minced (ground) meat: This can be cooked from frozen. If in a lump, scrape the browned meat away from the block as it cooks and break up the lump as soon as possible. Make sure every grain is separate and no longer pink before adding any other ingredients.

Never cook poultry or joints of meat from frozen: thaw as for home-frozen dishes (see previous page). To speed up the thawing of poultry or meat, immerse the wrapped product in cold water and change the water frequently. NEVER put it in hot water.

Don't re-freeze thawed raw food unless it is cooked through first.

Defrosting in the microwave

If you have a microwave, thawing food in it is quick, economical and hygienic. Many newer models have an automatic defrost facility, which makes everything really simple: you just select the item and the weight and the machine will calculate the defrosting and standing time required for you. All you have to do is follow the manufacturer's instructions.

If you don't have auto-defrost, here's how to do it yourself.

- Select the correct power setting. Thawing is usually carried out on Medium-Low (30 per cent power).

- Remove any metal twist ties or lids from packaging.

- Arrange the food (see the separate food categories below) in a suitable microwave-safe container.

- If the food contains a liquid that you won't want to use, place it on a microwave rack with a container underneath so that the liquid will drip away from the food as it thaws.

- Thaw in short bursts only, leaving to stand in between. If you microwave for too long, you will start to cook the outside before the centre has thawed.

- Keep checking the food and remember that it will continue to thaw when standing.

- When thawing a lump of minced (ground) meat, scrape off the meat as it thaws and remove from the oven so that it does not start to cook. Free-flow mince can be cooked from frozen.

- Break up blocks of food – such as casseroles and soups – as soon as possible and move the frozen pieces to the edges of the dish where they will thaw more quickly.

- If the food is in pieces – chops, diced meat, sliced bread, rashers (slices) of bacon, etc. – ease them apart as they thaw to allow more even distribution of the microwaves.

- If thawing food in a bag (such as frozen vegetables), flex the bag occasionally to distribute the microwaves evenly.

- Poultry portions, steaks and chops can be thawed completely in the microwave, but **never** try to defrost whole joints or poultry completely. Start the process in the microwave, then leave at room temperature, wrapped in foil, shiny side in, to finish thawing. Salmonella (a particularly nasty form of food poisoning) can occur if the flesh starts to cook before it is completely thawed.

- Protect bone ends and thin ends of meat, poultry and fish with tiny strips of smooth foil as they thaw, to stop them from beginning to cook. Don't use large pieces of foil or arcing will occur (sparks inside the microwave that can damage its mechanism).

- Put cakes, bread and desserts on a piece of kitchen paper (paper towel) to absorb moisture as they thaw.

- Don't try to thaw cream desserts, such as a cheesecake, completely. Start the process by microwaving, then leave it to complete thawing at room temperature.

Reheating in a conventional oven or on the hob

To make sure foods don't dry out while reheating, cover or wrap them in foil, or put in a casserole dish (Dutch oven) with a lid and cover in sauce or gravy. Reheat at the same temperature you used to cook the dish in the first place. The time will vary according to the quantity and density of the food. As a rough guide, allow 10–15 minutes for a single portion and about 30 minutes for a made-up dish for four people.

- You can reheat a plate of food by setting it over a pan of boiling water. Just cover it with a lid or foil and steam for about 10 minutes.

- Always make sure the food is piping hot right through, never just warm. To test if a made-up dish is hot through, insert a knife down through the centre, wait 5 seconds, then remove. The blade should feel burning hot. If not, heat a little longer.

- Cooked food should be reheated only once.

- To reheat chilled ready meals, follow the instructions on the packet.

Reheating in the microwave

Plated meals (including leftovers and take-aways)

- Always arrange plated meals with the densest, thickest foods nearest the outside of the plate. Ideally, leave the centre clear or fill with small, low-density items, such as peas. Potatoes, in particular, take a long time to reheat, so make sure they are not in large pieces.

- Cover the plate completely with a non-metallic lid, such as another plate, or clingfilm (plastic wrap), rolled back at one edge to prevent it from ballooning as it fills with steam.

- Microwave on High (100 per cent power).

- To test the food is hot right through, test the centre of the underneath of the plate with your hand. It should feel piping hot. If not, microwave for a little longer.

Ready meals

Many ready meals can be reheated in the microwave, including pizzas, baked beans, canned pasta, soups and stews and frozen and cook–chill meals. Follow the manufacturer's instructions on the packet or can.

- Always remove any foil containers, and empty canned food into a microwave-safe bowl.

- Pierce the bag of boil-in-the-bag foods.

- Stir canned foods several times during heating to distribute the heat evenly.

- To test whether a made-up dish is piping hot, insert a knife into the centre, wait 5 seconds, then remove and test its temperature – the blade should feel burning hot. If not, heat a little longer.

Pies

- You can't cook pies in the microwave, but they can be reheated successfully in just a minute or so.

- Take care not to overheat or the pastry (paste) will be unpalatably soggy.

- You can crisp the crust under a hot grill (broiler) after heating, but take care not to burn it.

- Beware, the filling can become searingly hot – especially a sweet sugary one.

BaSiC CooKinG TeRMS

I don't use incomprehensible jargon in this book, but there are some special terms you can't avoid. This section gives their definitions so that you know exactly what you are expected to do.

Bake: To cook uncovered in the oven.

Baste: To spoon the cooking fat, juices or marinade over food as it cooks to keep it moist.

Beat: To mix ingredients rapidly together in a circular motion, using a wooden spoon, wire whisk or electric beater, thus incorporating air to make the mixture light and fluffy. The same technique is also used to remove lumps from batters and sauces.

Bind: To add eggs, milk, cream or a sauce to dry ingredients so that they stick together.

Blend: To stir wet and dry ingredients together until smooth.

Boil: To cook in liquid at a temperature of at least 100°C/212°F.

Brown: To sear the outside of meat quickly to seal in the juices, usually in a little hot fat or a non-stick pan.

Carve: To cut joints of meat or poultry into slices with a sharp knife.

Casserole (Dutch oven): An ovenproof or flameproof cooking pot with a lid, used to slow-cook fish, meat and/or vegetables in liquid.

Chill: To cool food in the fridge until very cold before serving. Hot or warm food should be allowed to cool to room temperature **before** placing in the fridge.

Chop: To cut ingredients into small pieces with a sharp knife (see To chop an onion, page 24).

Coat: To cover food completely with seasoned flour, egg and breadcrumbs, batter or a sauce.

Deep-fry: To cook food by immersing it in hot oil. For most foods, 190°C/375°F is the correct temperature. To test the oil is hot enough, drop in a cube of day-old bread; it should brown in 30 seconds.

Dice: To cut into small cubes (see To dice root vegetables, page 25).

Dissolve: To mix a soluble substance such as salt, sugar or gelatine with liquid until no grains are left. This is particularly important with gelatine. If you can still see tiny jelly-like granules in the liquid, the finished dish will have unpleasant, gelatinous lumps in it.

Dot: To put small pieces of an ingredient, usually butter or margarine, all over the surface of a food before cooking.

Drain: To remove the liquid from food either by tipping into a colander or sieve (strainer) or by lifting the food out of liquid with a draining spoon.

Dredge: To sprinkle food liberally with flour or sugar.

Drizzle: To trickle liquids such as oil, syrup, melted butter or sauce over the surface of food.

Dry-fry: To cook foods in a non-stick frying pan (skillet) without the addition of extra oil or other fat.

Dry ingredients: Grainy or powdery ingredients, such as flour, sugar, spices, etc. Does not include foods such as fat, eggs, syrups, dried fruit, jams (conserves) or sauces.

Dust: To sprinkle lightly with flour, sugar, spices or other seasoning.

Dutch oven: *See* Casserole.

Fillet: The leanest, most tender cuts of any meats – the undercut of the sirloin of beef; a cut taken from the fleshy part of the buttocks of pork; the 'eye' of meat in the thick end of the neck of lamb; also, the boned flesh of fish and the boned breasts of poultry.

Flake: To separate cooked fish into individual flakes using a fork.

Fold in: To gently incorporate one ingredient or mixture into another mixture, using a metal spoon in a cutting and turning 'figure of eight' movement.

Fry (sauté): To cook food quickly over direct heat in a little oil, butter or other fat.

Grate: To shred into small pieces on a grater. A fine mesh is used for nutmeg and onion; a medium mesh for citrus zest, ginger, cheese, chocolate and breadcrumbs; and a coarse side for cheese, chocolate, vegetables and fat such as animal suet.

Hand-hot: At a temperature that feels bearably hot to the touch but not scalding.

Hull: To remove the green central calyx from strawberries, raspberries, tomatoes, etc.

Joint: A large piece of meat that is cooked and cut into slices for serving. Also, to cut poultry or game into pieces at the joints.

Knead: To push and stretch dough with the heel of your hand. For pastry (paste) this should be done briefly and gently, just to remove the cracks. For yeast dough it should be done much more firmly, for several minutes, until the dough is smooth and elastic.

Marinade: A mixture of liquids and flavourings, in which raw foods are soaked to add flavour and to tenderise them before cooking. May be spooned over food during cooking and any remainder may be made into a sauce to serve with the cooked dish. *See also* Baste.

Marinate: To soak foods in a marinade.

Mash: To use a fork or a potato masher to squash and beat cooked or soft foods to a pulp.

Mix: To stir ingredients together until combined.

Parboil: To part-cook in boiling water. The cooking process is then finished in another way, e.g. parboiled potatoes may then be roasted.

Pare: To cut off a thin layer of outer skin, particularly of citrus fruit.

Peel: To remove the skin of fruit and vegetables.

Poach: To simmer gently in just enough hot (not boiling) liquid to cover the food, until softly cooked.

Prove: To put yeast dough in a warm place to rise until doubled in bulk.

Pulses: Dried peas, beans and lentils.

Purée: To pass fruit or vegetables through a fine sieve (strainer) or process in a blender or food processor to make a smooth pulp.

Rind: The tough skin of bacon or pork. The oily, coloured skin (zest) of citrus fruit.

Rise: To expand and puff up. May be caused by the effect of heat on certain dishes with a lot of air incorporated, e.g. soufflés, puff and choux pastry (paste), Yorkshire pudding, breads and scones (biscuits), or by the fermentation of yeast.

Roast: To cook in the oven in fat or oil.

Roll out: To flatten and spread out dough with the help of a rolling pin.

Rub in: To incorporate fat into flour by working it gently between your fingertips and letting it drop back into the bowl until the mixture looks like breadcrumbs.

Sauté: *See* Fry.

Scrape: To use the edge of a knife blade to remove the skin from young vegetables, the scales of fish, etc., without damaging the flesh.

Sear: To brown meat or poultry quickly over a high heat to seal in the juices.

Seasoned flour: Flour to which a little salt and pepper have been added; used to dust meat, poultry, fish or vegetables before cooking.

Season: To flavour food with salt and pepper, plus in some cases other ingredients such as chilli powder, Tabasco sauce, etc.

Seasoning: Usually salt and pepper, but may include other flavourings, such as chilli powder, Tabasco sauce, etc.

Score: To make shallow cuts with a sharp knife at regular intervals over the surface of meats, such as steaks, to tenderise them before grilling (broiling) or frying (sautéing), or over the rind of pork to help it to 'crackle' when roasted.

Shallow-fry: To cook food in about 5 mm/¼ in of hot oil in a frying pan (skillet).

Sift: To pass flour, icing (confectioners') sugar or other dry ingredients through a sieve (strainer), using a wooden spoon, or through a flour sifter to remove the lumps.

Sieve (strain): To push soft ingredients, such as raspberries, through a wire- or nylon-meshed sieve (strainer), using a wooden spoon, to remove lumps or seeds.

Simmer: To cook gently in liquid just below boiling point, where occasional bubbles will rise to the surface.

Skim the surface: To spoon off the fat or scum floating on the surface of a soup, stew, casserole or gravy. Floating fat can also be removed by laying a sheet of kitchen paper (paper towel) lightly on the surface to absorb the fat. This may need to be repeated with several sheets.

Soft dropping consistency: Best illustrated by lifting a spoonful of the mixture: it should drop gently off the spoon when tilted, without being shaken.

Steam: To cook in steam by suspending food in a special steamer or a covered colander over a pan of simmering water, topping up the boiling water as necessary during cooking. The food should not come into contact with the water during cooking.

Stew: To cook food slowly in liquid, or its own juice, on the hob.

Stir-fry: To cook small, even-sized pieces of food quickly in a little oil or other fat in a wok or frying pan (skillet), tossing over a high heat.

Strain: To remove solids from liquid by tipping into a sieve (strainer) over a bowl, retaining the liquid for further use. *See also* Sieve.

Sweat: To soften vegetables without browning in fat in a covered pan over a gentle heat.

Toss: To turn foods over to coat them in a liquid, such as a marinade, dressing, melted butter or sauce, by gently lifting them with a spoon and fork or salad servers and letting them drop back into the bowl or pan. Also to turn a pancake by tossing it into the air so it turns over, then catching it again in the pan to cook the other side.

Whip: To stir rapidly or beat ingredients such as cream, using a fork, wire whisk or electric beater, to incorporate air quickly.

Whisk: To beat with a wire whisk or electric beater; usually used to add air to egg white or egg and sugar mixtures, also to remove the lumps from a sauce, gravy, etc., during cooking.

Zest: The oily, coloured rind of citrus fruit.

SiMPLe FooD PRePaRatioN

If you get beyond the knife and can opener chapter, you may want to try your hand at some real recipes. Most cookery books assume that you can prepare everything straight off without ever having done it before. It is easy – but only when you know how! So here is a step-by-step guide to the basic skills.

To chop an onion

1   Cut the point off the top of the onion. Pull off all the outer skin, leaving the root intact (this will help stop you crying).

2   Cut the onion in half from top to bottom, through the root. Hold one half at a time between your thumb and fingers, flat side down on a board, and cut at intervals from the root end to the tip.

3   Now cut across the first set of cuts. Discard the root end. To finely chop make the cuts closer together both ways. To coarsely chop, make the cuts wider.

To slice an onion into rings

1   Don't peel it. Hold the onion firmly between your thumb and middle finger, with the root end in the palm of your hand.

2   Starting at the tip end, cut into fairly thin slices. When you get to the root end, discard it.

3   Peel off the brown outer layer and the next layer, if it seems tough, from each slice.

4   Separate the slices into rings.

To prepare and slice (bell) peppers into rings

1   Cut off the stalk end of the pepper.

2   Pull out the core, seeds and any white pith.

3   Tap the pepper, cut side down, on the board to shake out any loose seeds.

4   Cut the pepper into rings.

To prepare and dice (bell) peppers

1 Cut the pepper in half lengthways, from the stalk end to the bottom.

2 Pull out the stalk, core, seeds and any white pith from both halves.

3 Tap the halves, cut sides down, on the board to remove any loose seeds.

4 Turn over the halves and cut into wide strips first in one direction and then, holding the strips together, cut across them to form dice.

To dice root vegetables

1 Peel thinly with a potato peeler or sharp knife, if necessary.

2 Cut in half lengthways.

3 Hold between your thumb and middle finger and cut into strips.

4 Still holding the vegetable together firmly, turn it and cut at right angles to the first cuts. For large dice, make the cuts wide apart. For smaller dice, make them closer together.

To chop fresh parsley and other herbs

1 Leave parsley on its stalks (they have a lot of flavour), but for other herbs, pull the leaves off the stalks unless they are very spindly and tender.

2 Put into a cup or small bowl.

3 Using a pair of scissors, snip them until chopped as finely as you wish.

To separate an egg

This is much easier than juggling with egg shells.

1 Crack the shell of the egg by tapping in the middle sharply with a knife.

2 Gently pull the two halves of the shell apart over a saucer so the contents fall on the saucer.

3 Invert an egg cup (or any other small cup) over the yolk. Hold firmly. Pick up the saucer and drain off the white into a small bowl.

Basic Cooking Methods

This section gives you a rundown on the most common ways of cooking different types of food. They come up over and over again in different recipes, so you'll soon get the hang of them, and then you can use them to make up your own dishes.

Meat, poultry and fish

Grill (broil)
Suitable for tender cuts, such as steaks, chops, fillets, kidneys, liver and sausages.

1   Cover a grill (broiler) rack with foil. Brush the food with a little oil or dot with butter or margarine. Season lightly.

2   Cook under a preheated grill (broiler) until done to your liking (see Top tips, page 35), turning over once when the first side is browned. The time will depend on the thickness.

Fry (sauté)
Suitable for tender cuts, such as steaks, chops, fillets, kidneys, liver and sausages.

1   Heat a little oil, or butter/margarine and oil, in a frying pan (skillet) until hot but not smoking.

2   Season the food and place in the pan. Cook quickly until brown underneath. Turn over and cook the other side until brown.

3   Reduce the heat and continue to cook, turning once until cooked to your liking (see Top tips, page 35). The cooking time will depend on the thickness.

Braise or casserole
Suitable for most meats, including braising or stewing meat that is diced or in slabs, plus chops, kidneys, liver, sausages, steaks, ribs and rashers (slices). Also suitable for whole fish, chicken portions or fillets.

1   Dip the meat, fish or poultry in flour mixed with a little salt and pepper, if liked.

2   Heat a little hot oil in a flameproof casserole (Dutch oven). Add the meat and cook over a high heat, turning it occasionally until brown all over. Remove from the pan with a draining spoon.

3   Add diced vegetables and stir in the hot oil for 2–3 minutes.

4   Replace the meat and add just enough stock or stock and wine to cover the meat. Add a bouquet garni sachet or bay leaf, if liked. Bring to the boil, then cover and transfer to a preheated oven at 160°C/325°F/gas 3/fan oven 145°C for 1½–2½ hours.

5   Remove the bouquet garni or bay leaf, if used. Taste and re-season if necessary.

Boil or stew
Suitable for stewing and braising meats, either diced or in slabs, plus joints, chops, sausages, whole chickens, chicken portions and fish.

1   Place the meat, poultry or fish in a saucepan or flameproof casserole (Dutch oven) with vegetables, cut into large, chunky pieces, and other flavourings of your choice.

2   Add just enough water or stock to cover.

3   Bring to the boil, then skim the surface with a draining spoon to remove any scum.

4   Turn down the heat until there are small bubbles just rising to the surface round the edges. Cover and cook at a very gentle simmer until really tender. Meat will take up to 1 hour per 450 g/1 lb. Fish cooks quickly and will need only about 10–15 minutes maximum.

5   Taste and re-season if necessary.

Roast
Suitable for whole poultry and joints of meat – of course – but also for fattier cuts, such as belly pork slices or breast of lamb. Joints for stuffing should have the bone removed.

1   If stuffing a joint, spread the meat with stuffing on the side where the bones were. Roll up and tie with string or secure with skewers.

2   Place the joint in a roasting tin (pan). Pork joints should be set on a rack or an upturned plate in the tin.

3   Smear beef or lamb with a little oil and season lightly. For pork, score the rind but slashing it with a sharp knife at regular intervals

all over. Rub the rind with oil and salt. This will help it 'crackle' as it cooks. For chicken or other birds, rub the skin with a little oil and sprinkle with salt.

4   Roast in a preheated oven at 220°C/425°F/gas 7/fan oven 200°C for 10 minutes, then reduce the heat to 190°C/375°F/gas 5/fan oven 170°C for the remaining cooking time.

Meat	Roasting time
Beef, rare	15 minutes per 450 g/1 lb plus 15 minutes over
medium	20 minutes per 450 g/1 lb plus 20 minutes over
well-done	30 minutes per 450 g/1 lb plus 30 minutes over
Pork	30 minutes per 450 g/1 lb plus 30 minutes over
Lamb	30 minutes per 450 g/1 lb plus 30 minutes over
Chicken	20 minutes per 450 g/1 lb plus 20 minutes over

For more information on cooking a roast dinner, see pages 349–51.

Pasta, rice and vegetables

To cook spaghetti and pasta

1   Three-quarters-fill a large pan with water and add a small teaspoonful of salt and a tablespoon of oil (this will help to stop it boiling over). Put over a high heat, cover with a lid and leave it until boiling, then remove the lid.

2   Hold the saucepan handle with one hand and the spaghetti with the other. Lower the ends of the spaghetti into the water.

3   Gently push the strands down. They will gradually curl round the pan as they soften. Do not push too hard or they will snap. Once the spaghetti is submerged, stir gently to separate the strands. Cook for 8–10 minutes, or according to the time given on the packet. Do not cover the pan.

4   To test whether the spaghetti is cooked, lift a strand out of the pan (be careful not to burn yourself) and bite it. It should feel just soft but still with a little bit of chewiness to it. Alternatively, you can try throwing it at the wall – it will stick if it is cooked. (Don't forget to remove it!)

5   Put a colander in the sink. Pour the contents of the saucepan into the colander and allow to drain well. Lift up the colander of spaghetti and place on top of the saucepan to finish draining while you get out the plates.

Note: Other pasta, such as tagliatelle, macaroni and other shapes, can be cooked in exactly the same way except you don't need to feed it gradually into the pan – simply add it to the boiling water and stir.

To cook plain rice
I like basmati rice, but American long-grain is cheaper.

1   Three-quarters-fill a large pan with water and add a small teaspoonful of salt. Put over a high heat, cover with a lid and leave it until it is boiling.

2   Meanwhile, measure the rice.

3   Remove the pan lid. Pour the rice in a thin stream into the boiling water and stir well to separate the grains. Do not cover the pan again. Reduce the heat so that the water is just boiling and cook for the time directed on the packet. Meanwhile, boil a kettle of water.

4   To test if it is cooked, lift out a few grains with a draining spoon and either taste or pinch a grain between your thumb and index finger. It should feel almost soft but still with some texture.

5   Place a colander in the sink and pour in the contents of the pan. Pour the kettle of boiling water all over the grains to rinse off any excess starch, then lift up the colander and place on top of the saucepan to finish draining. Stir gently with a fork to loosen (fluff up) the grains, then serve.

Note: To cook Thai fragrant rice, wash it well first, then cook as above. It will be stickier than other long-grain varieties.

Vegetables
There are many kinds of vegetables that you'll cook loads of times. Here's how ...

To prepare and boil potatoes and root vegetables
This is suitable for potatoes, carrots, turnips, parsnips, swede (rutabaga), etc.

1   Peel thinly with a potato peeler or sharp vegetable knife, or scrape or scrub, as necessary.

2   Cut into even-sized pieces (large chunks for potatoes, slices or sticks for carrots, chunky wedges for parsnips, for instance). Leave small new potatoes and baby carrots whole.

3   Place in a pan with just enough cold water to cover and add a very little salt.

4   Cover with a lid and bring up to the boil over a high heat. When bubbling, turn the heat down to moderate and let the vegetables boil gently until they feel tender when a knife is inserted in them. This could take anything from 5 to 15 minutes depending on the size of the pieces, so test every so often.

5   Tip into a colander in the sink to drain. (If you're making gravy, you can use the cooking water, so put the colander over a mixing bowl.)

To make chips
It's not easy to cook good chips, so oven chips are your best bet unless you are really keen.

1   Wash or scrub the potatoes (you don't have to peel them unless you want to). Cut each one in four thick slices, then cut the slices into strips to make chips (fries). Wrap in a clean tea towel (dish cloth) to dry.

2   Pour about 2.5 cm/1 in oil into a frying pan (skillet) and heat until your hand feels hot when held 5 cm/2 in above the surface.

3   Slide the chips down a fish slice into the pan (this stops the oil from splashing) and cook until golden, gently turning them occasionally.

Note: If you have a deep-fat fryer, follow the manufacturer's instructions.

To prepare and cook green leafy vegetables
Use this method for white and green cabbage, spring (collard) greens, etc. (Note that red cabbage is not suitable for cooking in this way.)

1   Pull or cut off any outer, damaged leaves.

2   Separate into leaves, discarding thick stalks. Cabbage may be cut in half and the thick central stump removed. Rinse in cold water and drain.

3   Cut the leaves into pieces or thin shreds as appropriate.

4   Put about 2.5 cm/1 in water in a saucepan with a good pinch of salt. Put the pan over a high heat until it is boiling rapidly.

5   Add the greens and push down well as they begin to soften. Boil over a high heat until they are just tender but still with some texture – it will take 3–5 minutes.

6   Drain in a colander in the sink or over a bowl if you want the cooking water for gravy.

Note: To cook spinach, wash well (it can be gritty). Place in a pan with no extra water and add a sprinkling of salt. Cover and cook for about 5 minutes. Drain thoroughly in a colander. Snip with scissors, if liked, before serving.

To cook peas and beans
This is suitable for shelled peas and beans, any type of green beans, mangetout (snow peas), baby corn cobs, etc.

1   Top and tail them, if necessary: snap off the stalk and the point where the flower was or remove the pods for fresh peas, broad (fava) beans, etc.

2   For runner beans, cut off the string all round the edge.

3   Leave mangetout, sugar snap peas, French (green) beans and baby cobs whole. Slice runner and flat beans into thin diagonal slices.

4   Put about 5 cm/2 in of water and a good pinch of salt in a saucepan. Bring to the boil over a high heat. Add the vegetable and boil until just tender – as little as 2–3 minutes for mangetout and up to 6 minutes for some thicker green beans. Drain the vegetable in a colander in the sink or over a bowl if you want the cooking water for gravy.

To stir-fry vegetables and/or meat
1   Cut all the ingredients into thin strips or small, even-sized pieces.

2   Heat a little oil in a frying pan (skillet) or wok.

3   Add meat or poultry, if using, and toss and stir for 2–3 minutes.

4   Add the vegetables, densest ones first, and continue to toss and stir until cooked to your liking.

5   Add flavourings, sauces, etc., of your choice.

Notes on the Recipes

- Most recipes serve one person but can easily be adjusted to serve more if you share a house and all cook together. Those that are designed for more just aren't worth cooking for only one, so are meant for sharing or making to eat over several days.

- Measurements have been kept simple. There's no need to bother with accurate weighing with measuring jugs, scales and so on – wet and dry ingredients are measured using an ordinary coffee mug and ordinary spoons (not measuring ones), and for things like grated cheese, I've used handfuls. See also the table on page 33 (opposite).

- When measuring dry ingredients, such as flour, it should be loosely packed, not pressed down.

- The words in brackets are the American equivalents.

- The ingredients are listed in the order you use them.

- I use medium eggs. If you use a different size, especially for baking, you may need to add a little more or less liquid to obtain the right consistency.

- Wash, peel, core and seed, if necessary, fresh fruit and vegetables before use. Make sure food is as fresh as possible and in good condition.

- Taste food (use a spoon!) as you cook and adjust the seasoning to suit your palate.

- Fresh herbs – especially parsley, basil and coriander (cilantro) – do give lots of recipes a lift. It is cheapest to buy pots of growing herbs from the supermarket. They will brighten up the kitchen as well as tasting good – but don't forget to water them!

- dried parsley are now widely available and are good enough to use for garnish.

- Can and packet sizes vary slightly between brands but it won't make any difference to the recipes.

- Where the recipe calls for half a large can of food such as tomatoes, baked beans, tuna, etc., you can use a small can if you prefer. (See Top tips for Value and Taste, page 34.)

- I tend to use sunflower or olive oil but you can use any good-quality oil. Corn and groundnut oil are best for deep-frying. Avoid the really cheap unspecified vegetable oils – they are only suitable for cooking and shouldn't be used in dressings as they taste pretty terrible.

- You can use butter or almost any kind of margarine for most recipes. However, some low-fat spreads are only for spreading and go slushy when heated, so check that the packet says it's okay for cooking.

- Conventional ovens should be turned on when you start preparing the food, to allow time to preheat. This does not apply to fan ovens.

- Different ovens will take different times to cook the same thing, so don't be afraid to take the food out as soon as you see it is ready, or – more likely in an old oven in a student house – give it a few more minutes.

- I have suggested Philadelphia as an example of soft white cheese, but supermarket own brands are much cheaper.

If you get keen and want to use 'proper' measurements or if you need to buy a block of cheese, for example, these are the equivalent weights and measures for those I have used:

Liquids:	1 mug = 250 ml/8 fl oz
Flour and bulghar (cracked wheat):	1 mug = 100 g/4 oz
Shelled or diced fresh or frozen vegetables, e.g. peas:	1 mug = 100 g/4 oz
Small pasta shapes:	1 mug = 100 g/4 oz
Large pasta shapes:	1 mug = 50 g/2 oz
Couscous and lentils:	1 mug = 175 g/6 oz
Sugar, rice, butter or margarine:	1 mug = 225 g/8 oz
Grated cheese, dried fruit, nuts:	1 small handful = 15 g/$\frac{1}{2}$ oz A handful = 25 g/1 oz A good handful = 50 g/2 oz
All spoon measurements are level unless stated otherwise	1 tsp = about 5 ml 1 tbsp = about 15 ml

TOP TIPS FOR VALUE AND TASTE

- Don't buy small cans of foods that you use often, such as tomatoes, baked beans, tuna, corned beef, salmon, pulses, etc. – larger sizes are always better value. Store any leftovers not required for a recipe in a covered container in the fridge for up to 3 days and don't forget they're there! Check the index of this book for lots of alternative recipes to use them up.

- Some of the recipes use unusual ingredients such as creamed coconut or tahini (sesame seed paste). These are not cheap but they do make the recipes much more interesting and they will keep for ages.

- White fish such as cod and haddock can be quite pricey – but coley, pollack and whiting are good substitutes and a lot cheaper and, believe it or not, farmed salmon is much cheaper than cod now!

- Market stalls are often cheaper than supermarkets for fresh fruit and veg. When you are shopping in a supermarket, look for economy ranges and always buy loose rather than prepacked produce – it's cheaper (unless there are special offers).

- Supermarket 'own brands' of breakfast cereals, soft white cheese, etc. are just as nutritious as the branded goods but much cheaper.

- Economy brands of foods like canned tomatoes, flour, red kidney beans and bread are great value. Beware of economy baked beans, however – lots of sauce and not many beans. Don't skimp on mince or sausages either: economy packs of sausages contain more rusk and fat and less actual meat and economy mince will be very fatty.

- If you buy a punnet of salad cress and keep watering it, it will keep regrowing for a while.

- If you want to freeze leftovers to eat at another time, make sure they are in tightly covered freezerproof containers or thick plastic bags, tied securely, with the air squeezed out. Always label the packet of food – all lumps of frozen food look the same and you won't remember what it is after a week or two! As a guide, most cooked foods can be safely frozen for up to 6 months but eat fish within 3 months. Don't try to freeze potatoes, cottage cheese, eggs, mayonnaise or single (light) cream.

- If freezing fresh meat or chicken, wrap tightly (unless prepackaged) and freeze it as soon as you get it home. Use within 12 months.

- Large loaves of sliced bread often go mouldy before they're finished. To avoid this, put them in the freezer. You can take out a slice or two at a time and toast it from frozen. If you toast it just briefly it will be just like warm fresh bread!

- Pastry (paste) can be safely re-frozen after it has thawed. Just cut off what you need, then wrap the remainder tightly in foil or clingfilm (plastic wrap) and return to the freezer.

- If salad greens go limp in the fridge, separate the leaves, rinse them in cold water and shake off the excess. Put them in a plastic bag (without holes), blow into the bag and tie it with a twist tie or elastic band to hold the air in like a balloon. Leave it in the fridge for several hours and it will revive. Rinse again before use!

- If you haven't got a fresh lemon or lime and the recipe calls for grated zest and juice, a dash of bottled lemon or lime juice will do.

- When cooking in oil, the temperature of the oil is very important. If it is not hot enough, the food will be unpleasantly soggy. If it is too hot (with smoke rising from the surface), the food will burn and you may end up setting the kitchen on fire. To test the temperature, for shallow-frying, hold your hand about 4 cm/2 in above the pan – it should feel hot but not unbearably so. For deep-frying, heat until a cube of day-old bread dropped into it browns in 30 seconds.

- To test if a steak or chop is cooked to your liking, press on it when browned on both sides. If it feels wobbly, it will be very rare. If firmer, but with a little 'give', it will be medium. If firm, it will be well done. (And if hard, it's dried out!) Don't keep prodding it with a fork or knife during cooking or all the juices will run out.

- Vegetarian recipes are marked with a **Ⓥ** symbol. Those who eat fish but not meat will find plenty of additional recipes containing seafood that they will enjoy. Note that vegetarian recipes may contain dairy products, which should be omitted or replaced with a vegetarian alternative, if preferred. Recipes may also use processed foods, and vegetarians should check the specific product labels to be certain of their suitability, especially items such as pastry, stock, stock cubes, soups and sauces, jellies or set desserts, ice-cream and chocolate products. Some alcoholic drinks also use animal-derived products in their production.

Recipes You can Do with ... a Knife and a Chopping Board

So either you don't want to be bothered to cook anything or you simply want to knock something up in a hurry. All the recipes in this section require no more than a bit of spreading, stirring or chopping – and occasionally grating!

Prawn and avocado cooler

If you're eating this straight away, you don't need to toss the avocado in lemon juice.

SERVES 1

2 slices of granary bread
Butter or margarine
2 tsp mayonnaise
A small handful of frozen prawns (shrimp), thawed and drained on kitchen paper (paper towels)
½ small ripe avocado, peeled, stoned (pitted) and thinly sliced
A dash of lemon juice
Pepper

1 Spread one side of each slice of bread with a little butter or margarine.

2 Top one slice with mayonnaise, then the prawns, then slices of avocado, tossed in lemon juice. Season well with pepper.

3 Top with the second slice.

Quick posh pâté with crispbreads

This is just as good on hot toast.

SERVES 1–2

1 small barrel of liver sausage
A knob of butter or margarine
1 small garlic clove, peeled and crushed, or 1 small squeeze of garlic purée (paste)
1 tbsp leftover beer or wine
A pinch of dried mixed herbs
Salt and pepper
A few lettuce leaves
Slices of tomato and cucumber
4 crispbreads

1 Peel the plastic off the liver sausage and discard.

2 Mash the liver sausage with the butter or margarine and garlic in a bowl. Add the beer or wine and mash thoroughly until well blended.

3 Add the herbs and season to taste with salt and pepper.

4 Spoon on to a plate with the lettuce, tomato and cucumber and eat with crispbreads.

Greek pitta pockets

SERVES 1

1 pitta bread
1 large spoonful of taramasalata
A little shredded lettuce
A few stoned (pitted) black olives, sliced
(optional)
A dash of lemon juice
Pepper

1 Cut the pitta in half across the middle and gently open to form two pockets.

2 Fill with the taramasalata, some shredded lettuce and the olives, if using. Add a dash of lemon juice and some pepper.

Smoked mackerel and soft cheese bagels

SERVES 1

1 smoked mackerel fillet
1 bagel, halved
1 tbsp soft white cheese,
such as Philadelphia
1 tsp horseradish relish
A little lemon juice
Pepper
A little salad cress

1 Cut the smoked mackerel fillet into small pieces, discarding the skin, if liked.

2 Spread the bagel halves with the soft cheese.

3 Add a thin spreading of horseradish relish, then top with the smoked mackerel.

4 Sprinkle with lemon juice, a good grinding of pepper and some salad cress.

Ⓥ Greek salad seedies Ⓥ

Use the pulled-out bread to make breadcrumbs. Store in a plastic bag until needed.

SERVES 1–2

1 small wedge of iceberg lettuce,
finely shredded
1 tomato, chopped
2.5 cm/1 in piece of cucumber, chopped
1 tbsp sliced stoned (pitted) black olives
½ small onion, peeled and thinly sliced
1 finger of feta cheese, crumbled
A good pinch of dried oregano
1 tbsp olive oil
1 tsp red wine vinegar
Salt and pepper
2 large seeded rolls

1 Put everything except the rolls in a large bowl and toss thoroughly, turning the mixture over with a spoon and fork until thoroughly blended.

2 Cut a slice off the top of each roll. Pull out most of the soft bread inside to leave a shell.

3 Pack the salad into each roll and top with the lids. Eat straight away.

Fragrant chicken and pesto baguette

Pesto is really useful to keep in the cupboard for a quick main meal.

SERVES 1

1 sandwich baguette
Butter or margarine
1 large crisp lettuce leaf
1 tbsp pesto, ready-made or see page 418
1 tbsp mayonnaise
2 slices of cooked pressed chicken, chopped
A few pine nuts

1 Split the baguette along one side. Spread inside with butter or margarine.

2 Line with the lettuce leaf.

3 Mix the pesto with the mayonnaise in a bowl with a spoon and stir in the chicken. Spread in the baguette and sprinkle with the pine nuts.

Italian lunch

You don't have to use ciabatta: any large white roll will do!

SERVES 1

1 ciabatta roll
2 slices of salami
1 tomato, sliced
2 torn fresh basil leaves
or a pinch of dried basil or oregano
1 tbsp olive oil
Black pepper

1 Split the roll along one side and gently open up slightly.

2 Lay the salami in the roll and top with the slices of tomato.

3 Scatter the herbs over. Trickle the olive oil on the tomatoes and add a little pepper.

Crunchy apple, walnut and ✓ goats' cheese baguette ✓

Walnut pieces are much cheaper than halves. They're highly nutritious and you can add them to all sorts of snacks and meals.

SERVES 1

1 eating (dessert) apple, quartered, cored and thinly sliced
1 little lemon juice (optional)
1 sandwich baguette
Butter or margarine
½ small cylinder of goats' cheese
4 walnut pieces, chopped

1 Mix the slices of apple with a little lemon juice, if liked, to prevent browning (this is not necessary if you're eating the baguette straight away).

2 Split the baguette, not right through, and spread inside with butter or margarine.

3 Slice the goats' cheese and place in the baguette (or, if very soft, spread it inside).

4 Sprinkle with the chopped walnuts, then add the slices of apple.

Red pepper and soft cheese ✓ sandwiches ✓

SERVES 1

2 slices of white bread
2 tbsp soft white cheese, such as Philadelphia
½ red (bell) pepper, sliced

1 Spread one side of each slice of bread with soft cheese.

2 Arrange the slices of pepper over one piece of bread.

3 Top with the other slice.

Peanut butter and orange Ⓥ sandwiches Ⓥ

SERVES 1

1 orange
2 slices of bread
Peanut butter
Pepper

1 Peel the orange and cut into round slices.

2 Spread the bread thickly with peanut butter.

3 Sandwich together with the slices of orange and add a sprinkling of pepper.

Banana, peanut butter and Ⓥ jam sandwiches Ⓥ

You can use other flavours of jam if you prefer.

SERVES 1

2 slices of bread
Peanut butter
Raspberry jam (conserve)
1 banana

1 Spread one slice of bread with peanut butter. Spread the other with jam.

2 Peel and slice the banana and arrange over the peanut butter. Top with the jam slice.

Cottage cheese, date and sesame seed Ⓥ sandwiches Ⓥ

SERVES 1

2 slices of bread
Butter or margarine
½ small tub of cottage cheese
A small handful of chopped cooking dates
1 tbsp sesame seeds

1 Spread the slices of bread on one side with butter or margarine.

2 Spread one slice with the cottage cheese and add the dates in an even layer. Sprinkle with the sesame seeds and top with the other slice of bread.

Kiwi and white cheese Ⓥ refresher Ⓥ

SERVES 1

1 kiwi fruit
2 slices of bread
2–3 tbsp soft white cheese, such as Philadelphia
A pinch of ground cinnamon

1 Peel the kiwi fruit and cut into slices.

2 Spread the bread with the cheese.

3 Arrange the kiwi fruit on one slice of bread, add a sprinkling of ground cinnamon, then top with the other slice of bread.

Ham sandwiches with chilli and tomatoes

You can use chilli relish instead of the ketchup and chilli sauce.

SERVES 1

2 slices of bread
Butter or margarine
2 tsp tomato ketchup (catsup)
½ tsp hot chilli sauce
1 slice of ham
1 tomato, cut into thick slices

1 Spread the bread on one side with butter or margarine.

2 Spread one slice with ketchup, then chilli sauce.

3 Top with the ham, then slices of tomato, then cover with the remaining slice of bread.

Cheese, ham and coleslaw jumbo bites

SERVES 1

1 large soft roll
or 2 thick slices of bread
Butter or margarine
1 tbsp sweet pickle
2 lettuce leaves
1–2 slices of Cheddar cheese
or 1 processed cheese slice
1 slice of ham
1 tbsp coleslaw, ready-made
or see page 47

1 Spread the split roll or the two slices of bread on one side with butter or margarine.

2 Spread one half of the roll or one slice of bread with the pickle, then top with the lettuce, then the cheese, then ham.

3 Spread evenly with the coleslaw, then add the remaining half roll or slice of bread.

Tomato and Mozzarella ⓥ munch ⓥ

For a more Italian feel, drizzle the bread with olive oil instead of spreading with butter or margarine.

SERVES 1

2 slices of bread
Butter or margarine
1 tomato, sliced
A handful of grated Mozzarella cheese
A pinch of dried basil
or 3 fresh basil leaves,
torn into small pieces
Pepper

1 Spread the bread with the butter or margarine.

2 Top one slice with the tomato, cheese and basil. Sprinkle with pepper and top with the other slice of bread.

Cheese and marmalade ⓥ magic ⓥ

SERVES 1

2 slices of bread
Butter or margarine
1 small carton of cottage cheese with pineapple
2 tsp orange marmalade

1 Spread the bread with butter or margarine.

2 Spread one slice with the cottage cheese.

3 Spread the other slice with the marmalade and sandwich them together.

♥ Christmas cracker ♥

SERVES 1

2 slices of bread
Butter or margarine
1–2 tbsp mincemeat
1–2 thick slices of Cheddar cheese
or 2 processed cheese slices

1 Spread the bread with butter or margarine.

2 Spread one slice with the mincemeat and top the other with the cheese, then sandwich them together.

Banana and
♥ date snack ♥

You can buy bags of ready-chopped dates in the dried fruit section at the supermarket. They're great as an energy-booster on cereal and in salads too.

SERVES 1

2 slices of bread
Butter or margarine
1 small banana, mashed
A small handful of chopped
cooking dates
A pinch of mixed (apple-pie) spice

1 Spread the bread with butter or margarine.

2 Top one slice with the banana, then scatter the dates over. Sprinkle with the spice and top with the other slice of bread.

Satay-style chicken
sandwiches

SERVES 1

2 slices of bread
Peanut butter
2 tsp chilli relish
2 slices of cooked pressed chicken
2 crisp lettuce leaves

1 Spread the bread with peanut butter, then with the chilli relish.

2 Sandwich together with the chicken and lettuce.

♥ Cheese blusher ♥

I prefer vacuum-packed, unpickled beetroot for this, but you can use the pickled kind if you prefer.

SERVES 1

1 bagel
Butter or margarine
1 cm/½ in stick of white cheese,
crumbled
2 baby beetroot (red beets), grated or
chopped
1 tbsp mayonnaise
½ small red onion, peeled and
thinly sliced

1 Split the bagel and spread with butter or margarine.

2 Mix the cheese with the beetroot and mayonnaise and pile on the bagel halves.

3 Top each with the thinly sliced onion.

Chinese chicken baguette

SERVES 1

A small handful of chopped cooked
chicken or 2 slices of cooked pressed
chicken, chopped
A small handful of fresh beansprouts
1 small carrot, peeled and
coarsely grated
½ small green (bell) pepper,
coarsely grated
2 tsp soy sauce
A pinch of ground ginger
1 sandwich baguette
2 tbsp soft white cheese,
such as Philadelphia

1 Mix the chicken with the beansprouts, carrot and pepper. Add the soy sauce and ginger and toss gently with your hands until well coated.

2 Split the baguette along one side and spread with the cheese. Fill with the chicken mixture.

🅥 Ploughman's lunch 🅥

You can use any sort of bread or roll for this – the fresher the better.

SERVES 1

1 chunk of French bread
A knob of butter or margarine
A good chunk of Cheddar
or other hard cheese
1 tomato, quartered
2.5 cm/1 in piece of cucumber,
cut into chunks
A few pickled onions
1 tbsp sweet pickle

Put everything on a plate and enjoy!

Savoury lettuce rolls

SERVES 1

3 tbsp soft cheese, flavoured with garlic
and herbs
1 tbsp milk
2 large lettuce leaves
2 slices of ham
5 cm/2 in piece of cucumber, cut into
thin matchsticks

1 Mix the cheese with the milk to make it spreadable, then spread it over the lettuce leaves, taking care not to tear them.

2 Top each with a slice of ham. Lay half the strips of cucumber in a small pile in the centre of one edge of each slice of ham.

3 Fold in the two sides of the lettuce, then roll up over the cucumber.

Ham and coleslaw rolls

SERVES 1–2

2 slices of bread, crusts removed
Butter or margarine
2 slices of ham
2 tbsp coleslaw, ready-made
or see page 47

1 Flatten the slices of bread slightly with a rolling pin.

2 Spread with butter or margarine, then top each with a slice of ham.

3 Spread with coleslaw and roll up.

Ⓥ Tzaziki with pittas Ⓥ

SERVES 1–2

5 cm/2 in piece of cucumber
5 tbsp Greek-style plain yoghurt
1 tsp olive oil
½ garlic clove, peeled and crushed,
or ½ tsp garlic purée (paste)
1 tsp dried mint
Salt and pepper
Pitta breads

1 Cut the cucumber into four strips lengthways, then cut the strips into small dice. Place in a bowl.

2 Add the yoghurt, oil, garlic and mint and mix thoroughly. Season to taste. Ideally, cover and chill for a while to allow the flavours to develop.

3 Cut the pittas into strips. Eat with the dip.

Ⓥ Cucumber raita Ⓥ

This is the Asian version of Tzaziki (above). You can use mint sauce from a jar instead of the dried mint.

SERVES 1–2

5 cm/2 in piece of cucumber
5 tbsp thick plain yoghurt
1 tsp grated onion
1 tsp dried mint
Salt and pepper

1 Grate the cucumber into a bowl. Squeeze with your hands to drain off the excess moisture.

2 Mix with the yoghurt, onion and mint and add salt and pepper to taste.

Cheese and pickle dip with Ⓥ vegetable sticks Ⓥ

SERVES 1

1 small tub of cottage cheese
2 pickled onions, chopped
2 tsp mayonnaise
Pepper
1 carrot, peeled and cut into fingers
5 cm/2 in piece of cucumber, cut into fingers
½ red or green (bell) pepper, cut into thick strips

1 Tip the cottage cheese into a small bowl. Mix with the pickled onions and mayonnaise, then season with pepper.

2 Eat with the vegetable sticks.

Pâté and horseradish dip with vegetable sticks

This is also good spread on crusty bread or toast. Any leftovers can be kept in the fridge for up to 3 days.

SERVES 4

½ small tub of soft white cheese, such as Philadelphia
4 tbsp single (light) cream or mayonnaise
1 tbsp horseradish relish
1 small barrel of smooth liver pâté
Milk
Salt and pepper
Carrot, cucumber and
red (bell) pepper sticks

1 Mix the cheese, cream, horseradish and pâté in a bowl until smooth, stirring briskly with a wooden spoon.

2 Thin with milk to a soft consistency that will drop easily off a spoon but is not runny. Season to taste.

3 Eat with carrot, cucumber and red pepper sticks to dip in.

Cheesy dip with tomatoes **(V)** and crackers **(V)**

SERVES 1

2 tbsp soft white cheese
A handful of grated Cheddar cheese
or crumbled blue cheese
½ tsp grated onion
½ tsp Worcestershire sauce
1 tbsp milk
2 tomatoes, chopped
Wheat or rye crackers

1 Mash the cheeses with the onion.
2 Stir in the Worcestershire sauce and milk, then add the tomatoes.
3 Eat with crackers.

Caerphilly and onion dip with crunchy **(V)** vegetables **(V)**

SERVES 1

A handful of grated Caerphilly cheese
1 tbsp butter or margarine
1 tbsp crème fraîche
½ tsp grated onion
1 tsp dried chives
Salt and pepper
¼ small cauliflower,
broken into tiny florets
2 carrots, peeled or scraped,
then cut into matchsticks
1 courgette (zucchini),
cut into matchsticks

1 Mix the cheese with the butter or margarine, crème fraîche and onion.
2 Stir in the chives and season to taste with salt and pepper. Tip into a small pot.
3 Use the chunks of vegetables to dunk into the mixture.

Salads

Salads are quick and easy to prepare and make excellent snacks. A good dressing will make a plain salad taste much more special, so I've included a recipe for that too.

French dressing

Use a small, clear glass jar with a tightly fitting screw-top lid.

SERVES 4–6

1 Quarter-fill the jar with red or white wine vinegar.
2 Top up with olive or sunflower oil (so that you have one part vinegar to three parts oil).
3 Add a good pinch of caster (superfine) sugar, a pinch of salt and some freshly ground black pepper.
4 Screw on the lid and shake thoroughly. Store in the fridge and use as required. Shake well before use.

Note: For added flavour, you can put in a squeeze of garlic purée (paste), a small teaspoonful of Dijon mustard or a good pinch of dried mixed herbs or oregano.

ⓥ Green salad ⓥ

You can use almost any salad ingredients you like for this, as long as they are green. You could try adding a couple of canned artichoke hearts, chopped, or some chopped avocado, if you are really pushing the boat out, and sprinkle the whole lot with some fresh herbs.

SERVES 1

2–3 lettuce leaves, torn
2.5 cm/1 in piece of cucumber, sliced or finely diced
½ green (bell) pepper, sliced or diced
2–3 spring onions (scallions), trimmed and chopped
French dressing (see page 44)

1 Put the lettuce leaves into a bowl.
2 Scatter the other ingredients over the top.
3 Add the French dressing and toss.

ⓥ Mixed salad ⓥ

SERVES 1

1 tomato, cut into small wedges
A few lettuce leaves,
torn into small pieces
1 cm/½ in piece of cucumber, sliced
½ red or green (bell) pepper,
cut into thin strips
1 tsp red wine vinegar
2 tsp sunflower or olive oil
A pinch of sugar
Salt and pepper

1 Put all the salad stuffs in a dish.
2 Sprinkle with the vinegar, oil, sugar, salt and pepper and toss gently together.

ⓥ Beansprout salad ⓥ

SERVES 1

½ red (bell) pepper, thinly sliced
1 spring onion (scallion), chopped
½ mug of beansprouts
1 tbsp olive oil
1 tsp wine vinegar
1 tsp soy sauce

1 Put the pepper and spring onion in a bowl with the beansprouts.
2 Sprinkle the remaining ingredients over and toss thoroughly.

ⓥ Village salad ⓥ

SERVES 1

1 small wedge of white cabbage, shredded
A few lettuce leaves, shredded
1 tomato, cut into wedges
1 cm/½ in piece of cucumber, diced
3 black olives
1 slice of onion, separated into rings, discarding the skin
1 cm/½ in finger of feta cheese, crumbled
A pinch of dried oregano
Salt and pepper
2 tsp olive oil
1 tsp red wine vinegar

1 Put the cabbage and lettuce in a dish. Scatter with the tomatoes, cucumber, olives, onion rings and cheese.
2 Sprinkle with the oregano and some salt and pepper.
3 Trickle the oil and vinegar all over the surface and leave to stand for 30 minutes before eating.

ⓥ Eastern tomato salad ⓥ

Eat this with naan bread for a light lunch or serve as an accompaniment to curries.

SERVES 1

1 large or 2 medium tomatoes, diced
¼ small red onion, peeled and finely chopped
2 tbsp desiccated (shredded) coconut
1 tbsp lemon juice
Salt and pepper
1 tsp chopped fresh parsley or coriander (cilantro) or ½ tsp dried parsley

1 Mix all the ingredients together.

2 Leave to stand for at least 30 minutes to allow the flavours to develop.

ⓥ French cabbage salad ⓥ

Eat this with bread on its own, or scattered with a handful of diced cheese, or with a few canned, drained anchovies laid on top.

SERVES 1

1 wedge of white cabbage
1 tbsp olive oil
1 tsp wine vinegar
Salt and pepper
A pinch of sugar
A few black or green olives (optional)

1 Shred the cabbage thinly or grate coarsely, discarding any thick central stump.

2 Put in a bowl with the oil, vinegar, a sprinkling of salt and pepper and the sugar.

3 Toss gently, then, if possible, leave to stand for 30 minutes to allow the flavours to develop.

4 Scatter a few olives over, if liked.

Tomato and onion ⓥ salad ⓥ

SERVES 1

2 tomatoes, sliced
1 onion, peeled and sliced into rings
A pinch of sugar
Salt and pepper
A pinch of dried mixed herbs
1 tsp red wine vinegar
2 tsp sunflower or olive oil

1 Put the slices of tomato into a serving dish.

2 Arrange the onion rings over the tomatoes.

3 Sprinkle with the sugar, salt, pepper and herbs, then trickle the vinegar and oil over.

Curried sweetcorn ⓥ salad ⓥ

SERVES 1

1 tbsp mayonnaise
1–2 tsp curry powder or paste
1 tsp tomato ketchup (catsup)
1 × 200 g/7 oz/small can of sweetcorn (corn), drained
2.5 cm/1 in piece of cucumber, cut into small chunks
½ tsp dried chives
Salt and pepper
3–4 crisp lettuce leaves, roughly torn
2 tomatoes, cut into wedges

1 Mix the mayonnaise with the curry powder or paste to taste and stir in the ketchup.

2 Stir in the sweetcorn, cucumber and chives and season to taste.

3 Put the lettuce in a bowl. Pile the corn mixture on top and arrange the tomato wedges around.

🅥 English-style coleslaw 🅥

This will keep in the fridge for several days.

SERVES 4

½ small white cabbage
2 carrots, peeled and grated
½ small onion, peeled and grated
3 tbsp mayonnaise
1 tbsp olive oil
1 tbsp white wine vinegar
A pinch of caster (superfine) sugar
Salt and pepper

1 Cut out the thick stalk of the cabbage and discard, together with any damaged outer leaves. Grate the cabbage into a salad bowl.

2 Put all the grated vegetables into the bowl.

3 Mix the remaining ingredients together in a small bowl, then pour over the vegetables.

4 Stir gently until well mixed. Chill, if time allows, before eating.

Middle Eastern 🅥 coleslaw 🅥

When cold, this will keep in the fridge. Serve as a side dish – it's good with sausages and chicken.

SERVES 4

½ small white cabbage
2 carrots, peeled and coarsely grated
2 tbsp raisins
2 tbsp sliced green olives
Salt and pepper
3 tbsp olive oil
2 tbsp black mustard seeds
1 tbsp lemon juice

1 Cut out the thick core from the cabbage and discard any damaged outer leaves.

2 Grate coarsely into a salad bowl.

3 Add the grated carrot, then the raisins and olives. Season lightly.

4 Heat the oil in a frying pan (skillet) over a high heat. Add the mustard seeds and fry (sauté) until they start to 'pop'.

5 Add the lemon juice, stir and pour over the salad. Lift and stir until well mixed. Serve warm or chilled.

ⓥ Italian coleslaw ⓥ

This will keep well in the fridge for a day or two and the flavour will improve as it stands.

SERVES 4

½ small white cabbage
½ small celeriac (celery root), thickly peeled
1 small garlic clove, peeled and crushed
4 tbsp olive oil
1½ tbsp white wine vinegar
A good pinch of dried oregano
¼ tsp celery salt
Salt and pepper

1 Cut out the thick core from the cabbage and discard, with any damaged outer leaves.

2 Shred the cabbage and celeriac finely with a sharp knife and place in a large bowl.

3 Put the oil, vinegar and seasonings in a small bowl and whisk together with a wire whisk. Pour over the salad and lift and stir to combine.

4 Leave to stand for at least 30 minutes, if possible, before eating.

ⓥ Fresh cucumber salsa ⓥ

Serve this salsa with flavoured tortilla chips or bagels spread with soft white cheese, or as an accompaniment to falafels, meat, fish or chicken dishes.

SERVES 1–2

¼ small onion, peeled,
or 1 spring onion (scallion), trimmed
5 cm/2 in piece of cucumber,
very finely chopped
½ tsp dried mint
2 tsp sugar
2 tsp wine vinegar
Salt and pepper

1 Chop the onion or spring onion very finely.

2 Mix all the ingredients in a bowl and season to taste.

3 Leave to stand for at least 1 hour, if possible, to allow the flavours to develop.

Marinated
Ⓥ mushrooms Ⓥ

Make these in the morning to eat at
night or prepare the day before, so
the flavours have time to develop.
If you like watercress or salad cress,
either makes a great accompaniment
for the mushrooms.

SERVES 1

8 small button mushrooms
1 spring onion (scallion), trimmed and
very finely chopped
5 tbsp sunflower or olive oil
2 tbsp vinegar
A good pinch each of salt, pepper
and sugar
¼ tsp dried basil
Crusty bread

1 Wipe the mushrooms and trim the
stalks but leave whole.

2 Put all the remaining ingredients
except the mushrooms into a
container with a lid.

3 Whisk the mixture thoroughly.

4 Add the mushrooms, put on the lid
tightly and give the container a good
shake to coat the mushrooms in the
dressing.

5 Chill in the fridge for at least
2 hours. Eat with crusty bread.

Ⓥ Cold salad soup Ⓥ

SERVES 1

Make in the same way as Cold
Tomato and Fresh Basil Soup (see
right) but add a small piece of
cucumber, grated or finely chopped,
and ¼ green or red (bell) pepper,
finely chopped.

Cold tomato and
Ⓥ fresh basil soup Ⓥ

Cold soup may sound a little strange,
but it is delicious – and quick!

SERVES 1

1¼ mugs of passata (sieved tomatoes)
5 tbsp water
1 tsp wine vinegar
1 tsp olive or sunflower oil
1 tbsp crème fraîche or plain yoghurt
A good pinch of caster (superfine) sugar
Salt and pepper
4 fresh basil leaves

1 Whisk all the ingredients except the
basil together in a bowl until
thoroughly blended, seasoning to
taste with salt and pepper.

2 Chop the basil and stir in. Chill, if
liked, before eating.

Refreshing cucumber
Ⓥ soup Ⓥ

SERVES 1

¼ cucumber, grated or very
finely chopped
Salt and pepper
½ tsp dried mint or dill (dill weed)
1½ tsp white wine vinegar
5 tbsp plain yoghurt
5 tbsp cold milk

1 Put the cucumber into a bowl.
Sprinkle with salt and leave to stand
for 10 minutes.

2 Squeeze the cucumber with your
hands to drain off all the moisture.

3 Stir in the mint or dill, the vinegar,
yoghurt and a sprinkling of pepper. If
possible, chill for a while.

4 When ready to eat, stir in the cold
milk.

Recipes you can do with ...
a knife and a can opener

No pans, no cooking – you may not even need a can opener for this chapter as more and more cans have ring-pulls! Apart from some more satisfying sandwiches, there are wraps, tacos and salads, and also some dips to enjoy with bread, crisps or vegetable dippers for tasty, nutritious no-bake meals. They would also be great as nibbles for a party when they would serve more people.

Crispy spiced tuna tacos

SERVES 1

1 tbsp chilli relish
1 × 185 g/6¹/₂ oz/small can of tuna, drained
Worcestershire sauce
3–4 corn taco shells
2 tomatoes, fairly thinly sliced
2.5 cm/1 in piece of cucumber, thinly sliced
3–4 good tsp mayonnaise

1 Mix the chilli relish with the drained tuna. Add a few drops of Worcestershire sauce to taste.

2 Line the taco shells with sliced tomato and cucumber, then spoon in the tuna mixture.

3 Top each with a spoonful of mayonnaise.

Sardine and cucumber mountains

SERVES 1–2

1 × 120 g/4¹/₂ oz/small can of sardines in oil, drained
1 tbsp salad cream or mayonnaise
2.5 cm/1 in piece of cucumber, finely chopped
¹/₂ small onion, peeled and finely chopped
Salt and pepper
2 soft bread rolls
Butter or margarine
A little paprika (optional)

1 Tip the sardines into a bowl and mash with a fork, bones and all.

2 Stir in the salad cream or mayonnaise, the cucumber and onion and season with salt and pepper.

3 Split the rolls in half and spread with butter or margarine.

4 Pile the sardine mixture on top and dust with paprika, if liked.

Pilchard stack

This is quite filling so you could use half and store the remaining pilchard mixture in the fridge for another day.

SERVE 1

1 × 155 g/5¼ oz/small can of pilchards
in tomato sauce
1 tbsp mayonnaise
1 tsp tomato purée (paste)
1 tbsp plain yoghurt
½ tsp white wine vinegar
A pinch of chilli powder
4 slices of bread
Butter or margarine, for spreading
Slices of tomato
Slices of cucumber
A little shredded lettuce

1 Empty the pilchards into a bowl and mash thoroughly (including the bones) with a fork.

2 Add the mayonnaise, tomato purée, yoghurt, vinegar and chilli powder, and stir briskly with a wooden spoon until well blended.

3 Spread the bread with butter or margarine.

4 Spread two slices with the pilchard mixture. Add some slices of tomato and cucumber and some shredded lettuce, then top with the remaining slices of bread.

Spicy sardine and bean pittas

If making for one, store the other portion in a covered container in the fridge. It will keep for 3 days.

SERVES 2

1 × 120 g/4½ oz/small can of sardines
in tomato sauce
1 small garlic clove, peeled and crushed
1 small fresh red chilli, seeded and
finely chopped,
or ¼ tsp chilli powder
1 × 215 g/7½ oz/small can of butter
(lima) beans, drained and mashed
Salt and freshly ground black pepper
4 wholemeal pitta breads
Shredded lettuce
Slices of cucumber

1 Mash the sardines, preferably including the bones. Add the garlic, chilli and mashed beans and season to taste.

2 Make a slit along one side of each to form a pocket. Spoon in the sardine mixture and add some shredded lettuce and sliced cucumber.

ⓥ Mandarin deckers ⓥ

Have the remaining fruit for dessert with yoghurt or custard, or for breakfast with cereal.

SERVES 1

3 slices of bread
3 tbsp soft white cheese,
such as Philadelphia
½ × 300 g/11 oz/medium can of broken mandarin segments, well-drained
½ punnet of salad cress
Black pepper

1 Spread the slices of bread with the cheese.

2 Dry the mandarin pieces on kitchen paper (paper towels), then spread half over one slice of bread. Top with half the cress and a sprinkling of pepper.

3 Add another layer of bread, then the remaining fruit and cress. Season again and top with the third slice, cheese-side down. Press down fairly firmly to stick it all together.

Cold chilli dogs

You can store the remaining hot dogs in the fridge to eat the next day.

SERVES 1

2 finger rolls
Butter or margarine, for spreading
Lettuce leaves
4 hot dog sausages from a can, drained
Chilli sauce or relish, to taste

1 Split the rolls and spread with butter or margarine.

2 Line the rolls with lettuce leaves, then add two hot dog sausages to each.

3 Spread with chilli sauce or relish and serve.

ⓥ Cold chilli bean wraps ⓥ

SERVES 1–2

1 × 425 g/15 oz/large can of red kidney beans, drained
1 green (bell) pepper, chopped
1 tbsp chilli relish
2.5 cm/1 in piece of cucumber, chopped
1 tomato, chopped
Salt and freshly ground black pepper
3 flour tortillas
A little shredded lettuce
3 tbsp plain yoghurt

1 Mash the beans.

2 Mix together all the ingredients except the tortillas, lettuce and yoghurt.

3 Spread the tortillas with the bean mixture.

4 Top with the lettuce, then the yoghurt. Roll up and eat.

Crunchy tuna corn pittas

For an extra nutty flavour, brown the pine nuts briefly in a frying pan – keep stirring them so they don't burn.

SERVES 1–2

A small handful of pine nuts
1 × 185 g/6½ oz/small can of tuna, drained
1 × 200 g/7 oz/small can of sweetcorn (corn), drained
1 celery stick, chopped
1 tbsp tomato relish
Salt and pepper
2 pitta breads

1 Mix all ingredients except the pitta breads together in a bowl and season to taste.

2 Cut the pitta breads in half, then carefully open to form pockets. Fill with the tuna mixture.

ⓥ Mixed bean salad ⓥ

Store any remaining pimientos in a covered container in the fridge and use within 3 days. Try them in salsa (see page 75), or chop them over a pizza or use instead of red pepper in any cooked dish.

SERVES 1

1 tbsp olive oil
2 tsp white wine vinegar
A pinch of sugar
Salt and pepper
1 × 275 g/10 oz/medium can of mixed beans, drained, rinsed and drained again
½ small onion, peeled and chopped
1 canned pimiento, drained and sliced
2 gherkins (cornichons), chopped
Crusty bread

1 Put the oil, vinegar, sugar and a sprinkling of salt and pepper in a bowl. Whisk with a wire whisk or fork until well blended.

2 Add the beans, onion, pimiento and gherkins.

3 Gently turn the ingredients over in the dressing to coat completely and chill for at least 1 hour to allow the flavours to develop. Eat with crusty bread.

Bean salad with ham

SERVES 1

Prepare as for Mixed Bean Salad (above) but add 1–2 slices of diced ham to the mixture.

Bean salad with tuna

SERVES 1

Prepare as for Mixed Bean Salad (left) but add an 85 g/3½ oz/very small can of tuna (or half a 185 g/6½ oz can) to the mixture.

Oriental chicken and beansprout salad

If eating alone, use the leftovers to fill pitta breads for another meal.

SERVES 2

1 × 225 g/8 oz/medium can of pineapple rings
1 green (bell) pepper, sliced
2 mugs of beansprouts
2 handfuls of cooked chicken, cut into bite-sized pieces
1 onion, peeled, halved and thinly sliced
1 tbsp soy sauce
1 tbsp sunflower oil
1 tsp tomato purée (paste)
Salt and pepper
Lettuce leaves
Prawn crackers

1 Drain the pineapple, reserving the juice, and cut into chunks.

2 Mix the pineapple with the pepper, beansprouts, chicken and onion.

3 Whisk the pineapple juice with the soy sauce, sunflower oil, tomato purée and seasoning in a small bowl with a wire whisk.

4 Pour over the salad, lift and stir gently until well mixed. Leave to stand for 30 minutes.

5 Line two bowls with lettuce leaves. Spoon in the salad and eat with prawn crackers.

Devilled tuna salad

If eating alone, make this in
two small bowls. It keeps well in
the fridge.

SERVES 2

3 tbsp olive oil
1 tbsp red wine vinegar
2 tbsp tomato ketchup (catsup)
½ tsp made English mustard
1 tsp Worcestershire sauce
A few drops of Tabasco sauce
1 tsp clear honey
1 × 185 g/6½ oz/small can of tuna,
drained
1 × 275 g/10 oz/medium can of
cut green beans, drained
¼ cucumber, thinly sliced
1 × 50 g/2 oz/small can of anchovy
fillets, drained and halved lengthways
6 stoned (pitted) olives, halved

1 Put the oil, vinegar, ketchup,
mustard, Worcestershire and Tabasco
sauces and honey in a bowl and
whisk together with a wire whisk
until well blended.

2 Stir in the tuna, breaking it up well
with a fork.

3 Put half the beans in a thin layer in
the base of a shallow serving dish.
Top with half the dressed tuna.
Repeat the layers. Top with a layer of
cucumber slices, then arrange the
anchovies over. Garnish with the
olives and chill for at least 1 hour
before eating.

Cheese and tuna croissants

Store the rest of the tuna in a covered
container in the fridge for
up to 3 days.

SERVES 1-2

2 croissants
½ × 185 g/6½ oz/small can of tuna,
drained
2 tsp mayonnaise
Pepper
2-4 thin slices of Cheddar cheese

1 Split the croissants but don't pull
completely apart.

2 Mash the tuna with the mayonnaise
and season with pepper.

3 Spread the mixture in the croissants
and top with slices of cheese.

Ⓥ Russian salad Ⓥ

SERVES 1

1 × 300 g/11 oz/medium can of
diced mixed vegetables
2 tbsp mayonnaise or salad cream
2 tsp olive or sunflower oil
2 tsp wine vinegar
1 tbsp caraway seeds

1 Drain the vegetables thoroughly.

2 Mix the mayonnaise with the oil
and vinegar in a salad bowl. Add half
the caraway seeds.

3 Add the drained vegetables, and stir
until they are well coated.

4 Sprinkle the salad with the
remaining caraway seeds.

Pineapple and beansprout ⓥ salad ⓥ

If eating alone, halve the ingredients. You can eat the pineapple as dessert.

SERVES 2

1 × 225 g/8 oz/small can of
pineapple chunks
1 small red (bell) pepper, diced
2 spring onions (scallions),
trimmed and chopped
2 mugs of beansprouts
1 tbsp soy sauce
1 tbsp sunflower oil
A pinch of Chinese five-spice powder

1 Drain the pineapple, reserving the juice.

2 Mix the pineapple and pepper with the spring onions and beansprouts in a salad bowl.

3 Put the soy sauce, sunflower oil and five-spice powder in a small bowl and add 1 tbsp of the pineapple juice. Whisk with a wire whisk until well blended.

4 Pour the dressing over the salad, then lift and stir everything gently until coated in the dressing.

ⓥ French bean salad ⓥ

This makes a good lunch with some crusty bread. For a more substantial dish, you could add some diced cheese or drained canned tuna.

SERVES 1

1 × 300 g/11 oz/medium can of
whole French (green) beans
½ small onion, peeled and
finely chopped
Salt and pepper
1 tbsp olive or sunflower oil
1 tsp wine vinegar

1 Drain the beans and put in a shallow dish.

2 Sprinkle the onion over, then season lightly, drizzle with the oil and vinegar and toss again. If possible, leave the salad to stand for up to an hour. It's not vital, but it will allow the flavours to develop.

Curried chicken and potato salad

This is a great way of making one cooked chicken portion do two meals. Eat half one day, half the next.

SERVES 2

1 cooked chicken portion
2 tbsp mayonnaise
1 tsp curry paste or powder
2 tsp mango chutney or sweet pickle
2 spring onions (scallions), trimmed
and finely chopped
1 × 300 g/11 oz/medium can of
new potatoes, drained and quartered
5 cm/2 in piece of cucumber,
cut into small dice
1 tbsp olive or sunflower oil
1 tsp vinegar
Salt and pepper

1 Pull all the meat off the chicken portion and cut into bite-sized pieces.

2 Mix the mayonnaise with the curry paste or powder and the chutney. Add the chicken and mix in gently.

3 Put the spring onion into a separate bowl with the potatoes and cucumber. Add the oil, vinegar and a sprinkling of salt and pepper and toss gently.

4 Spoon the potato salad on to a plate and top with the curried chicken mayonnaise.

Minted green pea and Ⓥ lettuce salad Ⓥ

This is delicious on its own as a snack or as an accompaniment. For a more substantial meal, add some diced ham and chopped tomato to the mixture.

SERVES 1

1 tbsp mayonnaise
A good pinch of dried mint
½ tsp lemon juice or vinegar
1 wedge of iceberg lettuce,
roughly chopped
1 × 200 g/7 oz/small can of
garden peas
Salt and pepper
Crusty bread

1 Mix the mayonnaise in a bowl with the mint and the lemon juice or vinegar.

2 Add the lettuce.

3 Drain the peas in a colander over the sink, shaking the colander well to remove the last of the liquid. Add to the bowl with a sprinkling of salt and pepper.

4 Toss gently until everything is combined. Eat with crusty bread.

Tomato, sweetcorn and Ⓥ onion salad Ⓥ

SERVES 1–2

2 spring onions (scallions), trimmed
and chopped
2 tomatoes, cut into small wedges
1 × 200 g/7 oz/small can of sweetcorn
(corn), drained
1 tbsp apple juice
2 tsp lemon juice
3 tbsp olive oil
Salt and pepper
Lettuce leaves

1 Mix the spring onions with the tomatoes and sweetcorn.

2 Whisk the apple juice, lemon juice and oil together with a little salt and pepper in a small bowl with a wire whisk.

3 Pour this dressing over the salad and lift and stir everything until well blended.

4 Line one or two individual bowls with lettuce leaves and add the salad.

Nutty cheese and Ⓥ pineapple salad Ⓥ

You can store the leftover pineapple in the fridge in a covered container for several days. Use it for another recipe, or eat it for dessert with some custard, yoghurt or cream. It will also make a quick supper, with grilled bacon and an egg.

SERVES 1

1 canned pineapple ring, chopped
1 small carton of cottage cheese
1 tbsp walnut pieces, chopped
1 tsp dried chives
Black pepper
A few lettuce leaves
Paprika
Crackers or bread

1 Mix the pineapple with the cheese, nuts, chives and some black pepper.

2 Put some lettuce leaves in a bowl and pile the cheese and nut mixture on top. Sprinkle with paprika and eat with crackers or bread.

Spicy mixed bean
Ⓥ salad Ⓥ

Any remainder will keep well in the fridge.

SERVES 2

*1 × 425 g/15 oz/large can of
mixed beans, drained, rinsed and
drained again
1 onion, peeled and chopped
1 × 170 g/6 oz/small can of pimiento
caps, drained and sliced
4 cornichons, chopped
2 tbsp olive oil
1 tbsp red wine vinegar
A pinch of caster (superfine) sugar
Salt and pepper
1 tsp dried chives*

1 Mix the beans with the onion,
pimientos and cornichons in a bowl.
2 Whisk the oil, vinegar, sugar,
seasoning and chives together in a
small bowl with a wire whisk and
pour over the salad.
3 Lift and stir gently until well
blended, then chill for at least 1 hour
to allow the flavours to develop.

Tuna cocktail salad

Try mixing the tuna with the
mayonnaise mixture for a delicious
sandwich filling.

SERVES 1–2

*2 tbsp mayonnaise
1 tbsp milk
2 tsp tomato ketchup (catsup)
1 tsp Worcestershire sauce
A few drops of Tabasco sauce
or a pinch of chilli powder
Pepper
A few lettuce leaves
Slices of cucumber and tomato
1 × 185 g/6½ oz/small can of tuna,
drained
Bread*

1 Mix the mayonnaise with the milk,
ketchup, Worcestershire and Tabasco
sauces and a little pepper in a small
bowl.
2 Put the lettuce and the slices of
cucumber and tomato on a plate.
3 Top with the tuna, then the sauce.
Eat with bread.

Tuna dip

This is also good with sticks of celery
and cucumber.

SERVES 2

*1 × 185 g/6½ oz/small can of tuna,
drained
4 tbsp mayonnaise
3 tbsp plain yoghurt
1 tbsp tomato ketchup (catsup)
1 tsp lemon juice
A good pinch of chilli powder
Tortilla chips*

1 Put all the ingredients except the
chips in a bowl and stir briskly with a
wooden spoon together until blended.
2 Eat with tortilla chips.

Tuna pâté

This can be stored in the fridge for
3 days. It's great spread on hot toast
or in sandwiches.

SERVES UP TO 3

*1 tbsp mayonnaise
1 × 185 g/6½ oz/small can of tuna,
drained
2 tbsp soft butter or margarine
1 tbsp plain yoghurt
Salt and pepper
A few drops of Tabasco sauce
or a pinch of chilli powder
1 tsp lemon juice*

Mash all the ingredients together in a
bowl, then beat with a wooden spoon
until well blended.

Tuna cheese

Use half this quantity for one meal
and store the remainder in the fridge
for up to 3 days.

SERVES 2

*1 × 185 g/6½ oz/small can of tuna,
drained
1 small carton of soft white cheese,
such as Philadelphia
1 tbsp lemon juice
A good pinch of paprika
Salt and pepper
2 chunks of French bread
A few lettuce leaves*

1 Put the tuna and cheese in a bowl
and stir briskly with a wooden spoon
until well blended, then add all the
remaining ingredients except the
bread and lettuce. Stir again, briskly.

2 Split the French bread along one
side. Gently open and spread with the
tuna cheese, then add some lettuce.

Ⓥ Chilli salsa dip Ⓥ

SERVES 1–2

*1 × 225 g/8 oz/small can of
chopped tomatoes
1 tsp clear honey
2 tbsp tomato purée (paste)
¼ tsp chilli powder
2.5 cm/1 in piece of cucumber,
finely chopped
½ small onion,
peeled and finely chopped
Salt and pepper
Tortilla chips or vegetable sticks*

1 Mix the tomatoes with the honey,
tomato purée and chilli powder in a
small bowl.

2 Stir in the chopped cucumber and
onion and season to taste.

3 Serve with tortilla chips or
vegetable sticks.

Ⓥ Bean and garlic dip Ⓥ

If you find the mixture curdles rather
than blending properly, add a
spoonful of mayonnaise and beat well
with a wooden spoon.

SERVES 1–2

*1 × 215 g/7½ oz/small can of
butter (lima) beans, drained
½ garlic clove, peeled and crushed,
or ½ tsp garlic purée (paste)
4 tbsp olive or sunflower oil
1 tsp lemon juice
Salt and pepper
A pinch of dried mint or oregano
Pitta breads
Vegetable sticks*

1 Put the beans in a bowl and mash
with a fork.

2 Work in the garlic, then gradually
whisk in the oil, using the fork, a
spoonful at a time until thoroughly
blended.

3 Add the lemon juice and salt and
pepper to taste.

4 Sprinkle with the herbs and eat
with pitta breads and vegetable sticks.

 Tomato dip

SERVES 1

1 × 225 g/8 oz/small can of
chopped tomatoes
½ tsp sugar
2 tbsp tomato purée (paste)
½ tsp dried basil
or 1 tsp chopped fresh basil leaves
A few drops of Worcestershire sauce
Salt and pepper
Crusty bread and vegetable sticks

1 Mix the tomatoes with the sugar and tomato purée in a small bowl.

2 Add the basil and Worcestershire sauce, salt and pepper to taste.

3 Eat with crusty bread and vegetable sticks.

Cool cassoulet

SERVES 1–2

1 × 400 g/14 oz/large can of
baked beans
1 pepperami stick
or 2 hot dog sausages
2 tomatoes, chopped
1 tsp Worcestershire or brown
table sauce
Bread

1 Empty the beans into a bowl.

2 Chop the pepperami or sausages.

3 Stir into the beans with the remaining ingredients until well blended.

4 Eat with bread.

Hash mash

Wrap the leftover corned beef in foil. It will keep for a few days in the fridge or for up to 3 months in the freezer.

SERVES 1–2

1 × 350 g/12 oz/large can of
corned beef
1 × 275 g/10 oz/medium can of
potatoes, drained
1 × 150 g/5 oz/small can of
garden peas, drained
1 tbsp sweet pickle
Pepper

1 Tip out the corned beef and cut in half. Put aside one half (see note above). Dice the other half and put in a bowl.

2 Chop the potatoes and add to the bowl with the peas.

3 Crush the mixture lightly with the back of a spoon or a fork and stir in the pickle and pepper to taste.

Recipes you can do with ...
a kettle and a toaster

A kettle and a toaster hardly qualify as sophisticated kitchen equipment but even if that's all you've got, you don't have to limit yourself to tea and toast.

Instant soups are a staple of most students' diets. They aren't very nutritious on their own, but they are great snack meals for emergencies and can be vastly improved if you add a few extra ingredients.

Any canned foods used in this section will have ring pulls, so you shouldn't even need a can opener.

Italian tomato and ⓥ Mozzarella soup ⓥ

SERVES 1

½ small round Mozzarella cheese,
cut into very small dice
1 tomato, finely chopped
2 fresh basil leaves, chopped,
or a pinch of dried basil
2–3 olives, stoned (pitted) and chopped
(optional)
1 sachet of instant tomato soup
Boiling water

1 Put the cheese in a mug and add the tomato, basil and olives, if using.

2 Tip in the soup powder, then top up with boiling water, stirring briskly until the cheese melts and the soup is well blended.

ⓥ Chilli bean soup ⓥ

Use any spicy vegetable soup for this. Add extra chilli powder or Tabasco sauce if you like it really hot.

SERVES 1

1 × 225 g/8 oz/small can of
baked beans
1 sachet of instant spicy tomato soup
1 mug of boiling water

1 Tip the beans into a bowl.

2 Add the soup powder, then mix in the boiling water, stirring briskly until thoroughly blended. Leave to stand for 1 minute (so that the beans heat through) before eating.

Broccoli and cauliflower 🅥 soup with cheese 🅥

SERVES 1

*1 small chunk of Cheddar, Edam or blue
cheese, cut into very small dice
1 sachet of instant broccoli and
cauliflower soup
Boiling water*

1 Put the cheese in a mug, then add
the soup powder.

2 Top up with boiling water, stirring
all the time. Stir thoroughly until the
cheese melts.

Double tomato and ham soup

SERVES 1

*1 slice of ham, cut into very small dice
1 tomato, chopped
1 sachet of instant tomato soup
A pinch of dried oregano
Boiling water*

1 Put the ham and tomato in a mug.

2 Add the sachet of soup powder and
the oregano.

3 Top up with boiling water, stirring
all the time until blended.

Tuna bisque

SERVES 1

*1 × 85 g/3½ oz/very small can of tuna,
drained
1 sachet of instant chicken and
sweetcorn (corn) soup
A pinch of dried mixed herbs
Boiling water*

1 Put the tuna in a mug with the
soup and herbs.

2 Top up with boiling water, stirring
briskly with a fork until well blended.

Oriental-style chicken and sweetcorn soup

SERVES 1

*1 spring onion (scallion), trimmed
and finely chopped
½ block of Chinese egg noodles
Boiling water
1 sachet of instant chicken and
sweetcorn (corn) soup
A few drops of soy sauce*

1 Put the spring onion in a bowl with
the noodles. Cover with boiling water,
stir and leave to stand for 5 minutes.
Drain off the water.

2 Empty the sachet of soup into a
fairly large soup bowl. Add a mug of
boiling water, stirring all the time
until well blended.

3 Add the noodles and spring onion
and stir gently but thoroughly.
Flavour with a few drops of soy sauce
to taste.

Rib-sticking lentil 🅥 mulligatawny soup 🅥

SERVES 1

*1 × 225 g/8 oz/small can of
pease pudding
½ tsp curry paste or powder
1 sachet of instant lentil and
tomato soup
1 tsp sweet pickle
1 mug of boiling water
1 tomato, finely chopped*

1 Empty the pease pudding into a
bowl, stir in the curry paste or
powder, then add everything except
the tomato.

2 Gradually pour in the boiling water,
stirring briskly with a fork. When it is
well blended, add the tomato.

ⓥ Real mushroom soup ⓥ

Use a cup mushroom with pink gills for this, not a flat one with black gills.

SERVES 1

1 large mushroom, very finely chopped
Boiling water
1 sachet of mushroom soup
with croûtons
A pinch of dried thyme or oregano
(optional)

1 Put the chopped mushroom in a mug and add 2 tbsp of boiling water. Leave to stand for 2 minutes.

2 Add the soup powder and croûtons and thyme or oregano, if using. Top up the mug with boiling water, stirring briskly until thoroughly blended.

Instant green Chinese noodles

SERVES 1

1 slab of Chinese egg noodles
1 chicken Oxo cube
2.5 cm/1 in piece of cucumber
½ green (bell) pepper, chopped
1 spring onion (scallion),
trimmed and chopped

1 Put the noodles in a bowl and crumble in the Oxo cube. Add just enough boiling water to cover, stir and leave to soak for 5 minutes.

2 Cut the cucumber into several strips lengthways, then into matchsticks, then very small dice.

3 Stir the noodles well, add all the chopped vegetables and serve.

Special chicken and mushroom soup

If you have any cooked chicken left from a meal, you can use that.

SERVES 1

1 mushroom, very finely chopped
Boiling water
1 slice of cooked pressed chicken,
cut into very small dice
1 sachet of instant chicken and
mushroom soup
A pinch of dried thyme (optional)

1 Put the chopped mushroom in a mug and add 2 tbsp of boiling water. Leave to stand for 2 minutes.

2 Add the chicken and the soup powder and thyme, if using. Top up the mug with boiling water, stirring briskly until thoroughly blended.

Hearty pea and bacon soup

SERVES 1

1 × 200 g/7 oz/small can of
garden peas
1 sachet of instant lentil and bacon soup
A pinch of dried mint (optional)
1 mug of boiling water

1 Drain the liquid from the can of peas, then tip them into a bowl. Mash thoroughly with a fork.

2 Sprinkle over the soup powder and mint, if using. With a fork, gradually work in the boiling water until well blended and thick.

Bumper golden **V** vegetable soup **V**

SERVES 1

1 × 225 g/8 oz/small can of diced
mixed vegetables
1 sachet of instant golden vegetable soup
1 mug of boiling water
1 tsp grated Parmesan cheese

1 Drain the liquid from the can of vegetables, then tip them into a bowl.

2 Sprinkle the soup powder over, then gradually stir in the boiling water until thoroughly blended.

3 Leave to stand for 1 minute, then sprinkle with the Parmesan cheese.

Butter bean soup with **V** garlic bread **V**

SERVES 1

1 slice of French bread
A small knob of butter or margarine
¼ tsp garlic purée (paste)
or a pinch of garlic granules
A pinch of dried mixed herbs
1 × 200 g/7 oz/small can of
butter (lima) beans
1 sachet of instant chicken soup
1 mug of boiling water

1 Toast the bread. Mash the butter or margarine with the garlic and herbs. Spread on the hot toast.

2 Drain off the liquid from the beans and tip them into a bowl. Mash thoroughly with a fork.

3 Sprinkle on the chicken soup powder, then gradually blend in the boiling water, stirring briskly all the time until thoroughly mixed.

4 Float the piece of garlic bread on top.

V Instant peanut soup **V**

SERVES 1

1 tbsp smooth peanut butter
1 sachet of instant golden vegetable or
chicken and vegetable soup
Boiling water

1 Put the peanut butter in a mug and add the soup powder.

2 Top up with boiling water, a little at a time, stirring briskly until well blended and thick.

Toasted bagels with cream **V** cheese and peppers **V**

If you don't like spicy relish, use tomato relish instead.

SERVES 1

1 bagel, split in half
½ small red (bell) pepper, chopped
2 tbsp soft white cheese,
such as Philadelphia
A little pepper
2 tsp chilli relish

1 Toast the bagel halves.

2 Mash the red pepper with the cheese and add a sprinkling of pepper.

3 Spread the cheese thickly on the bagel halves and top each with a spoonful of relish.

Toasted bagel with peanut ⓥ butter and cucumber ⓥ

SERVES 1

1 bagel, split in half
2 tbsp peanut butter
2.5 cm/1 in piece of cucumber,
finely chopped
Pepper
2 tsp thick plain yoghurt (optional)

1 Toast the bagel halves.

2 Mash the peanut butter with the cucumber and season with pepper.

3 Spread this mixture thickly on the bagels and top each with a spoonful of yoghurt, if liked.

Toasted bagel with salmon salad spread

SERVES 1

1 bagel, split in half
½ small jar of salmon paste or spread
1 tbsp mayonnaise
1 tomato, finely chopped
1 cm/½ in piece of cucumber,
finely chopped
A dash of Worcestershire sauce
Pepper

1 Toast the bagel.

2 Mash the salmon paste or spread with the mayonnaise until smooth, then mix in all the tomato and nearly all the cucumber. Season to taste with Worcestershire sauce and pepper.

3 Spread thickly on the bagels, then top each with the remaining cucumber.

Toasted bagel with citrus ⓥ cheese topping ⓥ

SERVES 1

1 bagel, split in half
1 satsuma or clementine
2 tbsp soft white cheese,
such as Philadelphia
A little sugar, to taste
2 tsp orange marmalade

1 Toast the bagel.

2 Peel the satsuma or clementine and chop the segments. Tip into a bowl and mix with the cheese and sweeten with a little sugar, if liked.

3 Spread the bagels with the marmalade, then top with the cheese mixture.

Toasted teacake with sunflower seed and ⓥ banana topping ⓥ

If you eat this straight away, you won't need to use the lemon juice.

SERVES 1

1 teacake, split in half
Butter or margarine
1 small banana
A squeeze of lemon juice
1–2 tsp clear honey
2 tsp sunflower seeds

1 Toast the teacake, then spread with a little butter or margarine.

2 Peel and mash the banana and add a squeeze of lemon juice, to prevent browning.

3 Pile on the teacake and trickle the honey over. Sprinkle with the sunflower seeds and serve.

Lemon cheese
Ⓥ teacakes Ⓥ

One of those tiny pots of fromage frais is just right for this recipe.

SERVES 1

1 teacake, split in half
1 tbsp lemon curd
2 tbsp of fromage frais

1 Toast the teacake.

2 Mix the lemon curd with the fromage frais and spoon on top of the toasted teacake halves.

Waffles with
Ⓥ strawberries Ⓥ

You can use any soft fruit you like, including blackberries, which you may be able to pick for free (but don't get them from beside a busy road, or they'll be covered in pollutants). Choose different flavoured yoghurts to go with different fruits.

SERVES 1–2

2 waffles
1 small carton of plain or strawberry-flavoured yoghurt
A handful of strawberries, halved or sliced if large
A little sugar, preferably caster (superfine)

1 Toast the waffles.

2 Place on a plate and spoon over the yoghurt. Top with the fruit and sprinkle with sugar.

Ⓥ Honey nut waffles Ⓥ

SERVES 1–2

2 waffles
2 tbsp chopped mixed nuts
1 tbsp clear honey
2 tbsp soft white cheese,
such as Philadelphia
A pinch of ground cinnamon

1 Toast the waffles.

2 Mix the nuts with the honey and spread over the toasted waffles.

3 Top each with a spoonful of soft cheese and sprinkle with cinnamon.

Chocolate orange
Ⓥ waffles Ⓥ

SERVES 1–2

2 waffles
2 satsumas or clementines
2 tbsp chocolate spread
1 small Flake chocolate bar

1 Toast the waffles.

2 Peel the satsumas or clementines and pull off any white pith.

3 Spread the waffles with the chocolate spread. Arrange the fruit segments on top and crumble the Flake bar over.

Honey cinnamon
Ⓥ toast Ⓥ

SERVES 1–2

2 knobs of soft butter or margarine
2 tsp clear honey
$\frac{1}{2}$ tsp ground cinnamon
2 slices of bread

1 Mash the butter or margarine with the honey and cinnamon.

2 Toast the bread and spread immediately with the cinnamon mixture. Eat warm.

Anchovy toast

Any leftover anchovies can be used for Salad Niçoise (see page 164). They will keep in the fridge for several days and can be frozen for up to 3 months.

SERVES 1–2

2 canned anchovy fillets
2 knobs of soft butter or margarine
¼ tsp tomato purée (paste)
Pepper
2 slices of bread

1 Put the anchovies in a mug or small bowl and snip with scissors until they almost form a paste (alternatively, chop them into very small pieces with a sharp knife).

2 Mash in the butter or margarine, tomato purée and a little pepper.

3 Toast the bread. Spread immediately with the anchovy mixture and eat warm.

Savoury white cheese and Ⓥ cress toastie Ⓥ

SERVES 1

1 slice of toast
Butter or margarine
Marmite or other yeast extract
1 tbsp soft white cheese,
such as Philadelphia
A small handful of salad cress

1 Toast the bread and spread with butter or margarine.

2 Add a thin scraping of Marmite, then spread with the cheese.

3 Sprinkle the cress over.

Ⓥ Tabbouleh Ⓥ

SERVES 1

½ mug of bulghar (cracked wheat)
½ small garlic clove, crushed,
or ¼ tsp garlic purée (paste)
A handful of chopped fresh parsley
A handful of chopped fresh mint
A squeeze of lemon juice
1 tbsp olive oil
Salt and pepper
2.5 cm/1 in piece of cucumber,
finely chopped
1 tomato, cut into small pieces

1 Put the bulghar in a bowl. Add just enough boiling water to cover the wheat and leave to stand for 30 minutes. Stir with a fork to fluff up.

2 Add the garlic, herbs, lemon juice, olive oil and seasoning. Lift and stir until thoroughly mixed and leave until cold.

3 Stir in the cucumber and tomatoes.

Bulghar salad with feta, pumpkin seeds ⓥ and apples ⓥ

Feta cheese is great for freezing: simply wrap it tightly in foil and freeze for up to 6 months. Even better, it can be used straight from the freezer. Just cut it up, using a large sharp knife, then crumble into the dish.

SERVES 1

½ mug of bulghar (cracked wheat)
1 spring onion (scallion), trimmed and chopped
1 small red eating (dessert) apple, quartered, cored and diced
1 cm/½ in finger of feta cheese, crumbled
1 tbsp pumpkin seeds
1 tbsp olive or sunflower oil
1 tsp vinegar
Salt and pepper
¼ tsp dried mint

1 Put the bulghar in a bowl and pour in just enough boiling water to cover it. Stir well and leave to stand until cold and all the water is absorbed.

2 Add all the remaining ingredients to the bulghar, mixing well.

Warm oriental sweetcorn ⓥ salad ⓥ

SERVES 1–2

¼ × 250 g/9 oz packet of rice noodles
Boiling water
½ small red (bell) pepper, sliced
A handful of fresh beansprouts
1 carrot, peeled and cut into very thin matchsticks
2.5 cm/1 in piece of cucumber, cut into very thin matchsticks
1 × 200 g/7 oz/small can of sweetcorn (corn), drained
2 tbsp sunflower oil
2 tsp wine vinegar
2 tsp soy sauce
A good pinch of sugar
A good pinch of pepper

1 Put the noodles in a bowl and cover with boiling water. Stir for 2 minutes. Add the vegetables to the bowl, stir again and leave to stand for 3 minutes. Drain off the water.

2 Add the oil, vinegar, soy sauce, sugar and pepper and lift and stir with a fork and spoon to mix thoroughly. Serve warm.

Eastern chicken and couscous salad

This is another great way to make two meals out of one cooked chicken portion. Store the remainder in the fridge and eat within 3 days.

SERVES 2

1 mug of boiling water
½ chicken stock cube
½ mug of couscous
1 small green or red (bell) pepper
or 1 courgette (zucchini)
1 cooked chicken portion
2 spring onions (scallions),
trimmed and chopped
A handful of dried apricots, quartered
¼ tsp dried mint or oregano
¼ tsp ground cinnamon
or mixed (apple-pie) spice
A handful of chopped fresh parsley
or coriander (cilantro)
1 tbsp olive oil
1 tsp lemon juice
Salt and pepper

1 Put the boiling water in a bowl and stir in the stock cube until dissolved. Add the couscous, stir, then leave to soak and cool.

2 If using a pepper, cut it in half, remove the stalk, white pith and seeds and cut into small pieces. If using a courgette, slice it, discarding the ends.

3 Pull all the meat off the chicken portion and cut into bite-sized pieces.

4 When the couscous is completely cold, add all the remaining ingredients and mix well.

Couscous with nuts **v** and raisins **v**

This is nutritious and filling and especially good when funds are low.

SERVES 1

½ mug of couscous
½ vegetable stock cube
1 mug of boiling water
½ tsp garam masala
1 × 50 g/2 oz/small packet of
peanuts and raisins
2.5 cm/1 in piece of cucumber, chopped
Salt and pepper

1 Put the couscous in a bowl.

2 Crumble the stock cube in the boiling water and stir until dissolved. Pour over the couscous, add the garam masala, stir well, then leave to soak for about 20 minutes or until all the liquid has been absorbed.

3 Stir in the remaining ingredients.

RECiPES YOU can DO WitH ...
a HanD BLenDeR

Electric hand blenders are really cheap, take up hardly any space and are simple to use: all you do is put them into a mixture and press the button for soups, smoothies and excellent drinks.

Cold smoothies are a great way to get loads of goodness in a glass. Have them for breakfast, a quick lunch or a snack to keep you going. All the smoothies in this section make about 600 ml/1 pt – so a 1-pint beer glass is ideal. If you haven't got one, make the mixture in a bowl, and drink it from a glass or mug. Either way, the washing-up is minimal.

This section also includes some great dips, cold soups and pâtés for you to enjoy.

Ⓥ Breakfast booster Ⓥ

SERVES 1

¼ mug of orange juice
¼ mug of milk
1 tbsp concentrated orange squash
(preferably high-juice)
1 small carton of any fruit- or nut-
flavoured yoghurt
1 Weetabix

1 Put the juice and milk into a large glass. Add the squash and yoghurt.
2 Crumble the Weetabix over the surface. Whizz with the blender until thick and smooth.

Mandarin morning
Ⓥ magic Ⓥ

SERVES 1

1 × 300 g/11 oz/small can of broken
mandarin segments
1 small carton of orange- or apricot-
flavoured yoghurt
1 tbsp instant oat cereal
½ mug of milk

1 Put the mandarins, yoghurt and cereal in a large glass. Blend until smooth.
2 Add the milk and blend again until frothy.

Banana with ⓥ attitude ⓥ

You can use oat or wheat bran instead of the oat cereal if you prefer.

SERVES 1

1 mug of milk
1 large or 2 small ripe bananas
1 tbsp instant oat cereal
1 tsp clear honey
½ tsp ground cinnamon

1 Measure the milk into a large glass.

2 Peel the banana, break it up and add to the milk.

3 Add the cereal, honey and cinnamon and whizz with the blender until smooth.

ⓥ Iced orange cream ⓥ

SERVES 1

1 mug of pure orange juice
A pinch of ground cinnamon
1 tsp lemon juice
2 scoops of vanilla ice cream
2 ice cubes (optional)

1 Put all the ingredients except the ice in a large glass. Blend until smooth and frothy.

2 Add the ice cubes, if using.

Fresh banana ⓥ milkshake ⓥ

SERVES 1

1 large ripe banana,
peeled and broken into pieces
1 tsp clear honey
1 mug of ice-cold milk

1 Put all the ingredients in a large glass.

2 Blend until smooth, thick and frothy.

Banana and strawberry ⓥ yoghurt smoothie ⓥ

SERVES 1

1 ripe banana,
peeled and broken into pieces
1 small carton of strawberry-flavoured yoghurt
2 tsp strawberry jam (conserve)
1 tsp lemon juice

1 Put all the ingredients in a large glass.

2 Blend until smooth, thick and frothy.

ⓥ Banana egg nog ⓥ

This is good shared with a mate – or you can drink the whole lot!

SERVES 1–2

1 ripe banana,
peeled and broken into pieces
2 tsp light brown sugar
1 egg
1 mug of ice-cold milk
1 tbsp brandy, vodka or rum

1 Put the banana and sugar in a bowl. Blend until smooth.

2 Add the remaining ingredients and blend again until thick and frothy. Pour into one or two glasses.

ⓥ Apricot ambrosia ⓥ

SERVES 1

1 × 225 g/8 oz/small can of apricots
¹/₂ mug of ice-cold milk
2 scoops of vanilla ice cream
Ice cubes
American dry ginger ale

1 Put all the apricots and their juice with the milk and ice cream in a large glass. Blend until smooth.

2 Add ice cubes, top up with ginger ale and stir well before drinking.

ⓥ Spiced peach soda ⓥ

SERVES 1

Prepare as for Apricot Ambrosia (above) but use canned peaches instead of apricots and add a good pinch of mixed (apple-pie) spice to the mixture.

ⓥ Chocolate pear soda ⓥ

SERVES 1–2

1 × 225 g/8 oz/small can of pear quarters
¹/₂ mug of apple juice
2 tbsp drinking (sweetened) chocolate powder
2 scoops of chocolate ice cream
Ice cubes
Cream soda

1 Put the pears and their juice, the apple juice and chocolate powder in a bowl.

2 Add the ice cream and blend until smooth and frothy.

3 Put the ice cubes in one or two glasses. Pour over the pear mixture and top up with cream soda. Stir again before drinking.

ⓥ Peach sunrise ⓥ

SERVES 1

¹/₂ mug of ice-cold milk
1 × 225 g/8 oz/small can of peach slices
1 very tiny tub of raspberry-flavoured fromage frais

1 Pour the milk into a large glass.

2 Add the can of peaches and the fromage frais.

3 Whizz with the blender until smooth.

ⓥ A trifle smooth ⓥ

If you don't have any trifle sponges, a slice of any plain cake will do – and it doesn't matter if it's a bit stale.

SERVES 1

1 trifle sponge
1 × 225 g/8 oz/small can of pineapple pieces
1 carton of raspberry-flavoured custard-style yoghurt
¹/₂ mug of milk
1 tsp raspberry jam (conserve)

1 Crumble the trifle sponge into a large glass.

2 Add the pineapple pieces, yoghurt, milk and jam. Blend until smooth.

ⓥ Tropical paradise ⓥ

SERVES 1

*¼ block of creamed coconut, cut into
small pieces*
½ mug of milk or water
1 banana, peeled and broken into pieces
*1 × 225 g/8 oz/small can of
pineapple pieces*
1 sponge (lady) finger

1 Put the coconut and milk or water in a large glass. Blend until smooth.

2 Add the banana and pineapple and blend again until thick and frothy.

3 Serve with the sponge finger to dunk in the mixture.

ⓥ Caffeine fix ⓥ

SERVES 1

½ mug water
1–2 tsp instant coffee granules
1 tsp clear honey
1 handful of chopped mixed nuts
*2 digestive biscuits (graham crackers),
crumbled*
*1 × 170 g/6 oz/small can of
evaporated milk, chilled*
2 scoops of vanilla ice cream

1 Mix the water with the coffee in a large glass. Add the honey, nuts, crumbled digestives and evaporated milk. Blend until smooth and thick.

2 Add the ice cream and blend again.

ⓥ Seriously tangoed! ⓥ

SERVES 1

*1 × 300 g/11 oz/medium can of broken
mandarin segments*
1 banana, peeled and broken into pieces
A few ice cubes
1 can of orange Tango

1 Put the mandarin segments and banana in a bowl. Blend until smooth and thick.

2 Put the ice cubes into a plastic bag and bash with a rolling pin or saucepan until crushed. Fill a large glass with the crushed ice.

3 Add the mandarin mixture and top up with orange Tango.

4 Stir well before drinking.

Strawberry yoghurt ⓥ cooler ⓥ

Fresh strawberries are great for a treat and you can often pick them up in the market quite cheaply. To crush ice, put it in a plastic bag and bash with a rolling pin.

SERVES 1

4–6 strawberries, hulled
*1 small carton of strawberry-flavoured
yoghurt*
½ mug of ice-cold milk
1 tsp clear honey
A squeeze of lime or lemon juice
Crushed ice

1 Put the strawberries and yoghurt in a bowl. Blend together, gradually adding the milk.

2 Add the honey and lime or lemon juice.

3 Fill a tall glass with crushed ice, then pour in the strawberry mixture.

Autumn hedgerow
ⓥ heaven ⓥ

SERVES 1

½ mug of ripe blackberries, hulled
½ mug of apple juice
2 scoops of vanilla ice cream
½ mug of milk
A good pinch of ground cinnamon
1 tsp clear honey

1 Put all the ingredients except the honey in a bowl and blend until thick and smooth.

2 Taste and add the honey if necessary, blending briefly again.

3 Strain the smoothie through a sieve (strainer) to remove the seeds, if you prefer. If not, just pour into a large glass and enjoy.

ⓥ Gazpachio in a glass ⓥ

SERVES 1

1 slice of bread, broken into pieces
½ mug of water
½ mug of passata (sieved tomatoes)
1 carrot, peeled and finely grated
½ red or green (bell) pepper, chopped
1 spring onion (scallion),
trimmed and chopped
A pinch of dried basil
A pinch of sugar
Salt and pepper
Ice cubes

1 Put the pieces of bread in a bowl or large glass and soak in the water for a minute or two.

2 Add the remaining ingredients and blend until smooth. Taste and adjust the seasoning.

3 Add some ice cubes.

ⓥ Vitamin booster ⓥ

This is the perfect morning pick-me-up (and it's pretty good as a hangover cure too). If you haven't got a fresh lemon, use 1 tbsp of bottled lemon juice.

SERVES 1

1 mug of tomato juice
½ lemon
1 tsp Marmite or other yeast extract
A few drops of Tabasco sauce
or a pinch of chilli powder
1 tsp clear honey

1 Pour the tomato juice into a large glass.

2 Squeeze the lemon juice into the glass (to get all the juice out, use a fork to pierce the flesh while you squeeze the lemon with the other hand).

3 Add the Marmite or other yeast extract, Tabasco sauce or chilli powder and the honey.

4 Whizz with the blender until smooth.

Cheese and tomato whizz

Eat the bread crusts while you blitz the shake!

SERVES 1

½ small tub of cheese spread
¾ mug of milk
1 slice of bread, crusts removed
2 tomatoes, cut into quarters
A good splash of Worcestershire sauce

1 Put the cheese spread in a large glass.

2 Add the remaining ingredients and blend until smooth.

Ⓥ Late-night reviver Ⓥ

SERVES 1

½ mug of ice-cold milk
1 good tbsp chocolate spread
1 satsuma, peeled and segmented
or 1 pear, peeled, quartered and cored
1 × 200 g/7 oz/small can of creamed
rice pudding

1 Put all the ingredients in a large glass.

2 Blend until thick and smooth.

English breakfast in a cup

Bread sticks make great nibbles and they can be stored for ages in their box wrapped tightly in a plastic bag or stored in an airtight container. Eat one or two with this smoothie for a more substantial meal. This also makes a good snack lunch.

SERVES 1

¾ mug of milk
1 tbsp mayonnaise (not salad cream)
1 × 225 g/8 oz/small can of baked
beans with sausages
A dash of Worcestershire
or brown table sauce

1 Pour the milk into a large glass.

2 Add the mayo, beans and sausages and a good dash of Worcestershire or brown table sauce.

3 Whizz with the blender until smooth.

Ⓥ Sangrita Ⓥ

This is seriously spicy. If you've finished your work and think you deserve a treat, add a shot of tequila – but not if you're studying!

SERVES 1

2 ripe tomatoes, quartered
1 fresh orange, halved
2 tsp lime or lemon juice
1 small piece of onion, peeled
¼ tsp sugar
¼ tsp chilli powder
A pinch of black pepper, preferably
freshly ground
Ice cubes

1 Put all the ingredients in a bowl. Blend until smooth.

2 Fill a glass with ice cubes and pour in the Sangrita.

Ⓥ Cool dude Ⓥ

SERVES 1

5 cm/2 in piece of cucumber,
roughly chopped
1 carrot, peeled and grated
1 slice of bread
1 small carton of plain yoghurt
2 good tbsp soft cheese
with garlic and herbs
1 tsp dried mint
1 tsp vinegar
½ mug of milk
Salt and pepper

1 Put everything except the salt and pepper in a large glass. Blend until smooth.

2 Season to taste.

Tangy carrot, tomato and ⓥ orange soup ⓥ

You can store this in the fridge to enjoy any time. It's good hot, too. For an extra dreamy result, add a spoonful of plain yoghurt or cream.

SERVES 2–4

1 × 275 g/10 oz/medium can of carrots, drained
1 × 400 g/14 oz/large can of tomatoes
½ mug of pure orange juice
1 tsp dried basil
or dried mixed herbs
Salt and pepper

1 Put all the ingredients in a bowl and blend until smooth.

2 Taste and re-season the soup, if necessary.

Fresh tomato and ⓥ pimento salsa ⓥ

This salsa will keep in the fridge for several days so it's not worth making less than this quantity. Serve it with cold meats, sausages, fish or falafels.

SERVES UP TO 4

4 ripe tomatoes, skinned
1 × 200 g/7 oz/small can of pimientos, drained
1 tbsp tomato purée (paste)
1 tbsp wine vinegar
1 tsp clear honey
Salt and pepper

1 Put all the ingredients except the salt and pepper in a bowl and blend together.

2 Season to taste. Use as required.

ⓥ Italian smoothie ⓥ

This is also really nice if you heat the mixture.

SERVES 1

1 × 225 g/8 oz/small can of tomatoes
1 × 225 g/8 oz/small can of spaghetti in tomato sauce
1 small red (bell) pepper, chopped
1 tbsp grated Parmesan cheese
or cheese spread
A good pinch of dried oregano
3 stoned (pitted) olives

1 Put all the ingredients in a large glass.

2 Blend until smooth.

Tuna and sweetcorn creation

SERVES 1

1 × 200 g/7 oz/small can of sweetcorn (corn), drained
½ × 185 g/6½ oz/small can of tuna, drained
1 good tbsp mayonnaise
¾ mug of ice-cold milk
A small handful of fresh parsley
A few drops of Tabasco
or other chilli sauce
A stick of celery

1 Put the corn, tuna, mayonnaise, milk and parsley in a large glass. Blend until smooth.

2 Add Tabasco or other chilli sauce to taste and blend again.

3 Serve with a celery stick as a stirrer.

Sardine pâté

Try this spread on bread with a few onion rings scattered over the top. It's also great spread on rye crispbread. If you don't eat it immediately, cover and keep in the fridge for up to 3 days.

SERVES 1–2

1 × 120 g/4¹/₂ oz/small can of sardines in oil, drained
A good knob of butter or margarine
2 tbsp plain yoghurt
¹/₂ tsp lemon juice
A few drops of Tabasco sauce or a pinch of chilli powder
Salt and pepper

1 Put all the ingredients in a bowl.

2 Blend until smooth, then use as required.

Tuna bean spread

If you don't eat all this in one go, store it in a container with a lid in the fridge for up to 3 days.

SERVES 1–2

1 × 425 g/15 oz/large can of cannellini beans, drained
1 garlic clove, peeled and crushed
1 × 85 g/3¹/₂ oz/very small can of tuna, drained
2 tbsp sunflower oil
1 tbsp lemon juice
A good pinch of cayenne or chilli powder
Pitta breads
A little shredded lettuce
A few slices of cucumber

1 Put all the ingredients except the breads and salad stuffs in a bowl and blend until fairly smooth.

2 Spoon the mixture into pitta breads, then add lettuce and cucumber.

Smoked mackerel pâté

Spread this on bread or eat with hot toast.

SERVES 1–2

1 smoked mackerel fillet
2 good knobs of butter or margarine
A squeeze of lemon juice (about ¹/₂ tsp)
Pepper

1 Pull the skin off the fish and remove any visible bones.

2 Put the fish in a bowl with the butter or margarine and lemon juice. Blend until smooth. Season with pepper.

ⓥ Hummus ⓥ

Tahini (sesame seed) paste is not cheap, but a jar of it will keep for ages. To be authentic, you should serve this with warm pitta breads but bread or crackers will do.

SERVES UP TO 4

1 × 425 g/15 oz/large can of chick peas (garbanzos), drained
2 tbsp lemon juice
5 tbsp tahini paste (optional)
1 garlic clove, peeled and crushed, or 1 tsp garlic purée (paste)
2 tbsp olive oil
Salt and pepper

1 Put the chick peas in a bowl with the lemon juice.

2 Blend until the mixture is a smooth purée.

3 Add the tahini paste, if using, then the garlic and all but 2 tsp of the olive oil. Blend again until smooth. Season to taste.

4 Spoon the hummus into a small bowl and trickle the remaining oil over.

Recipes You can Do With ... a Sandwich toaster

If you have a sandwich toaster in the kitchen, you can make yourself a hot snack in no time. And teamed with some fresh salad, those snacks can make a complete meal.

Most sandwich toasters need preheating for best results. Check the manufacturer's handbook if you have one – if not, it should take about 5 minutes.

If you don't have a sandwich toaster, you can still make hot sandwiches by cooking them in a frying pan (skillet). Simply prepare according to the instructions, then heat a frying pan and cook for about 2 minutes on each side, pressing down firmly with a fish slice until golden brown and hot through. Alternatively, you can grill (broil) them, again pressing down well and turning halfway through cooking (line the grill pan with foil to save on washing-up).

In most cases (except for panini) I have used four slices of bread, to make two large sandwiches. If you're hungry you'll eat both, but if not, you can eat one cold or reheat it briefly in the sandwich toaster or microwave the next day.

Top tip: If you haven't got a pastry brush and you need to oil the sandwich toaster's plates, pour a little oil on to a piece of kitchen paper (paper towel) and rub it all over the surface. Alternatively, you can smear it with your fingers – but only if the plates are cold!

Chicken and spinach panini

Use the leftover sauce with pasta to make another meal. Baby spinach tends to come in large bags, but you can eat the rest in salads or as a side vegetable. You can use lettuce if you haven't got spinach.

SERVES 1

A little sunflower oil
1 small part-baked baguette
2–3 tbsp ready-made tomato and basil pasta sauce
A few baby spinach leaves
2 slices of cooked pressed chicken
A small handful of grated Cheddar or Mozzarella cheese
Pepper

1 Oil the plates of the sandwich toaster, then preheat it.

2 Split the baguette and open it out slightly.

3 Spread the pasta sauce all over the inside.

4 Fill with the spinach, chicken and cheese.

5 Cook in the sandwich toaster for about 3 minutes until golden on both sides and hot through.

Cheese and ham panini

SERVES 1

A little sunflower oil
1 small part-baked baguette
1 slice of ham
3–4 slices of Cheddar cheese

1 Oil the plates of the sandwich toaster, then preheat it.

2 Split the baguette and open it out slightly.

3 Fill with the ham and cheese, cutting the slices to fit.

4 Cook in the sandwich toaster for about 3 minutes until golden on the outside and the cheese has melted.

Toasted curried chicken sandwiches

MAKES 2

4 slices of bread
Butter or margarine, for spreading
4 slices of cooked pressed chicken, cut into pieces
5 cm/2 in piece of cucumber, thinly sliced
2 tsp sweet pickle
1 tbsp mayonnaise
1 tsp curry paste
Salt and pepper

1 Preheat the sandwich toaster. Spread the slices of bread on one side with butter or margarine.

2 Mix all the rest of the ingredients together.

3 Put two slices of bread, buttered sides down, on the hot plates. Quickly spread the filling over, taking care not to get it too close to the edges.

4 Top with the remaining slices of bread, buttered sides up. Cook in the sandwich toaster for about 2–3 minutes until crisp and golden on the outside.

Toasted baked bean and ⓥ cheese sandwiches ⓥ

If you use half a large can of beans, they work out much cheaper. Put the rest in a covered container in the fridge and use them for another meal within 3 days.

MAKES 2

4 slices of bread
Butter or margarine, for spreading
A little brown table sauce
1 × 225 g/8 oz/small can of baked beans
4-6 thin slices of Cheddar cheese

1 Preheat the sandwich toaster. Spread the slices of bread on one side with butter or margarine. Put two slices, buttered sides down, on the hot plates.

2 Quickly spread lightly with brown sauce. Stir the beans, then spoon on to the bread and spread out, keeping it away from the edges all round. If the tomato sauce is very runny, add only a small amount. Sprinkle on the cheese.

3 Top with the remaining slices of bread, buttered sides up. Cook for about 2-3 minutes until golden.

Chicken Maryland sandwiches

Corn relish is great with sandwiches – especially tuna, bacon and, as here, chicken.

MAKES 2

4 slices of bread
Butter or margarine, for spreading
1 small banana
2 tbsp corn relish
4 slices of cooked pressed chicken
A sprinkling of ground cumin (optional)
A sprinkling of dried onion granules (optional)
A good pinch of dried mixed herbs
Salt and pepper

1 Preheat the sandwich toaster. Spread the slices of bread with butter or margarine on one side.

2 Peel the banana, break it up in a bowl and mash with a fork.

3 Put two slices of bread, buttered sides down, on the hot plates. Quickly spread with the corn relish and top with the chicken.

4 Spread the banana over the chicken.

5 Sprinkle with the cumin and the onion granules, if using, then the herbs and a little salt and pepper.

6 Top with the remaining slices of bread, buttered sides up. Cook in the sandwich toaster for about 2-3 minutes until golden.

Creamy mushroom and *V* herb toasties *V*

Store the leftover mushrooms in a covered container in the fridge. They make a good sauce with chicken or fish.

MAKES 2

4 slices of bread
Butter or margarine, for spreading
1 × 170 g/6 oz/small can of
creamed mushrooms
1/2 tsp dried oregano

1 Preheat the sandwich toaster. Spread the slices of bread with butter or margarine on one side.

2 Put two slices, buttered sides down, on the hot plates. Spread with the mushrooms, not quite to the edges, and sprinkle with the herbs.

3 Top with the remaining slices of bread, buttered sides up. Cook in the sandwich toaster for about 2–3 minutes until golden.

Croque Monsieur

MAKES 2

4 slices of bread
Butter or margarine, for spreading
2 slices of ham
Some thinly sliced Cheddar cheese

1 Preheat the sandwich toaster. Spread the slices of bread with butter or margarine on one side.

2 Put two slices, buttered sides down, on the hot plate. Cover with a slice of ham, then enough cheese to cover the ham.

3 Top with the other slices of bread, buttered sides up. Cook in the sandwich toaster for 2–3 minutes until golden and the cheese has melted.

V Croque Madame *V*

MAKES 2

4 slices of bread
Butter or margarine, for spreading
Some thinly sliced Cheddar cheese
1 small onion, sliced and separated
into rings
A good pinch of dried sage

1 Preheat the sandwich toaster. Spread the slices of bread with butter or margarine on one side.

2 Put two slices, buttered sides down, on the hot plate. Cover with cheese, then add the onion rings and a sprinkling of sage.

3 Top with the remaining slices of bread, buttered sides up. Cook in the sandwich toaster for 2–3 minutes until golden and the cheese has melted.

Beef and horseradish rolls

MAKES 4

4 slices of bread
Butter or margarine, for spreading
1 small jar of potted beef spread
4 tsp horseradish relish

1 Preheat the sandwich toaster. Cut the crusts off the bread and roll with a rolling pin (or a clean bottle) to flatten.

2 Spread one side of each slice with butter or margarine. Spread the beef paste over the other sides and then spread with a little horseradish sauce. Roll up, buttered sides out.

3 Cook in the sandwich toaster for 2–3 minutes until golden.

Hot dog rolls

MAKES 2

2 slices of bread
Butter or margarine, for spreading
2 hot dog sausages or frankfurters
2 tsp tomato ketchup (catsup)

1 Preheat the sandwich toaster. Cut the crusts off the bread and roll with a rolling pin (or a clean bottle) to flatten.

2 Spread butter or margarine on one side and ketchup on the other.

3 Put a sausage on the ketchup sides and roll up.

4 Cook in the sandwich toaster for 2–3 minutes until golden and piping hot.

Salmon tartare rolls

You can make your own tartare sauce – just mix 2 tsp salad cream with a chopped cornichon or a piece of dill pickle.

MAKES 4

4 slices of bread
Butter or margarine, for spreading
1 small jar of salmon paste
1 tbsp tartare sauce
or ready-made sandwich spread

1 Preheat the sandwich toaster. Cut the crusts off the bread and flatten with a rolling pin (or a clean bottle).

2 Spread each slice of bread on one side with butter or margarine. Spread the salmon paste over the other sides and then spread with a little tartare sauce. Roll up, buttered sides out.

3 Cook in the sandwich toaster for 2–3 minutes until golden.

Hawaiian munches

Eat the rest of the canned pineapple for dessert with yoghurt or breakfast cereal or to make any of the other recipes using pineapple in this book, such as Chicken and Pineapple Rice Salad (see page 161).

MAKES 2

2 slices of ham, chopped
A good handful of grated
Cheddar cheese
1 good tbsp coleslaw, ready-made
or see page 47
½ × 300 g/11 oz/medium can of
pineapple pieces, drained
4 slices of bread
Butter or margarine, for spreading

1 Preheat the sandwich toaster. Mix the ham with the cheese, coleslaw and pineapple.

2 Spread the slices of bread with butter or margarine on one side. Put two slices, buttered sides down, on the hot plates.

3 Top with the filling, spreading it out not quite to the edges. Cover with the other slices of bread, buttered sides up. Cook in the sandwich toaster for 2–3 minutes until golden.

Chicken and curried raisin mayo rolls

MAKES 4

4 slices of bread
Butter or margarine, for spreading
1 tbsp mayonnaise or salad cream
1 tsp curry powder or paste
A small handful of raisins
1 small jar of chicken spread

1 Preheat the sandwich toaster. Cut the crusts off the bread and roll with a rolling pin (or a clean bottle) to flatten. Spread one side of each slice with butter or margarine.

2 Mix the mayonnaise or salad cream with the curry powder or paste and the raisins.

3 Spread the chicken paste over the other sides of the bread and then spread with the curried raisin mixture. Roll up, buttered sides out.

4 Cook in the sandwich toaster for 2–3 minutes until golden.

Chicken and pesto rolls

MAKES 4

4 slices of bread
Butter or margarine, for spreading
2 tbsp pesto, ready-made,
or see page 418
4 slices of cooked pressed chicken

1 Preheat the sandwich toaster. Cut the crusts off the bread and roll with a rolling pin (or a clean bottle) to flatten. Spread one side of each slice with butter or margarine.

2 Spread the pesto over the other sides of the bread and then top each with a slice of chicken. Roll up, buttered sides out.

3 Place on the sandwich toaster plates. Lower the lid of the sandwich toaster and cook for 2–3 minutes until golden.

Indian take-away naans

You can, of course, make these with ordinary bread like the Chinese Take-away Slabs (see page 83), but using naans makes a delicious change – especially if you eat them with some home-made raita (see page 43). Like the Chinese option on page 83, these should never be reheated once cooked.

MAKES 2

2 individual naan breads
Oil, butter or margarine, for greasing
4–6 tbsp leftovers from a meat, chicken
or vegetable Indian take-away
Mango chutney or lime pickle (optional)

1 Preheat the sandwich toaster. Split the naans through the centre to make two slices.

2 Brush the outsides with oil or spread with a little butter or margarine.

3 Cut up any large pieces of meat, chicken or vegetable in the take-away.

4 Spread the insides of the naans with mango chutney or lime pickle, if liked.

5 Put two pieces of naan in the sandwich toaster, greased sides down. Spread the take-away over, not quite to the edges and top with the other slices, greased sides up.

6 Cook in the sandwich toaster for about 3 minutes until golden and hot through.

Chinese take-away slabs

These can be eaten hot or cold but you must not reheat them. The quantities will vary according to what leftovers you have, but this gives you a rough guide!

MAKES 2

4 slices of bread
Butter or margarine, for spreading
A few sesame seeds (optional)
4–6 tbsp leftovers from a meat, chicken or vegetable Chinese take-away or homemade stir-fry

1 Preheat the sandwich toaster.

2 Spread the slices of bread on one side with butter or margarine and sprinkle with sesame seeds, if liked.

3 Cut up any large pieces of meat or poultry.

4 Put two slices of bread, buttered side down, on the hot plates and top each with 2–3 spoonfuls of Chinese leftovers, not quite to the edges.

5 Top with the remaining slices of bread, buttered sides up. Cook in the sandwich toaster for 3 minutes until golden and hot through.

Creamy mushroom and ham toasties

MAKES 2

4 slices of bread
Butter or margarine, for spreading
2 slices of ham
1 × 170 g/6 oz/small can of creamed mushrooms
½ tsp dried mixed herbs

1 Preheat the sandwich toaster. Spread the slices of bread with butter or margarine on one side.

2 Put two slices of bread, buttered sides down, on the hot plates. Top with the ham, then spread with the mushroom mixture, not quite to the edges, and sprinkle with the herbs.

3 Top with the remaining two slices of bread, buttered sides up. Cook in the sandwich toaster for 2–3 minutes until golden.

Creamy mushroom and Ⓥ sweetcorn toasties Ⓥ

MAKES 2

4 slices of bread
Butter or margarine, for spreading
1 × 170 g/6 oz/small can of creamed mushrooms
1 × 200 g/7 oz/small can of sweetcorn (corn), drained
½ tsp dried oregano
Pepper

1 Preheat the sandwich toaster. Spread the slices of bread with butter or margarine on one side.

2 Put two slices, buttered sides down, on the hot plates.

3 Mix the mushrooms with the sweetcorn and spread on the bread, not quite to the edges. Sprinkle with the oregano and some pepper.

4 Top with the remaining slices of bread, buttered sides up. Cook in the sandwich toaster for 2–3 minutes until golden.

Tuna mayo toasties with cucumber

MAKES 2

*1 × 185 g/6½ oz/small can of tuna,
drained
2 tbsp mayonnaise
2.5 cm/1 in piece of cucumber,
finely chopped
Salt and pepper
4 slices of bread
Butter or margarine, for spreading*

1 Preheat the sandwich toaster.
Empty the tuna into a bowl and mash
with the mayonnaise. Stir in the
cucumber and season to taste.

2 Spread the slices of bread on one
side with butter or margarine.

3 Put two slices of bread, buttered
sides down, on the hot plates. Spread
with the tuna mixture, not quite to
the edges.

4 Top with the remaining slices of
bread, buttered sides up. Cook in the
sandwich toaster for about 3 minutes
until golden and hot through.

Sardine and cream cheese bites

MAKES 2

*1 × 120 g/4½ oz/small can of sardines
in tomato sauce
2 tbsp soft white cheese,
such as Philadelphia
Pepper, preferably black
4 slices of bread
Butter or margarine, for spreading*

1 Preheat the sandwich toaster.
Empty the fish into a bowl and mash
thoroughly (including the bones).
Mash in the cheese and season with
pepper.

2 Spread one side of each slice of
bread with butter or margarine. Place
two slices on the hot plates, buttered
sides down.

3 Top with the sardine mixture,
spreading it not quite to the edges.

4 Cover with the remaining slices,
buttered sides up. Cook in the
sandwich toaster for about 3 minutes
until golden.

Corned beef and ketchup toasties

Use the rest of the corned beef for the
hash on page 205.

MAKES 2

*4 slices of bread
Butter or margarine, for spreading
½ × 350 g/12 oz/large can of
corned beef
1–2 tbsp tomato ketchup (catsup)
Pepper*

1 Preheat the sandwich toaster.
Spread the slices of bread with butter
or margarine on one side.

2 Mash the corned beef with as much
ketchup as you like, until thoroughly
mixed.

3 Put two slices of bread, buttered
sides down, on the hot plates.

4 Top with the corned beef mixture,
not quite to the edges, then cover
with the remaining slices of bread,
buttered sides up. Cook in the
sandwich toaster for 2–3 minutes
until golden.

Corned beef and chilli toasties

MAKES 2

2 slices of bread
Butter or margarine, for spreading
½ × 350 g/12 oz/large can of
corned beef
1–2 tbsp chilli relish
½ red (bell) pepper, sliced

1 Preheat the sandwich toaster. Spread the slices of bread with butter or margarine on one side.

2 Mash the corned beef with the chilli relish until well blended.

3 Put two slices of bread, buttered sides down, on the hot plates.

4 Spread the corned beef mixture over the bread, not quite to the edges. Top with the slices of pepper.

5 Top with the remaining slices of bread, buttered sides up. Cook in the sandwich toaster for 2–3 minutes until golden.

Minced beef puffs

You may want to eat both puffs at one meal. If not, you can leave one to cool, then store, wrapped in foil or clingfilm (plastic wrap) in the fridge. You can then eat it cold the next day or reheat it in the preheated sandwich toaster for about 2 minutes until piping hot.

MAKES 2

½ × 350 g/12 oz block of frozen puff
pastry (paste), thawed
Flour, for dusting
A little sunflower oil
1 × 225 g/8 oz/small can of minced
(ground) beef with onion
2 pinches of dried mixed herbs

1 Preheat the sandwich toaster. Dust the work surface with a little flour and then, using a rolling pin (or a clean bottle), roll out the pastry to about 25 cm/10 in square. Cut into four squares.

2 Smear the squares lightly with oil and place two of them, oiled sides down, on the sandwich toaster plates.

3 Quickly spoon the meat mixture into the centres, spreading out not quite to the edges. Sprinkle with the herbs.

4 Top with the remaining squares, oiled sides up, then cook in the sandwich toaster for about 3 minutes until crisp and golden.

Cheese, celery and onion Ⓥ eggy specials Ⓥ

For extra crunch, add a small handful of chopped peanuts or walnuts instead of the celery.

MAKES 2

Sunflower oil
1/4 small carton of soft white cheese, such as Philadelphia
2 tsp instant onion soup powder
1 celery stick, chopped
2 tbsp milk
1 egg
Salt and pepper
4 slices of bread

1 Brush the sandwich toaster plates with oil and preheat.

2 Mix the cheese with the onion soup powder and the celery. Stir in 1 tbsp of the milk.

3 Using a fork, beat the egg on a plate with the remaining milk and a little salt and pepper.

4 Spread two of the slices of bread with the cheese mixture. Top with the remaining slices and press together. Dip both sides in the beaten egg.

5 Cook for about 3 minutes in the sandwich toaster until golden brown.

Chicken pies

Eat one hot and have the other one cold the next day. To store, cool it, then wrap in foil or clingfilm (plastic wrap) and keep in the fridge.

MAKES 2

1 × 225 g/8 oz/small can of chunky chicken
Flour, for dusting
1/2 × 350 g/12 oz block of frozen puff pastry (paste), thawed
A little sunflower oil
2 good pinches of dried sage or dried mixed herbs

1 Cut up any large pieces of chicken with scissors or a knife.

2 Preheat the sandwich toaster. Dust the work surface with a little flour, then, using a rolling pin (or a clean bottle), roll out the pastry to about 25 cm/10 in square. Cut into four squares.

3 Smear the squares lightly with oil and place two of them, oiled sides down, on the sandwich toaster plates.

4 Quickly divide the chicken among the squares and spread out slightly. Sprinkle with the sage or mixed herbs.

5 Top with the remaining squares, oiled sides up, and cook for about 3 minutes until crisp and golden. Eat hot or cold.

Creamy tuna and mushroom puffs

You can double the quantity to use all the tuna and mushrooms. Alternatively, keep them in the fridge and then heat in a saucepan with a little milk and stir into cooked pasta for a delicious supper dish.

MAKES 2

Flour, for dusting
½ × 350 g/12 oz block of frozen puff pastry (paste), thawed
A little sunflower oil
½ × 185 g/6½ oz/small can of tuna, drained
½ × 170 g/6 oz/small can of creamed mushrooms
½ tsp dried oregano or mixed herbs
Pepper

1 Preheat the sandwich toaster. Dust the work surface with a little flour, then, using a rolling pin (or a clean bottle), roll out the pastry to about 25 cm/10 in square. Cut into four squares.

2 Mix the tuna with the mushrooms and season with the herbs and a little pepper.

3 Smear the squares of the pastry lightly with oil and place two of them, oiled sides down, on the sandwich toaster plates.

4 Quickly spoon the tuna mixture into the centres, spreading out not quite to the edges.

5 Top with the remaining squares, oiled sides up and cook for about 3 minutes until crisp and golden. Eat hot or cold.

Cheese and onion ⓥ puffs ⓥ

Again, this makes two pies, so that you've got one to eat the next day – unless you polish off two in one go! Leave one to cool, then store, wrapped in foil or clingfilm (plastic wrap) in the fridge.

MAKES 2

Flour, for dusting
½ × 350 g/12 oz block of frozen puff pastry (paste), thawed
A little sunflower oil
2 good handfuls of grated Cheddar cheese
1 small onion, peeled and thinly sliced into rings

1 Preheat the sandwich toaster. Dust the work surface lightly with flour, then, using a rolling pin (or a clean bottle), roll out the pastry to about 25 cm/10 in square. Cut into four squares.

2 Smear the squares lightly with oil and place two of them, oiled sides down, on the sandwich toaster plates.

3 Quickly top with the cheese and scatter the onion rings over.

4 Top with the remaining squares, oiled sides up, and cook for about 3 minutes until crisp and golden. Eat hot or cold.

Steak, kidney and mushroom pies

If you are keeping one to eat cold the next day, leave it to cool, then store, wrapped in foil or clingfilm (plastic wrap) in the fridge.

MAKES 2

1 × 225 g/8 oz/small can of stewed steak and kidney
Flour, for dusting
½ × 350 g/12 oz block of frozen puff pastry (paste), thawed
A little sunflower oil
2–3 mushrooms, sliced

1 Cut up any large pieces of steak, using a knife or scissors.

2 Preheat the sandwich toaster. Dust the work surface lightly with flour, then, using a rolling pin (or a clean bottle), roll out the pastry to about 25 cm/10 in square. Cut into four squares.

3 Smear the squares lightly with oil and place two of them, oiled sides down, on the sandwich toaster plates.

4 Quickly top with the meat, then arrange the sliced mushrooms over.

5 Top with the remaining squares, oiled sides up, and cook for about 4 minutes until crisp and golden and piping hot through. Eat hot or cold.

Corned beef pasties

MAKES 2

Flour, for dusting
½ × 350 g/12 oz block of shortcrust pastry (basic pie crust), thawed if frozen
A little sunflower oil
1 × 170 g/6 oz/small can of mixed vegetables, drained
¼ × 350 g/12 oz/large can of corned beef, crumbled
A few drops of Worcestershire sauce (optional)
Salt and pepper

1 Preheat the sandwich toaster. Dust the work surface lightly with flour, then, using a rolling pin (or a clean bottle), roll out the pastry to about 25 cm/10 in square. Cut into four squares.

2 Smear the squares lightly with oil and place two of them, oiled sides down, on the sandwich toaster plates.

3 Quickly top with the vegetables and crumbled corned beef. Sprinkle with Worcestershire sauce, if using, and a little salt and pepper.

4 Top with the remaining squares and cook for about 3 minutes until crisp and golden. Eat hot or cold.

ⓥ Puff spring rolls ⓥ

MAKES 4

Flour, for dusting
½ × 350 g/12 oz block of frozen puff
pastry (paste), thawed
A little sunflower oil
1 × 425 g/15 oz/large can of stir-fry
vegetables, thoroughly drained
1–2 tsp soy sauce
¼ tsp Chinese five-spice powder
or ground ginger (optional)

1 Preheat the sandwich toaster. Dust the work surface lightly with flour, then, using a rolling pin (or a clean bottle), roll out each piece of pastry to about 25 cm/10 in square. Cut into four squares.

2 Smear the squares lightly with oil and turn them over.

3 Drain the vegetables on kitchen paper (paper towels) to remove any excess moisture. Tip into a bowl and mix with the soy sauce and spice, if using.

4 Spoon the vegetables in the centre of one edge of each piece of pastry. Fold in the sides and roll up.

5 Cook in the sandwich toaster for about 3–4 minutes until crisp, golden and cooked through. Eat hot.

Top tip: If you have a toaster that splits the sandwiches into two triangles, you can place one roll in each of the four triangular plates, to avoid squashing them.

Cheese and anchovy calzones

MAKES 2

1 packet of pizza base mix
Hot water
A little sunflower or olive oil
1 × 50 g/2 oz/small can of anchovies,
drained
2 tbsp tomato purée (paste)
2 handfuls of grated Mozzarella
or Cheddar cheese
¼ tsp dried oregano or basil

1 Make up the dough according to the packet directions. Knead it by stretching the dough with the heel of one hand, then folding it over and stretching it again. When it is smooth and stretchy, wrap it in an oiled plastic bag and leave it to rise for about 45 minutes.

2 Tip the anchovies into a bowl, cover with water and leave to soak – this will remove excess salt.

3 Knead the dough again, then cut it into quarters. Preheat the sandwich toaster.

4 Roll out each piece with a rolling pin (or a clean bottle) to 12.5 cm/5 in square. Smear one side with oil.

5 Turn over two of the squares and spread the unoiled sides with tomato purée.

6 Drain the anchovies and dry on kitchen paper (paper towels).

7 Place the tomato-covered dough on the hot plates, oiled sides down.

8 Add the cheese and lay the anchovies on top. Sprinkle with the oregano or basil.

9 Cover with the other pieces of dough, oiled sides up. Cook in the sandwich toaster for about 3 minutes until golden.

Salami, green pepper and olive calzones

MAKES 2

1 packet of pizza base mix
Hot water
A little sunflower or olive oil
2 tbsp tomato purée (paste)
4 slices of salami, diced
1 small green (bell) pepper,
finely chopped
4 stuffed or stoned (pitted) black olives,
sliced
2 handfuls of grated Mozzarella or
Cheddar cheese
¼ tsp dried oregano

1 Make up the dough according to the packet directions. Knead it by stretching the dough with the heel of one hand, then folding it over and stretching it again. When it is smooth and stretchy, wrap it in an oiled plastic bag and leave it to rise for about 45 minutes.

2 Knead it again, then cut it into quarters. Preheat the sandwich toaster.

3 Roll out each piece with a rolling pin (or a clean bottle) to about 12.5 cm/5 in square. Smear on one side with oil.

4 Turn over two of the squares and spread the unoiled sides with tomato purée. Place on the hot plates, oiled sides down.

5 Scatter the salami, pepper and olives over, then add the cheese and the oregano.

6 Cover with the other pieces of dough, oiled sides up. Cook in the sandwich toaster for about 3 minutes until crisp and golden.

Spinach and cheese
Ⓥ calzones Ⓥ

You should use ricotta cheese but cottage cheese is cheaper!

MAKES 2

1 packet of pizza base mix
Hot water
A little sunflower or olive oil
2 tbsp tomato purée (paste)
1 mug of frozen chopped spinach,
thawed
1 small tub of cottage cheese
Pepper
¼ tsp dried oregano

1 Make up the dough according to the packet directions. Knead it by stretching the dough with the heel of one hand, then folding it over and stretching it again. When it is smooth and stretchy, wrap it in an oiled plastic bag and leave it to rise for about 45 minutes.

2 Knead it again, then cut it into quarters. Preheat the sandwich toaster.

3 Roll out each piece with a rolling pin (or a clean bottle) to about 12.5 cm/5 in square. Smear on one side with oil.

4 Turn over two of the squares and spread the unoiled sides with tomato purée.

5 Squeeze the spinach thoroughly to remove excess moisture.

6 Place the tomato dough, oiled sides down, on the hot plates.

7 Spread the spinach over, then top with the cheese. Sprinkle well with pepper and add the oregano.

8 Cover with the other pieces of dough, oiled sides up. Cook in the sandwich toaster for about 3 minutes until crisp and golden.

Ham and mushroom calzones

MAKES 2

1 packet of pizza base mix
Hot water
A little sunflower or olive oil
2 tbsp tomato purée (paste)
2 slices of ham, chopped
4 mushrooms, sliced
2 handfuls of grated Mozzarella
or Cheddar cheese
¼ tsp dried oregano

1 Make up the dough according to the packet directions. Knead it by stretching the dough with the heel of one hand, then folding it over and stretching it again. When it is smooth and stretchy, wrap it in an oiled plastic bag and leave it to rise for about 45 minutes.

2 Knead it again, then cut it into quarters. Preheat the sandwich toaster.

3 Roll out each piece with a rolling pin (or a clean bottle) to about 12.5 cm/5 in square. Smear on one side with oil.

4 Turn over two of the pieces and spread the unoiled sides with tomato purée. Place on the hot plates, oiled sides down.

5 Top with the remaining ingredients, then cover with the other pieces of dough, oiled sides up. Cook in the sandwich toaster for about 3 minutes until crisp and golden.

Curried vegetable 🅥 pasties 🅥

For a milder flavour, use half the amount of curry powder or paste.

MAKES 2

Flour, for dusting
½ × 350 g/12 oz block of frozen puff pastry (paste), thawed
A little sunflower oil
1 × 170 g/6 oz/small can of mixed vegetables, well drained
1 tsp curry paste or powder
2 tsp mango chutney
or other sweet pickle
Salt and pepper
4 slices of bread

1 Preheat the sandwich toaster. Dust a work surface lightly with flour, and, using a rolling pin (or a clean bottle), roll out the pastry to about 25 cm/10 in square. Cut into four squares.

2 Mix the drained vegetables with the curry paste or powder, the chutney or pickle and a little salt and pepper.

3 Smear the squares of the pastry lightly with oil and place two of them, oiled sides down, on the sandwich toaster plates.

4 Quickly spoon the vegetable mixture on to the pastry squares.

5 Top with the remaining pastry, lower the lid of the sandwich toaster and cook for about 3 minutes until crisp and golden. Eat hot or cold.

Chocolate and banana
Ⓥ sweet toasts Ⓥ

For extra protein, add 1 tbsp of desiccated coconut to the mashed banana.

MAKES 2

4 slices of bread
Butter or margarine, for spreading
2 tbsp chocolate spread
1 banana, peeled and mashed

1 Preheat the sandwich toaster. Spread the slices of bread on one side with butter or margarine. Spread the other sides with chocolate spread.

2 Put two slices, chocolate-sides up, on the hot plates. Top with the banana, spreading it out not quite to the edges.

3 Top with the remaining slices of bread, chocolate-sides down. Lower the lid of the sandwich toaster and cook for about 2 minutes until golden.

Lemon cheesecake
Ⓥ bites Ⓥ

If you don't have a grater, just sharpen the mixture with 1 tbsp of bottled lemon juice instead of the zest and juice.

MAKES 2

1 small carton of plain cottage cheese
Grated zest and juice of ½ lemon
3 tbsp sugar
2 tbsp raisins
4 slices of raisin bread
Butter or margarine, for spreading

1 Preheat the sandwich toaster. Mix the cottage cheese with the lemon zest and juice, 2 tbsp of the sugar and the raisins.

2 Spread the slices of bread on one side with butter or margarine.

3 Put two slices on the hot plates, buttered sides down.

4 Spoon on the cheese mixture, spreading not quite to the edges.

5 Top with the remaining slices of bread, buttered sides up. Cook in the sandwich toaster for about 2 minutes until golden.

6 Sprinkle with the remaining sugar before eating.

Vanilla and walnut ⓥ cheesecake bites ⓥ

MAKES 2

1 small carton of plain cottage cheese
3 tbsp sugar
1 tbsp walnut pieces, chopped
1 tbsp sultanas (golden raisins)
or currants
½ tsp vanilla essence (extract)
4 slices of raisin or plain bread
Butter or margarine, for spreading

1 Preheat the sandwich toaster. Mix the cottage cheese with 2 tbsp of the sugar, the walnuts and the sultanas or currants.

2 Spread the slices of bread on one side with butter or margarine.

3 Put two slices on the hot plates, buttered sides down.

4 Spoon on the cheese mixture, spreading not quite to the edges.

5 Top with the remaining slices of bread, buttered sides up. Cook in the sandwich toaster for about 2 minutes until golden.

6 Sprinkle with the remaining sugar before eating.

Banana mallow energy ⓥ booster ⓥ

MAKES 2

8 pink marshmallows
4 slices of bread
Butter or margarine, for spreading
1 tbsp raspberry or strawberry jam
(conserve)
1 banana, peeled and mashed
1 tbsp sugar

1 Preheat the sandwich toaster. Put the marshmallows in a cup and snip with wet scissors to chop them. Alternatively, cut into pieces with a sharp, wet knife on a board.

2 Spread the slices of bread on one side with the butter or margarine. Spread the other sides with a little jam.

3 Put two of the slices, jam-sides up, on the hot plates.

4 Spread the banana over, not quite to the edges, then top with the marshmallow pieces.

5 Cover with the remaining bread, jam-sides down, and cook in the sandwich toaster for about 2 minutes until golden.

6 Sprinkle with the sugar before eating.

ⓥ Chocolate rice fillers ⓥ

I would recommend buying good-quality creamed rice. If you buy economy canned rice, it is too runny for this, but if it's all you've got you can drain off a lot of the milk or thicken it with instant oat cereal before making the recipe.

MAKES 2

4 slices of bread
Butter or margarine, for spreading
1 × 225 g/8 oz/small can of creamed rice
4 squares of plain (semi-sweet) or milk chocolate, chopped
1 tbsp sugar

1 Preheat the sandwich toaster. Spread the slices of bread on one side with butter or margarine.

2 Put two slices, buttered sides down, on the hot plates.

3 Stir the chocolate into the rice and spoon on to the bread, not quite to the edges.

4 Top with the remaining slices, buttered sides up. Cook in the sandwich toaster for 2–3 minutes until golden.

5 Sprinkle with sugar before serving.

ⓥ Muesli fillers ⓥ

These are great for keeping your energy levels up at exam time.

MAKES 2

6 white marshmallows
1 eating (dessert) apple, halved, cored and finely chopped
½ mug of muesli
2 tbsp clear honey
1 tbsp lemon juice
4 slices of bread
Butter or margarine, for spreading

1 Preheat the sandwich toaster. Put the marshmallows in a mug and snip with wet scissors or cut up on a board with a sharp, wet knife.

2 Mix the marshmallows with the apple, muesli, honey and lemon juice.

3 Spread the slices of bread on one side with butter or margarine.

4 Put two slices, buttered sides down, on the hot plates. Top with the muesli mixture, spreading out not quite to the edges.

5 Cover with the other slices, buttered sides up. Cook in the sandwich toaster for about 3 minutes until golden.

6 Eat warm or cold.

ⓥ Black Forest rolls ⓥ

MAKES 4

4 slices of bread
Butter or margarine, for spreading
2 tbsp chocolate spread
2 tbsp cherry jam (conserve)
1 tbsp sugar

1 Preheat the sandwich toaster. Cut the crusts off the bread and roll lightly with a rolling pin (or a clean bottle) to flatten.

2 Spread the slices of bread on one side with butter or margarine. Spread the other sides with chocolate spread, then jam.

3 Roll up the bread and place on the hot plates (put one in each section if separated into triangles). Cook in the sandwich toaster for 2–3 minutes until golden.

4 Sprinkle with the sugar before eating.

ⓥ Apple turnovers ⓥ

MAKES 2

*½ × 350 g/12 oz block of frozen puff
pastry (paste), thawed
1 cooking (tart) apple, quartered, peeled,
cored and very finely chopped
or thinly sliced
3 tbsp sugar
A good pinch of ground cinnamon
or mixed (apple-pie) spice
1 tsp cornflour (cornstarch)
A little sunflower oil*

1 Preheat the sandwich toaster. Dust
a work surface with a little flour,
then, using a rolling pin (or a clean
bottle), roll out the pastry to about
25 cm/10 in square. Cut into four
squares.

2 Mix the apple with 2 tbsp of the
sugar, all the spice and the cornflour.

3 Smear the squares of the pastry
lightly with oil and place two of them,
oiled sides down, on the sandwich
toaster plates.

4 Quickly spoon the apple mixture on
to the pastry and spread out evenly.

5 Top with the remaining pastry
squares, oiled sides up, and cook in
the sandwich toaster for about
4 minutes until crisp and golden and
cooked through.

6 Eat hot or cold, sprinkled with the
remaining sugar.

ⓥ Syrup turnovers ⓥ

MAKES 2

*Flour for dusting
½ × 450 g/1 lb block of shortcrust
pastry (basic pie crust), thawed if frozen
A little sunflower oil
3 tbsp golden (light corn) syrup
2 tsp lemon juice
1 slice of fairly stale bread, crumbled*

1 Preheat the sandwich toaster. Dust
a work surface with a little flour,
then, using a rolling pin (or a clean
bottle), roll out the pastry to about
25 cm/10 in square. Cut into four
squares.

2 Smear the squares of the pastry
lightly with oil.

3 Mix the syrup with the lemon juice
and the breadcrumbs.

4 Put two squares of pastry, oiled
sides down, on the hot plates. Spoon
the syrup mixture in the centres and
top with the remaining pastry, oiled
sides up.

5 Cook in the sandwich toaster for
about 3–4 minutes or until golden.

6 Eat warm or cold.

Snacks You can Do With ...
a Microwave

The cooking times in a microwave depend on the power output of your machine. This means that a 600 watt cooker will take longer to cook than an 800 watt one, so I have given a range of cooking times in each recipe in this section. Check after the shortest cooking time, then cook a little longer if necessary – on these quick cooking times, the extra needed can be as little as 15 seconds! Once you've cooked something in your microwave oven, pencil in the correct times for your microwave on the recipes, for future reference.

Some of these recipes may seem 'bog standard', but they're things that everyone wants to cook, and this is how to do them in a microwave.

Ⓥ Spaghetti on toast Ⓥ

SERVES 1

1 slice of bread
Butter or margarine (optional)
1 × 225 g/8 oz/small can of spaghetti in tomato sauce

1 Put the bread on a plate and microwave on High (100 per cent power) for 2 minutes. Alternatively, toast it on both sides in a toaster or under a preheated grill (broiler) then put on a plate.

2 Spread with butter or margarine, if liked.

3 Spoon the spaghetti over and spread out fairly evenly.

4 Microwave on High (100 per cent power) for 1–1½ minutes until piping hot.

Ⓥ Cheese on toast Ⓥ

SERVES 1

1 slice of bread
Butter or margarine (optional)
2–3 fairly thin slices of Cheddar cheese

1 Put the bread on a plate and microwave on High (100 per cent power) for 2 minutes. Alternatively, toast it on both sides in a toaster or under a preheated grill (broiler) then put on a plate.

2 Spread with butter or margarine, if liked.

3 Arrange the cheese slices in an even layer over the bread.

4 Microwave on High (100 per cent power) for 30–45 seconds until the cheese melts and bubbles. Do not overcook or the whole thing will become tough. Leave to stand for 1 minute to become crisp.

ⓥ Pizza toast ⓥ

SERVES 1

1 slice of bread
Butter, margarine or olive oil
1 tomato, sliced
2–3 fairly thin slices of Cheddar cheese
A pinch of dried oregano

1 Put the bread on a plate and microwave on High (100 per cent power) for 2 minutes. Alternatively, toast both sides in a toaster or under a preheated grill (broiler), then put on a plate.

2 Spread with butter or margarine or trickle a little olive oil over the surface.

3 Arrange the slices of tomato on top, then the cheese, in a single layer. Sprinkle with the oregano.

4 Microwave on High (100 per cent power) for 45 seconds to 1 minute until the cheese has melted.

5 Leave to stand for 1 minute to crisp before eating.

ⓥ Baked beans on toast ⓥ

SERVES 1

1 slice of bread
Butter or margarine (optional)
1 × 225 g/8 oz/small can of
baked beans

1 Put the bread on a plate and microwave on High (100 per cent power) for 2 minutes. Alternatively, toast it on both sides in a toaster or under a preheated grill (broiler), then put on a plate.

2 Spread with butter or margarine.

3 Spoon the beans over and spread out fairly evenly.

4 Microwave on High (100 per cent power) for 1–1½ minutes until piping hot.

Cheese and onion ⓥ slice ⓥ

You can use two pickled onions, sliced, instead of the onion, if you prefer.

SERVES 1

1 slice of bread
Butter or margarine (optional)
½ small onion, sliced and separated
into rings, discarding skin
A pinch of dried sage (optional)
1–3 fairly thin slices of Cheddar cheese

1 Put the bread on a plate and microwave on High (100 per cent power) for 2 minutes. Alternatively, toast it on both sides in a toaster or under a preheated grill (broiler), then put on a plate.

2 Spread with butter or margarine, if liked.

3 Arrange the onion rings in an even layer on the bread, then sprinkle with the sage, if using. Arrange the cheese slices evenly over the top.

4 Microwave on High (100 per cent power) for 40–50 seconds until the cheese melts and bubbles. Do not overcook.

5 Leave to stand for 1 minute to become crisp.

Beans and cheese
Ⓥ on toast Ⓥ

SERVES 1

1 slice of bread
Butter or margarine (optional)
1 × 225 g/8 oz/small can of
baked beans
2–3 fairly thin slices of Cheddar cheese

1 Put the bread on a plate and microwave on High (100 per cent power) for 2 minutes. Alternatively, toast it on both sides in a toaster or under a preheated grill (broiler), then put on a plate.

2 Spread with butter or margarine, if liked.

3 Spoon the beans over and spread out fairly evenly. Top with the cheese in an even layer.

4 Microwave on High (100 per cent power) for 1½–2 minutes until piping hot and the cheese has melted.

Wensleydale and beetroot
Ⓥ slice Ⓥ

You can, of course use Cheddar cheese, but Wensleydale goes really well with beetroot.

SERVES 1

1 slice of bread
Butter or margarine (optional)
1 baby pickled beetroot (red beet)
3 fairly thin slices of Wensleydale cheese
A pinch of dried chives

1 Put the bread on a plate and microwave on High (100 per cent power) for 2 minutes. Alternatively, toast it on both sides in a toaster or under a preheated grill (broiler), then put on a plate.

2 Spread with butter or margarine, if liked.

3 Slice the beetroot and arrange in an even layer on the bread, then arrange the cheese slices over the top. Sprinkle with the chives.

4 Microwave on High (100 per cent power) for 40–50 seconds until the cheese melts and bubbles. Do not overcook.

5 Leave to stand for 1 minute to become crisp.

Ham and cheese slice

SERVES 1

1 slice of bread
Butter or margarine (optional)
1 slice of cooked ham
1–3 fairly thin slices of Cheddar cheese

1 Put the bread on a plate and microwave on High (100 per cent power) for 2 minutes. Alternatively, toast it on both sides in a toaster or under a preheated grill (broiler), then put on a plate.

2 Spread with butter or margarine, if liked.

3 Lay the slice of ham on the bread, then arrange the cheese slices in an even layer over the top.

4 Microwave on High (100 per cent power) for 40–50 seconds until the cheese melts and bubbles. Do not overcook or the whole thing will become tough.

5 Leave to stand for 1 minute to become crisp.

Cheese and pickle
Ⓥ slice Ⓥ

SERVES 1

1 slice of bread
Butter or margarine (optional)
1 tbsp sweet pickle
1–3 fairly thin slices of Cheddar cheese

1 Put the bread on a plate and microwave on High (100 per cent power) for 2 minutes. Alternatively, toast it on both sides in a toaster or under a preheated grill (broiler), then put on a plate.

2 Spread with butter or margarine, if liked.

3 Spread the pickle on the bread, then arrange the cheese slices in an even layer over the top.

4 Microwave on High (100 per cent power) for 30–45 seconds until the cheese melts and bubbles. Do not overcook.

5 Leave to stand for 1 minute to become crisp.

Ⓥ Cheese dilly Ⓥ

SERVES 1

1 slice of bread
Butter or margarine (optional)
1 dill pickle
1–3 fairly thin slices of Cheddar cheese

1 Put the bread on a plate and microwave on High (100 per cent power) for 2 minutes. Alternatively, toast it on both sides in a toaster or under a preheated grill (broiler), then put on a plate.

2 Spread with butter or margarine, if liked.

3 Slice the pickle and arrange on the bread, then arrange the cheese slices in an even layer over the top.

4 Microwave on High (100 per cent power) for 40–50 seconds until the cheese melts and bubbles. Do not overcook.

5 Leave to stand for 1 minute to become crisp.

Hot dogs

My student son eats four hot dogs at a time easily but if your appetite isn't that huge, you can make half the quantity and microwave for half the time!

SERVES 1

4 hot dog sausages
4 finger rolls
Mustard
Tomato ketchup (catsup)

1 Prick the sausages with a fork.

2 Split the finger rolls and put a sausage in each. Wrap individually in kitchen paper (paper towels).

3 Arrange in a circle on the microwave turntable. Microwave on High (100 per cent power) for 1–3 minutes until the sausages are piping hot. Do not overcook or the bread will go rubbery.

4 Unwrap and add mustard and ketchup to taste.

Hot dogs with onions

SERVES 1

1 onion, peeled, halved and sliced
A knob of butter or margarine
4 hot dog sausages
4 finger rolls
Mustard
Tomato ketchup (catsup)

1 Put the sliced onion in a microwave-safe bowl with the butter or margarine and 1 tbsp of water. Microwave on High (100 per cent power) for 2–3 minutes, stirring twice, until soft. Remove from the microwave. Cover the bowl with a plate, cloth or foil. Leave to stand while cooking the hot dogs.

2 Prick the sausages with a fork.

3 Split the finger rolls and put a sausage in each. Wrap individually in kitchen paper (paper towels).

4 Arrange in a circle on the microwave turntable. Microwave on High (100 per cent power) for 1–3 minutes or until the sausages are piping hot. Do not overcook or the bread will go rubbery.

5 Unwrap and spoon some onions into each roll. Add mustard and ketchup to taste.

Hamburgers

If you have a microwave rack, put the burger on it and stand the rack over a plate to catch the fat as it runs out. Alternatively, use the method below. If cooking several burgers in one go, arrange them in a circle on the rack or on an upturned plate over another larger plate. Remember, if you cook four burgers, they will take between three and four times as long as cooking one (it's hard to be exact, so check frequently).

SERVES 1

1 frozen beefburger
1 round soft bread roll
Tomato ketchup (catsup)
Slices of dill pickle or cucumber

1 Put the frozen beefburger on an upturned saucer or small plate standing on a larger plate (this will let the fat run away from the meat as it cooks). Lay a sheet of greaseproof (waxed) paper over the top to prevent splattering or put another saucer or small plate over the top of the burger.

2 Microwave on High (100 per cent power) for 1–1½ minutes until cooked through, turning over once halfway through cooking.

3 Split the roll and spread a little ketchup inside. Add the burger. Top with slices of pickle or cucumber.

Cheeseburgers

SERVES 1

1 frozen beefburger
1 round soft bread roll
Tomato ketchup (catsup)
2 thin slices cut from an unpeeled onion
1 slice of Cheddar cheese
or 1 processed cheese slice

1 Put the frozen beefburger on an upturned saucer or small plate standing on a larger plate (this will let the fat run away from the meat as it cooks). Lay a sheet of greaseproof (waxed) paper over the top to prevent splattering or put another saucer or small plate over the top of the burger.

2 Microwave on High (100 per cent power) for 1–1½ minutes until cooked through, turning over once halfway through cooking.

3 Split the roll and spread a little ketchup inside.

4 Separate the onion into rings, discarding the brown outer one and the first white layer.

5 Add the burger to the bun and top with the onion rings, then the cheese slice and top with the other half of the roll.

6 Place on a plate and microwave for 10–20 seconds until the cheese is melting.

Micro-fried egg ⓥ sandwich ⓥ

SERVES 1

Butter or margarine
1 egg
2 slices of bread
Tomato ketchup (catsup) or brown
table sauce

1 Smear a saucer or small plate with a very little butter or margarine, just enough to grease the surface. Break the egg on to it.

2 Prick the yolk very gently once with the prongs of a fork.

3 Microwave on High (100 per cent power) for 30 seconds. Leave it to stand for 1 minute, then microwave for a further 20–30 seconds until the white is opaque and the yolk set.

4 Spread the bread with butter or margarine and ketchup or brown sauce.

5 Put one slice on a plate. Top with the egg, then the other slice of bread.

Egg and bacon butty

SERVES 1

2 slices of bread
Butter or margarine
Tomato ketchup (catsup)
or brown table sauce (optional)
2 rashers (slices) of back bacon, rinded
1 egg

1 Spread the bread with butter or margarine and then ketchup or brown sauce, if liked.

2 Put the rashers of bacon side by side on a plate. Cover the bacon with another plate or greaseproof (waxed) paper to prevent spluttering. Microwave on High (100 per cent power) for 40 seconds. Remove from the microwave.

3 Smear a very little butter or margarine on a saucer or small plate. Break the egg on to it and prick the yolk once gently with the prongs of a fork. Microwave on High (100 per cent power) for 30 seconds. Remove from the microwave.

4 Return the bacon and microwave for a further 20 seconds to 1½ minutes until cooked to your liking. Remove from the microwave.

5 Microwave the egg for a further 20–30 seconds until the white is opaque and the yolk set.

6 Transfer the bacon and egg to one slice of the bread and top with the remaining slice.

Bacon butty

SERVES 1

2 rashers (slices) of back bacon, rinded
2 slices of bread
Butter or margarine
Tomato ketchup (catsup)
or brown table sauce

1 Lay the rashers of bacon side by side on a plate. Cover with another plate or greaseproof (waxed) paper to prevent spluttering.

2 Microwave on High (100 per cent power) for 45 seconds to 2 minutes until cooked to your liking. Cook a few seconds more if you like your bacon crisp.

3 Spread the bread with butter or margarine and ketchup or brown sauce.

4 Lift the bacon on to one slice of bread and top with the other one.

BLT

SERVES 1

2 rashers (slices) of back bacon, rinded
2 slices of bread
Butter or margarine
2 tsp mayonnaise
1 tomato, sliced
1–2 crisp lettuce leaves

1 Lay the rashers of bacon side by side on a plate. Cover with another plate.

2 Microwave on High (100 per cent power) for 45 seconds to 2 minutes until cooked to your liking. Cook a few seconds more if you like your bacon crisp.

3 Spread the bread with butter or margarine, then spread one slice with the mayo and top with the tomato slices and lettuce.

4 Lay the bacon on top and cover with the other slice of bread.

ⓥ Micro-baked eggs ⓥ

You need a very small dish for each egg – an ordinary teacup will do. If cooking more than one egg, arrange the dishes in a circle on the microwave turntable. The cooking time given here is for one egg, so if you cook four, multiply the cooking time by 3 to 4 – it's not an exact science, so check once or twice. It's best to undercook, then cook for slightly longer, if necessary, than to overcook and end up with horrible rubbery eggs!

SERVES 1

A tiny knob of butter or margarine
1 egg
Salt and pepper
1 tbsp double (heavy) cream
Crusty bread

1 Grease a ramekin dish (custard cup), teacup or very small, shallow dish with the butter or margarine.

2 Break the egg into the dish and prick the yolk gently once with a fork. Season lightly.

3 Spoon the cream over. Cook on High (100 per cent power) for 1–1½ minutes and leave to stand for 2 minutes. For a firmer egg, cook for 30 seconds more.

ⓥ Micro-scrambled eggs ⓥ

As with all microwave cooking, the cooking time varies with the quantity. In general, allow about 45 seconds to 1 minute per egg when scrambling them.

SERVES 1

2 eggs
2 tbsp milk
A small knob of butter or margarine
Salt and pepper

1 Break the eggs into a microwave-safe bowl. Whisk with a balloon whisk or fork until well blended.

2 Whisk in the milk and add the butter or margarine and a sprinkling of salt and pepper.

3 Microwave on High (100 per cent power) for about 1½ minutes, stirring with a fork every 30 seconds, until almost set.

4 Leave to stand for 2 minutes to complete cooking. You may have to microwave them for a few seconds more, but don't overcook or they will go rubbery and watery.

Ravioli special

SERVES 1

1 × 410 g/14½ oz/large can of ravioli in tomato or meat sauce
1 tbsp grated Parmesan cheese

1 Tip the ravioli into a bowl. Microwave on High (100 per cent power) for 4–5 minutes, stirring once or twice, until piping hot.

2 Sprinkle with the cheese and leave to stand for 1 minute before eating.

Stuffed jacket potatoes

Jacket potatoes are quick and easy to cook in the microwave and make a nutritious and filling snack any time of day.

Top tips: Allow about 4 minutes per large potato. If you're cooking more than one at a time in the microwave, add extra time. Cook until they feel soft when squeezed.

When handling cooked potatoes, be sure to use an oven glove to protect your hand, or wrap it in a tea towel (dish cloth).

If you have a grill (broiler), you can put the stuffed potatoes under to reheat and brown on top instead of putting them back in the microwave.

ⓥ Cheesy stuffed jackets ⓥ

SERVES 1

1 large potato, scrubbed
A knob of butter or margarine
2 tbsp soft white cheese,
such as Philadelphia
A small handful of grated
Cheddar cheese
Salt and pepper

1 Prick the potato all over and wrap in kitchen paper (paper towels). Microwave on High (100 per cent power) for about 4 minutes, turning over once, until soft when squeezed.

2 Halve the cooked potato and scoop out most of the flesh into a bowl. Using a fork, mash with the butter or margarine and the cheeses. Add salt and pepper to taste.

3 Pack the potato mixture back into the shells. Microwave for a further 30 seconds to 1 minute to heat through.

Tuna mayonnaise jackets

You can store the remaining tuna in a covered container in the fridge for up to 3 days.

SERVES 1

1 large potato, scrubbed
A knob of butter or margarine
¹/₂ × 185 g/6¹/₂ oz/small can of tuna,
drained
2 tbsp mayonnaise
A pinch of dried mixed herbs
Salt and pepper

1 Prick the potato all over and wrap in kitchen paper (paper towels). Microwave on High (100 per cent power) for about 4 minutes, turning over once, until soft when squeezed.

2 Halve the cooked potato and scoop out most of the flesh into a bowl.

3 Using a fork, mash with the butter or margarine, the tuna, half the mayonnaise, the herbs and a little salt and pepper.

4 Pile the potato mixture back into the shells and place in a bowl. Microwave for 45 seconds to 1 minute until hot through. Top with the remaining mayonnaise.

Cheesy sweetcorn
ⓥ jackets ⓥ

SERVES 1

1 large potato, scrubbed
A knob of butter or margarine
A handful of grated Cheddar cheese
or 1 tbsp cheese spread
1 × 200 g/7 oz/small can of sweetcorn
(corn), drained
Pepper

1 Prick the potato all over and wrap in kitchen paper (paper towels). Microwave on High (100 per cent power) for about 4 minutes, turning over once, until soft when squeezed.

2 Halve the cooked potato and scoop out most of the flesh into a bowl.

3 Using a fork, mash with the butter or margarine, and the cheese. Work in the sweetcorn and season with pepper.

4 Pile the potato mixture back into the shells and place in a bowl. Microwave for 1–1½ minutes until hot through.

Ham, pepper and pickle
jackets

SERVES 1

1 large potato, scrubbed
A knob of butter or margarine
1 small green (bell) pepper, finely diced
2 slices of cooked ham, chopped
1 tbsp sweet pickle or chilli relish

1 Prick the potato all over and wrap in kitchen paper (paper towels). Microwave on High (100 per cent power) for about 4 minutes, turning over once, until soft when squeezed.

2 Halve the cooked potato and scoop out most of the flesh into a bowl.

3 Using a fork, mash with the butter or margarine.

4 Mix into the potato with the pepper, ham and pickle or relish.

5 Pile the potato mixture back into the shells and place in a bowl. Microwave for 1–1¼ minutes until hot through.

Bean-stuffed
ⓥ jackets ⓥ

Don't put this one under the grill to reheat or the beans will go hard.

SERVES 1

1 large potato, scrubbed
A knob of butter or margarine
A handful of grated Cheddar cheese
or 1 tbsp cheese spread
Pepper
1 × 225 g/8 oz/small can of
baked beans

1 Prick the potato all over and wrap in kitchen paper (paper towels). Microwave on High (100 per cent power) for about 4 minutes, turning over once, until soft when squeezed.

2 Halve the cooked potato and scoop out most of the flesh into a bowl.

3 Using a fork, mash with the butter or margarine and cheese. Season with pepper.

4 Pack the potato mixture back into the shells. Put the stuffed potatoes in a bowl and spoon the beans over. Microwave for about 2 minutes until piping hot.

Marmite and grated cheese ⓥ jackets ⓥ

SERVES 1

1 large potato, scrubbed
A knob of butter margarine
1 tsp Marmite or other yeast extract
A small handful of grated
Cheddar cheese
Pepper

1 Prick the potato all over and wrap in kitchen paper (paper towels). Microwave on High (100 per cent power) for about 4 minutes, turning over once, until soft when squeezed.

2 Halve the cooked potato and scoop out most of the flesh into a bowl.

3 Using a fork, mash with the butter or margarine and the Marmite or other yeast extract.

4 Pile the potato mixture back into the shells and place in a bowl. Sprinkle with the cheese. Microwave for 30 seconds to 1 minute until hot through.

Oxo spuds

SERVES 1

1 large potato, scrubbed
A knob of butter or margarine
1 red Oxo cube
Pepper
2 tbsp soft white cheese,
such as Philadelphia

1 Prick the potato all over and wrap in kitchen paper (paper towels). Microwave on High (100 per cent power) for about 4 minutes, turning over once, until soft when squeezed.

2 Halve the cooked potato and scoop out most of the flesh into a bowl.

3 Using a fork, mash with the butter or margarine. Crumble the Oxo cube over and stir in. Season with pepper.

4 Pile the potato mixture back into the shells and place in a bowl. Microwave for 30 seconds to 1 minute until hot through. Top each half with a spoonful of soft cheese and serve.

Sardine jackets

SERVES 1

1 large potato, scrubbed
A knob of butter or margarine
1 × 120 g/4½ oz/small can of sardines
in tomato sauce
1 tsp lemon juice
A splash of Worcestershire sauce
(optional)
Pepper
2 tsp salad cream or mayonnaise

1 Prick the potato all over and wrap in kitchen paper (paper towels). Microwave on High (100 per cent power) for about 4 minutes, turning over once, until soft when squeezed.

2 Halve the cooked potato and scoop out most of the flesh into a bowl.

3 Using a fork, mash with the butter or margarine. Add the sardines (including the bones) and mash in thoroughly. Add the lemon juice and Worcestershire sauce, if using.

4 Pile the potato mixture back into the shells and place in a bowl. Microwave for 1–1¼ minutes until hot through. Top each half with a spoonful of salad cream or mayonnaise.

ⓥ Cottage jackets ⓥ

SERVES 1

1 large potato, scrubbed
A knob of butter or margarine
1 small carton of plain or flavoured
cottage cheese
Salt and pepper
1 tsp salad cream

1 Prick the potato all over and wrap in kitchen paper (paper towels). Microwave on High (100 per cent power) for about 4 minutes, turning over once, until soft when squeezed.

2 Place the potato in a bowl and make a 'cross' cut in the top. Squeeze gently to open up slightly. Put a knob of butter or margarine in the top and sprinkle with salt and pepper.

3 Spoon over the cottage cheese. Top with the salad cream and eat straight away.

ⓥ Hummus jackets ⓥ

SERVES 1

1 large potato, scrubbed
2 good tbsp hummus,
ready-made or see page 76
1 tbsp olive oil
Pepper, preferably black
A few slices of black olive (optional)

1 Prick the potato all over and wrap in kitchen paper (paper towels). Microwave on High (100 per cent power) for about 4 minutes, turning over once, until soft when squeezed.

2 Place the potato in a bowl and make a 'cross' cut in the top. Squeeze gently to open up slightly.

3 Spoon over the hummus. Trickle the olive oil over, sprinkle with pepper and add a few slices of black olive, if liked.

Black pepper, cheese and ⓥ walnut jackets ⓥ

If you can't get soft cheese with black pepper, use cheese with chives.

SERVES 1

1 large potato, scrubbed
1 good tbsp of soft cheese with
black pepper
1 tbsp walnut pieces, chopped

1 Prick the potato all over and wrap in kitchen paper (paper towels). Microwave on High (100 per cent power) for about 4 minutes, turning over once, until soft when squeezed.

2 Place the potato in a bowl and make a 'cross' cut in the top. Squeeze gently to open up slightly.

3 Add the spoonful of cheese, pressing it gently into the hot potato to encourage it to melt. Sprinkle the walnuts over the top.

ⓥ Pesto potatoes ⓥ

SERVES 1

1 large potato, scrubbed
1 tbsp pesto, ready-made or see page 418
1 tomato, chopped
A small handful of grated
Mozzarella cheese

1 Prick the potato all over and wrap in kitchen paper (paper towels). Microwave on High (100 per cent power) for about 4 minutes, turning over once, until soft when squeezed.

2 Place the potato in a bowl and make a 'cross' cut in the top. Squeeze gently to open up slightly.

3 Mix the pesto with the tomato and cheese and spoon into the potato. Microwave for a further 30 seconds to melt the cheese.

Thai noodle soup

If you're into Thai food, you can buy jars of minced lemon grass from the spices and herbs section in the supermarket – it'll keep for months in the fridge. Use about ½ tsp instead of the lemon zest. Alternatively use ½ stalk of fresh lemon grass, finely chopped. You can make a more filling meal by adding more stock and noodles and eating it with bread.

SERVES 1

1½ mugs of water
1 chicken stock cube
1 tsp grated lemon zest
1 tsp soy sauce
¼ slab of fine Chinese egg noodles
or 1 nest of vermicelli
Thai rice crackers

1 Put the water and stock cube in a microwave-safe bowl with the lemon zest and soy sauce. Heat on High (100 per cent power) until the stock is boiling. Stir to dissolve the stock cube.

2 Break the noodles or vermicelli into small pieces and add to the stock. Microwave for 5 minutes, stirring once or twice.

3 Taste and add a dash more soy sauce, if liked. Eat with Thai rice crackers.

Ⓥ Green vegetable soup Ⓥ

You can make this in a saucepan too. Cook for the same amount of time.

SERVES 2

1 small onion, peeled and chopped
1 potato, peeled and chopped
½ mug of frozen broad (fava) beans
½ mug of frozen spinach
2 mugs of water
1 vegetable stock cube
Salt and pepper
Grated nutmeg
1–2 tbsp plain yoghurt

1 Put all the ingredients except the nutmeg and yoghurt in a large microwave-safe bowl. Cook on High (100 per cent power) for 10 minutes until everything is really tender, stirring occasionally.

2 Mash the soup with a potato masher or fork or purée with a hand blender. Add salt, pepper and nutmeg, to taste. Reheat.

3 Ladle into warm bowls and add a spoonful of yoghurt.

Ⓥ Poppadoms Ⓥ

The best way to cook poppadoms is in the microwave with no added oil. Place one at a time on a plate. Microwave for about 20–30 seconds until beginning to puff up. Turn over and microwave until puffy all over. Repeat with as many as you like.

Reheated leftover Chinese or Indian take-away

You can reheat last night's leftovers very successfully – but only once. First tip the food out of the foil containers on to a plate. Make sure the food is spread out fairly evenly. Cover with another plate or clingfilm (plastic wrap), folded back slightly at one edge to allow steam to escape. Microwave on High (100 per cent power) following the times given below. Remember, reheat for the shortest time first, then check and heat for a little longer as necessary.

1 portion: 1½–3½ minutes

2 portions: 3–6 minutes

1 large plateful of rice and a selection of other dishes: 4–7 minutes

Ⓥ Curried naan snack Ⓥ

This makes enough for two, but you can eat the second portion the next day either cold or reheated in a microwave on High (100 per cent power) for about 30 seconds.

SERVES 2

1 × 225 g/8 oz/small can of pease pudding
2 tsp curry paste or powder
2 tbsp mango chutney or sweet pickle
2 naan breads
A handful of shredded lettuce

1 Put the pease pudding, curry paste or powder and chutney or pickle in a microwave-safe bowl. Microwave on High (100 per cent power) for 1–2 minutes until piping hot, stirring once.

2 Remove the bowl from the microwave. Wrap the naan breads in kitchen paper (paper towels) and microwave on High for 30 seconds to 1 minute.

3 Spread the breads with the pease pudding mixture and cover with the lettuce. Fold in half, and cut each into four wedges. Hold in a piece of kitchen paper for easy eating.

Ⓥ Porridge Ⓥ

Porridge is cheap and very good for you – but it can look a bit dull. Zip it up by adding a handful of chopped nuts, raisins, chopped dried apricots or any other dried fruit before cooking. You may need to increase the cooking time by 30 seconds.

SERVES 1

3 tbsp porridge oats
½ mug of milk and water, mixed
A pinch of salt
Milk and sugar, golden (light corn) syrup or clear honey

1 Mix the oats with the measured milk and water. Stir in the salt.

2 Microwave on High (100 per cent power) for 2–3 minutes, stirring once until thick and creamy.

3 Eat with milk and sugar, syrup or honey.

Main Courses You can Do With ... a Microwave

Microwaves are fantastic – they take up very little space, they're easy and fast to use and they really do cut down on the washing-up.

Make sure any crockery or utensils you use are safe for putting in the microwave – so no metal, thin glass or ironstone pottery. Heatproof glass – like Pyrex – is ideal. Most polythene bowls are fine, provided you don't use them with foods with a high sugar content or they'll get too hot and melt.

Some recipes include standing time at the end. This is necessary to allow certain foods to complete cooking before serving, so don't ignore it.

Remember that cooking times vary according to the output of your oven, and if you've got a really old microwave with only 600 watt output, you may need to add on a minute or two to the cooking times I've given. Just test after the shorter time and add on a little at the end if necessary.

Smoked mackerel and rice pot

SERVES 1

*1 spring onion (scallion),
trimmed and chopped*
¹/₄ mug of long-grain rice
A handful of frozen peas
6 tbsp passata (sieved tomatoes)
6 tbsp water
¹/₄ tsp dried basil
¹/₄ tsp sugar
Salt and pepper
1 small smoked mackerel fillet

1 Mix everything except the mackerel in a dish with a lid. Cover and microwave on High (100 per cent power) for 10 minutes until almost tender and most of the liquid has been absorbed.

2 Cut the fish into cubes, discarding the skin. Stir into the rice, cover again and microwave for 1–2 minutes or until the rice is cooked.

3 Leave to stand for 5 minutes before eating.

Tuna and mushroom jackets

SERVES 1

1 large potato, scrubbed
1 tbsp mayonnaise
1 tsp tomato ketchup (catsup)
1 tsp brown table sauce
Salt and pepper
½ × 185 g/6½ oz/small can of tuna,
drained
3 button mushrooms, sliced
Salad, to serve

1 Prick the potato all over and wrap in kitchen paper (paper towels). Microwave on High (100 per cent power) for about 4 minutes, turning over once, until soft when squeezed.
2 Mix the mayonnaise with the ketchup and brown sauce. Season to taste.
3 Stir the tuna and mushrooms into the sauce.
4 Put the potato in a bowl. Cut a large cross in the top. Squeeze the potato to open it up a bit and spoon the tuna mixture on top. Eat with salad.

Prawn cocktail jackets

Prawns may sound a bit of a luxury, but bags of frozen prawns are often on special offer and a few go a long way (a 400 g/14 oz bag will do you for about six meals!)

SERVES 1

1 large potato, scrubbed
1 tbsp mayonnaise
1 tsp tomato ketchup (catsup)
A few drops of Worcestershire sauce
or soy sauce
A few drops of Tabasco
or other chilli sauce
Salt and pepper
A handful of frozen peeled prawns
(shrimp), thawed
Salad, to serve

1 Prick the potato all over and wrap in kitchen paper (paper towels). Microwave on High (100 per cent power) for about 4 minutes, turning over once, until soft when squeezed.
2 Mix the mayonnaise with the ketchup, Worcestershire or soy sauce and the Tabasco or other chilli sauce. Season to taste.
3 Drain the prawns on kitchen paper (paper towels), then stir into the sauce.
4 Put the potato in a bowl. Cut a large cross in the top. Squeeze the potato to open it up a bit, then spoon the prawn mixture on top. Eat with salad.

Blue cheese, celery and mushroom jackets with ⓥ baked tomatoes ⓥ

If you don't have (or like) celery, try 1 tbsp of chopped walnuts, peanuts or cucumber instead.

SERVES 1

1 large potato, scrubbed
A good knob of butter or margarine
1 cm/¹/₂ in wedge of blue cheese,
crumbled
1 celery stick, finely chopped,
removing any strings
2–3 mushrooms, sliced
Salt and pepper
4 small tomatoes
1 tbsp balsamic vinegar and ¹/₂ tsp sugar
or 1 tbsp wine vinegar and 1 tsp sugar

1 Prick the potato all over with a fork. Wrap in kitchen paper (paper towels) and microwave on High (100 per cent power) for about 4 minutes, turning over once, or until soft when squeezed.

2 Cut the potato in half and, holding the halves in an oven-gloved hand, scoop out most of the potato into a bowl, leaving a shell.

3 Mash with the butter or margarine and cheese, then stir in the celery and mushrooms. Taste and season.

4 Pack the mixture back into the potatoes and place on a plate.

5 Put the tomatoes in a small bowl, make a 'cross' cut into the top of each and sprinkle with the vinegar and sugar.

6 Microwave on High for 1 minute until softened but still holding their shape. Remove from the microwave.

7 Put the potatoes back in and microwave for 1–1¹/₂ minutes until piping hot. Eat with the tomatoes.

Goulash

SERVES 1

2 tsp sunflower oil
1 onion, peeled and chopped
1 carrot, peeled and finely chopped
A handful of minced (ground) lamb
or beef
1 tsp paprika
1 × 225 g/8 oz/small can of
chopped tomatoes
1 × 275 g/10 oz/small can of
new potatoes, drained
¹/₄ tsp sugar
Salt and pepper
Plain yoghurt

1 Put the oil, onion, carrot and meat in a dish. Cover with a lid or plate and microwave on High (100 per cent power) for 2–3 minutes, stirring once, until the grains of meat are no longer pink.

2 Add all the remaining ingredients except the yoghurt. Stir well. Cover and microwave on High for 5 minutes until everything is cooked and bathed in a rich sauce.

3 Top with a spoonful of yoghurt.

Fish in cider on carrot mash

SERVES 1

1 potato, peeled and cut into
small chunks
1 carrot, peeled and sliced
2 knobs of butter or margarine
1 small onion, peeled and thinly sliced
2-3 button mushrooms, sliced
1 small piece of white fish fillet
3 tbsp cider or apple juice
2 tbsp milk
Salt and pepper
1 tsp cornflour (cornstarch)
½ tsp dried parsley

1 Put the potato and carrot in a dish
with a lid. Add 3 tbsp of water. Cover
and microwave on High (100 per cent
power) for about 6 minutes or until
tender. Remove from the oven and
leave to stand while cooking the fish.

2 Put a knob of butter or margarine
in a separate shallow dish. Add the
onion and mushrooms and
microwave on High for 2 minutes.

3 Add the fish and pour over the
cider or apple juice. Season lightly.
Cover with a lid, plate or clingfilm
(plastic wrap), peeled back slightly at
one edge, and microwave for
1-2 minutes until the fish is cooked.

4 Drain the potatoes and carrots and,
using a potato masher or fork, mash
with the remaining butter or
margarine and 1 tbsp of the milk.
Season with salt and pepper and pile
on a plate.

5 Lift the fish out of the dish,
retaining the cooking juices, and put
on top.

6 Mix the cornflour with the
remaining milk and stir into the
cooking juices. Return to the

microwave and cook for 30 seconds.
Stir, taste and re-season if necessary,
then spoon over the fish.

Fast fresh fish pie

SERVES 1

1 small piece of white fish fillet
5 tbsp milk
1 tsp cornflour (cornstarch)
2 knobs of butter or margarine
1 × 200 g/7 oz/small can of diced mixed
vegetables, drained
A good pinch of dried mixed herbs
Salt and pepper
1 portion of instant mashed potatoes
A handful of grated Cheddar cheese
A small handful of cornflakes

1 Put the fish in a shallow dish and
add 4 tbsp of the milk. Cover with a
lid or plate and microwave on High
(100 per cent power) for 1-2 minutes
until cooked through. Carefully lift
out the fish, and remove the skin.

2 Blend the cornflour with the
remaining milk in a cup or mug. Tip
into the fish juices and stir to thicken.

3 Stir in a knob of butter or
margarine, the drained vegetables, the
herbs and the fish. Taste and season.
Microwave on High for 1 minute. Stir
again.

4 Meanwhile, make up the mashed
potato according to the packet
directions, adding a knob of butter or
margarine. Pile on top of the fish
mixture and sprinkle with the cheese
and then crush the cornflakes over.
Microwave on High for a further
1-2 minutes until the cheese has
melted.

Trout with almonds, new potatoes and broccoli

This tastes equally good with mackerel, which is even cheaper!

SERVES 1

6 small new potatoes,
scrubbed or scraped
1 small head of broccoli,
cut into small florets
Salt
1 trout, cleaned
1 tsp lemon juice
Salt and pepper
A knob of butter or margarine
½ tsp dried parsley
1 tbsp flaked (slivered) almonds

1 Cut the potatoes in half. Put in a dish with 3 tbsp of water. Cover and microwave on High (100 per cent power) for 3 minutes.

2 Add the broccoli, re-cover and cook for a further 3–5 minutes or until the broccoli and potatoes are tender. Sprinkle lightly with salt, then cover and leave to stand.

3 Put the fish in a dish. Sprinkle with the lemon juice and a little salt and pepper. Cover and microwave for 3–4 minutes until cooked through. Remove from the microwave and leave to stand.

4 Put the butter or margarine in a small bowl or mug with the parsley and almonds. Microwave on High for 1 minute, stirring once, until the nuts are brown.

5 Drain the potatoes and broccoli. Put the fish on a plate, spoon the nut mixture over and put the potatoes and broccoli to one side.

Hot crab supper

SERVES 1

A knob of butter or margarine
1 spring onion (scallion),
trimmed and chopped
1 × 225 g/8 oz/small can of butter
(lima) beans, drained and mashed
with a fork
2.5 cm/1 in piece of cucumber, chopped
4 crabsticks, chopped
1 tbsp white wine or apple juice
½ tsp Worcestershire sauce
½ tsp soy sauce
½ tsp dried parsley
Salt and pepper
1 small packet of cheese and onion
crisps (potato chips)
A small handful of grated Emmental
(Swiss) or Cheddar cheese
A Green Salad (see page 45), to serve

1 Put the butter or margarine in a shallow dish and add the spring onion. Microwave on High (100 per cent power) for 30 seconds.

2 Add all the other ingredients except the crisps and cheese, stir, then microwave on High for 1–2 minute. Stir again.

3 Crush the crisps and sprinkle over, then scatter the cheese on top. Return to the microwave and cook for 1 minute until the cheese has melted.

4 Eat with a Green Salad.

Warm salmon and potato salad

SERVES 1

6 small new potatoes,
scrubbed or scraped
Salt and pepper
1/4 small iceberg lettuce, torn into pieces
1 tomato, cut into small wedges
2.5 cm/1 in piece of cucumber, cut into
small chunks
1/4 small onion, peeled and thinly sliced
A handful of radishes, halved
1 tbsp olive oil
1 tsp lemon juice
1/2 tsp Worcestershire sauce
A pinch of sugar
1 small piece of salmon fillet,
about 150 g/5 oz
Mayonnaise

1 Cut the potatoes in half, then place in a small dish and add 3 tbsp of water. Cover and microwave on High (100 per cent power) for 3–4 minutes or until tender. Sprinkle with salt and leave to stand.

2 Put the lettuce, tomato, cucumber, onion and radishes in a bowl. Sprinkle the oil, lemon juice and Worcestershire sauce over, then add a sprinkling of salt, pepper and sugar.

3 Drain the potatoes and add to the bowl. Toss everything together, lifting and turning with a spoon and fork.

4 Put the fish into the dish you cooked the potatoes in, with 1 tbsp of water. Cover and cook on High for about 2 minutes until just cooked. Leave to stand for 1 minute.

5 Pile the salad on a plate, sit the fish on top and add a dollop of mayonnaise.

Macaroni special

SERVES 1

1/2 mug of macaroni
Boiling water
Salt and pepper
A good knob of butter or margarine
1 rasher (slice) of streaky bacon, rinded
and diced
1 green (bell) pepper, diced
1 small onion, peeled and chopped
2 tsp cornflour (cornstarch)
1/2 mug of milk
A good handful of grated
Red Leicester cheese

1 Put the pasta in a dish. Add plenty of boiling water (allowing enough room for it to boil). Microwave on High (100 per cent full power) for 6–8 minutes until just tender, stirring once during cooking. Add a pinch of salt and leave to stand.

2 Put the butter or margarine, bacon, pepper and onion in a bowl. Microwave on High for 2 minutes, stirring once or twice.

3 Stir in the cornflour, then the milk, and continue stirring until no lumps of cornflour remain. Return to the microwave and cook on High for 2 minutes, stirring twice.

4 Add the cheese and stir until melted. Drain the pasta and mix into the sauce. Season to taste, then microwave on High for 1 minute.

Chicken in red wine with sweetcorn and jacket potato

SERVES 1

1 large potato, scrubbed
1 small onion, peeled and sliced
1 rasher (slice) of streaky bacon, rinded and diced
4 mushrooms, sliced
2 tsp plain (all-purpose) flour
2 tbsp water
2 tbsp red wine
1 chicken breast
A good pinch of dried mixed herbs
Salt and pepper
¼ tsp sugar
1 × 200 g/7 oz/small can of sweetcorn (corn)
A knob of butter or margarine
½ tsp dried parsley

1 Prick the potato all over with a fork. Wrap in a piece of kitchen paper (paper towel) and microwave on High (100 per cent power) for about 4 minutes, turning over once, until soft when squeezed. Wrap in foil or a clean cloth and leave to stand while cooking the rest of the dish.

2 Put the onion, bacon and mushrooms in a small dish with a lid and microwave on High for 2 minutes, stirring.

3 Blend the flour with the water and stir into the dish with the wine.

4 Add the chicken, herbs, a little salt and pepper and the sugar. Stir. Cover and microwave on High for 4–5 minutes or until the chicken is tender, stirring the sauce and turning the chicken over once halfway through cooking.

5 Remove the casserole from the microwave. Tip the sweetcorn on to a large plate. Cover loosely with a piece of kitchen paper and microwave for 30 seconds to heat through. Stir.

6 Put the jacket potato on the plate and make a slit in the top. Add a knob of butter or margarine. Spoon the chicken and sauce to the side and sprinkle with the dried parsley.

Ⓥ Scrambled beans Ⓥ

This doesn't look very beautiful but it's quick, tasty and full of goodness.

SERVES 1

2 eggs, beaten
2 tbsp milk
A knob of butter or margarine
1 small red or green (bell) pepper, cut into small dice
½ × 425 g/15 oz/large can of mixed beans, drained
A good pinch of cayenne or chilli powder
Salt and pepper
A few lettuce leaves (optional)
Bread, to serve

1 Break the eggs into a microwave-safe bowl. Whisk in the milk until well blended.

2 Add the butter or margarine, pepper and drained beans.

3 Microwave on High (100 per cent power) for 1½ minutes. Stir well, then cook for a further 2–3 minutes until the mixture is just set but still slightly creamy. Stir well, season to taste with cayenne or chilli powder and a little salt and pepper and leave to stand for 1 minute.

4 Line a bowl with lettuce leaves, if liked. Spoon the mixture into the bowl and eat with bread.

Chicken cacciatore with pasta

SERVES 1

½ mug of pasta shapes
Boiling water
Salt and pepper
1 small onion, peeled and thinly sliced
½ small garlic clove, peeled and crushed,
or ½ tsp garlic purée (paste)
4 mushrooms, sliced
1 courgette (zucchini), sliced
1 tsp olive or sunflower oil
3 tbsp white wine or cider
3 tbsp water
1 tbsp tomato purée
¼ tsp dried basil
¼ tsp dried parsley
Salt and pepper
½ tsp clear honey
1 chicken portion
A knob of butter or margarine

1 Put the pasta in a dish and cover with plenty of boiling water. (The dish should be large enough for it to boil.) Stir, then cook on High (100 per cent power) for 7–9 minutes until almost tender, stirring once during cooking. Remove from the oven, sprinkle with salt and leave to stand.

2 Put the onion, garlic, mushrooms and courgette in a dish with the oil. Stir, then cook on High for 2 minutes, stirring once.

3 Add all the remaining ingredients except the chicken and stir well. Add the chicken and spoon the sauce over it. Cover with a lid or plate and microwave on Medium-High (70 per cent power) for 5–7 minutes, spooning the sauce over twice during cooking. Leave to stand for 5 minutes.

4 Pop the pasta back in the microwave on High for 1 minute to heat through. Drain and stir in the butter or margarine.

5 Spoon the pasta on to a plate and add the chicken and sauce.

Ham and broccoli bake

SERVES 1

1 small head of broccoli,
cut into small florets
2 slices of bread
2 slices of ham
A good handful of grated
Cheddar cheese
1 egg
5 tbsp milk
Salt and pepper
1 tomato, sliced, to serve

1 Put the broccoli in a shallow individual dish. Add 3 tbsp of water. Cover with a lid or small plate and microwave on High (100 per cent power) for 3–4 minutes until tender. Drain in a colander in the sink.

2 Wipe out the dish, then line with the bread, cutting it to fit. Lay the ham in the dish, then add the broccoli and sprinkle with the cheese.

3 Break the egg into a small bowl or mug. Whisk in the milk with a fork or balloon whisk. Season well, then pour over the cheese. Leave to stand for 30 minutes, if time allows, so that the egg mixture soaks into the bread.

4 Microwave on High for 2 minutes. Turn the setting to Medium (50 per cent power) and cook for a further 5–7 minutes or until set.

5 Leave to stand for 2 minutes before serving with slices of tomato.

Chicken fingers with saucy jacket potato and fresh tomato salsa

SERVES 1

1 large potato, scrubbed
3 tbsp crème fraîche
2 tsp dried chives
Salt and pepper
1 small garlic clove, peeled and crushed,
or ½ tsp garlic purée (paste)
1 skinless chicken breast,
cut into 4 fingers
5 tbsp dried breadcrumbs
1 tbsp grated Parmesan cheese
¼ tsp paprika
For the salsa:
2 tomatoes, chopped
½ small onion, peeled and
finely chopped
1 tsp tomato purée (paste)
A pinch of sugar
1 tsp olive oil
1 tsp lemon juice
A pinch of chilli powder

1 Prick the potato all over with a fork. Wrap in kitchen paper (paper towels) and microwave on High (100 per cent power) for about 4 minutes, turning over once, until soft when squeezed. Wrap in foil or a clean cloth and leave to stand.

2 Mix 2 tbsp of the crème fraîche with half the chives and season with a little salt and pepper.

3 Mix the rest of the crème fraîche with a little salt and pepper, the remaining chives and the garlic. Stir in the chicken.

4 Mix the breadcrumbs with the Parmesan and the paprika. Roll each piece of chicken in the crumb mixture to coat completely. Repeat the rolling, if necessary, to coat thoroughly.

5 Mix the salsa ingredients together with a pinch of salt and pepper in a small bowl.

6 Ideally, place the chicken fingers on a microwave rack over a plate. If you don't have one, put straight on the plate. Microwave on Medium (50 per cent power) for 2 minutes. Rearrange the pieces and microwave for a further 1–2 minutes until cooked through.

7 Make a 'cross' cut in the top of the potato. Squeeze gently, then spoon in the crème fraîche and chives. Put on a plate with the chicken fingers and the salsa on one side.

Creamy mushroom chicken with pasta

Check the cooking time of the pasta on the packet. If it is labelled 'quick-cook', it will take only 4–5 minutes.

SERVES 1

½ mug of small pasta shapes
Boiling water
Salt and pepper
1 skinless chicken breast, cubed
1 × 170 g/6 oz/small can of
creamed mushrooms
1 tbsp milk
A pinch of dried thyme
A little dried parsley
A Green Salad (see page 45), to serve

1 Put the pasta in a dish and cover with plenty of boiling water. (The dish should be large enough for it to boil in the microwave.) Microwave on High (100 per cent power) for 6–8 minutes or until almost tender. Add a pinch of salt and stir, then cover and leave to stand.

2 Put the chicken with the mushrooms, milk and thyme in a separate dish with a lid. Cover and microwave on High for 3–4 minutes until the chicken is cooked through. Taste and season, if necessary.

3 Check that the pasta is completely cooked (if not, return to the microwave for a minute or two). Drain in a colander in the sink, then add to the chicken, stir well and pile on a plate. Sprinkle with dried parsley and eat with a Green Salad.

Chicken and peanut pilaf

SERVES 1

1 tbsp olive or sunflower oil
4 spring onions (scallions),
trimmed and chopped
½ green (bell) pepper, chopped
1 small garlic clove, peeled and crushed,
or ½ tsp garlic purée (paste)
1 skinless chicken breast,
cut into small chunks
¼ mug of long-grain rice
½ chicken stock cube
½ mug of boiling water
A handful of roasted peanuts
1 tsp soy sauce

1 Put the oil, spring onions, pepper, garlic and chicken in a bowl. Stir to coat in the oil, then microwave on High (100 per cent power) for 3 minutes, stirring once.

2 Add the rice, stir and cook on High for 1 minute.

3 Stir the stock cube into the water until dissolved and add to the rice with the peanuts. Stir well, then microwave on Medium-High (70 per cent power) for about 10 minutes, stirring twice, until the rice is cooked and has absorbed the liquid and the chicken is tender.

4 Stir in the soy sauce and season with pepper. Sprinkle with more soy sauce, if liked.

Chinese pork with oriental vegetables

The remaining beansprouts can be frozen in their bag to use in any other Chinese-style cooked recipe in this book. For added sustenance, have some prawn crackers with this.

SERVES 1

1 egg white

2 tsp cornflour (cornstarch)

A pinch of sugar

1 pork shoulder steak,
cut into small cubes

1 carrot, peeled and cut into
thin matchsticks

2.5 cm/1 in piece of cucumber,
cut into matchsticks

1 red (bell) pepper, cut into matchsticks

2 good handfuls of beansprouts

1 tbsp sunflower oil

A pinch of ground ginger
or Chinese five-spice powder

1 tsp soy sauce

1 tsp apple juice or white wine

1 small garlic clove, peeled and crushed,
or ½ tsp garlic purée (paste)

1 Lightly beat the egg white with a fork. Add the cornflour and sugar and beat again. Drop in the pieces of pork, stir, then leave in the fridge for at least 30 minutes.

2 Put the carrot, cucumber and pepper in a dish. Add 1 tbsp of water. Cover and microwave on High (100 per cent power) for 2 minutes. Add the beansprouts, re-cover and cook for 30 seconds. Remove from the microwave and tip into a bowl.

3 Wipe out the vegetable cooking dish and pour in the oil. Remove the pork from the egg mixture with a draining spoon and arrange the pieces in the dish. Microwave on High for 2 minutes, turning the cubes once.

4 Add the vegetables and remaining ingredients. Stir, then cover and microwave on High for a further 2–3 minutes or until the pork is tender.

Tasty midweek mince

SERVES 1

2 smallish potatoes, scrubbed
2 tsp sunflower oil
1 small onion, peeled and
finely chopped
1 carrot, peeled and thinly sliced
3 mushrooms, thinly sliced
A good handful of minced (ground) beef
or lamb
1 × 225 g/8 oz/small can of
chopped tomatoes
½ beef stock cube, crumbled
A handful of frozen peas
Salt and pepper
1 tsp cornflour (cornstarch)
2 tsp water

1 Prick the potatoes with a fork. Wrap in kitchen paper (paper towels) and microwave on High for 4–5 minutes, turning over once, until cooked through. Wrap in foil or a clean cloth and leave to stand.

2 Put the oil, onion, carrot, mushrooms and mince in a dish. Microwave on High (100 per cent power) for 2 minutes, stirring once, until the meat is no longer pink.

3 Stir in all the remaining ingredients except the cornflour and water. Cook on High for 3 minutes, stirring twice, until the carrot is tender. Blend the cornflour with the water and stir into the mixture. Microwave for 30 seconds to thicken. Taste and re-season.

4 Spoon the mixture into a shallow bowl. Cut the potatoes in half and put on top.

Cottage pie

SERVES 1

Prepare as for Tasty Midweek Mince (left) but instead of cooking jacket potatoes, peel and cut a large potato into small dice. Cook it in 3 tbsp of water in a covered dish in the microwave for 3–4 minutes until tender. Drain and mash with a knob of butter or margarine and 1 tbsp of milk. Season to taste. Pile the potato on top of the cooked mince, then add a few flakes of butter or margarine or a handful of grated cheese. Return to the microwave for a minute or two to melt, or flash under a hot grill (broiler) to brown.

Chilli con carne

SERVES 1

Prepare as for Tasty Midweek Mince (left), but omit the potatoes and peas and add ½ × 425 g/15 oz/large can of economy red kidney beans, drained (you can keep the rest in the fridge in a covered container for up to 3 days, for use in for another recipe). Stir in a good pinch each of dried oregano, cumin and chilli powder. Spoon the mixture into crispy tacos and top with a little grated cheese or eat with crusty bread.

Ribs with carrot noodles

If you can't find small pork ribs, use belly pork slices, cut in half. If you like a richer, dark colour, use dark brown sugar instead of golden syrup.

SERVES 1–2

A knob of butter or margarine
½ small green or red (bell) pepper, finely chopped
1 small onion, peeled and finely chopped
1 small garlic clove, peeled and crushed, or ½ tsp garlic purée (paste)
¼ tsp dried chives
1 tbsp cornflour (cornstarch)
1 tbsp vinegar
½ beef stock cube
½ mug of boiling water
4 tsp soy sauce
2 tbsp golden (light corn) syrup
400 g/14 oz short pork ribs
½–1 slab of Chinese egg noodles
1 large carrot, peeled and grated

1 Put the butter or margarine in a fairly large, shallow dish with the pepper, onion, garlic and chives. Microwave on High for 2 minutes, stirring once.

2 Stir in the cornflour, then the vinegar. Crumble the stock cube into the mug of water and stir until dissolved. Blend into the bowl of vegetables and add 3 tsp of the soy sauce and all the syrup. Microwave on High for 1 minute. Stir well and microwave for 1 further minute until thick.

3 Add the ribs and turn each one to coat in the sauce. Spread out and microwave on High for 10–12 minutes, turning twice during cooking. Cover and leave to stand.

4 Put the noodles in a bowl and pour boiling water over. Stir and leave to stand for 5 minutes. Stir, then drain in a colander in the sink. Tip into a bowl and add the carrot and remaining soy sauce. Lift and stir with a spoon and fork to mix. Top with the ribs.

Sausage and apple braise

SERVES 1

2–4 thick pork sausages
1 onion, peeled and thinly sliced
1 eating (dessert) apple, quartered, peeled, cored and thinly sliced
1 tsp plain (all-purpose) flour
1 tsp Dijon mustard
1 tsp Worcestershire sauce
1 tsp clear honey
1 tbsp vinegar
2 tbsp tomato purée (paste)
5 tbsp water
Salt and pepper
½ mug of frozen peas
Crusty bread, to serve

1 Cut each sausage into two or three pieces. Put in a dish with the onion and apple. Cover and microwave on High (100 per cent power) for 3 minutes, stirring once.

2 Put all the remaining ingredients except the salt and pepper and the peas into a bowl and blend together. Pour over the sausages and stir. Cover and microwave on High for 2–3 minutes, stirring once or twice, until the sauce is thick and richly flavoured. Remove from the microwave and leave to stand.

3 Add 1 tbsp of water to the mug of peas. Microwave on High for 2 minutes, then stir and cook for a further 1 minute, if necessary.

4 Drain the peas, stir into the sausage mixture. Taste and add salt and pepper. Eat with crusty bread.

✪ Mushroom quiche ✪

If this is too much for one meal, have the rest cold for lunch the next day.

SERVES 1-2

Flour, for dusting
¼ × 450 g/1 lb block of frozen shortcrust
pastry (basic pie crust), thawed
6 mushrooms, sliced
1 small onion, peeled and sliced
A knob of butter or margarine
¼ tsp dried oregano
1 egg
½ mug of milk
A good handful of grated
Cheddar cheese

1 Dust a work surface with a little flour and, using a rolling pin or clean bottle, roll out the pastry (paste) to a round large enough to fit a 15 cm/ 6 in shallow dish. Press gently into the dish.

2 Prick the base with a fork. Line the pastry with a sheet of kitchen paper (paper towel) and microwave on High (100 per cent power) for 3 minutes. Remove the paper and cook for a further 1 minute until set. Remove from the oven.

3 Put the mushrooms, onion and butter or margarine in a small bowl. Microwave on High for 2 minutes. Stir, then microwave for a further 1 minute. Tip into the pastry case (pie shell) and sprinkle with the oregano.

4 Break the egg into the mushroom bowl. Whisk in the milk and a little salt and pepper. Cover the mushroom mixture with the cheese, then pour in the egg and milk.

5 Microwave on Medium (50 per cent power) for 10–15 minutes until set.

Spiced sweet lamb with couscous

SERVES 1

½ mug of couscous
1 lamb or chicken stock cube
Boiling water
A good handful of minced (ground) lamb
1 small onion, peeled and
finely chopped
1 small garlic clove, peeled and crushed,
or ½ tsp garlic purée (paste)
2 tsp sunflower or olive oil
2 mushrooms, sliced
1 × 225 g/8 oz/small can of
apricot halves
A good pinch of ground cumin
A good pinch of ground cinnamon
Salt and pepper

1 Put the couscous in a bowl. Stir half the stock cube into a mugful of boiling water, then pour over the couscous. Stir well, then microwave on High (100 per cent power) for 5 minutes. Remove from the microwave, cover with foil and leave to stand.

2 Mix the lamb, onion, garlic, oil and mushrooms in a dish. Cover with a lid or plate and microwave on High for 2–3 minutes, stirring once or twice, until the grains of meat are no longer pink.

3 Blend the remaining half stock cube with 4 tbsp of boiling water. Add to the lamb mixture with the apricots and their juice, the cumin, cinnamon and a sprinkling of pepper. Stir well, cover and microwave on High for 5–6 minutes until cooked and tender. Taste and add salt, if necessary.

4 Fluff up the grains of couscous with a fork. Tip on to a plate and spoon the lamb over.

Lasagne

SERVES 2

1 small onion, peeled and chopped
½ small garlic clove, peeled and crushed,
or ¼ tsp garlic purée (paste)
1 tsp sunflower oil
A good handful of minced (ground) beef
1 × 225 g/8 oz/small can of
chopped tomatoes
2 tsp tomato purée
¼ tsp dried oregano
A good pinch of sugar
Salt and pepper
1 tbsp plain (all-purpose) flour
½ mug of milk
A knob of butter or margarine
A good handful of grated
Cheddar cheese
3 sheets of lasagne
1 tbsp grated Parmesan cheese (optional)
A Green Salad (see page 45),
to serve

1 Put the onion, garlic, oil and meat in a bowl and microwave on High (100 per cent power) for 3 minutes, stirring twice, until the meat is no longer pink.

2 Add the tomatoes, tomato purée, oregano, sugar and some salt and pepper. Microwave on High for 4–5 minutes until rich and thick, stirring twice. Remove from the microwave.

3 In a separate bowl, blend the flour with the milk and add the butter or margarine. Microwave on High for 1–2 minutes, stirring every 30 seconds, until thick. Season to taste and stir in the Cheddar cheese.

4 Spread a spoonful of the meat mixture in the base of a shallow dish, large enough to hold a sheet of lasagne. Cover with a sheet of lasagne. Put half the remaining meat on top, then another sheet of lasagne. Repeat the layers. Spoon the sauce over and sprinkle with the Parmesan, if using.

5 Microwave on Medium-High (70 per cent power) for 7–10 minutes until the pasta feels tender when a knife is inserted down the centre. Serve with a Green Salad.

Micro-roast chicken with scalloped vegetables

SERVES 1

1 potato, scrubbed and thinly sliced
1 carrot, peeled and thinly sliced
1 courgette (zucchini), thinly sliced
½ mug of vegetable or chicken stock,
made with ½ stock cube
Salt and pepper
1 chicken portion
½ tsp paprika

1 Arrange the vegetables in thin layers in a dish. Pour the stock over and sprinkle with pepper. Cover with a lid or plate and microwave on High (100 per cent power) for about 10 minutes or until the vegetables are tender. Remove from the microwave and leave to stand.

2 Rub the chicken all over with paprika. Place upside-down in a dish and cover with a lid or plate. Microwave on Medium-High (70 per cent power) for 4–5 minutes until cooked through. Turn the chicken over halfway through cooking. Leave to stand for 5 minutes.

3 Return the vegetables to the microwave and reheat for 1 minute. Transfer the chicken and vegetables to a plate and pour any chicken juices over.

Spiced prawns and mushrooms with noodles

SERVES 1

1 slab of Chinese egg noodles
1 spring onion (scallion),
trimmed and chopped
4 mushrooms, sliced
1 tbsp sunflower oil
2 tsp tomato purée (paste)
A good pinch of ground ginger
A good pinch of chilli powder
1 tbsp water
2 tsp soy sauce
A good handful of frozen peeled prawns
(shrimp), thawed

1 Put the noodles in a bowl, cover with boiling water and leave to stand.

2 Put everything except the prawns in a bowl. Microwave on High (100 per cent power) for 1 minute until bubbling.

3 Put the prawns in the bowl and microwave on High for 1–1½ minutes until piping hot, stirring once during cooking. Remove from the microwave.

4 Put the bowl of noodles in the oven and microwave for 30 seconds, then drain thoroughly.

5 Tip the noodles into a bowl and top with the prawns.

Snacks Yeu can De WitH ... ene Pan

ou may think that your repertoire is going to be very limited if you only have one gas or electric ring. But take a look at this section – loads of ideas, with the added advantage that you end up with only one pan to wash up.

True to the title, I have kept strictly to the idea of making everything for the snack in just one pan, even using it to fry (sauté) bread before cooking the rest of the snack. If you have a toaster or grill (broiler), you can toast the bread instead, if you prefer, then spread with butter or margarine after cooking, if liked.

Ⓥ Boiled eggs Ⓥ

Soft-boiled: Everyone has a different method. Mine works well, but don't cook more than six at once. Start with the eggs at room temperature, as they are less likely to crack.

1 Place the egg(s) in a saucepan just large enough to hold them in a single layer.

2 Add just enough cold water to cover. Put on a lid and bring to the boil.

3 As soon as the water is bubbling rapidly, start timing the eggs.

4 After exactly 3½ minutes, lift the eggs out of the water with a draining spoon and place in egg cups.

5 Tap the tops gently with a spoon to prevent further cooking.

Hard-boiled (hard-cooked):
Prepare as for soft-boiled but cook for 7 minutes. If serving cold, drain off the boiling water and cover with cold water to prevent a black ring forming round the yolk. Leave until cold before shelling.

Barbecued beans Ⓥ on fried bread Ⓥ

SERVES 1

2 tbsp sunflower oil
1 slice of bread
½ × 400 g/14 oz/large can of baked beans
1 tsp tomato ketchup (catsup)
1 tsp brown table sauce
1 tsp clear honey
1 tsp vinegar

1 Heat the oil in a saucepan or frying pan (skillet) until hot but not smoking (see page 35). Add the bread and fry (sauté) for 1–2 minutes on each side until golden brown. Remove from the pan and place on a plate.

2 Add the beans, ketchup, brown sauce, honey and vinegar to the pan and heat through, stirring, until piping hot and well blended.

3 Spoon the mixture on to the fried bread and serve.

Beans and bacon on fried bread

Store the remaining beans in a covered container in the fridge for up to 3 days. Alternatively, if you're very hungry, use the whole can!

SERVES 1

1–2 rashers (slices) of streaky bacon, rinded and chopped
1 slice of bread
2 tbsp sunflower oil
½ × 400 g/14 oz/large can of baked beans

1 Place the bacon in a frying pan (skillet) or saucepan and cook over a fairly high heat, stirring until browned. Remove from the pan and reserve.

2 Add the oil to the pan, then, when hot but not smoking (see page 35), fry (sauté) the bread for 1–2 minutes on each side until golden brown. Remove from the pan and place on a plate.

3 Tip the beans into the pan and add the bacon. Heat, stirring until piping hot. Spoon on to the fried bread.

Fried egg on Ⓥ fried bread Ⓥ

SERVES 1

A little oil
1 slice of bread
1 egg

1 Heat just enough oil in a medium frying pan (skillet) to cover the base.

2 When hot but not smoking (see page 35), add the bread and fry (sauté) on one side until golden. Turn over and push to one side of the pan. Break the egg into a cup or mug, then gently slide it into the pan beside the bread.

3 Cook until the white is just firm but the yolk is still soft. If you like crisp edges, cook over a fairly high heat (but be careful as the fat may splutter). If you like them soft-cooked, use a lower heat.

4 Remove the bread from the pan with a fish slice and place it on a plate. Lift out the egg in the same way, then transfer to the bread.

Ⓥ Fried egg sandwich Ⓥ

SERVES 1

2 slices of bread
Butter or margarine
Tomato ketchup (catsup)
or brown table sauce
A little sunflower oil
2 eggs

1 Spread the bread with butter or margarine and a little ketchup or sauce, if liked. Put one slice on a plate.

2 Put just enough oil in a frying pan (skillet) to cover the base. Heat until hot, but not smoking (see page 35).

3 One at a time, break the eggs into a cup or mug, then gently slide into the pan.

4 Tilt the pan slightly and spoon the hot oil over the eggs as they cook (this is called 'basting').

5 Cook until the whites are just firm but the yolk is still soft. If you like crisp edges, cook over a fairly high heat (but be careful as the fat may splutter). If you like them soft-cooked, use a lower heat.

6 Remove from the pan with a fish slice to allow the fat to drain off, then place on a slice of bread. Top with the other slice.

Hot dogs, beans and mushrooms

You can store the remaining beans and frankfurters in covered containers in the fridge for up to 3 days.

SERVES 1

2–3 mushrooms, sliced
A small knob of butter or margarine
4 hot dog sausages from a can, drained
1/2 × 400 g/14 oz/large can of baked beans
A splash of Worcestershire sauce (optional)
Bread

1 Put the mushrooms in the saucepan with the butter or margarine. Heat, stirring for 2 minutes, until the mushrooms are cooked.

2 Cut each sausage into three pieces, then add to the pan with the beans and Worcestershire sauce, if using. Heat, stirring gently occasionally, until bubbling hot.

3 Spoon into a bowl and eat with bread.

Poached egg
ⓥ on a slice ⓥ

This is the traditional way to poach eggs, giving a soft, delicate result.

SERVES 1

1 egg
1 tbsp lemon juice or vinegar
1 slice of bread or toast
A knob of butter or margarine

1 Put about 2.5 cm/1 in water in a heavy-based frying pan (skillet) and add the lemon juice or vinegar.

2 Bring the water to the boil, then reduce the heat until the water is just bubbling round the edges.

3 Break the egg into a cup or mug. Swirl the water round with a spoon to cause a mini 'whirlpool', then gently slide the egg into the centre (the circular motion of the water should prevent it from breaking up).

4 Cover with a lid or a piece of foil and poach for about 3 minutes for a soft-cooked egg, 4–5 minutes for a firm one.

5 Spread the bread or toast with butter or margarine, then put it on a plate.

6 Lift the egg out of the pan with a draining spoon, allowing the water to drain off, and set it on top.

ⓥ Scrambled eggs ⓥ

SERVES 1

2 eggs
2 tbsp milk
A knob of butter or margarine, plus extra for spreading
Salt and pepper
1 slice of bread or toast

1 Break the eggs into a saucepan and add the milk. Whisk with a fork or small whisk until blended. Add the butter or margarine and season lightly.

2 Cook over a gentle heat, stirring all the time, until the mixture is just set but still creamy. Do not allow the mixture to boil or it will curdle.

3 Spread the bread or toast with a little butter or margarine.

4 Place on a plate and top with the eggs.

Scrambled eggs with kippers

SERVES 1

2 eggs
2 tbsp milk
A knob of butter or margarine,
plus extra for spreading
Salt and pepper
1 × 120 g/4½ oz/small can of kipper
fillets, drained
1 slice of bread or toast

1 Break the eggs into a saucepan and add the milk. Whisk with a fork or small whisk until blended. Add the butter or margarine. Season lightly.

2 Cook over a gentle heat, stirring all the time, until partially set.

3 Break up the fish into small pieces and add to the eggs. Continue to scramble over a gentle heat until just set. Do not allow the mixture to boil or it will curdle.

4 Spread the bread or toast with a little butter or margarine.

5 Place on a plate and top with the egg mixture.

Scrambled egg with bacon

SERVES 1

A knob of butter or margarine,
plus extra for spreading
2 rashers (slices) of bacon,
cut into small pieces
2 eggs
2 tbsp milk
Salt and pepper
1 slice of bread or toast

1 Melt the butter or margarine in a saucepan. Add the bacon and cook, stirring, for 2 minutes until lightly golden. Remove from the pan.

2 Break the eggs into the pan and add the milk. Whisk with a fork or small whisk until blended. Add the bacon and season lightly.

3 Cook over a gentle heat, stirring all the time, until the mixture is scrambled but still creamy. Do not allow it to boil or it will curdle.

4 Spread the bread or toast with a little butter or margarine.

5 Place on a plate and top with the egg mixture.

Scrambled egg with Ⓥ mushrooms Ⓥ

SERVES 1

A large knob of butter or margarine,
plus extra for spreading
4 mushrooms, sliced
2 eggs
2 tbsp milk
Salt and pepper
1 slice of bread or toast

1 Melt the butter or margarine in a saucepan. Add the mushrooms and cook, stirring, for 2 minutes. Remove from the pan.

2 Break the eggs into the pan and add the milk. Whisk with a fork or small whisk until blended. Add the mushrooms and season lightly.

3 Cook over a gentle heat, stirring all the time, until the mixture is scrambled but still creamy. Do not allow it to boil or it will curdle.

4 Spread the bread or toast with a little butter or margarine.

5 Place on a plate and top with the egg mixture.

Scrambled egg with tomatoes and ham

SERVES 1

2 eggs
2 tbsp milk
A knob of butter or margarine,
plus extra for spreading
Salt and pepper
1 tomato, cut into small pieces
1 slice of bread or toast
1 slice of ham

1 Break the eggs into a saucepan and add the milk. Whisk with a fork or small whisk until blended. Add the butter or margarine and season lightly.

2 Cook over a gentle heat, stirring all the time, until the mixture is partially scrambled. Add the tomato and continue to cook, stirring, until just set. Do not allow the mixture to boil or it will curdle.

3 Spread the bread or toast with a little butter or margarine.

4 Place on a plate and top with the ham. Spoon the egg and tomato mixture on top.

Ⓥ French toast Ⓥ

You might know this as 'eggy bread'!

SERVES 1

1 egg
2 tsp milk
Salt and pepper
2 slices of bread
A little sunflower oil

1 Beat the egg and milk together with a sprinkling of salt and pepper in a shallow dish.

2 Cut the slices of bread in half and dip each half in the egg mixture until completely soaked.

3 Heat just enough oil in a frying pan (skillet) to cover the base. When hot but not smoking (see page 35), fry (sauté) the bread on both sides until golden brown.

4 Sprinkle with a little more salt, if liked, and eat while very hot.

Mixed bean and cheese
Ⓥ scramble Ⓥ

This is actually nourishing enough for a main meal but quick enough for a snack! Store the other half of the can of mixed beans in a covered container in the fridge for up to 3 days.

SERVES 1

½ × 430 g/15½ oz/large can of mixed
beans, drained
A knob of butter or margarine
1 egg, beaten
A handful of grated Cheddar cheese
Salt and pepper
A pinch of chilli powder
Bread or toast
Slices of tomato

1 Put everything except the bread or toast and tomato in a pan.

2 Cook over a moderate heat, stirring all the time, until scrambled. Do not allow to boil.

3 Pile on to bread or toast and serve with slices of tomato.

ⓥ Pan-roasted ⓥ vegetable slabs

You can use oregano instead of basil.

SERVES 1

3 tbsp oil
1 long bread roll or sandwich baguette,
halved lengthways
1 small red (bell) pepper, sliced
1 small green pepper, sliced
1 small onion, peeled and sliced
1 tbsp tomato purée (paste)
Salt and pepper
A good pinch of sugar
A good pinch of dried basil

1 Heat 2 tbsp of the oil in a frying pan (skillet) until hot but not smoking (see page 35). Add the baguette halves and fry (sauté) on both sides until brown. Remove from the pan and put on a plate.

2 Heat the remaining oil in the pan. Add the peppers and onion and fry (sauté), stirring for about 4 minutes until softened but still with a little bite.

3 Add the tomato purée, a sprinkling of salt and pepper, the sugar and basil. Stir well until blended.

4 Pile the pepper mixture on top of the fried bread.

ⓥ Everyday rarebit ⓥ

SERVES 1

1 slice of bread
Butter or margarine
A small handful of grated
Cheddar cheese
1 tsp made English mustard
1 tbsp apple juice
Slices of tomato

1 Spread the bread lightly with butter or margarine on both sides. Heat a frying pan (skillet) or saucepan and fry (sauté) the bread on both sides until browned. Transfer to a plate.

2 Put everything else in the pan and heat, stirring, until melted and blended.

3 Spoon on to the fried bread and serve straight away with slices of tomato.

ⓥ Somerset rarebit ⓥ

SERVES 1

1 Prepare Everyday Rarebit (above), substituting cider or white wine for the apple juice.

2 Quarter and peel an eating (dessert) apple. Cut out the core and slice it over the fried (sautéed) bread before spooning the cheese mixture on top.

Welsh rarebit

If you have a grill, toast the bread instead of frying it and when you've made the cheese mixture, spread it on the toast and put it back under the grill to brown.

SERVES 1

1 slice of bread
Butter or margarine
2 tsp plain (all-purpose) flour
A small handful of grated
Cheddar cheese
A pinch of salt
A pinch of chilli powder
1 tbsp beer
A few drops of Worcestershire sauce
(optional)

1 Spread the bread with butter or margarine on both sides and fry (sauté) in a saucepan or frying pan (skillet) until browned on both sides. Place on a plate.

2 Blend all the rest of the ingredients in the pan. Heat gently, stirring all the time, until thick and bubbling.

3 Spread the cheese mixture over the fried bread.

Buck rarebit

SERVES 1

After cooking the bread as for Welsh Rarebit (above), fry (sauté) an egg in a little more butter or margarine. Slide it on to the fried bread, then cook the cheese as above and spoon over.

ⓥ Simple pancakes ⓥ

Try sprinkling these with grated cheese, then roll them up. You can also eat them as a dessert with syrup or sugar and lemon. For more sophisticated main-meal pancakes, see pages 257–60, and for more pancake desserts, see page 395.

MAKES 4 PANCAKES

½ mug of plain (all-purpose) flour
A pinch of salt
1 egg
½ mug of milk
or milk and water mixed
A little sunflower oil

1 Mix the flour and salt in a bowl.

2 Make a hollow in the centre and add the egg and half the milk (or milk and water). Beat with a whisk or wooden spoon until thick and smooth. Stir in the remaining liquid.

3 Heat a little oil in a frying pan (skillet) until very hot but not smoking (see page 35). Pour off the excess into a small bowl to use for the next pancake.

4 Pour in just enough batter to coat the base of the pan when tipped and swirled gently. Cook until the mixture has set and the base of the pancake is golden brown. Toss or flip over with a fish slice or knife. Cook the other side.

5 Slide out on to a plate. Wrap in foil to keep warm while cooking the remainder. Use as required.

American pancakes
Ⓥ with syrup Ⓥ

These are great for breakfast – or at any time of day! If you're not a vegetarian, you can serve them as the Americans do, with bacon as well, if you like.

MAKES 8 PANCAKES

1 mug of plain (all-purpose) flour
A good pinch of salt
2 tsp caster (superfine) sugar
2 tsp baking powder
1 egg
2 tbsp melted butter or margarine
1 scant mug of milk
A little sunflower oil
Golden (light corn) syrup

1 Mix the flour, salt, sugar and baking powder together in a bowl.

2 Beat the egg with the melted butter or margarine and milk and gradually work into the flour mixture to form a thick batter.

3 Heat a little oil in a frying pan (skillet) until very hot but not smoking (see page 35). Pour off the excess. Add enough batter to make a 10 cm/4 in pancake. Cook until golden underneath and bubbles are breaking on the surface. Flip over and cook the other side. Wrap in foil to keep warm while making the remainder.

4 Serve hot with syrup trickled over.

Ⓥ Rosti Ⓥ

SERVES 1

1 large potato, scrubbed
1 small onion, peeled
Salt and pepper
1 tbsp sunflower oil

1 Grate the potato into a bowl. Squeeze out the excess moisture. Grate the onion into the bowl and add some salt and pepper. Mix well.

2 Heat the oil in a large frying pan (skillet). Divide the potato mixture into three flat cakes.

3 Fry (sauté) the cakes, pressing them down firmly with a fish slice for about 5 minutes, then turn over and cook the other sides for a further 5 minutes or until golden and cooked through.

4 Transfer to warm plates and eat while hot.

Fried fish sanger

SERVES 1

1 frozen breaded cod or haddock fillet
A little sunflower oil
2 thick slices of crusty white bread
A good knob of butter or margarine
2 tsp tomato ketchup (catsup)
Lemon juice or vinegar
Salt and pepper

1 Fry (sauté) the fish fillet in the oil as directed on the packet.

2 Spread both slices of bread with butter or margarine and top with ketchup.

3 Put one slice of the bread on a plate. Top with the cooked fish fillet, sprinkle with lemon juice or vinegar and a little salt and pepper and top with the second slice of tomato buttered bread. Eat while it's hot.

ⓥ Egg rosti ⓥ

SERVES 1

1 egg
1 large potato, scrubbed
1 small onion, peeled
Salt and pepper
1 tbsp sunflower oil

1 Whisk the egg in a bowl with a fork or balloon whisk.

2 Grate the potato into a separate bowl. Squeeze out the excess moisture. Add the potato to the egg.

3 Grate the onion into the bowl and add some salt and pepper. Mix well.

4 Heat the oil in a large frying pan (skillet) until hot but not smoking (see page 35). Spoon the mixture into the pan to make three cakes.

5 Fry (sauté) the cakes, pressing them down firmly with a fish slice for 3 minutes until browned underneath. Turn over, turn down the heat and cook the other sides for a further 5–8 minutes or until golden and cooked through.

ⓥ Hot potato salad ⓥ

SERVES 1

1 large potato, scrubbed and
cut into chunks
Salt and pepper
1 tbsp mayonnaise
1 tomato, diced
2.5 cm/1 in piece of cucumber, diced

1 Cook the potato in boiling water with a pinch of salt added, for about 10 minutes. The pieces should be tender but still holding their shape. Drain in a colander in the sink and return to the pan.

2 Stir in the mayonnaise and season with pepper. Lift and stir with a spoon and fork until blended with the mayonnaise. Tip into a bowl and scatter the tomato and cucumber on top.

Cinnamon ⓥ French toast ⓥ

SERVES 1–2

1 egg
1 tbsp milk
2 slices of white bread, crusts removed
A good knob of butter or margarine
1 tbsp sunflower oil
1 tbsp sugar
¼ tsp ground cinnamon

1 Beat the egg and milk together in a shallow dish.

2 Soak the bread on both sides in the egg and milk until thoroughly coated.

3 Heat the butter or margarine and oil in a large frying pan (skillet). Add the slices of bread and fry (sauté) for about 2 minutes on each side until golden.

4 Mix the sugar and cinnamon together on a plate. Dip the fried bread on either side in the sugar mixture. Cut into fingers and eat while still warm.

ⓥ Sauté potatoes ⓥ

These are good on their own for a snack, or as an accompaniment to an egg, a couple of sausages or even a sprinkling of grated cheese. They're also great as part of a main meal to accompany any meat, chicken or fish.

SERVES 1

A good knob of butter or margarine
1 tbsp sunflower or olive oil
1–2 potatoes, peeled and sliced
Salt
Tomato ketchup (catsup)

1 Heat the butter or margarine and oil in a frying pan (skillet). Add the potatoes and fry (sauté), turning occasionally, for about 6 minutes until golden brown and cooked through.

2 Drain on kitchen paper (paper towels), sprinkle with salt and eat while hot with ketchup.

ⓥ Scrumpets ⓥ

MAKES 1

1 crumpet
A knob of butter or margarine
1 tbsp sugar
A few fresh sliced strawberries or any other soft fruit

1 Spread the crumpet on both sides with the butter or margarine, then dust liberally with the sugar.

2 Heat a frying pan (skillet). Add the crumpet and fry (sauté) for about 2 minutes on each side until golden and sizzling.

3 Serve hot, topped with fruit of your choice.

Sauté potatoes with ⓥ sesame seeds ⓥ

SERVES 1

Cook as for Sauté Potatoes (left) but sprinkle with 2 tsp of sesame seeds before serving.

Sauté potatoes ⓥ with garlic ⓥ

SERVES 1

Prepare as for Sauté Potatoes (left) but cut a small garlic clove in half and add to the pan. Discard before serving.

Sauté potatoes ⓥ with spices ⓥ

SERVES 1

Prepare as for Sauté Potatoes (left) but mix a pinch each of chilli and mixed (apple-pie) spice with a pinch of celery salt and toss the potatoes in this before serving.

ⓥ Bubble and squeak ⓥ

I had a flatmate who loved this so much she would cook cabbage and potatoes specially so she could make it! If you want to do this, cut the potato up small and cook for 5 minutes, then add the cabbage to the same water and cook for about 5 minutes until both are tender, then drain really well before use. It's great on its own, with cold meats and salad or with eggs, bacon, sausages, etc.

SERVES 1

1 tbsp sunflower oil
A small knob of butter or margarine
3–4 pieces of boiled cooked potato, chopped
2–3 tbsp cooked cabbage, chopped
Salt and pepper
Tomato ketchup (catsup)
or brown table sauce

1 Heat the oil and butter or margarine in a frying pan (skillet) until hot but not smoking (see page 35). Add the potato and cabbage and season well.

2 Press down with the back of a fish slice and cover tightly with a plate that will fit just inside the rim of the pan, to keep the mixture pressed down well.

3 Cook over a moderate heat for about 15 minutes until the base is crisp and brown. Loosen with the fish slice, then invert on to the plate.

4 Serve with ketchup or brown sauce.

ⓥ Bobbed and squashed ⓥ

This is a variation on the traditional Bubble and Squeak (left), made with cooked, leftover potatoes, peas and carrots, with fried onions.

SERVES 1

1 tbsp sunflower oil
1 small onion, peeled and chopped
A good pinch of ground cumin
3–4 pieces of cooked potato, chopped
1–2 tbsp cooked carrots, chopped
1–2 tbsp cooked peas
Salt and pepper

1 Heat the oil in a frying pan (skillet). Add the onion and cumin and fry (sauté), stirring, for 3 minutes until softened and lightly golden.

2 Mix the potato and carrots with the peas. Add to the pan and stir well. Season the mixture liberally with salt and pepper. Press down well with the back of a fish slice, then cover with a plate that will fit just inside the rim of the frying pan to keep the mixture pressed down firmly. Fry over a moderate heat for 10–15 minutes until piping hot and crisp and golden underneath.

3 Loosen the base with the fish slice, invert on to the plate and serve piping hot.

ⓥ Re-fried beans ⓥ

Serve these in crisp tacos or rolled up in flour tortillas. They also make a great dip with tortilla chips. The fresh herbs are not vital but they do add a very good flavour.

SERVES 1–2

1 tbsp sunflower oil
1 × 425 g/15 oz/large can of pinto or red kidney beans, drained
1 tbsp chopped fresh parsley or coriander (cilantro)
½ tsp dried oregano
A pinch of chilli powder
A pinch of ground cumin
Salt and pepper
A good handful of grated Cheddar cheese

1 Heat the oil in a frying pan (skillet).

2 Mash the beans with a fork or purée them briefly with a hand blender.

3 Add to the hot oil and sprinkle with all the remaining ingredients except the cheese. Cook, stirring, until piping hot.

4 Either spoon on to plates and sprinkle with the cheese or stir in the cheese until melted, then serve.

Fried red beef sandwich

You can make this in a sandwich toaster but, somehow, it tastes much better fried in a pan.

SERVES 1

2 slices of white bread
Butter or margarine
1 tsp horseradish relish
2 slices of cold roast beef
2 tbsp pickled red cabbage
Salt and pepper

1 Spread the bread on one side with butter or margarine.

2 Spread the other sides lightly with the horseradish.

3 Put the roast beef on top of one horseradish-spread slice.

4 Drain the pickled cabbage on kitchen paper (paper towels), then spread over the beef and season with pepper.

5 Top with the other slice of bread, buttered side up.

6 Heat a frying pan (skillet) over a moderate heat. Add the sandwich and fry (sauté), pressing down lightly with a fish slice until golden brown underneath. Don't have the heat to high or the sandwich will burn before the filling is hot.

7 Carefully turn over and fry, pressing again, until golden. Serve straight away.

Colcannon

This is an Irish version of Bubble and
Squeak (see page 136), which is
traditionally cooked in beef or pork
dripping. I use sunflower oil, which is
better for you!

SERVES 1

2 tbsp sunflower oil
1 small onion, peeled
and finely chopped
1–2 rashers (slices) of streaky bacon,
rinded and diced
3–4 pieces of cooked potato, mashed
2–3 tbsp cooked cabbage, chopped
Salt and pepper
A little flour, for dusting

1 Heat half the oil in a frying pan
(skillet) over a fairly high heat. Add
the onion and bacon and cook,
stirring, for about 3 minutes until
lightly golden.

2 Remove from the pan with a
draining spoon and place in a bowl
with the potatoes and cabbage. Season
well and mix together with a wooden
spoon.

3 With floured hands, shape the
mixture into two small cakes and
flatten to about 1 cm/½ in thick.

4 Heat the remaining oil in the same
frying pan over a fairly high heat.
Add the cakes and cook for
3–4 minutes on each side until golden
brown.

5 Serve hot.

ⓥ Onion bhajis ⓥ

You may as well make a batch of
these. You can keep any leftovers in
the fridge (wrap them well) for
several days.

SERVES 4

½ mug of gram (besan) or plain
(all-purpose) flour
½ tsp salt
A good pinch of ground turmeric
¼ tsp chilli powder
1 tbsp chopped fresh coriander (cilantro)
About ½ mug of water
2 onions, peeled and chopped
Oil, for deep-frying

1 Mix the flour, salt and turmeric in a
bowl. Stir in the chilli and coriander.

2 Using a wire whisk, mix in the
water, a little at a time, to form a
thick batter (you may need slightly
more or less than I have suggested,
depending on the flour you use).
Leave to stand for 30 minutes.

3 Stir in the onions.

4 Heat about 2.5 cm/1 in oil in a
large frying pan (skillet). To test if it
is hot enough, add a cube of day-old
bread – it should brown in
30 seconds. Gently slide spoonfuls of
the batter into the pan and cook for
about 3 minutes until golden brown,
turning them over if necessary. Drain
on kitchen paper (paper towels) and
keep warm while cooking the
remainder.

5 Serve warm.

ⓥ Mushroom bhajis ⓥ

SERVES 4

Prepare as for Onion Bhajis (see page 138) but omit the onions. When the batter has been standing, stir in 1 tsp of bicarbonate of soda (baking soda) and 2 handfuls of button mushrooms. Drop the coated mushrooms one at a time into the hot oil and cook as before.

ⓥ Potato bhajis ⓥ

SERVES 4

Prepare as for Onion Bhajis (see page 138) but omit the onion. Cut a large potato into thin slices and dry well on kitchen paper (paper towels). Dip the slices into the batter and deep-fry as before.

Cheesy beany bite

For economy, you can use half a 400 g/14 oz/large can of beans and store the rest in a covered container in the fridge for up to 3 days.

SERVES 1

1 × 225 g/8 oz/small can of baked
beans with pork sausages
¹/₂ Weetabix
2 pitta breads
1 tomato, sliced
A handful of grated Cheddar cheese

1 Heat the beans and sausages in a saucepan.

2 Crumble in the Weetabix and stir until thickened.

3 Make a slit along the edge of each pitta and gently open up.

4 Line with tomato slices and cheese. Spoon in the bean mixture and eat straight away.

ⓥ Pan haggerty ⓥ

If you have a grill, you can brown the top of the Pan Haggerty after cooking and serve it from the pan, rather than turning it out.

SERVES 1

2 tbsp sunflower oil
1 large potato, scrubbed and
very thinly sliced
1 onion, peeled and very thinly sliced
A good handful of grated
Cheddar cheese
Salt and pepper

1 Heat the oil in a heavy-based frying pan (skillet) over a low heat.

2 Layer the potato slices, onion and cheese in the pan, seasoning each layer of potatoes with salt and pepper and finishing with a layer of cheese.

3 Cover the pan with a lid or foil and cook over a very low heat for about 35 minutes until golden underneath and the potatoes are tender.

4 Loosen the base with a fish slice and turn the Pan Haggerty out on to a plate.

Ⓥ Egg 'n' cheese waffles Ⓥ

SERVES 1

A little sunflower oil
2 frozen potato waffles
2 slices of Cheddar cheese
2 eggs
A little shredded lettuce
2 good tsp mayonnaise

1 Heat just enough oil to cover the base of a large frying pan (skillet).

2 When hot but not smoking (see page 35), fry (sauté) the waffles until golden underneath.

3 Turn the waffles over and push to one side of the pan. Top with the cheese. Break the eggs into a cup and slide into the pan. Fry until cooked to your liking and the cheese has melted.

4 Transfer the waffles to a plate with a fish slice. Top with a little lettuce and a spoonful of mayonnaise, then put an egg on top of each.

Ham and Red Leicester waffles

SERVES 1

A little sunflower oil
2 frozen potato waffles
1–2 slices of ham
4 slices of cheese
A sprinkling of Worcestershire sauce
(optional)

1 Heat just enough oil to cover the base of a frying pan (skillet). When hot but not smoking (see page 35), fry (sauté) the waffles until golden brown on one side. Turn them over.

2 Cut the ham in half, if necessary, and put a slice on top of each waffle. Cover with the cheese and a sprinkling of Worcestershire sauce, if using. Cover with a lid or foil.

3 Cook until the cheese melts and bubbles. Serve straight away.

Devilled mushrooms on fried bread

SERVES 1

3 tbsp sunflower oil
1 slice of bread
1 small onion, peeled and finely chopped
6–8 button mushrooms
1 tomato, chopped
1 tsp tomato ketchup (catsup)
1 tsp Worcestershire sauce
A few drops of Tabasco sauce or a pinch of chilli powder

1 Heat 2 tbsp of the oil in a frying pan (skillet). When hot but not smoking (see page 35), add the bread and fry (sauté) until golden on both sides. Remove from the pan and keep warm.

2 Add the remaining oil and the onion and fry for 2 minutes, stirring, until softened.

3 Add the mushrooms and tomato and cook, stirring, for 2 minutes.

4 Add the remaining ingredients, turn down the heat to fairly low, cover with a lid, plate or foil and cook for 5 minutes.

5 Spoon on to the fried bread and serve.

ⓥ Spicy potato cakes ⓥ

SERVES 1

1 egg
1 large potato, peeled
½ small onion, peeled
¼ tsp garam masala or curry powder
A good pinch of chilli powder
1 tbsp plain (all–purpose) flour
Salt and pepper
Oil, for cooking
Mango chutney or sweet pickle

1 Break the egg into a mixing bowl and beat with a fork until blended.

2 Grate the potato and onion into the bowl.

3 Stir in the spices, flour and a little salt and pepper.

4 Heat enough oil to cover the base of a frying pan (skillet). When hot but not smoking (see page 35), put spoonfuls of the mixture in the pan and press down with a fish slice. Cook for 2–3 minutes until golden brown underneath.

5 Turn over the cakes with a fish slice and cook the other sides for a further 2–3 minutes until brown and cooked through.

6 Serve straight away with mango chutney or sweet pickle.

ⓥ Hash browns ⓥ

You can leave the potato unpeeled if you like, to add extra texture and fibre.

SERVES 1

2 tbsp sunflower oil
1 large potato, peeled and cut into small dice
1 small onion, peeled and chopped
Salt and pepper

1 Heat the oil in a frying pan (skillet). When hot but not smoking (see page 35), add the potato and fry (sauté), stirring, for about 10 minutes until golden on the outside and soft in the middle.

2 Add the onion and a good sprinkling of salt and pepper and continue to fry for a further 5 minutes until the mixture is soft and brown. Press down firmly with a fish slice to form a cake.

3 Serve hot.

Hash browns ⓥ with egg ⓥ

SERVES 1

2 tbsp sunflower oil
1 large potato, peeled and cut into small dice
1 small onion, peeled and chopped
Salt and pepper
1–2 eggs

1 Heat the oil in a frying pan (skillet). When hot but not smoking (see page 35), add the potato and fry (sauté), stirring, for about 10 minutes until golden on the outside and soft in the middle.

2 Add the onion and a good sprinkling of salt and pepper and continue to fry for a further 3 minutes until the mixture is soft and golden.

3 Make a hole in the mixture, easing it out with a spoon. Break an egg into a mug, then slide it into the hole. Cover the pan with a lid or foil and cook for about 5 minutes until set. Cook a little longer if you like your egg hard.

4 Serve hot.

Hash browns with bacon and mushroom topping

If liked, you can simply cook the potatoes, then add the bacon, mushrooms and onions and cook everything together.

SERVES 1

3 tbsp sunflower oil
4 mushrooms, sliced
2 rashers (slices) of streaky bacon, rinded and cut into small pieces
1 large potato, peeled and cut into small dice
1 small onion, peeled and chopped
Salt and pepper

1 Heat 1 tbsp of the oil in a frying pan (skillet). When hot but not smoking (see page 35), add the mushrooms and bacon and fry (sauté) for 2–3 minutes until golden and cooked. Remove from the pan with a fish slice and reserve.

2 Heat the remaining oil in the pan. Add the potato and fry, stirring, for about 10 minutes until golden on the outside and soft in the middle.

3 Add the onion and a good sprinkling of salt and pepper and continue to fry for a further 5 minutes until the mixture is soft and brown. Press down firmly with a fish slice to form a cake. Turn down the heat, spoon the bacon mixture on top, cover with foil or a lid and cook for 1 minute to heat through.

4 Serve hot.

Creamy pan mushrooms V with eggs V

SERVES 1

A knob of butter or margarine
6–8 mushrooms, sliced
1 small garlic clove, peeled and crushed, or ½ tsp garlic purée (paste)
3 tbsp water
A good pinch of dried mixed herbs
Salt and pepper
1–2 eggs
1–2 tbsp double (heavy) cream
Crusty bread

1 Melt the butter or margarine in a frying pan (skillet), add the mushrooms and garlic and cook, stirring, for 2 minutes until softened.

2 Add the water, herbs and a little salt and pepper and cook over a gentle heat until the water has nearly all evaporated.

3 Make one or two wells in the mushroom mixture and break in the eggs. Pour the cream over.

4 Cover the pan with a lid or foil and cook gently for 4–8 minutes until the eggs are cooked to your liking.

5 Serve with crusty bread.

Saucy mushrooms on ⓥ golden bread ⓥ

SERVES 1

1 slice of bread
Butter or margarine
6–8 button mushrooms, thickly sliced
¼ tsp dried mixed herbs
1 tsp cornflour (cornstarch)
½ mug of milk
Salt and pepper

1 Spread the bread with butter or margarine on both sides.

2 Heat a frying pan (skillet) and fry (sauté) the bread on both sides until golden. Remove from the pan and keep warm.

3 Melt another knob of butter or margarine in the pan, add the mushrooms and cook, stirring and turning, for 3 minutes. Sprinkle with the herbs.

4 Mix the cornflour with the milk and stir into the pan. Cook, stirring all the time, until thick and bubbling, then cook gently for another minute and season to taste with salt and pepper.

5 Spoon on to the golden bread.

Egg and vegetable ⓥ fry ⓥ

You can use frozen mixed vegetables and instant mash for this but it's worth cooking extra veg one day ready to cook this the next.

SERVES 1

1 mug of cooked leftover vegetables,
including potato
Pepper
A knob of butter or margarine
1 tbsp barbecue sauce
or brown table sauce
A little sunflower oil
2 eggs

1 Chop the vegetables, if necessary. Season with pepper.

2 Melt the butter or margarine in a frying pan (skillet) and When hot but not smoking (see page 35), add half the vegetables and press down flat.

3 Spread with the sauce, then top with the remaining vegetables and press down again.

4 Cover the pan with a plate and cook for about 10–15 minutes until crisp and golden on the base. Loosen underneath with a fish slice and then tip out on to the warm plate. Keep warm if possible.

5 Quickly heat just enough oil to cover the base of the pan and fry (sauté) the eggs until cooked to your liking. Slide on top of the vegetable cake and serve.

Roasted mustard seed, raisin and carrot salad

This is a great accompaniment to curries as well as a delicious snack.

SERVES 1

2 carrots
A small handful of raisins
1 tbsp olive or sunflower oil
2 tsp mustard seeds
1 tsp lemon juice
Salt and pepper

1 Coarsely grate the carrot into a bowl. Add the raisins.

2 Heat the oil in a frying pan (skillet). When hot but not smoking (see page 35), add the mustard seeds and heat until they 'pop'.

3 Add the lemon juice, swirl round and pour over the carrot. Sprinkle with salt and pepper, toss and eat while still warm.

Ratatouille with Ⓥ blue cheese Ⓥ

If you don't like blue cheese, use Cheddar, Red Leicester or even some sliced Camembert.

SERVES 1–2

1 × 425 g/15 oz/large can of ratatouille
A good handful of crumbled blue cheese
(or 2–3 slices, if creamy)
Crusty bread

1 Empty the ratatouille into a saucepan and heat through, stirring.

2 Scatter the cheese over the surface, turn down the heat to low and cover the pan with a lid, foil or a plate. Heat for 3–4 minutes until the cheese has completely melted.

3 Serve with crusty bread.

Fake cheese and onion Ⓥ focaccia Ⓥ

SERVES 1

1 tbsp olive oil
1 onion, peeled and sliced
1 small garlic clove, peeled and crushed,
or ½ tsp garlic purée (paste)
1 pitta bread
2–3 slices of Cheddar
or Mozzarella cheese
Slices of tomato

1 Heat half the oil in a frying pan (skillet). Add the onion and garlic and cook, stirring, over a moderate heat for 3–4 minutes until the onion is soft and lightly golden.

2 Spoon on to a pitta bread and spread out evenly.

3 Put the pan back over a low heat and add the remaining oil. Add the pitta bread, onion-side up, and top with the cheese. Cover the pan with a lid, plate or foil and cook gently for about 4 minutes until the cheese has completely melted.

4 Serve hot with slices of tomato.

Veggie cheese
 sausages

SERVES 1

A good handful of grated
Cheddar cheese
2 crusts of bread, grated
½ small onion, peeled and grated
½ tsp Dijon mustard
A good pinch of dried mixed herbs
Salt and pepper
3 tbsp milk
3–4 tbsp dried breadcrumbs
A little sunflower oil
Slices of tomato
Tomato ketchup (catsup)

1 Mix the cheese, bread, onion, mustard, herbs and a sprinkling of salt and pepper together with 1–2 tsp of the milk. Squeeze the mixture firmly together and shape into three small sausages.

2 Roll in the remaining milk, then the dried breadcrumbs, to coat completely.

3 Heat enough oil to cover the base of a small frying pan (skillet). Fry (sauté) the sausages for about 3 minutes, turning occasionally, until golden brown all over.

4 Serve with tomatoes and ketchup.

Pan garlic bread

The fresh parsley is optional but it does add extra flavour.

SERVES 1

A good knob of butter or margarine
1 tbsp sunflower oil
1 small garlic clove, peeled and crushed,
or ½ tsp garlic purée (paste)
2 tsp chopped fresh parsley
¼ tsp dried oregano
2 slices of French bread

1 Heat the butter or margarine and oil in a frying pan (skillet) until the fat melts. Stir in the garlic and herbs over a fairly gentle heat.

2 Quickly dip the bread in the mixture on both sides. Fry (sauté) for about 2 minutes on each side until just beginning to turn golden at the edges but still soft in the middle.

3 Remove from the pan and serve straight away.

Omelettes

There are two types: plain (French-style) and fluffy (soufflé). To make fluffy omelettes, you really need a grill (broiler) – see the recipe under Quick Fixes, page 439.

Plain omelettes can be adapted by adding all sorts of fillings and flavourings, but the basic method is always the same.

Ⓥ Plain omelette Ⓥ

SERVES 1

2–3 eggs
Salt and pepper
1 tbsp water
A small knob of butter or margarine

1 Beat the eggs in a bowl with a little salt and pepper and the water.

2 Melt the butter or margarine in an omelette pan over a moderate heat.

3 Add the egg mixture. Cook, lifting the set mixture to let the runny egg trickle underneath, until the omelette is golden brown underneath and the top is just set.

4 Fold the omelette in half, then slide out on to a warm plate.

Ⓥ Cheese omelette Ⓥ

SERVES 1

Prepare as for a plain omelette (above). Scatter a handful of grated Cheddar cheese over one half when about half-set. When melted and cooked, fold the other half over and slide on to a warm plate.
Alternatively, stir the cheese into the eggs before cooking.

Ⓥ Mushroom omelette Ⓥ

SERVES 1

Stew 4 sliced mushrooms in a little water for 2 minutes, then remove from the pan. Prepare and cook a plain omelette (left), then scatter the mushrooms over one half when nearly set. Fold the other half over, then slide on to a warm plate.

Ham omelette

SERVES 1

Prepare a plain omelette (left). Sprinkle a handful of chopped ham over the surface when it is almost cooked. Cook for a minute or two longer before folding and sliding on to a warm plate.

Chicken omelette

SERVES 1

Prepare a plain omelette (left). Scatter a handful of chopped cooked chicken and a pinch of dried thyme over the surface when it is almost cooked. Cook for a minute or two longer, then fold and slide on to a warm plate.

ⓥ Tomato omelette ⓥ

SERVES 1

Prepare a plain omelette (see page 146). Arrange slices of tomato over one half when it is almost cooked. Cook for a minute or two longer to heat through, sprinkle with a few chopped fresh basil leaves or a pinch of dried basil, then fold and slide on to a warm plate.

Prawn omelette

SERVES 1

Prepare a plain omelette (see page 146). Scatter 2 tbsp of thawed frozen cooked peeled prawns (shrimp) over one half when almost cooked. Sprinkle with a few drops of soy sauce. Cook for a minute or two longer, then fold and slide on to a warm plate.

ⓥ Spinach omelette ⓥ

SERVES 1

Thaw ¼ × 450 g/1 lb packet (about 1 mug) of frozen chopped spinach. Squeeze it thoroughly to remove excess moisture. Add to the eggs when preparing the plain omelette (see page 146). Sprinkle the cooked, folded omelette with a little grated Parmesan.

Cucumber oriental ⓥ omelettes ⓥ

SERVES 1

2 eggs
2 tbsp cold water
A good pinch of Chinese five-spice
powder (optional)
Soy sauce
2 knobs of butter or margarine
5 cm/2 in piece of cucumber,
cut into matchsticks

1 Break the eggs into a bowl and, using a fork or balloon whisk, whisk in the water until blended. Add the five-spice powder, if using, and 1 tsp of soy sauce. Whisk again.

2 Heat a knob of butter or margarine in a small frying pan (skillet). When bubbling, pour in half the omelette mixture and cook, lifting the edges and letting the uncooked egg run underneath until setting. Carefully flip over in the pan and cook the other side briefly.

3 Slide the omelette out on to a plate and cook the other omelette in the same way.

4 Scatter the cucumber sticks over both the omelettes, then sprinkle with a little soy sauce. Roll up and eat in your fingers.

ⓥ Piperade ⓥ

SERVES 1

1 tbsp olive oil
A knob of butter or margarine
1 onion, peeled and sliced
1 green (bell) pepper, sliced
2 ripe tomatoes, roughly chopped
½ garlic clove, peeled and crushed,
or ¼ tsp garlic purée (paste)
2 eggs, beaten
Salt and pepper

1 Heat the butter or margarine and oil in a large frying pan (skillet) over a fairly high heat.

2 Add the onion, pepper, tomatoes and garlic and cook, stirring, for 5 minutes until soft.

3 Turn down the heat. Add the eggs and some salt and pepper and cook gently, stirring, until scrambled.

French omelette ⓥ lunch ⓥ

SERVES 1

A large chunk of French bread
Butter or margarine
1 tsp tomato purée (paste)
1 egg
1 tbsp milk
A good pinch of dried mixed herbs
Salt and pepper
A small handful of shredded lettuce
1 tbsp mayonnaise

1 Split the French bread along one edge and spread inside with butter or margarine, then the tomato purée.

2 Beat the egg with the milk, herbs and a sprinkling of salt and pepper.

3 Heat a knob of butter or margarine in a small frying pan (skillet). Add the egg mixture and cook, stirring gently from time to time, until set. If liked, flip over the omelette to brown the other side.

4 Fold the omelette in half and place in the baguette.

5 Add some shredded lettuce and the mayonnaise.

Soups

Soups, served with lots of bread, are an excellent way to fill up cheaply and to get lots of nourishment inside you in one easy go. They're particularly good when you're studying for exams as you can make a large quantity that will last for two or even three days.

Remember, if you're not going to eat all the soup in one go, pour it into a cold, clean container, cover it and, as soon as it's cold, store it in the fridge. Make sure you reheat it until piping hot too.

Thick winter lentil Ⓥ soup Ⓥ

You can use an onion, peeled and chopped, instead of the leek.

SERVES 2

¼ mug of red lentils
2 mugs of water
1 leek, peeled, washed well and chopped
1 potato, peeled and
cut into small dice
1 carrot, peeled and
cut into small dice
¼ small swede (rutabaga), peeled and
cut into small dice
1 vegetable stock cube
Salt and pepper

1 Put everything in a saucepan. Bring to the boil, stir, reduce the heat until just gently bubbling round the edges, then part-cover and cook for 20 minutes until everything is tender.
2 Taste and re-season, if necessary. The soup can be eaten just as it is, or puréed with a hand blender or mashed with a potato masher.

No-effort vegetable Ⓥ soup Ⓥ

This is a great way of using up anything in the veg rack that's a bit past its best. To make it more filling, add a can of beans or lentils, or sweetcorn.

SERVES 4

About 4 handfuls of prepared vegetables
3 mugs of water
1 vegetable, chicken or beef stock cube
Dried mixed herbs
Salt and pepper

1 Peel and prepare the vegetables. Cut root vegetables such as carrots, potatoes, parsnips and swede (rutabaga) into small dice or grate them; slice onion and leeks, chop celery and beans, grate or shred cabbage. The smaller the pieces, the quicker they will cook.
2 Place them in a saucepan and cover with the water. Add the stock cube and a sprinkling of herbs, salt and pepper.
3 Bring to the boil over a high heat, turn down the heat to moderate, part-cover with a lid and cook gently for about 10–15 minutes until the vegetables are really tender. Taste and add more seasoning, if necessary.

Cheese and vegetable
ⓥ soup ⓥ

For a tasty alternative, use crumbled blue cheese instead of Cheddar and leeks instead of onions – but make sure you wash the leeks really well as they often contain lots of grit.

SERVES 4

2 carrots, peeled and cut into
small pieces
2 onions, peeled and cut into
small pieces
3 potatoes, peeled and cut into
small pieces
2½ mugs of water
1 vegetable stock cube
2 large handfuls of grated
Cheddar cheese
1 mug of milk
½ tsp dried mixed herbs
Salt and pepper

1 Put the vegetables with the water and stock cube in a large saucepan.

2 Bring to the boil, reduce the heat, then part-cover and simmer for about 15 minutes until really soft.

3 Mash with a potato masher or fork or liquidise with a hand-held blender, then stir in the cheese and milk, and add herbs and salt and pepper to taste.

4 Heat through, stirring, until the cheese melts.

ⓥ Peasant soup ⓥ

SERVES 4

1 × 400 g/14 oz/large can of
chopped tomatoes
¼ small cabbage, cut into thin slices
1 onion, peeled and cut into small dice
1 large carrot, peeled and cut into
small dice
1 large potato, peeled and cut into
small dice
3 mugs of water
2 vegetable stock cubes
1 × 425 g/15 oz/large can of haricot
(navy) beans, drained
½ tsp dried mixed herbs
Salt and pepper
Grated cheese (optional)

1 Empty the contents of the can of tomatoes into a large pan.

2 Separate the cabbage into shreds, removing any thick pieces of stalk, and add to the pan with all the remaining ingredients. Bring to the boil, reduce the heat, until bubbles are gently appearing round the edge, part-cover and cook for 20–30 minutes until all the vegetables are really tender. Taste and re-season if necessary.

3 Sprinkle grated cheese over, if liked.

ⓥ Brown onion soup ⓥ

SERVES 4

1 tbsp butter or margarine
4 large onions, peeled and
roughly chopped
2 tsp sugar
3 mugs of water
2 beef or vegetable stock cubes
Salt and pepper
4 small handfuls of grated
Cheddar cheese

1 Melt the butter or margarine in a saucepan and fry (sauté) the onions for 5 minutes, stirring until turning brown.

2 Add the sugar and continue frying for 3–4 minutes, stirring all the time, until a rich golden brown.

3 Stir in the stock and a little salt and pepper, bring to the boil, reduce the heat, part-cover and cook very gently for 15–20 minutes until the onions are really soft. Taste and re-season.

4 Spoon the soup into bowls and sprinkle with the cheese.

ⓥ French onion soup ⓥ

SERVES 4

If you have a grill (broiler), you can make authentic French Onion Soup. Prepare Brown Onion Soup as above. Toast four slices of French bread. Top with grated Gruyère (Swiss) or Cheddar cheese and toast until melted. Float one piece of the cheese toast in each bowl of soup.

Oriental soup ⓥ with noodles ⓥ

To turn this into a more filling main meal, add a fried or poached egg (see pages 127 and 128) to each soup bowl before pouring on the hot soup.

SERVES 4

5 mugs of water
2 chicken or vegetable stock cubes
2 nests of vermicelli
or 1 slab of Chinese egg noodles
A pinch of ground ginger (optional)
Soy sauce

1 Put the water and stock cubes in a saucepan and bring to the boil, stirring until the cubes dissolve.

2 Break up the vermicelli or noodles into small pieces and add to the pan.

3 Add the ginger, if using, and soy sauce to taste. Bring back to the boil. Boil uncovered for 5 minutes until the noodles are cooked. Taste and add more soy sauce, if liked.

Creamy chicken and vegetable soup

This is a good way to use up the carcass and any leftover veg after you've made a roast chicken (see page 349). Don't use roast potatoes or parsnips as they don't have a very good flavour when reheated. Before making the soup, pick any meat off the carcass – it's fine for sandwiches. The milk powder makes the soup creamy but you can omit it.

SERVES 4

1 roast chicken carcass
5 mugs of water
1 bay leaf
1 chicken stock cube
Salt and pepper
Any quantity of leftover boiled
vegetables, chopped
4 tbsp dried milk powder
(non-fat dry milk)
2 tbsp plain (all-purpose) flour

1 Break the carcass into pieces and place in a saucepan.
2 Cover with the water, add the bay leaf, stock cube and some salt and pepper.
3 Bring to the boil over a high heat, then turn down the heat so it is just bubbling gently around the edges. Cover with a lid and cook for 1 hour.
4 Put a colander over a large bowl. Tip everything carefully into the colander and leave to let all the liquid drip through. Rinse out the saucepan, and then tip the liquid back into the pan. Throw away the carcass (it's a good idea to wrap it well in newspaper to stop the local cats or foxes from tearing open your bin bags to get at it).

5 Add the vegetables to the liquid and heat gently for 5 minutes.
6 If you have a hand blender, add the dried milk powder and flour and blend until the mixture is smooth. If not, mix the milk powder and flour with a little water and add to the pan.
7 Cook, stirring, over a high heat until boiling, then turn down the heat and cook for a further 2 minutes, still stirring. Taste and re-season.

Oriental vegetable and
Ⓥ noodle soup Ⓥ

SERVES 4

5 mugs of water
2 vegetable stock cubes
1 carrot, peeled and coarsely grated
1 potato, peeled and coarsely grated
1 courgette (zucchini)
or a 5 cm/2 in piece of cucumber,
coarsely grated
2 nests of vermicelli
or 1 slab of Chinese egg noodles
A pinch of ground ginger (optional)
Soy sauce

1 Put the water and stock cubes in a saucepan and bring to the boil, stirring until the cubes dissolve.
2 Add the grated vegetables.
3 Break up the vermicelli or noodles into small pieces and add to the pan.
4 Add the ginger, if using, and soy sauce to taste. Bring back to the boil. Simmer uncovered for 5 minutes until the noodles are cooked. Taste and add more soy sauce if liked.

🅥 Mulligatawny soup 🅥

You can use 1 tbsp of instant oat cereal instead of instant mash.

SERVES 2

1 tbsp sunflower oil
2 mugs of frozen mixed vegetables
½ garlic clove, peeled and crushed,
or ½ tsp garlic purée (paste)
1–2 tsp curry powder or paste
2 mugs of water
1 vegetable or beef stock cube
1 tbsp tomato purée
1 tbsp desiccated (shredded) coconut
1 tbsp instant mashed potato powder
Salt and pepper

1 Heat the oil in a saucepan. When hot but not smoking (see page 35), add the vegetables, garlic and curry powder or paste and cook, stirring, for about 1 minute.

2 Add the water, stock cube, tomato purée and coconut. Bring to the boil, turn down the heat, part-cover and cook gently for 5 minutes or until the vegetables are cooked.

3 Sprinkle over the mashed potato and stir in to thicken the soup. Season to taste.

Frankfurter warmer

It's not worth making this just for one and, anyway, the flavour improves if you cool it, then store it in the fridge and reheat it another day. The caraway seeds are not essential, but they do give it a lovely mellow flavour.

SERVES 4

1 onion, peeled and chopped
A knob of butter or margarine
¼ small white cabbage, cut into fine shreds
4 mugs of water
2 chicken stock cubes
1 tsp caraway seeds
1 × 400 g/14 oz/large can of frankfurters, drained and cut into small chunks
Salt and pepper
Grated cheese

1 Fry (sauté) the onion in the butter or margarine for 2 minutes, stirring, until softened and lightly golden.

2 Add the cabbage, water, stock cubes and caraway seeds. Bring to the boil over a high heat, stirring until the stock cubes have dissolved. Turn down the heat until gently bubbling round the edges and cook for 15 minutes.

3 Add the frankfurters and season to taste. Heat for a further 2 minutes.

4 Pour into warm bowls and sprinkle with grated cheese.

Cheese and broccoli
ⓥ potage ⓥ

You can try this with the remains of
Camembert, Cheddar or even blue
cheese for a change, and substitute
cauliflower for the broccoli.

SERVES 4

1 tbsp butter or margarine
1 large onion, peeled and chopped
2 large potatoes, peeled and diced
4 mugs of vegetable stock,
made with 2 stock cubes
Salt and pepper
2 thick fingers of Brie, chopped
2 good handfuls of raw or cooked
broccoli, chopped
2 tbsp milk or double (heavy) cream

1 Melt the butter or margarine in a
saucepan over a moderate heat. Add
the onion and potato and fry (sauté)
for 2 minutes until slightly softened
but not browned, stirring all the time
with a wooden spoon.

2 Add the stock and sprinkle in a
little salt and pepper.

3 Turn up the heat until the soup
boils. Turn it down again until just
gently bubbling around the edges and
cook for 20 minutes.

4 Add the cheese and broccoli and
stir well. Cook for a further
5 minutes, stirring occasionally.

5 Mash the soup with a potato
masher or liquidise with a hand
blender. Taste and add more salt and
pepper if necessary. Add the milk or
cream.

6 Heat through over a gentle heat.

ⓥ Red Leicester soup ⓥ

SERVES 4

1–2 carrots, peeled and grated
1 onion, peeled and grated
1 potato, peeled and grated
3 mugs of water
2 chicken or vegetable stock cubes
2 good handfuls of grated
Red Leicester cheese
Salt and freshly ground black pepper
1 tbsp cornflour (cornstarch)
²/₃ mug of milk

1 Put the grated carrots, onion and
potato into a saucepan. Add the water
and stock cubes.

2 Put over a high heat until boiling.
Stir until the stock cubes are
dissolved, then turn down the heat
until bubbling gently around the
edges and cook for 15 minutes.

3 Stir in the cheese.

4 Blend the cornflour with the milk.
Stir into the pan, bring to the boil
over a high heat and cook for
1 minute, stirring all the time.

5 Taste the soup and re-season, if
necessary.

Chicken and sweetcorn chowder

Mix up the soup then, before heating (Step 2), spoon half in a rigid container, cover and store in the fridge for the next day (unless you can eat it all in one go!)

SERVES 2

1 × 300 g/11 oz/medium can of cream of chicken soup
1 × 200 g/7 oz/small can of sweetcorn (corn)
A pinch of chilli powder

1 Mix the ingredients together in a saucepan.

2 Heat through, stirring gently until piping hot.

Tomato and carrot soup

SERVES 2–4

2 large carrots, peeled and grated
1 onion, peeled and grated
1 × 400 g/14 oz/large can of chopped tomatoes
1½ mugs of chicken or vegetable stock, made with 1 stock cube
1 tsp dried oregano
1 bay leaf (optional)
1 tsp sugar
Salt and pepper

1 Put all the ingredients in a saucepan. Bring to the boil over a high heat.

2 When bubbling, turn down the heat until gently bubbling round the edges, part-cover with a lid and cook for 30 minutes.

3 Discard the bay leaf, if used, then taste and re-season, if necessary.

Double tomato and bean
Ⓥ soup Ⓥ

Make up the whole quantity in the saucepan then, before heating (Step 4), if you're not going to eat it all, spoon half into a rigid container, cover and store in the fridge for use the next day.

SERVES 2–4

1 × 295 g/10½ oz/medium can of condensed tomato soup
1 × 400 g/14 oz/large can of chopped tomatoes
1 × 425 g/15 oz/large can of haricot (navy) beans, drained
½ tsp dried basil

1 Empty the can of condensed tomato soup into a saucepan.

2 Whisk in one canful of water with a fork or a wire whisk.

3 Stir in the tomatoes, beans and basil.

4 Heat through until almost boiling.

Easy tomato and orange ⓥ soup ⓥ

This will give you a good burst of vitamin C – great if you've got a cold lurking.

SERVES 2–3

2 tbsp sunflower or olive oil
1 onion, peeled and finely chopped
2 mugs of passata (sieved tomatoes)
Juice of 1 orange
or 4 tbsp pure orange juice
Juice of ½ lemon
or 1 tbsp bottled lemon juice
1 mug of water
1 tsp sugar
Salt and pepper

1 Heat the oil in a saucepan and add the onion. Cook, stirring, for 2 minutes until softened but not browned.

2 Add all the remaining ingredients and bring to the boil, stirring. Turn down the heat until gently bubbling round the edges and cook gently for 20 minutes.

3 Taste and re-season, if necessary.

Cheese, celery and ⓥ sweetcorn chowder ⓥ

Mix up the soup (Steps 1–3). Then, if you're not going to eat it all, spoon what you can't eat into a rigid container, cover and store in the fridge for the next day.

SERVES 2–3

1 × 295 g/10½ oz/medium can of
condensed celery soup
About 1 mug of milk
1 × 200 g/7 oz/small can of
sweetcorn (corn)
2 large handfuls of grated
Cheddar cheese
Pepper

1 Empty the condensed soup into a saucepan.

2 Use the empty can to measure a canful of milk, add to the pan and stir with a wire whisk until completely blended.

3 Stir in the contents of the can of sweetcorn and the cheese.

4 Heat through, stirring over a fairly high heat until piping hot.

5 Thin with a little more milk, if liked, and heat through again. Season the soup to taste with pepper.

Clam bisque

Clams are quite cheap and they're really good brain food! Have half the soup for one meal, then tip the rest into a rigid container, cover and leave to cool before storing in the fridge.

SERVES 2

1 tbsp butter or margarine
1 onion, peeled and cut into small dice
1 carrot, peeled and cut into small dice
1 potato, peeled and cut into small dice
1 mug of chicken stock,
made with 1 stock cube
2 tbsp cornflour (cornstarch)
1 mug of milk
1 × 300 g/11 oz/medium can of
minced (ground) clams
Salt and pepper

1 Melt the butter or margarine in a saucepan over a moderate heat. Add the vegetables and cook, stirring, for 2 minutes until softened but not browned.

2 Add the stock. Bring to the boil, then turn down the heat, part-cover and let it bubble gently for 15 minutes.

3 Blend the cornflour with the milk. Stir into the pan, turn up the heat and cook, stirring until boiling and thickened.

4 Stir in the minced clams with their liquid and season with salt and pepper to taste.

5 Cook the soup for a further minute, before serving.

Curried parsnip and ⓥ potato soup ⓥ

You can use carrots instead of the parsnips and potatoes if you prefer. And if you've got any leftover cooked rice, put that in before reheating (end of Step 2) for an even more filling meal.

SERVES 4

2 large parsnips, peeled and sliced
2 large potatoes, peeled and sliced
1 onion, peeled and chopped
3 mugs of vegetable stock,
made with 2 stock cubes
1 tsp curry powder or paste
Salt and pepper
A little milk

1 Put all the ingredients except the milk in a saucepan. Bring to the boil, reduce the heat, part-cover and simmer for about 15 minutes or until the vegetables are really soft.

2 Tip the stock through a sieve (strainer) into a bowl. Let all the liquid drain through, then mash the vegetables well, and stir into the stock again. Thin with a little milk, if liked.

3 Taste and re-season, if necessary. Reheat and serve.

Tomato rice special

Worcestershire sauce contains
anchovies, so is not suitable for strict
vegetarians – use Tabasco instead.

SERVES 2–4

1 handful of long-grain rice
1 × 400 g/14 oz/large can of
chopped tomatoes
1 × 295 g/10½ oz/small can of cream of
tomato soup
Worcestershire sauce

1 Put the rice in a saucepan, then add
the tomatoes.

2 Half-fill the tomato can with water
and add to the pan. Bring to the boil,
reduce the heat and simmer for about
10 minutes, stirring occasionally,
until the rice is just tender.

3 Stir in the can of tomato soup and
spike to taste with Worcestershire
sauce. Heat through and serve.

Simple sweetcorn ⓥ chowder ⓥ

SERVES 4

1 onion, peeled and chopped
4 potatoes, peeled and thinly sliced
1 × 350 g/12 oz/large can of
sweetcorn (corn)
3 mugs of vegetable stock,
made with 2 stock cubes
Salt and pepper
⅔ mug of milk

1 Put all the ingredients except the
milk in a saucepan. Bring to the boil,
reduce the heat, part-cover and
simmer for 30 minutes or until the
potatoes are really soft.

2 Stir well with a balloon whisk so
the potatoes break up and thicken the
liquid. Stir in the milk.

3 Taste and re-season if necessary.
Heat thoroughly before serving.

ⓥ Minted pea soup ⓥ

Cheap economy peas are ideal for
this tasty soup.

SERVES 2–4

2 mugs of frozen peas
1 potato, peeled and cut into
small pieces
2 mugs of water
1 vegetable stock cube
1 tsp sugar
1 tsp dried mint
Salt and pepper
2 tbsp double (heavy) cream
or crème fraîche (optional)

1 Put all the ingredients except the
cream or crème fraîche in a
saucepan. Bring to the boil, turn
down the heat until gently bubbling
round the edges and cook for
15 minutes.

2 Mash with a potato masher or fork
or, preferably, liquidise with a hand
blender. Season to taste and stir in the
cream or crème fraîche, if using.

Country vegetable ⓥ soup ⓥ

For an even more filling combination, add a large peeled, diced potato to the mixture and serve with grated Cheddar cheese.

SERVES 4

1 small cauliflower, cut into small florets
1 small swede (rutabaga), cut into
small pieces
1 onion, peeled and chopped
5 mugs of vegetable stock,
made with 2 stock cubes
Salt and pepper
1 tbsp tomato purée (paste)
1 tsp dried mixed herbs

1 Put all the ingredients in a large saucepan. Bring to the boil, reduce the heat, part-cover and simmer gently for 1 hour until the vegetables are really tender.

2 Taste and re-season, if necessary.

ⓥ Spinach and rice soup ⓥ

SERVES 2

2 mugs of frozen chopped spinach
1 chicken or vegetable stock cube
2 mugs of water
A knob of butter or margarine
¼ mug of long-grain rice
Salt and pepper
Grated Parmesan cheese

1 Put the spinach, stock cube, water and butter or margarine in a pan.

2 Bring to the boil over a high heat, then add the rice and stir. Turn down the heat, part-cover and allow to bubble gently for 10 minutes until the rice is just tender.

3 Season to taste and sprinkle with lots of grated Parmesan cheese.

ⓥ Smooth peanut soup ⓥ

If you have a grill, make some toast, top with cheese and grill until melted. Cut into pieces and serve with the soup.

SERVES 4

1 small onion, peeled
A knob of butter or margarine
1 tbsp plain (all-purpose) flour
3 mugs of vegetable stock,
made with 2 stock cubes
8 tbsp smooth peanut butter
⅔ mug of milk
Salt and pepper

1 Grate the onion straight into a saucepan. Add the knob of butter or margarine and fry (sauté), stirring, for 30 seconds. Stir in the flour.

2 Remove from the heat and gradually blend in the stock, stirring all the time.

3 Bring to the boil, stirring, then blend in the peanut butter, stirring until it has melted.

4 Stir in the milk and season to taste. Heat through.

Main Courses You can Do With ... one Pan

These are the type of recipes that appeal to everyone: dead easy to make, with very little washing-up! They are ideal for anyone with minimal facilities – and that's most students. Most are pretty quick to prepare too, which makes them perfect for eating after a hard day's studying.

For any of the recipes calling for diced cooked chicken, you can buy a ready-cooked portion or even a slice of cooked chicken breast from the deli counter, or use leftovers from a roast.

Summer beach chicken salad

SERVES 1

¼ mug of long-grain rice
1 rasher (slice) of streaky bacon, rinded and cut into small pieces
1 small banana, peeled and cut into chunky slices
1 tsp lemon juice
1 tbsp mayonnaise
1 tsp sunflower or olive oil
A small handful of diced cooked chicken
½ small green (bell) pepper, diced
Salt and pepper
Lettuce leaves
1 tomato, cut into small wedges

1 Cook the rice in boiling water according to the packet directions. Drain in a colander in the sink, rinse with cold water and drain again and place in a bowl.

2 Cook the bacon in the same pan, stirring, until crisp and brown. Drain on kitchen paper (paper towels).

3 Mix the banana chunks with the lemon juice. Add to the rice.

4 Mix the mayonnaise with the oil to make it slightly thinner. Add to the bowl with the chicken and pepper. Lift and stir gently, turning the ingredients over until thoroughly mixed, adding salt and pepper to taste.

5 Line a bowl with lettuce leaves. Pile the salad on top and sprinkle with the bacon and tomato wedges before serving.

Apple, chicken and walnut salad

SERVES 1

¼ mug of long-grain rice
1 small green eating (dessert) apple,
quartered, cored and diced
2 tsp lemon juice
1 celery stick, chopped
A small handful of walnut pieces,
roughly chopped
A small handful of diced cooked chicken
2 tsp sunflower or olive oil
1 tbsp mayonnaise
Salt and pepper
½ tsp dried chives (optional)

1 Cook the rice in boiling water according to the packet directions. Drain in a colander in the sink, rinse with cold water and drain again.

2 Mix the apple in a large bowl in a teaspoon of the lemon juice to prevent browning. Add the rice, celery, nuts and chicken and stir gently until well mixed.

3 Using a wire whisk, whisk the oil, the remaining lemon juice and the mayonnaise together in a small bowl with a little salt and pepper and add to the salad. Lift and stir gently until completely coated, then serve sprinkled with the chives, if using.

Chicken and pineapple rice salad

Use the rest of the pineapple slices for another recipe. Alternatively eat them with yoghurt, custard or ice cream for dessert. If you prefer, use just half a larger can of sweetcorn, using the rest for a salad or in a soup, or as a vegetable accompaniment for another meal.

SERVES 1

¼ mug of long-grain rice
1 canned pineapple ring, cut into
small pieces
1 × 200 g/7 oz/small can of sweetcorn
(corn), drained
2.5 cm/1 in piece of cucumber, diced
A small handful of diced cooked chicken
1 tbsp mayonnaise or salad cream
Salt and pepper
Lettuce leaves

1 Cook the rice according to the packet directions. Drain in a colander in the sink, rinse with cold water and drain again.

2 Tip the rice into a bowl and add all the remaining ingredients except the lettuce, with salt and pepper to taste. Mix gently but thoroughly.

3 Line a bowl with lettuce leaves and pile the salad in the centre.

Chicken, potato and spiced almond salad

SERVES 1

3–4 small new potatoes, scrubbed or
scraped and halved
1 tbsp mayonnaise
1 tbsp plain yoghurt
1 tsp tomato purée (paste)
A few drops of Worcestershire sauce
2.5 cm/1 in piece of cucumber, chopped
A small knob of butter or margarine
1 tbsp blanched almonds
A good pinch of mixed (apple-pie) spice
A good pinch of chilli powder
1 ready-cooked chicken portion
Lettuce leaves

1 Cook the potatoes in boiling water with a pinch of salt added for about 10 minutes until tender. Drain in a colander, rinse with cold water and drain again.

2 Mix the mayonnaise in a small bowl with the yoghurt, tomato purée and Worcestershire sauce. Season lightly and stir in the cucumber.

3 Melt the butter or margarine in the potato pan over a moderate heat. Fry (sauté) the almonds, stirring and turning, until golden brown. Remove from the heat. Sprinkle with the spices and stir well until coated. Drain on kitchen paper (paper towels).

4 Arrange the lettuce leaves on a plate. Put the chicken on top with the potatoes around. Spoon the mayonnaise mixture on top and scatter with the almonds.

Tuna pasta salad

Store the leftover tuna in a covered container in the fridge, not in the can.

SERVES 1

½ mug of conchiglie (pasta shells)
or other small pasta shapes
Salt
½ × 185 g/6½ oz/small can of
tuna, drained
½ small onion, peeled and
finely chopped
½ small green (bell) pepper,
finely chopped
1 tomato, cut into small pieces
2.5 cm/1 in piece of cucumber, diced
1 tbsp olive oil
1 tsp lemon juice
1 tsp caster (superfine) sugar
Salt and pepper
Lettuce leaves

1 Cook the pasta according to the packet directions. Drain in a colander in the sink, rinse with cold water and drain again. Place in a bowl.

2 Add the tuna to the pasta with the onion, pepper, tomato and cucumber.

3 Whisk the oil and lemon juice together with the sugar and a little salt and pepper.

4 Pour over the salad, lift and stir gently until everything is coated in the dressing and chill until ready to eat.

5 Put the lettuce leaves into a bowl and top with the pasta mixture.

Smoked mackerel and potato salad

SERVES 1

4–6 baby new potatoes,
scrubbed and halved
A sprig of fresh mint
or ¼ tsp dried mint
A handful of frozen peas
1 tbsp mayonnaise
2 tsp sunflower oil
1 tsp lemon juice
½ tsp horseradish sauce
Salt and pepper
1 ready-to-eat smoked mackerel fillet,
skinned and cut into bite-sized pieces
1 cooked beetroot (red beet), diced
(optional)

1 Put the potatoes in a pan of salted water with the mint. Bring to the boil and cook for 5 minutes. Add the peas and boil for a further 5 minutes or until the potatoes are tender. Drain in a colander in the sink. Discard the sprig of mint if necessary.

2 Put the mayonnaise, oil, lemon juice, horseradish sauce and a little salt and pepper in a bowl. Whisk with a wire whisk or fork until well blended.

3 Tip the warm potatoes and peas into the dressing and add the fish. Lift and stir gently with a spoon and fork until everything is lightly coated in dressing.

4 Spoon the beetroot round the edge of the bowl, if using.

Big filling salad

The seeds are optional but they do add interesting texture and flavour.

SERVES 1

½ mug of wholewheat pasta shapes
1 tbsp olive or sunflower oil
1 tsp lemon juice
¼ tsp Dijon mustard
A good pinch of salt and pepper
1 tomato, quartered
1 spring onion (scallion),
trimmed and chopped
½ small green (bell) pepper, diced
1 small eating (dessert) apple, quartered,
cored and diced
1 slice of cooked ham, diced
A small chunk of Cheddar cheese, diced
A small handful of sunflower
or pumpkin seeds

1 Cook the pasta according to the packet directions. Drain in a colander in the sink, rinse with cold water and drain again.

2 Whisk the oil, lemon juice, mustard, salt and pepper together in a fairly large bowl.

3 Add all the salad ingredients except the seeds.

4 Lift and stir the salad gently until well blended. Chill for at least 1 hour to allow the flavours to develop, if possible. Sprinkle with the sunflower or pumpkin seeds before serving.

Salade niçoise

If you use half a larger can of tuna (which is cheaper), store the remainder in a covered container, not the can, in the fridge.

SERVES 1

4 baby new potatoes,
scrubbed and halved
1 egg, scrubbed under cold water
A small handful of French (green)
beans, topped and tailed
and cut into short lengths
1 tomato, quartered
2.5 cm/1 in piece of cucumber, diced
A wedge of iceberg lettuce,
torn into bite-sized pieces
1 × 85 g/3½ oz/very small can of
tuna, drained
2 black olives
1 tbsp olive oil
2 tsp wine vinegar
A pinch of dried mixed herbs
A pinch of sugar
¼ tsp Dijon mustard
Salt and pepper
2 slices of peeled onion,
separated into rings

1 Bring a saucepan of lightly salted water to the boil. Add the potatoes and egg and cook for 5 minutes. Add the beans and cook for a further 5 minutes or until the vegetables are tender. Lift out the egg with a draining spoon and place in a bowl of cold water. Drain the vegetables in a colander in the sink, rinse with cold water and drain again.

2 Put the potatoes and beans in a salad bowl with the tomato, cucumber, lettuce, tuna and olives.

3 Shell the egg, cut into quarters and set aside.

4 Whisk together the oil, vinegar, mixed herbs, sugar, mustard and some salt and pepper.

5 Pour over the salad and lift and stir the ingredients very gently with a spoon and fork until well mixed and the ingredients are all coated with the dressing.

6 Scatter the onion rings and egg quarters over the top.

Hot potato and bacon salad

SERVES 1

8 baby new potatoes,
scrubbed and halved
Salt and pepper
2 rashers (slices) of streaky bacon,
rinded and diced
2 tbsp boiling water
1 tbsp white wine vinegar
1 tbsp crème fraîche
1 spring onion (scallion),
trimmed and finely chopped

1 Cook the potatoes in boiling water with a pinch of salt added for about 10 minutes until tender. Drain in a colander in the sink.

2 Heat the same pan to remove any moisture, then add the bacon and fry (sauté) until crisp and brown. Remove from the pan with a draining spoon.

3 Add the measured boiling water to the pan with the vinegar and boil for a few seconds. Stir in the crème fraîche, spring onion, bacon and some salt and pepper. Add the potatoes, stir and turn to coat in the dressing and tip into a bowl.

Curried chicken and pasta salad

SERVES 1

½–1 mug of pasta shapes
1 tbsp mayonnaise
½ tsp curry powder or paste
1 × 225 g/8 oz/small can of
baked beans
A small handful of diced cooked chicken
½ green (bell) pepper, diced
Lettuce leaves
1 tomato, diced
2 tsp desiccated (shredded) coconut
or a few coconut flakes (optional)

1 Cook the pasta according to the packet directions. Drain in a colander, rinse with cold water and drain again.
2 Mix the mayonnaise with the curry powder or paste and the baked beans. Add the pasta, chicken and green pepper and lift and stir gently.
3 Pile the salad on to a bed of lettuce leaves.
4 Scatter the tomato over the salad. Sprinkle with the coconut, if using, and serve.

ⓥ Summer pasta salad ⓥ

SERVES 1

½ mug of small pasta shapes
1–2 tomatoes, chopped
2.5 cm/1 in piece of cucumber, diced
A finger or wedge of Cheddar or Edam
cheese, diced
1 × 200 g/7 oz/small can of sweetcorn
(corn), drained
1 tbsp sunflower or olive oil
1 tsp vinegar or lemon juice
A good pinch of sugar
A good pinch of dried oregano
Salt and pepper

1 Cook the pasta according to the packet directions. Drain in a colander in the sink, rinse with cold water and drain again.
2 Place the pasta in a bowl and add all the remaining ingredients. Toss and stir gently until well mixed.

Warm bacon and avocado salad

You can use three good handfuls of fresh spinach instead of the lettuce if you like. This is also fantastic topped with a soft-cooked boiled, poached or microwaved egg
(see pages 126, 128 and 103).

SERVES 1

¼ small round lettuce, torn into pieces
½ avocado, peeled and cut into
small dice
2.5 cm/1 in piece of cucumber, diced
1 tomato, cut into dice
2 rashers (slices) of streaky bacon,
rinded and diced
2 tbsp olive oil
2 tsp vinegar
½ tsp Worcestershire sauce
Salt and pepper
Crusty bread, to serve

1 Put the lettuce in a bowl and scatter the avocado, cucumber and tomato over.
2 Dry-fry the bacon in a small frying pan (skillet) until crisp and golden. Scatter over the salad.
3 Add the oil, vinegar and Worcestershire sauce to the pan and heat, stirring, until bubbling. Season lightly and spoon over the salad.
4 Eat with crusty bread.

Egg, pea and potato ⓥ salad ⓥ

SERVES 1

4–6 new potatoes, scrubbed and cut into
bite-sized pieces
1 egg, scrubbed under
cold running water
1 tbsp mayonnaise
1 tsp white wine vinegar
¼ tsp made English mustard
Salt and pepper
2 tsp chopped fresh mint
or ½ tsp dried mint
1 × 170 g/6 oz/small can of minted
garden peas, drained

1 Put the potatoes in a saucepan and
cover with cold, salted water. Add the
egg, bring to the boil and cook for
10 minutes.

2 Lift out the egg with a draining
spoon and place immediately in a
bowl of cold water.

3 Test the potatoes and cook a little
longer, if necessary, until just tender,
then drain.

4 Mix the mayonnaise in a bowl with
the vinegar, mustard, a little salt and
pepper and half the mint.

5 Shell the egg and cut into chunks.

6 Add the potatoes to the mayonnaise
mixture and stir gently until
completely coated. Add the peas and
egg and stir in very gently.

7 Sprinkle with the remaining mint.
Serve warm or cold.

ⓥ Stuffed tomato salad ⓥ

Use the rest of the Weetabix to
crumble over a dish instead of
cornflakes or breadcrumbs before
grilling or baking. Or just eat it
for breakfast!

SERVES 1

1 egg
1 beefsteak tomato
½ Weetabix, crumbled
Salt and pepper
2 tsp olive oil
2 tsp mayonnaise
1 tsp snipped fresh chives
or ½ tsp dried chives
A good handful of fresh beansprouts
A little soy sauce
Crusty bread, to serve

1 Hard-boil (hard-cook) the egg (see
page 126) and put straight away into
cold water.

2 Cut the tomato in half and scoop
out the seeds into a bowl.

3 Add the Weetabix, a little salt and
pepper, the oil and mayonnaise.

4 Shell the egg and chop. Add to the
bowl and mix everything together
thoroughly. Pack into the tomato
halves.

5 Put the beansprouts on a plate and
sprinkle with the soy sauce. Put the
stuffed tomato halves in the centre
and chill until ready to eat.

6 Serve with crusty bread.

Hot lentil and bacon salad

SERVES 1–2

*4 rashers (slices) of smoked streaky
bacon, rinded and cut into pieces
4 tbsp sunflower or olive oil
1 × 400 g/14 oz/large can of lentils
3 tbsp wine vinegar
1 tsp Dijon mustard
½ tsp sugar
Salt and pepper
½ punnet of salad cress
Crusty bread, to serve*

1 Fry (sauté) the bacon in 1 tbsp of
the oil in a saucepan, stirring until
golden and cooked through. Tip the
oil and bacon into a bowl.

2 Tip the lentils into the pan and
heat through, stirring. Drain in a
colander in the sink, then add to the
bacon.

3 Away from the heat, whisk the
remaining oil with the vinegar,
mustard, sugar and a little salt and
pepper in the pan. Pour over the
lentils and mix everything together.

4 Sprinkle with the salad cress and
serve with crusty bread.

West Indian bean and ⓥ fruit salad ⓥ

Store the leftover kidney beans in the
fridge for another recipe.

SERVES 1

*¼ mug of long-grain rice
1 satsuma, peeled and all pith removed
½ × 425 g/15 oz/large can of red kidney
beans, drained
A finger of Cheddar cheese, cubed
1 tsp chilli relish
2 tbsp plain yoghurt
Salt and pepper
Lettuce leaves*

1 Cook the rice according to the
packet directions. Drain in a colander
in the sink, rinse with cold water and
drain again.

2 Place in a bowl and add the fruit,
beans and cheese.

3 Using a wire whisk, mix the relish
in a small bowl with the yoghurt, a
little salt and plenty of pepper. Add to
the bowl and mix gently.

4 Pile on to a bed of lettuce leaves
and serve.

Ⓥ Potato and tofu sauté Ⓥ

The rest of the block of tofu will keep in the fridge, provided you wrap it well in foil or clingfilm.

SERVES 1

6 new potatoes, scraped and cut into
bite-sized pieces
A good knob of butter or margarine
2 tsp olive oil
2 spring onions (scallions),
trimmed and chopped
1 small green (bell) pepper, sliced
1 × 200 g/7 oz/small can of sweetcorn
(corn) with peppers, drained
¼ × 250 g/9 oz block of
smoked tofu, cubed
1 tsp paprika
¼ tsp dried thyme or mixed herbs
Salt and pepper

1 Cook the potatoes in boiling, salted water for about 10 minutes until tender. Drain in a colander.

2 Heat the butter or margarine and oil in the same saucepan. Add the spring onions and pepper and fry (sauté) for 2 minutes, stirring.

3 Add the potatoes and continue to fry, stirring and turning, for 5 minutes until turning golden.

4 Add the remaining ingredients to the pan, seasoning to taste with salt and pepper, and continue to cook, stirring and turning, for 3 minutes until everything is piping hot.

Ⓥ Curried rice salad Ⓥ

SERVES 1

¼ mug of long-grain rice
A small handful of frozen peas
1 tsp mild curry powder or paste
1 tbsp mayonnaise
A small handful of sultanas
(golden raisins)
A small handful of roasted
or raw peanuts
Salt and pepper

1 Cook the rice according to the packet directions, adding the peas after 5 minutes' cooking time. Drain in a colander in the sink, rinse with cold water and drain again.

2 Mix the curry powder or paste with the mayonnaise in a bowl.

3 Stir in the rice, sultanas and nuts. Season to taste with salt and pepper.

Curried rice and baked Ⓥ bean salad Ⓥ

SERVES 1–2

Prepare as for the Curried Rice Salad (above) but omit the peas. Stir in a 225 g/8 oz/small can of baked beans with the rice, fruit and nuts.

Curried rice, bean and Ⓥ cheese salad Ⓥ

SERVES 1

Prepare as for the Curried Rice Salad (above) but omit the peas and nuts and stir in a 225 g/8 oz/small can of baked beans and a chunk of Cheddar or Edam cheese, cut into small dice.

ⓥ Quick pan pizza ⓥ

Add other toppings of your choice
before adding the cheese, if you like.
If you have a grill, you can put the
cooked pizza, still in the pan, under it
for a few minutes to brown the top
before serving.

SERVES 1

1 mug of self-raising (self-rising) flour
A pinch of salt
3 tbsp sunflower or olive oil
About 4 tbsp cold water
1 × 225 g/8 oz/small can of chopped
tomatoes, drained
¼ tsp dried oregano
A handful of grated Cheddar cheese
A Mixed Salad (see page 45),
to serve

1 Mix the flour and salt in a bowl.
Add 2 tbsp of the oil and mix with
cold water, a little at a time, to form a
soft but not sticky dough (you may
need slightly more or less water,
depending on the flour).

2 Squeeze the dough gently into a
ball, then put it on a lightly floured
surface and roll out with a rolling pin
or clean bottle to a round the size of a
medium frying pan (skillet).

3 Heat the remaining oil in the frying
pan and add the pizza base. Cook for
3 minutes until golden brown
underneath.

4 Turn over and top with the
tomatoes, oregano and cheese. Cover
with a lid or foil and cook over a
fairly gentle heat for about 5 minutes
until the cheese has melted.

5 Serve with a Mixed Salad.

Quick paella

If eating alone, eat half hot for supper
and the rest cold the next day.

SERVES 2

1 packet of savoury vegetable rice
1 tsp ground turmeric
2 mugs of boiling water
1 skinless chicken breast,
cut into bite-sized pieces
1 × 170 g/6 oz/small can of prawns
(shrimp), drained
A good pinch of dried oregano

1 Put the rice, turmeric, water and
chicken pieces in a large frying pan
(skillet). Bring to the boil, then turn
down the heat to fairly low and
bubble gently for 15 minutes.

2 Add the prawns and oregano, stir
well, then cover and cook over a very
low heat for a further 5 minutes until
the liquid has been absorbed and the
rice is tender.

Sausage and corn salad with garlic croûtons

SERVES 1

2 thick pork sausages
2 tbsp sunflower oil
1 slice of bread, cut into cubes
1 garlic clove, cut in half,
or 1 tsp garlic purée (paste)
1 × 200 g/7 oz/small can of sweetcorn
(corn) with (bell) peppers, drained
5 cm/2 in piece of cucumber, diced
4–6 radishes, halved
2 tbsp plain yoghurt or mayonnaise
1 tsp dried chives
Salt and pepper

1 Heat a frying pan (skillet) and dry-fry the sausages for about 8 minutes, turning occasionally, until golden and cooked through. Drain on kitchen paper (paper towels). Wipe out the pan with more kitchen paper.

2 Heat the oil in the pan and add the garlic clove or paste. Fry (sauté) the bread cubes in the garlic oil until golden all over, turning as necessary. Drain on kitchen paper. Discard the garlic clove, if used.

3 Put the sweetcorn, cucumber and radishes in a bowl. Cut the sausages into bite-sized chunks and add. Stir in the yoghurt or mayonnaise and the chives and season to taste with salt and pepper.

4 Sprinkle the croûtons over and serve.

Bacon and mushroom risotto

If you use proper risotto rice, the mixture will be creamer but it should still have some 'bite'.

SERVES 1

A good knob of butter or margarine
1 small onion, peeled and
finely chopped
2 rashers (slices) of streaky bacon,
rinded and diced
4–6 mushrooms, sliced
½ mug of risotto or long-grain rice
A good handful of frozen peas
1 mug of hot chicken stock,
made with 1 stock cube
½ mug of boiling water
4 tbsp single (light) cream (optional)
Salt and pepper
1 tbsp grated Parmesan cheese

1 Melt the butter or margarine in a saucepan over a fairly high heat. Add the onion, bacon and mushrooms and fry (sauté) for 3 minutes until the onion is golden.

2 Stir in the rice and cook for 1 minute. Add the peas. Turn down the heat to fairly low. Stir in about ¼ of the stock and cook, stirring, until it has been absorbed. Repeat, adding a little stock at a time, then the water, until the rice is tender and the liquid has all been absorbed. It should take about 20 minutes.

3 Stir in the cream, if using, season to taste and add the Parmesan. Serve straight away.

Spanish rice

This tastes similar to paella but is much easier to make. If it's too much for one, any leftovers taste great cold the next day.

SERVES 1

A knob of butter or margarine
1 small chicken breast, diced
1 small onion, peeled and chopped
1 small red (bell) pepper, diced
¼ mug of long-grain rice
A good pinch of ground turmeric
⅔ mug of chicken stock,
made with ½ stock cube
1 tomato, roughly chopped
A handful of frozen peas
1 small handful of frozen cooked peeled prawns (shrimp)
A pinch of dried oregano
Salt and pepper

1 Melt the butter or margarine in a frying pan (skillet) over a moderate heat. Add the chicken, onion and pepper and fry (sauté), stirring, for 3 minutes. Stir in the rice and cook for 1 minute.

2 Add the turmeric and the stock, turn up the heat and bring to the boil, stirring. Turn down the heat until the mixture is just bubbling gently round the edges. Cover and cook for 10 minutes.

3 Stir in the tomato, peas, prawns, oregano and a little salt and pepper and a little more water, if becoming too dry already. Cover and continue cooking for a further 10 minutes over a low heat until the rice is cooked and has absorbed all the liquid.

4 Stir well and serve.

Creamy rice with ham and peas

If you want to reheat the rest the next day, put it in a saucepan with 2 tbsp of milk and heat, stirring gently, until piping hot. Alternatively, reheat in a microwave in a bowl with a plate over the top for 2–3 minutes. Stir well before serving.

SERVES 2

1 small onion, peeled and chopped
A knob of butter or margarine
½ mug of long-grain rice
1 mug of water
1 chicken or vegetable stock cube
½ mug of milk
¼ mug of frozen peas
1 × 225 g/8 oz/small can of ham,
cut into dice
A good pinch of dried mint
1 tbsp single (light) cream
or mayonnaise
Salt and pepper

1 Put the onion and butter or margarine in a saucepan and cook over a moderate heat, stirring, for 2 minutes until the onion is softened but not browned.

2 Stir in the rice until all the grains are glistening.

3 Add the water and stock cube and bring to the boil, stirring until the stock cube has dissolved. Stir in the milk and cook over a fairly gentle heat for 10 minutes, stirring occasionally.

4 Add the peas, ham and mint and continue to cook, stirring, for about 5 minutes until the rice is tender and the liquid has been absorbed.

5 Stir in the cream or mayonnaise and season with salt and pepper.

One-pot yellow kedgeree

This is traditionally served for breakfast, but is equally good for lunch of supper. You can use smoked haddock, cod or whiting.

SERVES 1

1 egg, scrubbed under cold water
¼ mug of long-grain rice
A good pinch of salt
A good pinch of ground turmeric
1 small fillet of any yellow smoked fish, about 150 g/5 oz
¼ mug of frozen peas
A pinch of curry powder
1 tbsp chopped fresh parsley
1 tbsp milk
Pepper

1 Put the egg in a large saucepan of water. Bring to the boil.

2 Add the rice, salt and turmeric. Stir, then cook over a high heat for 5 minutes. Add the fish and peas and cook for a further 5 minutes or until the rice and fish are tender.

3 Lift out the egg and fish with a fish slice. Put the egg in a bowl of cold water. Drain the rice in a colander over the sink and return to the pan. Stir in the curry powder.

4 Remove the skin from the fish and break the flesh into chunks. Add to the rice.

5 Shell the egg and cut into chunks. Add to the rice.

6 Add the parsley, milk and season with pepper. Stir gently over a fairly low heat until piping hot.

White fish kedgeree

SERVES 1

Prepare as for One-pot yellow Kedgeree (left) but use a small white fish fillet – pollack and coley are the cheapest – instead of the smoked fish.

Kipper kedgeree

SERVES 1

Prepare as for One-pot Yellow Kedgeree (left) but use a kipper fillet instead of yellow fish.

Sausage and vegetable pilaf

SERVES 1

¼ mug of long-grain rice
½ mug of frozen mixed vegetables
A knob of butter or margarine
1 small onion, peeled and finely chopped
2–3 thick pork or spicy sausages, cut into chunks
A pinch of chilli powder
¼ tsp dried mixed herbs
Salt and pepper

1 Cook the rice according to the packet directions. Add the vegetables halfway through cooking. Drain in a colander in the sink and rinse with boiling water.

2 Melt the butter or margarine in the rice pan. Add the onion and sausages and fry (sauté), stirring, over a fairly high heat for about 5 minutes until golden and cooked through.

3 Add the rice and vegetables, chilli powder and herbs. Stir and turn over a gentle heat for 2 minutes. Season to taste.

Chicken pilaf

Make the mixed salad while the pilaf is cooking. Any leftovers can be eaten cold the next day.

SERVES 1–2

A knob of butter or margarine
1 onion, peeled and thinly sliced
1 small chicken breast,
cut into chunks
1 tbsp peanuts
1 tomato, chopped
1 small green (bell) pepper, cut into
small dice
1 small handful of sultanas
(golden raisins)
½ tsp paprika
½ mug of long-grain rice
1¼ mugs of water
¼ tsp dried basil
1 chicken stock cube
Salt and pepper
A Mixed Salad (see page 45), to serve

1 Heat the butter or margarine in a frying pan (skillet). Fry (sauté) the onion for 3 minutes until lightly golden.

2 Add the chicken, peanuts, tomato, pepper, sultanas and paprika and cook for 1 minute.

3 Stir in the rice, water and basil and crumble in the stock cube. Cook over a high heat, stirring, until boiling, then turn down the heat until gently bubbling round the edges.

4 Cover with a lid, plate or foil and cook very gently for 20 minutes, stirring once or twice, until the chicken and rice are tender and the liquid has been absorbed.

5 Season with salt and pepper, stir and serve with a Mixed Salad.

Riviera cod and rice

To skin fish, put it skin-side down on a board. Loosen the skin at one edge, hold the loosened piece of skin firmly and, using the sharpest knife you have, push the flesh away from the skin.

SERVES 1

1 tbsp olive or sunflower oil
1 small onion, peeled and chopped
1 small garlic clove, peeled and crushed,
or ½ tsp garlic purée (paste)
1 red (bell) pepper, sliced
½ mug of passata (sieved tomatoes)
1 tsp tomato purée
4 tbsp water
¼ mug of long-grain rice
Salt and pepper
1 small piece of cod fillet,
about 150 g/5 oz, skinned and cubed
A few sliced olives

1 Heat the oil in a saucepan. Add the onion, garlic and pepper and fry (sauté), stirring, for 2 minutes. Stir in the passata, tomato purée, water, rice and a little salt and pepper. Bring to the boil over a high heat, then cover, turn down the heat to moderate and cook, stirring occasionally, for 10 minutes.

2 Add the fish and, if the mixture is getting dry, a little more water. Season with more salt and pepper and cook for a further 5 minutes until all the liquid has been absorbed and the rice and fish are cooked.

3 Serve sprinkled with a few sliced olives.

Spanish rice with tuna

SERVES 1

1 tbsp olive or sunflower oil
1 small green (bell) pepper, diced
1 small onion, peeled and chopped
¹/₄ mug of long-grain rice
²/₃ mug of water
¹/₂ chicken stock cube
¹/₄ mug of frozen peas with
sweetcorn (corn)
1 tomato, chopped
¹/₂ × 185 g/6¹/₂ oz/small can of
tuna, drained
Salt and pepper
A few sliced stoned (pitted) olives

1 Heat the oil in a frying pan (skillet). Add the pepper and onion and stir-fry for 2 minutes.

2 Add the rice and stir until the grains are glistening with oil.

3 Add the water and stock cube and stir until the cube dissolves. Bring to the boil, turn down the heat until gently bubbling round the edges, cover with a lid or foil and cook over a low heat for 10 minutes.

4 Stir the rice, add the peas and sweetcorn, the tomato and the tuna. Re-cover and cook for a further 10 minutes until the rice is cooked and has absorbed nearly all the liquid but the rice is moist.

5 Season to taste and top with the olives.

Okra and prawn pilaf

SERVES 1

1 small onion, peeled and chopped
2 rashers (slices) of streaky bacon,
rinded and diced
1 tbsp sunflower or olive oil
4 okra, cut into chunky slices
¹/₄ mug of long-grain rice
¹/₄ tsp ground cumin
²/₃ mug of water
¹/₂ chicken stock cube
Salt and pepper
¹/₄ mug of frozen peeled prawns (shrimp)
1 tbsp chopped fresh parsley
or 1 tsp dried parsley

1 In a saucepan, fry (sauté) the onion and bacon in the oil for 2 minutes, stirring.

2 Stir in the okra, rice and cumin and cook, stirring, for about 1 minute until everything is glistening in the oil.

3 Add all the remaining ingredients except the prawns and parsley, stir well, cover and cook over a fairly gentle heat for about 15 minutes.

4 Add the prawns and, if the mixture is getting too dry, a little more water. Cover and cook for a further 5 minutes or until the rice is tender and has absorbed the liquid. Taste and re-season if necessary.

5 Sprinkle with the parsley.

ⓋVegetable risotto Ⓥ

SERVES 1–2

1 onion, peeled and chopped
1 carrot, peeled and chopped
1 green (bell) pepper, chopped
2 tbsp olive or sunflower oil
½ mug of long-grain rice
1 mug of vegetable stock,
    made with 1 stock cube
1 × 400 g/14 oz/large can of
    chopped tomatoes
A good pinch of dried basil
Salt and pepper
A good handful of grated
    Cheddar cheese

1 Fry (sauté) all the prepared vegetables in the oil in a large saucepan or frying pan (skillet) for 5 minutes, stirring all the time.

2 Add the rice and continue to cook and stir for 1 minute.

3 Add the stock, tomatoes, basil and seasoning and bring to the boil over a high heat. Stir well, turn down the heat to very low, cover and cook for 20 minutes without stirring. If there is any excess liquid, turn up the heat and boil rapidly for a minute or two to evaporate it. If it seems too dry, add a little more water.

4 Stir well and serve sprinkled with grated cheese.

Creamy salami and mushroom risotto

SERVES 1

A knob of butter or margarine
2 tsp sunflower or olive oil
1 small onion, peeled and
    finely chopped
4–6 mushrooms, sliced
½ mug of risotto or long-grain rice
1 mug of hot chicken stock,
    made with 1 stock cube
½ mug of boiling water
1 pepperami stick, cut into small chunks
3 tbsp single (light) cream
Salt and pepper
A little chopped fresh parsley
    or ½ tsp dried chives
Grated Parmesan cheese

1 Heat the butter or margarine with the oil in a saucepan over a moderate heat.

2 Add the onion and mushrooms and fry (sauté), stirring, for 2 minutes.

3 Add the rice and cook, stirring, until glistening.

4 Pour on about a quarter of the stock and simmer, stirring occasionally, until the liquid is absorbed.

5 Repeat, adding the stock and then the water in this way until all the liquid is used and the rice is just tender, but still with some 'bite'. This should take about 20 minutes.

6 Stir the pepperami and cream into the rice and heat through, stirring. Do not boil. Add salt and pepper, to taste.

7 Pile the creamy mixture on to a plate, sprinkle with the parsley or chives and some grated Parmesan cheese.

Rice and vegetable Ⓥ stir-fry Ⓥ

SERVES 1

¼ mug of long-grain rice
1 tbsp sunflower oil
1 spring onion (scallion), trimmed and
cut into short lengths
1 small carrot, peeled and cut into
thin matchsticks
2.5 cm/1 in piece of cucumber, cut into
thin matchsticks
1 red (bell) pepper, cut into thin strips
4 button mushrooms, sliced
A good pinch of ground ginger
or Chinese five-spice powder
1 small garlic clove, peeled and crushed,
or ½ tsp garlic purée (paste)
1 tbsp soy sauce

1 Cook the rice according to the
packet directions. Drain, rinse with
boiling water and drain again.

2 Heat the oil in the rice pan. Add all
the remaining ingredients except the
rice and soy sauce and stir-fry for
5 minutes.

3 Add the rice and toss until heated.
Sprinkle in the soy sauce, adding
more if liked, toss again and serve.

Ⓥ Mushroom risotto Ⓥ

SERVES 1

2 tsp olive oil
1 small onion, peeled and chopped
1 small garlic clove, peeled and crushed,
or ½ tsp garlic purée (paste)
6 mushrooms, sliced
½ mug of risotto or long-grain rice
1 mug of hot vegetable stock,
made with 1 stock cube
½ mug of boiling water
A good pinch of dried oregano
Salt and pepper
A small handful of chopped fresh
parsley
Grated Parmesan cheese
A Mixed Salad (see page 45) and crusty
bread, to serve

1 Heat the oil in a saucepan. Add the
onion, garlic and mushrooms and cook
gently, stirring, for 2 minutes until the
onion is softened but not browned.

2 Add the rice and stir until every
grain of rice is glistening.

3 Pour in a quarter of the stock and
add the oregano. Cook over a
moderate heat, stirring occasionally,
until the liquid has been absorbed.
Repeat, adding a little stock at a time,
then the water until all the liquid is
used and the risotto is creamy but
still with some 'bite'. This should take
about 20 minutes.

4 Season to taste, then sprinkle the
risotto with parsley and some grated
Parmesan and serve with a Mixed
Salad and crusty bread.

Okra, bacon and mushroom pilaf

SERVES 1

2 tsp sunflower oil
1 small onion, peeled and chopped
2 rashers (slices) of streaky bacon,
rinded and cut into small pieces
4 okra (ladies' fingers)
¼ mug of long-grain rice
¼ tsp ground cumin
⅔ mug water
½ chicken stock cube
4 mushrooms, sliced
Salt and pepper

1 Heat the oil in a saucepan. Add the onion and bacon and fry (sauté), stirring, for 2 minutes.

2 Cut each okra pod into four pieces. Add to the pan with the rice and cumin and cook, stirring, for about 1 minute until everything is glistening in oil.

3 Add the water and stock cube and stir until the cube dissolves.

4 Add the mushrooms and a little salt and pepper and bring to the boil. When bubbling, turn down the heat, cover and cook gently for 20 minutes.

5 Taste and add more salt and pepper, if necessary, then serve.

ⓥ Peanut paella ⓥ

You can leave out the turmeric and parsley, if you prefer.

SERVES 1

2 tsp olive oil
1 small leek, trimmed, washed well and
thinly sliced
1 small red (bell) pepper, diced
¼ mug of long-grain rice
¼ tsp ground turmeric
3–4 mushrooms, sliced
A handful of raw peanuts
⅔ mug of vegetable stock,
made with ½ stock cube
Salt and pepper
¼ tsp dried oregano
A little chopped fresh or dried parsley

1 Heat the oil in a frying pan (skillet). Add the leek and pepper and cook, stirring, for 2 minutes.

2 Stir in the rice and cook for about 1 minute until every grain is glistening.

3 Add all the remaining ingredients except the parsley. Cook, stirring gently, over a high heat until bubbling.

4 Turn down the heat as low as possible. Cover with a lid and cook very gently for 20 minutes. Remove the lid and stir well. The rice should have absorbed all the liquid and be just tender. If not, add a little more water if necessary and cook over a high heat for a few more minutes.

5 Spoon on to a plate and sprinkle with parsley.

Ⓥ Egg fried rice Ⓥ

SERVES 1

¹/₄ mug of long-grain rice
A small handful of frozen peas
2 tbsp sunflower oil
2 eggs, beaten
A pinch of Chinese five-spice powder
(optional)
¹/₂ tsp soy sauce

1 Cook the rice according to the packet directions. Add the peas halfway through cooking. Drain in a colander, rinse with cold water and drain again thoroughly.

2 Add the oil to the pan and heat over a fairly high heat.

3 Add the rice and peas and cook, stirring and turning, for 2 minutes.

4 Push the mixture to one side and tilt the pan. Pour in the beaten eggs.

5 Cook the eggs, stirring, then gradually draw in the rice until it is filled with tiny strands of egg. Add a pinch of Chinese five-spice powder, if liked, and a sprinkling of soy sauce.

6 Stir gently and serve.

Savoury rice Ⓥ with eggs Ⓥ

If eating on your own, serve half the rice and eggs, and leave the remainder covered in the frying pan until cold (the eggs will go hard).

Break up the eggs and store everything in an airtight container in the fridge. Eat cold the next day with some mayonnaise and lettuce.

SERVES 2

1 packet of savoury rice (any flavour)
4 eggs
Crusty bread, to serve

1 Empty the rice into a large frying pan (skillet). Add water as directed on the packet.

2 Bring to the boil, stir, cover with a lid or foil, turn down the heat to fairly low and cook for 15 minutes.

3 Make four holes in the rice. Break the eggs one at a time into a mug and slide them into the holes. Re-cover and cook for 5–10 minutes or until the eggs are just set.

4 Serve with crusty bread.

Mushroom, nut and ⓥ raisin pilaf ⓥ

SERVES 1

¼ mug of long-grain rice
1 tbsp sunflower oil
½ green or red (bell) pepper, diced
1 small onion, peeled and sliced
½ garlic clove, peeled and crushed,
or ½ tsp garlic purée (paste)
5–6 button mushrooms, sliced
1 × 50 g/2 oz/small packet of
peanuts and raisins
1 tsp soy sauce or to taste
A Beansprout Salad (see page 45),
to serve

1 Cook the rice in a pan according to the packet directions. Drain in a colander in the sink. Rinse with boiling water and drain again.

2 Heat the oil in the rice saucepan. Add the pepper, onion, garlic and mushrooms and fry (sauté), stirring, for 3 minutes until softened.

3 Add the rice, peanuts and raisins and the soy sauce and cook, stirring, for 2 minutes.

4 Spoon on to a plate and serve with the salad.

Tuscan macaroni

Eat half of this hot and the rest as a salad the next day. The olives and chives are optional but they do give it extra flavour.

SERVES 2

½ mug of macaroni
4 tbsp olive or sunflower oil
2 tbsp lemon juice
1 small garlic clove, peeled and crushed,
or ½ tsp garlic purée (paste)
1 × 425 g/15 oz/large can of black-eye
beans, drained
2 tbsp chopped fresh parsley
1 × 185 g/6½ oz/small can of
tuna, drained
Salt and pepper
A few black olives
1 tsp dried chives

1 Cook the macaroni in plenty of boiling, lightly salted water according to the packet directions. Drain in a colander in the sink and return to the pan.

2 Add the oil, lemon juice, garlic, beans and parsley. Cook over a fairly gentle heat for 5 minutes, stirring occasionally until hot through.

3 Gently stir in the tuna and a little salt and pepper and heat through, taking care not to break up the chunks of tuna.

4 Spoon into bowls and garnish with a few black olives and some dried chives, if liked.

ⓥ Neapolitan tortellini ⓥ

If you find this is too much for one meal, store the remainder in a covered container in the fridge and reheat it the following day, either in the microwave for about 2 minutes or in a saucepan with a couple of spoonfuls of water added to prevent sticking.

SERVES 1–2

½ packet of dried tortellini, stuffed with cheese or mushrooms
1 mug of passata (sieved tomatoes)
Salt and pepper
½ tsp dried basil
Grated Parmesan cheese
A Mixed Salad (see page 45), to serve

1 Cook the tortellini according to the packet directions. Drain in a colander in the sink and return to the pan.

2 Add the passata, basil, salt and plenty of pepper. Heat through, stirring, until bubbling and the tortellini is bathed in the sauce.

3 Spoon the pasta and sauce into a warm bowl, sprinkle with Parmesan cheese and serve with salad.

Garlic and pepperami pasta

SERVES 1

½ mug of small pasta shapes
1 pepperami stick, cut into small chunks
½ garlic clove, peeled and crushed, or ¼ tsp garlic purée (paste)
1 × 200 g/7 oz/small can of garden peas, drained
1 egg
2 tbsp milk
Salt and pepper
Crusty bread, to serve

1 Cook the pasta according to the packet directions. Drain and return to the pan.

2 Add the pepperami, garlic and peas and heat through, stirring, for 2 minutes.

3 Whisk the egg with the milk and stir into the pan with a sprinkling of salt and pepper (don't add too much as the pepperami is salty).

4 Cook over a gentle heat, stirring, until creamy but don't let the egg scramble. Spoon into a bowl and eat with crusty bread.

Mushroom macaroni with ⓥ melted cheese ⓥ

SERVES 1

½ mug of macaroni
½ × 170 g/6 oz/small can of creamed mushrooms
2 tbsp milk
A good handful of Edam cheese, grated
A good pinch of dried oregano
Salt and pepper
A Mixed Salad (see page 45), to serve

1 Cook the macaroni according to the packet directions until just tender. Drain in a colander in the sink.

2 Put the mushrooms and milk in the same saucepan and heat through, stirring, until blended and hot. Add the pasta, cheese, oregano and a sprinkling of pepper. Lift and stir with a spoon and fork until the cheese has melted and the pasta is coated in the sauce.

3 Taste and add a little more salt and pepper if necessary. Serve with a Mixed Salad.

Chick pea and carrot 🅥 pasta pot 🅥

If this is too much for one meal, cool the remainder and store it in a covered container in the fridge. Either reheat or eat as a cold salad the next day.

SERVES 1–2

¹/₂–1 mug of pasta shapes
1 large carrot, peeled and cut into thin slices
Salt and pepper
1 tbsp sunflower or olive oil
1 onion, peeled and chopped
¹/₂ mug of passata (sieved tomatoes)
1 tbsp tomato purée (paste)
¹/₂ tsp sugar
1 × 425 g/15 oz/large can of chick peas (garbanzos), drained
¹/₂ tsp dried mixed herbs

1 Cook the pasta and carrots in boiling water with a pinch of salt added for 10 minutes until just tender. Drain in a colander in the sink.

2 Heat the oil in the same saucepan and fry (sauté) the onion, stirring, for 3 minutes until soft and lightly golden.

3 Return the pasta and carrots to the pan, add the remaining ingredients and cook over a moderate heat, stirring gently, until piping hot.

4 Season to taste before serving.

Chick pea and garlic sausage pasta pot

Have half of this for one meal, then cool the remainder and store in a sealed container in the fridge. Eat cold or reheated until piping hot the following day.

SERVES 2

¹/₂–1 mug of pasta shapes
10 cm/4 in piece of garlic sausage
1 tbsp sunflower or olive oil
1 onion, peeled and chopped
1 green (bell) pepper, diced
¹/₂ mug of passata (sieved tomatoes)
1 tbsp tomato purée (paste)
¹/₂ tsp sugar
1 × 425 g/15 oz/large can of chick peas (garbanzos), drained
¹/₂ tsp dried oregano
Salt and pepper

1 Cook the pasta according to the packet directions, then drain in a colander in the sink.

2 Peel off any outer skin from the garlic sausage and cut the sausage into small dice.

3 Heat the oil in the same saucepan and add the onion and pepper. Cook, stirring, for 3 minutes until softened and lightly golden.

4 Add all the remaining ingredients except the pasta and bring to the boil. Simmer for 2 minutes, then stir in the pasta and season to taste.

Macaroni with bacon and Red Leicester

Ask for bacon pieces at the deli counter. They are very cheap and you can store any you don't use in the fridge for another recipe.
If you can't get bacon pieces, use 2–3 rashers of streaky bacon, rinded and diced, instead.

SERVES 1

½ mug of macaroni
A handful of bacon pieces, trimmed and cut into bite-sized pieces
A good handful of grated Red Leicester cheese
1 tsp Worcestershire sauce
Salt and pepper
1 tbsp butter or margarine
A Tomato and Onion Salad (see page 46), to serve

1 Cook the macaroni according to the packet directions. Drain in a colander in the sink.

2 Dry-fry the bacon in the same pan, stirring until cooked.

3 Return the macaroni to the pan and add the cheese, Worcestershire sauce, a sprinkling of salt and pepper and the butter or margarine. Lift and stir gently until everything is well blended.

4 Serve with a Tomato and Onion Salad.

Broad bean and pine nut Ⓥ pasta Ⓥ

The smaller the pasta shapes, the less you will need.

SERVES 1

1 tbsp pine nuts
½–1 mug of pasta shapes
½ mug of fresh shelled or frozen baby broad (fava) beans
A good knob of butter or margarine, cut into small pieces
3 tbsp single (light) cream or crème fraiche
2 tsp chopped fresh parsley or 1 tsp dried parsley
A pinch of grated nutmeg
Salt and pepper
1 tbsp grated Parmesan cheese

1 Put the pine nuts in a saucepan. Cook over a high heat, stirring until golden. Tip out of the pan straight away to prevent over-browning.

2 Cook the pasta according to the packet directions in the same pan. Add the broad beans for the last 5 minutes' cooking time. Drain in a colander in the sink, then return to the saucepan.

3 Add the butter or margarine and stir gently until melted.

4 Stir in the cream or crème fraiche, parsley, nutmeg and a little salt and lots of pepper. Cook, stirring, over a very gentle heat until piping hot. Do not allow to boil.

5 Spoon the pasta on to a plate, sprinkle with the pine nuts and the Parmesan and serve.

Fishy pan pasta

If you have a grill, you can put the cooked pasta mixture into a flameproof dish, then cover with the cheese and tomatoes and grill until browned and bubbling.

SERVES 1

½–1 mug of pasta shapes
1 × 155 g/5¼ oz/small can of pilchards
in tomato sauce, mashed
1 tbsp olive or sunflower oil
½ tsp lemon juice
4 tbsp passata (sieved tomatoes)
Salt and pepper
A good handful of grated
Cheddar cheese
1 tomato, sliced

1 Cook the pasta according to the packet directions. Drain in a colander and return to the saucepan.

2 Add all the remaining ingredients except the cheese and sliced tomatoes. Lift and stir gently over a low heat until well combined. Season to taste. Add a little more passata to moisten if necessary.

3 Cover with the grated cheese and arrange the tomato slices around the top. Cover the pan with a lid and cook over a very gentle heat for 2–3 minutes until the cheese has melted.

Salmon macar

Use the rest of the salmo sandwiches the following day. in a covered container in the r not in the can.

SERVES 1

2 tbsp plain (all-purpose) flour
½ mug of milk
A knob of butter or margarine
½ × 200 g/7 oz/small can of
pink salmon
1 tbsp tomato ketchup (catsup)
Salt and pepper
½ mug of macaroni
A handful of grated Cheddar cheese
Slices of cucumber, sprinkled with
pepper and vinegar, to serve

1 Whisk the flour with the milk in a saucepan until smooth, using a wire whisk. Add the butter or margarine. Bring to the boil over a high heat and cook for 2 minutes, stirring with the whisk all the time.

2 Remove the skin from the fish but, ideally, leave the bones in as they are very good for you. Stir the salmon and its juices into the sauce. Add the ketchup and salt and pepper to taste.

3 Cook the macaroni according to the packet directions. Drain in a colander in the sink, then stir into the fish sauce.

4 Tip on to a plate and sprinkle with the cheese. Serve with the sliced cucumber.

Tagliatelle with pesto and 🟥 mushrooms 🟥

SERVES 1

3–4 tagliatelle nests
A good knob of butter or margarine
4–6 mushrooms, sliced
1 small onion, peeled and
finely chopped
1 tbsp pesto, ready-made or see page 418
A Mixed Salad (see page 45), to serve

1 Cook the tagliatelle according to the packet directions, stirring occasionally. Drain in a colander in the sink.

2 Melt the butter or margarine in the same pan. Add the mushrooms and onion and cook for 3–4 minutes until soft and lightly golden.

3 Add the pasta and pesto to the onion mixture and toss over a gentle heat until every strand is coated.

4 Pile on to a warm plate and serve with a Mixed Salad.

Rigatoni beef supper

SERVES 2

1 mug of rigatoni
1 × 175 g/6 oz/small can of minced
(ground) steak with onions
½ tsp dried mixed herbs
2 handfuls of grated Cheddar cheese
A Tomato and Onion Salad
(see page 46), to serve

1 Cook the rigatoni according to the packet directions. Drain in a colander in the sink and return to the pan.

2 Add the minced steak and herbs and heat through, stirring until piping hot.

3 Spoon on to plates and sprinkle with the cheese.

4 Serve with a Tomato and Onion Salad.

Spaghetti con 🟥 salsa Alfredo 🟥

This is traditionally made with fresh pasta but dried is cheaper!

SERVES 1

¼ × 450 g/1 lb packet of spaghetti
½ mug of double (heavy) cream
A good knob of butter or margarine
3 tbsp grated Parmesan cheese
Pepper (preferably freshly ground black)
Crusty bread and a Green Salad
(see page 45), to serve

1 Cook the spaghetti according to the packet directions. Drain in a colander in the sink.

2 Put the cream and butter or margarine in the saucepan and bring to the boil over a high heat. Reduce the heat until just bubbling very gently and cook for 1 minute.

3 Add half the cheese and some pepper and whisk with a wire whisk until smooth.

4 Add the cooked spaghetti with the remaining cheese and lift and stir gently over a fairly low heat.

5 Pile on to a plate or into a bowl and serve with crusty bread and salad.

Vermicelli with smoked salmon and broccoli

This sounds grand but smoked salmon trimmings are cheap and go a long way. This recipe serves four people, so it's great if you're cooking for friends – it'll certainly impress them! If you want to cook it for one, use a quarter of the ingredients (but 1 whole egg).

SERVES 4

½ × 450 g/1 lb packet of vermicelli
1 large head of broccoli, cut into tiny florets
1 × 150 g/5 oz packet of smoked salmon trimmings
1 small carton of single (light) cream
2 eggs
Salt and pepper
A small handful of chopped fresh parsley
Lemon juice
Grated Parmesan cheese

1 Bring a large pan of water with a pinch of salt to the boil. Add the vermicelli and broccoli, bring back to the boil and cook for 5 minutes until just tender. Drain in a colander in the sink and return to the pan.

2 Separate the pieces of salmon and add to the pan.

3 Using a wire whisk or a fork, mix the cream and eggs together with a pinch of salt and lots of pepper until well blended. Add to the pan.

4 Cook, stirring gently, over a very low heat until the mixture is piping hot and creamy. Do not allow the mixture to boil or it will scramble.

5 Stir in the parsley and add lemon juice and salt and pepper to taste.

6 Pile on warm plates and serve sprinkled with grated Parmesan.

Spaghetti with pine nuts, mushrooms, Mozzarella and ⓥ fresh basil ⓥ

It really is worth buying pots of fresh herbs, such as basil and parsley, and keeping them on the windowsill. Just remember to water them every other day.

SERVES 1

¼ × 450 g/1 lb packet of spaghetti
2 good knobs of butter or margarine
1 tbsp sunflower or olive oil
6 button mushrooms, sliced
½ garlic clove, peeled and crushed, or ½ tsp garlic purée (paste)
A handful of pine nuts
8 fresh basil leaves, shredded
A handful of grated Mozzarella cheese
Salt and pepper
A Mixed Salad (see page 45), to serve

1 Cook the spaghetti according to the packet directions. Drain in a colander in the sink.

2 Melt the butter or margarine in the spaghetti saucepan with the oil. Add the mushrooms and garlic and fry (sauté), stirring, for 2 minutes. Add the pine nuts and fry for 1 further minute until lightly golden.

3 Return the spaghetti to the pan, add the basil, Mozzarella and a sprinkling of salt and pepper and toss gently until well mixed.

4 Pile on to a plate and serve with a Mixed Salad.

Tagliatelle with ⓥ aubergine ⓥ

SERVES 1

½ aubergine (eggplant)
1 tbsp plain (all-purpose) flour
Salt and pepper
¼ tsp dried oregano
4 tbsp olive oil
1 small garlic clove, peeled and crushed,
or ½ tsp garlic purée (paste)
3–4 tagliatelle nests
A handful of grated Mozzarella cheese

1 Cut the aubergine into slices, then cut each slice into matchsticks.

2 Put the flour in a bowl and mix with a little salt and pepper and the oregano. Add the aubergine and mix with your hands to coat completely.

3 Cook the tagliatelle according to the packet directions. Drain in a colander in the sink.

4 Heat half of the oil in the pan over a high heat. Add the aubergine and garlic and fry (sauté), stirring, until golden and tender, about 5 minutes. Turn down the heat.

5 Add the pasta and the remaining oil and lift and stir gently using a spoon and fork until piping hot.

6 Spoon on to a warm plate and scatter the cheese over.

Simple chicken pasta

As large cans of tomatoes are much cheaper than small ones, it makes sense to cook enough for two meals at one go. The alternative is to halve the quantity of ingredients and put half the tomatoes in a covered container in the fridge for use in another recipe.

SERVES 2

1 mug of small pasta shapes
1 tbsp sunflower or olive oil
1 small onion, peeled and chopped
1 small garlic clove, peeled and crushed,
or ½ tsp garlic purée (paste)
¾ mug of minced (ground) chicken
1 × 400 g/14 oz/large can of
chopped tomatoes
½ tsp dried mixed herbs
Salt and pepper
2 handfuls of grated Cheddar cheese
A Green Salad (see page 45), to serve

1 Cook the pasta according to the packet directions. Drain in a colander in the sink and reserve.

2 Heat the oil in the pasta pan. Add the onion and garlic and fry (sauté), stirring, for 2 minutes. Add the minced chicken and fry, stirring, until the meat is no longer pink and all the grains are separate.

3 Add the tomatoes, herbs and some salt and pepper to taste. Allow to boil, then turn down the heat to moderate and let the mixture bubble for 10 minutes until a rich sauce is formed.

4 Stir in the pasta and heat through.

5 Sprinkle with grated cheese and serve with a Green Salad.

Tortellini with Italian cheese and tomato ❤ sauce ❤

This is traditionally made with Mascarpone cheese but any soft white cheese will do.

SERVES 1

½ packet dried stuffed tortellini, any flavour
½ mug passata (sieved tomatoes)
2 tsp tomato purée (paste)
A pinch of sugar
½ tsp dried basil
or 1 tbsp chopped fresh basil
¼ tub of soft white cheese, such as Philadelphia
Salt and pepper
Grated Parmesan cheese
A Green Salad (see page 45), to serve

1 Cook the tortellini according to the packet directions. Drain in a colander in the sink.

2 Put the remaining ingredients in the pan and whisk with a fork or balloon whisk until smooth. Add the pasta to the mixture and heat through gently until almost boiling.

3 Tip into a bowl, sprinkle with Parmesan and serve with a Green Salad.

Minted bacon and pea penne

You can, of course, use any pasta shapes you like.

SERVES 1

½ mug of penne
A knob of butter or margarine
1 small onion, peeled and chopped
2 rashers (slices) of streaky bacon, rinded and diced
¼ mug of frozen peas
½ tsp dried mint
Salt and pepper
5 tbsp crème fraîche
A Tomato and Onion Salad (see page 46), to serve

1 Cook the pasta according to the packet directions. Drain in a colander in the sink.

2 Melt the butter or margarine in the pasta pan. Add the onion and bacon cook, stirring, for 2 minutes. Add the peas, mint and a sprinkling of salt and pepper. Turn down the heat to low, cover the pan with a lid and cook very gently for 6–8 minutes, stirring occasionally, until the peas are cooked.

3 Return the pasta to the pan and add the crème fraîche. Cook, lifting and stirring the mixture, until hot through. Taste and add more salt and pepper, if necessary.

4 Pile on to a plate and serve with a Tomato and Onion Salad.

ⓥ Macaroni cheese ⓥ

If you have a grill, you can spoon the macaroni cheese into a flameproof dish, sprinkle it with a little extra cheese and grill until golden. It is also nice with some canned tomatoes, heated in a separated pan.

SERVES 1

½ mug of macaroni
2 tbsp plain (all-purpose) flour
⅔ mug of milk
A knob of butter or margarine
½ tsp made English mustard
*A good handful of grated
Cheddar cheese*
Salt and pepper
Slices of tomato, to serve

1 Cook the macaroni according to the packet directions. Drain in a colander in the sink.

2 Put the flour and milk in the same saucepan and whisk with a balloon whisk or fork until smooth.

3 Add the butter or margarine and cook over a fairly high heat, stirring all the time, until boiling, thick and smooth. Allow to bubble, stirring, for 2 minutes.

4 Stir in the mustard, cheese and salt and pepper to taste.

5 Tip the cooked macaroni into the sauce and stir well over a fairly gentle heat until piping hot.

6 Spoon on to a plate and serve with slices of tomato.

Spaghetti carbonara

SERVES 1

¼ × 450 g/1 lb packet of spaghetti
2 tbsp olive or sunflower oil
*1 small onion, peeled and
finely chopped*
*½ small garlic clove, peeled and crushed,
or ¼ tsp garlic purée (paste)*
*2 rashers (slices) of streaky bacon,
rinded and diced*
4 mushrooms, sliced
1 egg
2 tbsp milk
Salt and pepper
1 tbsp chopped fresh parsley
Grated Parmesan cheese
A Mixed Salad (see page 45), to serve

1 Cook the spaghetti according to the packet directions. Drain in a colander in the sink.

2 Heat the oil in the pasta pan. Add the onion, garlic and bacon and cook, stirring, over a moderate heat for 3 minutes until cooked but not browned. Add the mushrooms and cook for 1–2 minutes.

3 Whisk the egg with the milk.

4 Return the spaghetti to the pan and toss and stir until the bacon mixture is mixed into the pasta. Add the egg and milk and season well with salt and pepper. Add the parsley.

5 Cook over a fairly low heat, lifting and stirring the mixture gently, for 1–2 minutes until hot but still creamy (not scrambled).

6 Turn into a bowl, sprinkle with a little grated Parmesan and serve with a Mixed Salad.

Middle Eastern cottage ⓥ cheese pasta ⓥ

SERVES 1

3–4 tagliatelle nests
A knob of butter or margarine
1 small tub of cottage cheese
1 tbsp caraway seeds
1 tbsp poppy seeds
Salt and pepper
Chilli powder, to taste
A Tomato and Onion salad
(see page 46), to serve

1 Cook the tagliatelle according to the packet directions, stirring occasionally to separate the strands. Drain in a colander in the sink, tip back into the pan and return to the heat, turned down fairly low.

2 Add the remaining ingredients and toss and stir until hot through.

3 Serve with a Tomato and Onion Salad.

Golden crabstick macaroni

SERVES 1

2 tsp sunflower oil
1 small onion, peeled and chopped
1 small garlic clove, peeled and crushed,
or ¹/₂ tsp garlic purée (paste)
¹/₂ mug of macaroni
1 mug of fish, chicken or vegetable stock,
made with 1 stock cube
A good pinch of ground turmeric
A good pinch of dried oregano
A handful of frozen peas
4 crabsticks, cut into chunks
Salt and pepper
Chopped fresh parsley
or a few dried chives
French bread, to serve

1 Heat the oil in a frying pan (skillet). Add the onion and garlic and cook gently, stirring, for 2 minutes until softened but not browned.

2 Add the macaroni and stir for a few seconds until coated in the oil.

3 Add the stock, turmeric and oregano and bring to the boil, stirring. Reduce the heat until bubbling gently round the edges, cover and cook for 10 minutes, stirring once or twice.

4 Add the peas and crabsticks, stir again, re-cover and cook for a further 10 minutes until the pasta is tender and has absorbed nearly all the liquid. Season to taste with salt and pepper and stir gently again.

5 Sprinkle with the parsley or chives and serve with French bread.

ⓥ Tagliatelle with cheese ⓥ

SERVES 1

3–4 tagliatelle nests
A good knob of butter or margarine
A good handful of grated Cheddar cheese
1 tbsp mayonnaise
Salt and pepper
Grated Parmesan cheese
A Tomato and Onion Salad
(see page 46)

1 Cook the tagliatelle according to the packet directions, stirring occasionally to separate the strands. Drain in a colander in the sink and return to the pan.

2 Add the butter or margarine and lift and stir until melted. Add the cheese and mayonnaise and lift and stir again until every strand is coated. Season to taste with salt and pepper.

3 Tip into a bowl or on to a plate and sprinkle with Parmesan before serving with the salad.

One-pot chicken

A whole chicken is great if you are cooking for several people. If on your own, it still makes sense because you can use any leftover vegetables in stock, puréed with a hand blender or mashed with a potato masher for soup, and the rest of the chicken can be stored in the fridge for up to 3 days and eaten cold. Alternatively, you can put it in any dish that calls for cooked chicken.

SERVES 4

1.25 kg/2½ lb oven-ready chicken
2 tsp salt
Pepper
2 mugs of water
1 bouquet garni sachet or bay leaf
2 onions, peeled and quartered
2 carrots, peeled and cut into chunks
2 leeks, trimmed, washed well and cut into chunks
1 parsnip, peeled and cut into chunks
8 fairly small potatoes, scrubbed

1 Remove any giblets from the chicken and pull off any fat from just inside the rim of the body cavity.

2 Place in a large saucepan with the salt, a good grinding of pepper, the water and the bouquet garni sachet or bay leaf. Bring to the boil, then turn down the heat until just bubbling round the edges, cover with a lid and cook for 30 minutes.

3 Add all the prepared vegetables around the chicken. Bring quickly back to the boil, turn down the heat again, then cover and cook gently for 30 minutes until the vegetables and chicken are tender.

4 Lift the bird and vegetables out of the stock. Discard the bouquet garni or bay leaf. Cut the chicken into pieces and serve with the vegetables and a little of the broth.

Chicken and cauliflower stir-fry

You can buy ready-cooked chicken or use leftovers.

SERVES 1

½ slab of Chinese egg noodles
1 tbsp sunflower oil
¼ small cauliflower, cut into tiny florets
1 small onion, peeled, cut into wedges and separated into layers
1 small carrot, peeled and cut into ribbons with a potato peeler
A handful of frozen peas
1 tomato, cut into wedges
A small handful of diced cooked chicken
2 tsp soy sauce
1 tsp vinegar
2 tsp tomato ketchup (catsup)
½ tsp sugar
A good pinch of dried rosemary or dried mixed herbs

1 Put the noodles in a bowl and cover with boiling water. Stir to break up, then leave them to stand while you cook the stir-fry.

2 Heat the oil in a frying pan (skillet) or wok. Add the cauliflower and onion and stir-fry for 3 minutes. Add the carrot, peas and tomato and stir-fry for a further 2 minutes.

3 Add all the remaining ingredients except the noodles, stir well, cover with a lid, plate or foil and cook over a gentle heat for 10 minutes.

4 Drain the noodles. Pile into a bowl and top with the chicken mixture.

Chinese-style chicken with sesame soy noodles

Chicken thighs are cheaper than ready-prepared stir-fry meat.

SERVES 1

½ slab of Chinese egg noodles
2 chicken thighs
1 tbsp sunflower oil
1 small onion, peeled and sliced
1 carrot, peeled and cut into
thin matchsticks
5 cm/2 in piece of cucumber, cut into
thin matchsticks
½ mug of beansprouts
1 tsp cornflour (cornstarch)
5 tbsp apple juice
2 tsp soy sauce
2 tsp sesame seeds

1 Put the noodles in a bowl and cover with boiling water, stir to break up, then leave to stand while you cook the chicken.

2 Pull the skin off the chicken, then cut all the meat off the bones. Cut it into thin strips.

3 Heat the oil in a frying pan (skillet) and add the chicken and onion. Stir-fry for 3 minutes. Add the carrot and cucumber and continue to cook, stirring, for a further 3 minutes. Add the beansprouts and stir-fry for 1 minute.

4 Mix the cornflour with the apple juice and 1 tsp of the soy sauce. Add to the pan and cook, stirring, until thickened.

5 Drain the noodles in a colander in the sink. Return to the bowl and add the remaining soy sauce and the sesame seeds. Toss gently to coat.

6 Put the stir-fry on top of the noodles and serve.

Monday chicken sag

SERVES 1

2 tsp sunflower oil
1 small onion, peeled, halved and
thinly sliced
1 tsp mild curry paste or powder
1 small garlic clove, peeled and crushed,
or ½ tsp garlic purée (paste)
2 tbsp water
1 tbsp chopped fresh coriander (cilantro)
1 tomato, finely chopped
Salt
¼ tsp sugar
1 mug of frozen leaf spinach, thawed
A handful of diced cooked chicken
1 cooked potato, cut into small chunks
Naan bread, to serve

1 Heat the oil in a saucepan over a high heat. Fry (sauté) the onion for 3 minutes, stirring.

2 Add the curry paste or powder, the garlic, water, coriander, and tomato and season lightly with salt. Fry for 1 minute.

3 Add the sugar, spinach, chicken and potato, stir well, cover and cook gently for 5 minutes.

4 Tip into a bowl and serve with naan bread.

Winter chicken pot

If you have any cabbage in the fridge, shred a small wedge and add it with the potatoes.

SERVES 1

A knob of butter or margarine
2 chicken thighs
1 small onion, peeled and sliced
1 carrot, peeled and sliced
1 small turnip, sliced
A small handful of pearl barley
or brown rice
1 mug of chicken stock,
made with ½ stock cube
Salt and pepper
1 potato, scrubbed and cut into
bite-sized chunks

1 Melt the butter or margarine in a saucepan over a high heat. Add the chicken and brown on all sides. Remove from the pan with a draining spoon.

2 Add the onion, carrot and turnip and fry (sauté) for 2 minutes, stirring. Add the barley or rice and stock and return the chicken to the pan. Season to taste. Bring to the boil, reduce the heat until gently bubbling round the edges, part-cover and cook for 30 minutes.

3 Add the potatoes, cover and continue cooking for 10 minutes or until everything is tender.

4 Tip into a bowl and serve.

Fast-food chicken chow mein

SERVES 1-2

½ slab of Chinese egg noodles
1 tbsp sunflower oil
1 chicken breast, cut into thin strips
or a handful of chicken stir-fry meat
1 × 425 g/15 oz/large can of stir-fry
mixed vegetables, drained
½ garlic clove, peeled and crushed,
or ¼ tsp garlic purée (paste)
2 tsp soy sauce
2 tsp vinegar
½ tsp ground ginger
2 tsp clear honey

1 Put the noodles in a bowl and cover with boiling water. Stir, then leave to stand while you cook the rest of the dish.

2 Heat the oil in a frying pan (skillet). Add the chicken and stir-fry for 3 minutes until almost cooked.

3 Add the remaining ingredients and stir-fry for a further 3 minutes.

4 Stir the noodles, drain in a colander in the sink, then stir into the frying pan. Heat through for 1–2 minutes, then serve.

Chicken and potato stew

SERVES 1

2 tsp sunflower or olive oil
1 small onion, peeled and chopped
1 chicken portion
1 small garlic clove, peeled and crushed,
or ¹/₂ tsp garlic purée (paste)
¹/₂ mug of water
¹/₂ chicken stock cube
Salt and pepper
¹/₄ tsp dried mixed herbs
1 large tomato, chopped
1 large potato, peeled and cut into
small chunks
A handful of French (green) beans,
topped and tailed and cut in half
Crusty bread, to serve

1 Heat the oil in a saucepan. Add the onion and cook, stirring, for 2 minutes. Add the chicken, skin-side down, and brown for 2 minutes. Turn over and cook the other side for 2 minutes.

2 Add the garlic, water, stock cube, a sprinkling of salt and pepper and the herbs. Bring to the boil, stirring to dissolve the stock cube. Turn down the heat until bubbling gently round the edges, part-cover and cook for 15 minutes.

3 Add the tomato, potato and beans and cook for a further 15 minutes until the chicken and vegetables are tender.

4 Serve with crusty bread.

Warming turkey casserole

If you add a bit more turkey, this is easily enough to serve two people.

SERVES 1

1 tbsp plain (all-purpose) flour
Salt and pepper
A handful of diced turkey thigh meat
2 tsp sunflower oil
1 small onion, peeled and chopped
4 button mushrooms,
left whole or halved
¹/₄ small swede (rutabaga), peeled and
cut into chunks
1 small carrot, cut into chunks
1 small leek, trimmed, washed well and
cut into chunks
1 large potato, cut into chunks
1 mug of beef or vegetable stock,
made with 1 stock cube
¹/₄ tsp dried mixed herbs
Crusty bread, to serve

1 Mix the flour with a little salt and pepper in a plastic bag. Add the turkey, hold the bag closed and shake it to coat all the meat with the flour.

2 Heat the oil in a saucepan over a fairly high heat. Add the turkey and onion and cook, stirring and turning, until the turkey is lightly coloured all over.

3 Add all the other vegetables, then stir in the stock and herbs and bring to the boil, stirring all the time. Turn down the heat until the mixture is only just bubbling round the edges.

4 Cover with a lid and cook for 1–1¹/₂ hours or until everything is really tender, stirring once or twice to prevent sticking. Taste and re-season if necessary.

5 Serve with crusty bread.

Fish, pea and potato fry

SERVES 1

A knob of butter or margarine
1 tbsp sunflower oil
1 large potato, scrubbed and
coarsely grated
Salt and pepper
1 small piece of cod fillet,
about 150 g/5 oz, skinned and cubed,
discarding any bones
1 × 200 g/7 oz/small can of
garden peas, drained
Slices of tomato, to serve

1 Melt the butter or margarine in a fairly small frying pan (skillet) over a moderate heat and add the oil. Add half the grated potato and press down well. Sprinkle with salt and pepper.

2 Scatter the fish and peas over the top, then add the remaining potato. Press down well again. Season lightly. Cover with foil or a lid and cook over a fairly gentle heat for 30 minutes until cooked through and the base is golden brown.

3 Turn the fish cake out on to a plate and serve with sliced tomatoes.

Turkey stir-fry with noodles and beans

You can use cooked leftover chicken for this dish instead of the raw turkey. Simply add it after you have fried the onions and beans.

SERVES 1

A handful of French (green) beans,
½ tbsp oil
½ red (bell) pepper, thinly sliced
A handful of turkey stir-fry meat
1 tsp sugar
1 tsp vinegar
1 tsp soy sauce
A pinch of chilli powder
3 tbsp water
½ slab of Chinese egg noodles

1 Cut off the tops and tails from the beans, then cut each one into three pieces.

2 Heat the oil in a frying pan (skillet). Add the beans, pepper and turkey meat and stir-fry for 5 minutes.

3 Add the sugar, vinegar, soy sauce, chilli powder and water. Cover with a lid or foil, turn down the heat and cook gently for 7 minutes.

4 Put the noodles in a bowl and cover with boiling water. Stir to break up and leave to stand for at least 5 minutes.

5 When the turkey mixture is cooked, drain the noodles and place in a bowl. Top with the turkey and bean mixture and serve.

Smoked fish pot

You can use white fish instead of
smoked, if you prefer.

SERVES 1

A good knob of butter or margarine
1 small onion, peeled and sliced
1 small carrot, peeled and thinly sliced
1 potato, peeled and diced
1 wedge of cabbage, shredded, thick
stalk removed
$^1/_2$ × 400 g/14 oz/large can of
chopped tomatoes
$^1/_2$ mug of chicken or fish stock,
made with $^1/_2$ stock cube
1 small piece of smoked fish fillet,
about 150 g/5 oz,
skinned and cut into chunks
Salt and pepper
Snipped fresh chives or dried chives

1 Melt the butter or margarine in a
saucepan. Add the prepared
vegetables and cook, stirring, for
5 minutes.

2 Add the tomatoes and the stock.
Bring to the boil over a high heat,
reduce the heat to fairly low, cover
with a lid and cook gently for
15 minutes.

3 Add the fish, re-cover and continue
to cook for 5 minutes until the fish
and vegetables are tender. Season to
taste.

4 Serve sprinkled with chives.

Fast fish stew for two

If you're eating alone, simply cool the
leftovers and store in the fridge.
Reheat in a saucepan the next day.

SERVES 2

1 large piece of fish fillet,
about 250 g/9 oz
1 × 400 g/14 oz/large can of
chopped tomatoes
$^1/_2$ mug of water
1 vegetable or chicken stock cube,
crumbled
1 × 275 g/10 oz/medium can of new
potatoes, drained and quartered
1 × 275 g/10 oz/medium can of sliced
carrots, drained
1 × 200 g/7 oz/small can of peas,
drained
Salt and pepper
Crusty bread, to serve

1 Loosen the skin of the fish with a
sharp knife at one end then pull it
off, easing it with the knife, if
necessary (this is much easier if the
fish is frozen).

2 Cut the fish into chunks, discarding
any bones.

3 Put all the remaining ingredients
except the fish into a pan.

4 Bring to the boil over a high heat
and stir gently to dissolve the stock
cube. Add the fish, cover with a lid,
turn down the heat to low and cook
for 5 minutes until the fish is cooked.

5 Stir, taste and re-season if
necessary. Spoon into large bowls and
serve with crusty bread.

Stewed spiced tuna and beans

Eat half one day, half the next, if eating on your own.

SERVES 2

1 × 400 g/14 oz/large can of chopped tomatoes
1 garlic clove, peeled and crushed, or 1 tsp garlic purée (paste)
1 × 425 g/15 oz/large can of mixed beans, drained
1 × 185 g/6½ oz/small can of tuna, drained
¼ tsp chilli powder
Salt and pepper
2 tsp red wine vinegar
½ tsp caster (superfine) sugar
1 tsp snipped fresh chives
Crusty bread, to serve

1 Put everything except half the chives into a saucepan. Bring to the boil over a high heat, stirring, then turn down the heat to moderate and cook for 4 minutes.

2 Stir the mixture and season to taste, if necessary, then spoon into warm bowls.

3 Sprinkle with the remaining chives and serve with crusty bread.

Cheesy cod supper

SERVES 1

1 small piece of cod fillet, about 150 g/5 oz
Salt and pepper
A few drops of Worcestershire sauce
2 tbsp sunflower or olive oil
1 slice of bread
2 tomatoes, sliced
A handful of grated Cheddar cheese
A small handful of cornflakes, crushed
1 × 300 g/11 oz/medium can of French (green) beans

1 Wipe the fish and season with salt and pepper. Sprinkle on both sides with a few drops of Worcestershire sauce.

2 Heat half the oil in a frying pan (skillet). Fry (sauté) the bread on both sides to brown. Remove from the pan and place on a plate.

3 Heat the remaining oil and cook the fish, skin-side up, for 2 minutes. Carefully turn over.

4 Lay the tomato slices on top of the fish. Mix the cheese and cornflakes together and pile on top.

5 Drain the beans, reserving 2 tbsp of the liquid. Arrange the beans round the sides of the fish and add the bean liquid. Turn down the heat. Cover with a lid or foil and cook for 3–5 minutes until the cheese melts and bubbles.

6 Carefully transfer the cheese-topped fish to the fried bread and arrange the beans around.

Smoked trout and mushroom rosti

SERVES 1

A knob of butter or margarine
1 tbsp sunflower oil
1 large potato, scrubbed and
coarsely grated
Salt and pepper
1 small smoked trout fillet,
about 150 g/5 oz, skinned and cubed,
discarding any bones
3 mushrooms, thinly sliced
½ tsp dried basil
5 tbsp passata (sieved tomatoes)

1 Melt the butter or margarine in a fairly small frying pan (skillet) over a moderate heat and add the oil. Add half the grated potato and press down well. Sprinkle with salt and pepper.

2 Scatter the fish and mushrooms over the top, sprinkle with the basil, then add the remaining potato. Press down well again. Season lightly. Cover with foil or a lid and cook over a fairly gentle heat for 30 minutes until cooked through and the base is golden brown.

3 Turn the fish cake out on to a plate. Quickly pour the passata into the pan and heat, stirring until hot.

4 Pour over the potato cake and serve.

Smoked haddock rosti

You can also use smoked cod or whiting for this recipe.

SERVES 1

1 large potato, scrubbed and
coarsely grated
Salt and pepper
1 mug of frozen chopped spinach,
thawed
A knob of butter or margarine
1 tbsp sunflower oil
1 small piece of smoked haddock fillet,
about 150 g/5 oz, skinned and cubed,
discarding any bones
5 tbsp passata (sieved tomatoes)

1 Put the grated potato in a bowl with a little salt and pepper. Squeeze the spinach well to remove excess moisture and add to the potato. Mix well.

2 Melt the butter or margarine in a fairly small frying pan (skillet) over a moderate heat and add the oil. Add half the potato and spinach mixture and press down well.

3 Spread the fish over the top, then add the remaining potato and spinach. Press down well again. Cover with foil or a lid and cook over a fairly gentle heat for 30 minutes until cooked through and the base is golden brown.

4 Turn the fish cake out on to a plate. Quickly add the passata to the pan and heat through. Pour over the cake and serve.

ⓥ Tortilla ⓥ

This is the traditional Spanish omelette. For an extra tasty variation, add a red or green pepper, thinly sliced, to the potatoes before cooking.

SERVES 1

1 tbsp olive oil
1 small onion, peeled and thinly sliced
1 potato, peeled and thinly sliced
2 eggs
Salt and pepper

1 Heat the oil in a small frying pan (skillet) over a fairly high heat.

2 Add the onion and potato and cook gently, stirring, for 2 minutes. Turn down the heat to low, cover with a lid and cook gently for about 8 minutes until softened but not browned, stirring occasionally. Spread out evenly.

3 Break the eggs into a bowl and whisk gently with a wire whisk or fork, adding a little salt and pepper. Pour into the pan. Cook, lifting and stirring until the egg is golden brown underneath and just set.

4 Slide out of the pan on to a plate, then invert back into the pan to cook the other side.

5 Serve hot or cold.

Tuna omelette

SERVES 1

3 eggs
1 tbsp water
Salt and pepper
A small knob of butter or margarine
½ × 185 g/6½ oz/small can of tuna, drained
1 tbsp chopped fresh parsley
2 tsp tomato ketchup (catsup)
A few drops of Worcestershire sauce
Crusty bread and a Mixed Salad (see page 45), to serve

1 Break the eggs into a bowl, add the water with a little salt and pepper. Mix well with a fork or wire whisk until well blended.

2 Melt the butter or margarine in a small omelette pan over a moderate heat. Add the egg mixture and cook, lifting and stirring gently, until the base is golden and the egg mixture is almost set.

3 Mix the tuna with the parsley, ketchup and a few drops of Worcestershire sauce. Spoon over half the omelette. Sprinkle with a little more Worcestershire sauce.

4 Fold the omelette over the filling and cook for a minute or two more to heat through.

5 Slide on to a warm plate and serve with bread and salad.

Camembert and walnut ⓥ omelette ⓥ

Make the salad before you prepare the omelette. An individual portion of Camembert is equivalent to about one-sixth of a whole round one.

SERVES 1

3 eggs
2 tbsp milk
Salt and pepper
1 tbsp sunflower oil
1 small onion, peeled and chopped
A good pinch of dried mixed herbs
A knob of butter or margarine
1 individual portion of Camembert, thinly sliced
1 tbsp chopped walnuts
1 tbsp cranberry sauce (optional)
French bread and a Green Salad (see page 45), to serve

1 Break the eggs into a bowl and whisk with the milk and a little salt and pepper until thoroughly blended.

2 Heat the oil in a frying pan (skillet) and fry (sauté) the onion for 2–3 minutes, stirring until lightly golden and softened.

3 Tip the onion into the egg, add the herbs and mix well.

4 Melt the butter or margarine in the frying pan, pour in the egg mixture and cook, lifting and stirring to allow the uncooked egg to run underneath, until the base is golden brown and the omelette is still creamy on top.

5 Lay the cheese in a single layer over half the omelette, sprinkle with the nuts and dot with cranberry sauce, if using. Cook for 1minute.

6 Tilt the pan slightly, fold the omelette in half and slide on to a plate.

7 Serve with French bread and salad.

ⓥ Egg and vegetable fry ⓥ

If you like Brussels sprouts, they work particularly well in this dish instead of the cabbage – use about eight for one person.

SERVES 1

A knob of butter or margarine
1 tbsp sunflower oil
1 wedge of cabbage, finely shredded and any thick stalk removed
1 small onion, peeled and thinly sliced
1 medium potato, peeled and thinly sliced
1 tomato, sliced
Salt and pepper
2 eggs
Brown table sauce and crusty bread, to serve

1 Heat the butter or margarine and oil in a frying pan (skillet). Add the cabbage, onion and potato and cook, stirring, for 3 minutes until softening slightly.

2 Add the tomato and a sprinkling of salt and pepper. Stir, then cover with a plate, lid or foil. Turn down the heat to fairly low and cook for about 10–15 minutes, stirring once or twice to prevent sticking, until everything is tender.

3 Make two wells in the mixture and break in the eggs. Cover again and cook for 5–10 minutes until the eggs are cooked to your liking.

4 Serve straight from the pan with brown sauce and crusty bread.

Spinach and bacon omelette

SERVES 1

1 mug of frozen chopped spinach, thawed
A good knob of butter or margarine
1 small onion, peeled and chopped
1 rasher (slice) of streaky bacon, rinded and diced
A pinch of dried mixed herbs
Salt and pepper
2 eggs
1 tbsp milk
A Tomato and Onion Salad (see page 46), to serve

1 Put the spinach in a colander and squeeze it well to remove excess moisture.

2 Melt the butter or margarine in a small frying pan (skillet). Add the onion and bacon and cook, stirring, for 2 minutes. Add the spinach and herbs.

3 Break the eggs into a bowl and beat in the milk and some salt and pepper. Pour into the pan and cook, stirring gently, until almost set.

4 Slide the omelette out of the pan on to a plate. Tip it back into the pan, browned side up, and cook for a minute or two to set the other side.

5 Cut into wedges and serve hot or cold with salad.

Ⓥ Mexican eggs Ⓥ

SERVES 1

2 tsp olive or sunflower oil
1 small onion, peeled and chopped
½ aubergine (eggplant), diced
½ small green (bell) pepper, diced
¼ tsp chilli powder
1 × 225 g/8 oz/small can of butter (lima) beans, drained
2 tsp tomato relish
4 tbsp water
Salt and pepper
2 eggs
Tortilla chips and a Green Salad (see page 45), to serve

1 Heat the oil in a frying pan (skillet). Add the onion, aubergine, pepper and chilli powder and fry (sauté), stirring, for 4 minutes until softened.

2 Add the beans, relish, water and some salt and pepper and stir well. Cover and simmer gently for 10 minutes until the vegetables are tender and nearly all the liquid has evaporated.

3 Make a well for each egg in the mixture and break an egg into each. Cover with a lid or foil and cook for 5–10 minutes until cooked to your liking.

4 Serve with tortilla chips and salad.

Sausage, potato and sweetcorn skillet

A jar of passata will keep in the fridge for a week or more.

SERVES 1

2 tsp sunflower oil
2–3 chipolata sausages, cut into chunks
1 × 300 g/11 oz/medium can of
new potatoes, drained
A good pinch of dried mixed herbs
Salt and pepper
5 tbsp passata (sieved tomatoes)
1 × 200 g/7 oz/small can of sweetcorn
(corn), drained
Crusty bread, to serve

1 Heat the oil in a frying pan (skillet). Add the sausages and fry (sauté) for 2 minutes, stirring, until the fat runs.

2 Add the potatoes and continue to fry and stir for 5 minutes until golden.

3 Add the herbs, a sprinkling of salt and pepper, the passata and sweetcorn. Stir well, cover with a lid or foil, then turn down the heat and cook for a further 5 minutes.

4 Spoon into a bowl and eat with lots of crusty bread.

Pan-scrambled eggs with beans and bacon

SERVES 1

1 thick slice of bread
A knob of butter or margarine
2 rashers (slices) of bacon,
rinded and chopped
2 eggs
Salt and pepper
2 tbsp milk or single (light) cream
1 × 225 g/8 oz/small can of
butter (lima) beans, drained

1 Spread the bread with half the butter or margarine. Fry (sauté) in a frying pan (skillet) on both sides until golden. Remove from the pan and keep warm.

2 Add the bacon to the pan and fry for 2 minutes, stirring, until cooked through.

3 Break the eggs into a bowl and whisk in just a pinch of salt, lots of pepper and the milk or cream.

4 Pour the egg mixture into the pan, add the beans and cook over a moderate heat, stirring all the time, until scrambled.

5 Spoon the egg mixture on to the toast and serve.

Sausage soup

This will feed one very hungry person, or two ordinary human beings. If serving two, use the whole can of beans. If for one, store the remaining beans in a covered container in the fridge and mix with mayonnaise or a little oil and vinegar as a salad with some tuna or diced cheese.

SERVES 1–2

A knob of butter or margarine
2 thick pork sausages, cut into
small chunks
1 onion, peeled and thinly sliced
1½ mugs of beef stock,
made with 1 stock cube
1 tsp Dijon mustard
A good pinch of dried sage
1 × 425 g/15 oz/large can of haricot
(navy) beans, drained
Salt and pepper
1 small handful of grated
Cheddar cheese
Crusty bread, to serve

1 Melt the butter or margarine in a large saucepan over a fairly high heat, add the sausages and onions and brown, stirring all the time, for 3–4 minutes.

2 Add the stock, mustard and the sage, bring to the boil, reduce the heat until gently bubbling around the edges, and cook for 15 minutes. Add the beans and cook for a further 5 minutes. Season to taste.

3 Stir in the cheese until melted and serve piping hot with crusty bread.

French-style stir-fry

Look out in the supermarket for bacon pieces – the off-cuts from sliced bacon. They're cheap and ideal for any recipe calling for diced bacon. Simply remove any rinds and cut into small, even-sized pieces.

The cheese should be kept in the fridge until you're ready to use it, or it will become runny.

Use the other half of the packet of stir-fry vegetables for the recipes on page 192 or 208.

SERVES 1

1 tbsp sunflower oil
2–3 rashers (slices) of streaky bacon,
rinded and diced
1 small onion, thinly sliced
½ × 450 g/1 lb packet of ready-prepared
stir-fry vegetables with beansprouts
1 individual portion of Camembert
or Brie, cut into small dice
2 tsp soy sauce
1 tsp balsamic vinegar
1–2 large crisp lettuce leaves
French bread, to serve

1 Heat the oil in a large frying pan (skillet). Add the bacon and onion and fry (sauté), stirring, for 4 minutes until golden.

2 Add the stir-fry vegetables and cook, lifting and stirring, for 4 minutes.

3 Add the cheese, soy sauce and balsamic vinegar and stir gently for 30 seconds until the cheese is melting, adding a little more soy or vinegar, if you like.

4 Put the lettuce leaves on a plate. Spoon the stir-fry on top and serve straight away with French bread.

Extra-goodness quarter-pounders

Make two, then either share them with a mate or keep one raw, wrapped in clingfilm or foil, in the fridge to cook the next day. You can grill the burgers, if you prefer.

MAKES 2

1 small onion
1 carrot
2 good handfuls of minced (ground) beef
1 Weetabix
½ tsp tomato purée (paste)
1 tsp Worcestershire sauce
Salt and pepper
1 egg, beaten
2 tbsp sunflower oil
2 burger buns
Tomato ketchup (catsup), mustard and salad, to serve

1 Peel the onion and carrot and grate them into a mixing bowl.

2 Add the beef. Crumble in the Weetabix and add the tomato purée, Worcestershire sauce and a sprinkling of salt and pepper.

3 Mix well with your hands (or a wooden spoon, if you prefer). Add the egg and mix again thoroughly.

4 Shape the mixture into two burgers. Chill in the fridge until ready to cook.

5 Heat the oil in a frying pan (skillet). When hot but not smoking (see page 35), add the burgers and fry (sauté) for about 5 minutes on each side until golden and cooked through, pressing down gently with a fish slice during cooking.

6 Serve each burger in a bun, spread with ketchup and mustard, if liked, with plenty of salad on the side.

Crispy chilli con carne tacos

SERVES 1

¼ quantity of Chilli con Carne
(see page 121)
3–4 corn taco shells
Shredded lettuce
Chopped tomato
Chopped cucumber
Chopped onion
Soured (dairy sour) cream
or plain yoghurt
Grated Cheddar cheese

1 Prepare the Chilli con Carne.

2 Warm the tacos as directed on the packet.

3 Fill the tacos with the chilli and top with a little lettuce, chopped tomato, cucumber and onion, a small spoonful of soured cream or yoghurt and a little grated cheese.

Crispy chilli bean tacos

SERVES 1

1 small green chilli
or ¼ tsp chilli powder
1 × 425 g/15 oz/large can of
red kidney beans
½ small green (bell) pepper, diced
½ garlic clove, peeled and crushed,
or ½ tsp garlic purée (paste)
3–4 corn taco shells
A handful of shredded lettuce
3–4 spoonfuls of plain yoghurt

1 If using a fresh chilli, cut it in half and remove all the seeds and the stalk. Chop finely.

2 Drain the kidney beans in a colander. Rinse with cold water and drain again. Tip into a saucepan and mash with a fork.

3 Add the pepper, garlic and chilli or chilli powder. Heat, stirring, until hot through.

4 Spoon the mixture into taco shells, top each with some shredded lettuce and a spoonful of yoghurt.

Sausage burger with melted cheese filling

If eating on your own, cook only one burger. Wrap the other in foil or clingfilm and store in the fridge for up to 3 days. The remaining sausagemeat can be rolled into balls and cooked like sausages. Alternatively, make more burgers and freeze them – they will keep for up to 2 months.

MAKES 2

½ × 450 g/1 lb packet of
pork sausagemeat
2 Baby Bel cheeses, rinds removed
A little sunflower oil
2 burger buns
Tomato relish
Slices of cucumber
Plain potato crisps (chips) and a Mixed
Salad (see page 45), to serve

1 Divide the sausagemeat into four portions and flatten each to a cake about 5 mm/¼ in thick.

2 Put a cheese in the centre of two of the cakes and top with the remaining cakes, squeezing the edges well together to seal the cheeses inside.

3 Put a few drops of oil in a frying pan (skillet) and wipe round with a piece of kitchen paper (paper towel) to spread over the base. Heat, and when hot but not smoking add the burgers and fry (sauté) for 4–5 minutes on each side until crisp and golden on the outside and cooked through. Drain on kitchen paper.

4 Spread the buns with tomato relish, add the burgers and top with sliced cucumber. Serve with potato crisps and salad.

Chilli winter warmer

Tip any leftover soup into a rigid container. Cover, cool, then store in the fridge.

SERVES 2–4

2 onions, peeled and finely chopped
2 carrots, peeled and finely chopped
2 handfuls of minced (ground) beef
¹/₂ tsp chilli powder
1 tbsp tomato puree (paste)
4 mugs of beef stock,
made with 2 stock cubes
1 tsp yeast extract
¹/₂ tsp dried oregano
Salt and pepper
¹/₂ mug of small pasta shapes
1 tbsp cornflour (cornstarch)

1 Put the onions, carrots and beef in a large saucepan and cook over a fairly high heat, stirring, until the grains of meat are separate and no longer pink.

2 Add everything except the pasta and cornflour. Bring to the boil, stirring over a high heat, reduce the heat until gently bubbling around the edges and cook for 20 minutes, stirring occasionally.

3 Add the pasta and cook for a further 10 minutes.

4 Mix the cornflour in a cup with 2 tbsp of water until smooth. Stir into the soup, turn up the heat and bring back to the boil. Continue to cook, stirring, for 1 minute. Season to taste, then serve.

Corned beef hash

If you have some leftover cooked potatoes, use them instead. You can use a small can of corned beef, but it's nearly as expensive as a large one, so I recommend buying the bigger one and using the other half for stuffed pancakes (see page 258), toasted sandwiches (see pages 84–5) or the salad recipe on page 59. If you use half a larger can of beans, store the remainder in the fridge in a covered container and use within 3 days.

SERVES 1

1 tbsp sunflower oil
1 large potato, peeled and finely diced
1 small onion, peeled and
finely chopped
¹/₂ × 350 g/12 oz/large can of corned beef, diced
1 × 225 g/8 oz/small can of baked beans
A good pinch dried oregano
1 tsp brown table sauce
Salt and pepper
Crusty bread and a Green Salad
(see page 45), to serve

1 Heat the oil in a large frying pan (skillet) over a fairly high heat. Add the potato and onion and cook, stirring, for 2 minutes. Cover with a lid, turn down the heat to low and cook for 10 minutes, stirring occasionally.

2 Add the remaining ingredients and cook, stirring, for 5 minutes. Press down and cook for a further 5 minutes until crispy and golden underneath.

3 Serve the hash with crusty bread and the salad.

Moroccan lamb

Couscous is easy to cook and makes a very impressive dish with this delicious lamb casserole. You can buy bags of frozen stewing lamb, so you can store it in the freezer for another day. If you haven't got the fresh herbs, use ½ tsp of dried mixed herbs and add it all at Step 3.

SERVES 1

A good handful of diced stewing lamb
1 small onion, peeled and
cut into wedges
½ small garlic clove, peeled and crushed,
or ¼ tsp garlic purée (paste)
½ green chilli, seeded and chopped
A good pinch of ground cinnamon
A good pinch of ground ginger
Salt and pepper
1 mug of lamb or chicken stock,
made with ½ stock cube
1 tsp tomato purée (paste)
½ mug of couscous
4 ready-to-eat dried apricots, halved
1 small courgette (zucchini), diced
1 small carrot, peeled and diced
½ green (bell) pepper, diced
2 tsp chopped fresh coriander (cilantro)
2 tsp chopped fresh parsley

1 Put the lamb and onion in a large saucepan with the garlic, chilli, spices, a little salt and pepper, the stock and tomato purée. Bring to the boil, stirring over a high heat. Reduce the heat until just bubbling gently round the edges, cover and cook gently for 1½ hours, stirring occasionally.

2 While it is cooking, put the couscous in a bowl with just enough boiling water to cover. Cover with a plate or lid and leave to stand.

3 Add the apricots and vegetables to the lamb mixture with half the fresh herbs. Cover and cook for a further 15 minutes.

4 Stir the couscous with a fork to fluff it up. If necessary, boil the stew rapidly without a lid, stirring all the time, to reduce the liquid to a thick sauce. Taste and re-season, if necessary.

5 Spoon the couscous on to a plate. Spoon the lamb mixture on top and sprinkle with the remaining herbs before serving.

Butter beans with tomatoes ⓥ and cheese ⓥ

If this is too much for one meal, cool the remainder and store it in a covered container in the fridge. It's delicious cold or reheated.

SERVES 1–2

1 × 425 g/15 oz/large can of
butter (lima) beans
½ × 400 g/14 oz/large can of
chopped tomatoes
1 tbsp tomato purée (paste)
1 small garlic clove, peeled and crushed,
or ½ tsp garlic purée (paste)
½ tsp sugar
Salt and pepper
A good handful of grated
Cheddar cheese
A Green Salad (see page 45) and crusty
bread, to serve

1 Drain the beans and place in a saucepan with all the remaining ingredients except the cheese.

2 Heat gently, stirring until piping hot.

3 Stir in the cheese until melted.

4 Serve with the salad and crusty bread.

Pork with cabbage and caraway

You'll have to buy at least half a small white cabbage so use the rest for coleslaw (see page 47), or a Village Salad (see page 45). Alternatively, add it to a soup or cook it as a vegetable with any fried or grilled meat or chicken.

SERVES 1

¼ small white cabbage
1 potato, peeled and thinly sliced
2 tsp sunflower oil
1 pork shoulder chop
1 tsp caraway seeds
Salt and pepper
½ chicken stock cube
¼ mug of boiling water

1 Thinly shred the cabbage, discarding any tough central core and damaged outer leaves.

2 Cook the potato slices in boiling, lightly salted water in a frying pan (skillet) for about 4 minutes until almost cooked. Drain in a colander in the sink and reserve.

3 In the same frying pan, heat the oil and When hot but not smoking (see page 35), fry (sauté) the chop on both sides to brown. Take out of the pan.

4 Add the cabbage to the pan and cook, stirring and turning it over in the oil, for 2 minutes until beginning to soften. Press down with a fish slice.

5 Put the chop back on top and sprinkle with the caraway seeds and a little salt and pepper. Cover with a layer of the sliced potatoes.

6 Mix the half stock cube with the boiling water until dissolved. Pour into the pan. Cover with a lid or foil and cook over a fairly gentle heat for 30 minutes until the meat and cabbage are tender.

7 Spoon on to a plate and serve.

Cheesy sweetcorn
Ⓥ mash Ⓥ

SERVES 1

1 large potato, peeled and
cut into small chunks
A good knob of butter or margarine
1 × 200 g/7 oz/small can of
sweetcorn (corn)
A good handful of grated
Cheddar cheese
Salt and pepper

1 Boil the potato in plenty of boiling water with a pinch of salt added for about 10 minutes until tender. Drain and return to the pan. Mash with the butter or margarine, using a potato masher or fork.

2 Beat in the corn, cheese and some salt and pepper and serve.

Pork and vegetable stir-fry with rice noodles

Rice noodles are white and semi-transparent. Like egg noodles, they cook very quickly.

SERVES 1

$^1/_4$ × 250 g/9 oz packet of rice noodles
1–2 belly pork slices
1 tbsp sunflower oil
2 spring onions (scallions), trimmed and cut into short lengths
1 carrot, peeled and cut into matchsticks
4 mushrooms, sliced
5 cm/2 in piece of cucumber, cut into matchsticks
1 tbsp vinegar
1 tbsp soy sauce
2 tsp sugar
$^1/_4$ tsp Chinese five-spice powder
Pepper

1 Put the noodles in a bowl and cover with boiling water. Leave to stand while you cook the pork.

2 Using scissors or a sharp knife, cut the rind and any bones from the belly pork, then cut it into bite-sized pieces.

3 Heat the oil in a frying pan (skillet). Add the pork and stir-fry for 4 minutes.

4 Add the vegetables and stir-fry for a further 4 minutes.

5 Add the remaining ingredients and the noodles. Lift and stir gently until everything is blended.

6 Taste and add a little more soy sauce, if liked, then serve.

French-style cannellini ⓥ beans ⓥ

You can use cider or apple juice instead of the white wine.

SERVES 1

1 onion, thinly sliced
1 tbsp olive oil
1 small garlic clove, peeled and crushed, or $^1/_2$ tsp garlic purée (paste)
$^1/_2$ × 400 g/14 oz/large can of chopped tomatoes
1 tbsp tomato purée
$^1/_2$ tsp caster (superfine) sugar
1 tbsp white wine
$^1/_4$ tsp dried mixed herbs
1 × 425 g/15 oz/large can of cannellini beans, drained
6 stoned (pitted) black olives, halved
1 tbsp chopped fresh parsley
Crusty bread, to serve

1 Put the onions and oil in a saucepan and fry (sauté) for 4 minutes, stirring, until golden.

2 Add the garlic, tomatoes, tomato purée, sugar, wine and herbs. Cook over a high heat until the mixture is boiling, turn down to moderate and continue to cook for 5 minutes, stirring occasionally, until pulpy.

3 Stir in the beans, olives and half the parsley and cook for 5 minutes, stirring.

4 Sprinkle with the remaining parsley and serve with crusty bread.

Warming Baltic stew

If you're eating alone, keep the remainder in the fridge and reheat in a saucepan the following day.

SERVES 2

2 tbsp sunflower or olive oil
1 leek, trimmed, halved, washed well
and chopped
½ garlic clove, peeled and crushed,
or ½ tsp garlic purée (paste)
1 onion, peeled and chopped
½ small green cabbage, shredded and
any thick stalk removed
1 smoked pork ring, thickly sliced
1 mug of water
1 chicken stock cube
1 large potato, peeled and cut into dice
½ tsp dried mixed herbs
Salt and pepper
1 tsp poppy seeds
1 tsp dried chives
Crusty bread, to serve

1 Heat the oil in a large saucepan over a fairly high heat. Add the leek, garlic and onion and fry (sauté), stirring, for 3 minutes.

2 Stir the cabbage into the pot and cook for a further 2 minutes until beginning to soften slightly.

3 Add all the remaining ingredients except the poppy seeds and chives, then stir well, turn down the heat until gently bubbling round the edges, cover and cook for 30 minutes until everything is tender.

4 Taste the stew and re-season, if necessary.

5 Sprinkle with the seeds and chives and serve with lots of crusty bread.

Greek-style
Ⓥ mushrooms Ⓥ

SERVES 1

2 tbsp olive or sunflower oil
1 small onion, peeled and chopped
½ mug of dry white wine
1 bay leaf
A good pinch of dried oregano
½ garlic clove, peeled and crushed,
or ½ tsp garlic purée (paste)
8 small button mushrooms
½ × 400 g/14 oz/large can of
chopped tomatoes
Crusty bread and a Green Salad
(see page 45), to serve

1 Heat the oil in a large saucepan. Add the onion and cook over a fairly gentle heat for 3 minutes until softened but not browned, stirring all the time.

2 Add the wine, bay leaf, oregano, garlic, mushrooms and tomatoes and bring to the boil over a high heat. Turn down the heat until just bubbling gently round the edges and cook for 15 minutes. Leave to cool slightly, then remove the bay leaf.

3 Spoon into a bowl and serve warm with crusty bread and salad. Alternatively, leave until cold, then chill before serving.

Frankfurters with chunky tomato sauce

If you use part of a larger can of tomatoes, store them in a covered container in the fridge for use in another recipe. The remaining frankfurters can also be stored for another recipe.

SERVES 1

1 small onion, peeled and chopped
2 tsp sunflower or olive oil
½ × 400 g/14 oz/large can of
chopped tomatoes
½ small garlic clove, peeled and crushed,
or ¼ tsp garlic purée
A good pinch of dried sage
or mixed herbs
¼ tsp Dijon mustard
Salt and pepper
½ tsp clear honey
4 frankfurters from a can
or 2 larger vacuum-packed ones
Crusty bread, to serve

1 Put the onion and oil in a saucepan and cook over a fairly high heat, stirring, for 2 minutes to soften.

2 Add the tomatoes, garlic, herbs, mustard, a little salt and pepper and the sugar. Bring to the boil and simmer for 5 minutes, stirring until pulpy.

3 Add the frankfurters and heat through for 3 minutes.

4 Serve with crusty bread.

Sweet and sour beans

True vegetarians will need to buy their Worcestershire sauce from a health food shop – the traditional one contains anchovies.

SERVES 1

A good handful of French (green) beans,
topped and tailed
½ slab of Chinese egg noodles
A large knob of butter or margarine
1 small onion, peeled and sliced
4–6 button mushrooms, sliced
2 tsp Worcestershire sauce
2 tsp soy sauce
2 tsp clear honey
2 tsp wine vinegar

1 Cut the beans into short lengths. Bring a saucepan of water to the boil over a high heat. Add a pinch of salt and the beans and noodles. Bring back to the boil, then boil for 5 minutes until just tender, stirring occasionally. Drain in a colander in the sink.

2 Melt the butter or margarine in the same saucepan. Add the onion and cook, stirring, for 2 minutes. Add the mushrooms and cook for a further 2 minutes.

3 Add the Worcestershire sauce, soy sauce, honey and vinegar and stir well. Return the runner beans and noodles to the pan. Cook over a low heat, stirring gently, for 2 minutes until piping hot.

4 Serve in a bowl.

ⓥ Vegetable dolmas ⓥ

It's difficult to make this for one person without having a lot of ratatouille left over, so make it when friends come round or eat some and have the rest cold or reheated over the next couple of days. If you're really hungry, you'll probably manage three or even four rolls!

SERVES 4

8 large outer cabbage leaves
1 × 425 g/15 oz/large can of ratatouille
2 tbsp long-grain rice
1 mug of vegetable stock,
made with 1 stock cube
1 tbsp tomato purée (paste)
Salt and pepper
A handful of grated Cheddar cheese
Crusty bread, to serve

1 Cut a V-shape out of the base of the thick stalk on each of the cabbage leaves.

2 Bring a pan of water to the boil. Drop in the leaves and blanch for 3 minutes. Drain, rinse with cold water and drain again. Dry on kitchen paper (paper towels).

3 Mix the ratatouille with the rice.

4 Lay a leaf on a chopping board and draw together the two points where the stalk was, so that they overlap. Put an eighth of the filling on top. Fold in the sides and roll up, then place in a flameproof casserole (Dutch oven) or heavy-based saucepan.

5 Repeat with the remaining cabbage leaves and filling.

6 Mix the stock and tomato purée together and pour around the cabbage rolls. Season lightly.

7 Bring to the boil, cover, reduce the heat until bubbling very gently round the edges and cook for about 30 minutes or until the cabbage and rice are tender. Transfer to warm plates and spoon any juices over.

8 Sprinkle with grated cheese and serve with lots of crusty bread.

Cheese-topped
ⓥ aubergine layer ⓥ

This is a version of moussaka, cooked in a frying pan. If it is too much for one, cool one portion and store in the fridge. Reheat in the microwave on High (100 per cent power) for about 3 minutes or on a plate, covered with another plate or a saucepan lid over a pan of simmering water for 10 minutes.

SERVES 1-2

1 small aubergine (eggplant), sliced
2 tbsp olive oil
6 tbsp water
1 small onion, peeled and chopped
½ mug minced (ground) lamb
½ garlic clove, peeled and crushed,
or ½ tsp garlic purée (paste)
Salt and pepper
¼ tsp dried basil
½ mug of passata (sieved tomatoes)
½ tsp sugar
1 egg
½ tub of soft white cheese,
such as Philadelphia
1 tbsp milk
A Mixed Salad (see page 45),
to serve

1 Put the aubergine in a bowl and add the oil. Mix with your hands until the slices are coated.

2 Heat a small frying pan (skillet). Add the aubergine slices and fry (sauté) for 1 minute on each side. Add the water and cook for a further 2–3 minutes until the water is absorbed and the aubergine is tender. Remove from the pan.

3 Add the onion, lamb and garlic to the pan. Cook, stirring, until the meat is no longer pink and all the grains are separate.

4 Add a sprinkling of salt and pepper, the basil, passata and sugar. Cook over a high heat, stirring, until bubbling, turn down the heat to moderate and continue to cook, stirring occasionally, for 5 minutes. Turn the heat down low.

5 Arrange the aubergine slices over the top.

6 Whisk the egg with a fork or balloon whisk and whisk in the cheese and milk. Sprinkle with a little salt and pepper and spoon over the aubergine.

7 Cover the pan with foil or a lid and cook gently for 12–15 minutes until the topping is set.

8 Serve with a Mixed Salad.

Sweet and sour peanut
ⓥ stir-fry ⓥ

Ideally, cook this for two people – by doubling all the ingredients – and so use the whole can of pineapple. If not, store it in the fridge in a covered container and use within 3 days.

SERVES 1

½ slab of Chinese egg noodles
1 tbsp sunflower oil
½ red (bell) pepper
½ bunch of spring onions (scallions)
4 mushrooms, sliced
½ × 225 g/8 oz/small can of
pineapple pieces
1 tbsp tomato purée (paste)
1 tbsp soy sauce
1 tbsp wine vinegar
1 tbsp clear honey
2 tbsp water
1½ tsp cornflour (cornstarch)
Pepper
½ mug of beansprouts
A good handful of raw peanuts

1 Put the noodles in a bowl. Cover with boiling water, stir, then leave to stand while you cook the stir-fry.

2 Heat the oil in a wok or large frying pan (skillet).

3 Add the pepper, spring onions and mushrooms and stir-fry for 3–4 minutes.

4 Add the pineapple and its juice, the tomato purée, soy sauce, vinegar and honey.

5 Mix the water and cornflour together in a cup and stir in. Bring to the boil and cook for 1 minute, stirring.

6 Add the beansprouts and nuts and stir in carefully. Cook for a further 2–3 minutes.

7 Drain the noodles. Spoon into a bowl and spoon the stir-fry over.

ⓥ Pea and lentil curry ⓥ

Make this as hot or mild as you like by adjusting the amount of curry powder or paste.

SERVES 1–2

1 onion, peeled and sliced
3 tbsp sunflower oil
1 large potato, scrubbed and diced
2 tsp curry powder or paste
⅔ mug of vegetable stock,
made with ½ stock cube
1 × 425 g/15 oz/large can of green or
brown lentils, drained
1 × 275 g/10 oz/medium can of
garden peas, drained
Salt and pepper
1 small carton of plain yoghurt
Naan bread, to serve

1 Fry (sauté) the onion in the oil for 2 minutes in a large saucepan. Add the potato and curry powder or paste and cook, stirring, for 3 minutes.

2 Add the stock, cover with a lid, turn down the heat and cook gently for 5 minutes or until the potato is tender.

3 Stir in the lentils, peas, some salt and pepper and the yoghurt. Continue to cook gently, uncovered, for a further 15 minutes until everything is tender and bathed in sauce. The mixture will curdle before it blends and thickens.

4 Taste and add more salt and pepper if necessary. Serve hot with naan bread.

Farmhouse main-meal potage

Any remaining soup can be cooled, then kept in a covered container in the fridge for up to 3 days.

SERVES 2

A knob of butter or margarine
1 onion, peeled and cut into small dice
1 carrot, peeled and cut into small dice
1 potato, peeled and cut into small dice
1½ mugs of chicken stock,
made with 1 stock cube
1 × 400 g/14 oz/large can of
chopped tomatoes
1 × 400 g/14 oz/large can of
baked beans
A good pinch of dried oregano
Salt and pepper
2 small handfuls of grated
Cheddar cheese
Bread, to serve

1 Melt the butter or margarine in a saucepan over a fairly high heat. Fry (sauté) the diced vegetables for 2 minutes, stirring.

2 Add the stock, bring to the boil, then reduce the heat until gently bubbling around the edges, part-cover and cook for 15 minutes.

3 Add the tomatoes, beans, oregano and seasoning, turn up the heat and bring back to the boil, then turn it down again as before and cook for a further 5 minutes. Taste and re-season, if necessary.

4 Ladle into warm bowls, sprinkle with grated cheese and serve with bread.

Ⓥ Baked bean hash Ⓥ

Large cans of beans are better value than small ones. If you're really hungry, you can use the whole lot, but if not, you can store the unused half in a covered container in the fridge for later use. This is also good topped with fried eggs.

SERVES 1

A knob of butter or margarine
1 large potato, peeled and cut into
small pieces
1 small onion, peeled and chopped
½ × 400 g/14 oz/large can of
baked beans
1 tsp brown table sauce
Salt and pepper
A little chopped fresh parsley
or a few dried chives
Crusty bread, to serve

1 Heat the butter or margarine in a frying pan (skillet) over a fairly high heat. Add the potato and onion and fry (sauté), stirring, for 2 minutes.

2 Cover with a lid, turn down the heat to low and cook for 10 minutes, stirring once or twice until the potatoes are soft.

3 Add the beans, sauce and some salt and pepper and cook, stirring, for 2–3 minutes.

4 Spoon into a warm bowl, sprinkle with parsley or chives and serve with crusty bread.

Ⓥ Black-eyed bean tacos Ⓥ

If you like avocado, try adding half a small one, peeled and chopped, to the mixture instead of the cucumber.

SERVES 1–2

1 tbsp olive oil
1 small onion, peeled and
finely chopped
1 × 425 g/15 oz/large can of black-eyed
beans, drained
½ tsp hot chilli sauce
1 tomato, diced
2.5 cm/1 in piece of cucumber, diced
4 taco shells
A good handful of grated
Cheddar cheese

1 Heat the oil in a large frying pan (skillet) over a fairly high heat. Add the onion and cook, stirring, for 3 minutes until golden. Turn down the heat to moderate.

2 Add the beans and mash with a fork or potato masher. Fry (sauté), stirring, for 2 minutes.

3 Stir in the tomato, cucumber and chilli sauce. Heat through, stirring.

4 Spoon into the taco shells and top with grated cheese.

Ⓥ Cheesy dhal Ⓥ

The fresh herbs are optional, but they do make it taste much better.

SERVES 1

A good knob of butter or margarine
2 tsp sunflower oil
1 small onion, peeled and chopped
½ tsp mild curry powder or paste
¼ mug of red lentils
¾ mug of water
½ vegetable stock cube
1 small bay leaf
Salt and pepper
2.5 cm/1 in finger of mild Cheddar
cheese, cubed
1 tsp chopped fresh coriander (cilantro)
or parsley
Garlic and coriander naan bread,
to serve

1 Heat the butter or margarine in a saucepan. Add the onion and cook, stirring, for 2 minutes.

2 Stir in the curry powder or paste, lentils, water, stock cube, bay leaf and seasoning. Cook until bubbling, then turn down the heat, cover and cook gently for 20 minutes, stirring occasionally, until the lentils are tender and have absorbed the liquid, adding a little more water, if necessary.

3 Stir in the cheese and continue to heat until the cheese is just beginning to melt. Spoon the dhal into a bowl, sprinkle with the coriander or parsley and serve straight away with the naan bread.

Ⓥ Falafels Ⓥ

These are also delicious cold. Try them with sticks of carrot, cucumber or cherry tomatoes.

MAKES 20

1 large onion
1 × 425 g/15 oz/large can of chick peas (garbanzos), drained
1 garlic clove, peeled and crushed, or 1 tsp garlic purée (paste)
1 tsp ground coriander (cilantro)
1 tsp ground cumin
1 egg, beaten
2 tbsp milk
5 tbsp plain (all-purpose) flour
Oil, for deep-frying
Fresh Tomato and Pimento Salsa (see page 75) and salad stuffs of your choice, to serve

1 Peel and grate the onion into a bowl.

2 Add the chick peas and garlic and mash thoroughly with a potato masher or fork (or use a hand blender).

3 Stir in the coriander, cumin and half the beaten egg. Squeeze thoroughly together, then shape into 20 small balls.

4 Whisk the remaining beaten egg with the milk on a plate. Put the flour on a separate plate. Roll the balls in the flour, then the egg and milk, then the flour again. Chill for at least 30 minutes, if possible.

5 Heat about 2.5 cm/1 in oil in a frying pan (skillet). When hot but not smoking (see page 35), deep-fry the balls for about 3 minutes, turning once until crisp and golden. Drain on kitchen paper (paper towels).

6 Serve warm with Fresh Tomato and Pimento Salsa and salad.

Ⓥ Rice and corn cakes Ⓥ

SERVES 1-2

¼ mug of long-grain rice
½ tsp ground turmeric
1 × 200 g/7 oz/small can of sweetcorn (corn), drained
2 eggs, beaten
Salt and pepper
A good pinch of chilli powder
A little sunflower oil
Eastern Tomato Salad (see page 46), to serve

1 Cook the rice according to the packet directions, adding the turmeric to the cooking water. Drain and return to the pan.

2 Stir in the sweetcorn, eggs, some salt and pepper and the chilli powder.

3 Heat about 5 mm/¼ in oil in a large frying pan (skillet). Drop in spoonfuls of the mixture and fry (sauté) for about 2 minutes on each side until golden brown and set.

4 Drain on kitchen paper (paper towels) and keep warm while cooking the remainder.

5 Serve with Eastern Tomato Salad.

Corn, pepper and cheese Ⓥ fritters Ⓥ

It's not worth making less than this amount. If you are eating on your own, leave any leftovers to get cold, then wrap in foil and store in the fridge. Reheat by frying in a little hot oil for a minute or two the next day.

SERVES 2

Sunflower or olive oil for cooking
1 red (bell) pepper, chopped
1 leek, trimmed, washed well
and chopped
½ mug of plain (all-purpose) flour
A good pinch of salt
1 tbsp baking powder
7–8 tbsp water
1 × 200 g/7 oz/small can of sweetcorn
(corn), drained
1 cm/½ in finger of Edam (Dutch) or
Cheddar cheese, cut into small dice
A Mixed Salad (see page 45), to serve

1 Heat 1 tbsp of oil in a frying pan (skillet) over a fairly high heat and fry (sauté) the pepper and leek, stirring, for 2–3 minutes until lightly golden. Remove the pan from the heat.

2 Mix the flour, salt and baking powder in a bowl. Using a wire whisk, stir in enough of the water to form a thick, creamy batter. Stir in the pepper mixture with any fat and juices, then the sweetcorn and cheese.

3 Wipe out the frying pan with kitchen paper (paper towels), then heat about 5 mm/¼ in oil in the pan. When hot but not smoking (see page 35), drop in spoonfuls of the batter. Fry for 2–3 minutes until golden underneath. Turn over with a fish slice and cook for 2 minutes or until crisp.

4 Drain on kitchen paper and serve with the salad.

Ⓥ Pan dauphinoise Ⓥ

SERVES 1

1 large potato, thinly sliced
A knob of butter or margarine
1 small garlic clove, peeled and crushed,
or ½ tsp garlic purée (paste)
A good handful of grated Emmental
(Swiss) or Cheddar cheese
Salt and pepper
1 egg
5 tbsp single (light) cream, crème
fraîche, plain yoghurt or milk

1 Put the potato slices in a frying pan (skillet). Cover with water, bring to the boil and boil for 4 minutes. Drain in a colander in the sink.

2 Wipe out the pan with kitchen paper (paper towels). Spread the butter or margarine all over the base.

3 Layer the potato slices with tiny flecks of the garlic, the cheese and salt and pepper.

4 Break the egg into a small bowl and add the cream, crème fraîche, yoghurt or milk. Whisk with a fork or balloon whisk until well blended and pour over the potatoes and cheese.

5 Cook over a high heat until beginning to bubble round the edges, then turn down the heat, cover with a lid, plate or foil and cook for 30 minutes until set. If liked, flash under a hot grill (broiler) to brown.

ⓥ Fasoulia ⓥ

SERVES 1–2

2 tbsp olive oil
1 onion, peeled and finely chopped
1 garlic clove, peeled and crushed,
or 1 tsp garlic purée (paste)
1 bay leaf
½ tsp dried oregano
1 large tomato, chopped
1 tbsp tomato purée
1 tbsp lemon juice
1 × 425 g/15 oz/large can of haricot
(navy) beans, drained
Salt and pepper
1 tbsp chopped fresh parsley

1 Heat the oil in a saucepan over a moderate heat. Add the onion and garlic and cook for 2–3 minutes until softened but not browned.

2 Add all the remaining ingredients except the parsley, stir well and cook over a moderate heat for 10 minutes, stirring gently.

3 Leave to cool, then remove the bay leaf. Taste and re-season if necessary. Sprinkle with chopped parsley and serve cold.

Chick pea and pepperami goulash

This is very substantial for one person but you can cool and store any leftovers in a covered container in the fridge and reheat the following day.

SERVES 1–2

1 tbsp olive or sunflower oil
1 small onion, peeled and chopped
2 tsp paprika
A good pinch of dried mixed herbs
1 garlic clove, peeled and crushed,
or 1 tsp garlic purée (paste)
1 × 400 g/14 oz/large can of
chopped tomatoes
1 × 425 g/15 oz/large can of chick peas
(garbanzos), drained
1 pepperami stick, cut into small chunks
1–2 spoonfuls of plain yoghurt
Crusty bread and a Green Salad
(see page 45), to serve

1 Heat the oil in a large saucepan. Add the onion and cook over a fairly gentle heat for 3 minutes until softened but not browned, stirring all the time.

2 Add the remaining ingredients and bring to the boil over a high heat. Turn down the heat until just bubbling gently round the edges and cook for 15 minutes.

3 Spoon into one or two bowls, top with a spoonful of yoghurt and serve warm with crusty bread and salad.

Baked bean and Ⓥ cheese tacos Ⓥ

SERVES 1-2

1 tbsp sunflower oil
1 onion, peeled and chopped
4 mushrooms, sliced
1 tsp chilli powder
1 × 400 g/14 oz/large can of
baked beans
1 tomato, chopped
2.5 cm/1 in piece of cucumber, chopped
Salt and pepper
4-6 crispy taco shells
A handful of grated Cheddar cheese
A Mixed Salad (see page 45), to serve

1 Heat the oil in a frying pan (skillet). Add the onion and mushrooms and fry (sauté) for 2 minutes.

2 Add the chilli powder and cook for 1 further minute.

3 Add the beans and mash with a fork or wooden spoon against the sides of the pan. Cook, stirring occasionally, for 2 minutes. Stir in the tomato and cucumber and season lightly.

4 Spoon the mixture into taco shells and top each with a little grated cheese.

5 Serve with a Mixed Salad.

Ⓥ Ratatouille Ⓥ

If there is any left over, have it cold the following day. For a more substantial meal, add some cooked ham, diced cheese or drained canned tuna, or serve it on a bed of rice or pasta.

SERVES 1-2

1 tbsp olive or sunflower oil
1 small aubergine (eggplant), sliced
1-2 courgettes (zucchini), sliced
1 onion, peeled and sliced
1 green or red (bell) pepper, sliced
2 tomatoes, quartered
1 garlic clove, peeled and crushed,
or 1 tsp garlic purée (paste)
1 tbsp tomato purée
5 tbsp water
A good pinch of sugar
½ tsp dried mixed herbs
Salt and pepper
Grated Parmesan cheese
French bread, to serve

1 Put the oil in a saucepan. Add all the prepared vegetables and the garlic and cook, stirring, for 2-3 minutes until they start to soften.

2 Mix the tomato purée with the water and add with the sugar, herbs and a sprinkling of salt and pepper.

3 Cover with a lid and cook over a moderate heat for 15 minutes, stirring occasionally, until everything is soft and bathed in a tomato sauce. Spoon the ratatouille into a bowl and sprinkle with Parmesan cheese.

4 Serve hot with French bread.

Greek-style broad beans ⓥ with feta cheese ⓥ

If it's too much for one meal, eat the rest cold, piled on lettuce leaves or packed into pitta breads.

SERVES 1–2

2 mugs of frozen broad (lima) beans
1 mug of passata (sieved tomatoes)
1 small garlic clove, peeled and crushed,
or ¹/₂ tsp garlic purée (paste)
Salt and pepper
2 tbsp olive or sunflower oil
5 tbsp water or white wine
A good pinch of dried oregano
A small handful of crumbled feta cheese
2–3 black olives
Crusty bread, to serve

1 Put all the ingredients except the cheese and olives in a saucepan. Bring to the boil over a high heat, stirring.

2 Turn down the heat to fairly low so that the mixture is just bubbling gently round the edges. Part-cover with a lid and cook gently for 15 minutes, stirring occasionally, until the beans are cooked and bathed in a rich sauce.

3 Spoon into a bowl, sprinkle the cheese over and add the olives, if using. Eat with crusty bread.

Greek-style ⓥ chick peas ⓥ

Any leftovers will make a delicious cold salad the next day. You can use cider or apple juice instead of the white wine.

SERVES 1–2

2 tbsp olive or sunflower oil
1 small onion, peeled and chopped
¹/₂ mug of dry white wine
1 bay leaf
A good pinch of dried oregano
1 garlic clove, peeled and crushed,
or 1 tsp garlic purée (paste)
1 × 425 g/15 oz/large can of chick peas
(garbanzos)
1 × 400 g/14 oz/large can of
chopped tomatoes
Crusty bread and a Green Salad
(see page 45), to serve

1 Heat the oil in a large saucepan. Add the onion and cook over a fairly gentle heat for 3 minutes until softened but not browned, stirring all the time.

2 Add the wine, bay leaf, oregano, garlic, chick peas and tomatoes and bring to the boil over a high heat. Turn down the heat until just bubbling gently round the edges and cook for 15 minutes. Leave to cool slightly, then remove the bay leaf.

3 Spoon into bowls and serve warm with crusty bread and a salad.

Snacks You can Do with ...
a Grill

The grill (broiler) is quick and versatile for tasty snacks or light lunches. You can, of course, use it to cook any of the sandwiches from the sandwich toaster section, starting on page 77.

Sausage toasties

SERVES 1

2 thick pork sausages
2 slices of bread, crusts removed
Tomato ketchup (catsup)

1 Preheat the grill (broiler) and cook the sausages for about 10 minutes, turning occasionally, until golden and cooked through.

2 Spread the bread on one side with tomato ketchup. Add a sausage to each and roll up. Secure with cocktail sticks (toothpicks) and grill (broil), turning occasionally, until the bread is toasted all over.

Cheese and peanut butter
Ⓥ toast Ⓥ

SERVES 1

1 slice of bread
1–2 tbsp peanut butter
A handful of grated Red Leicester
or Cheddar cheese

1 Preheat the grill (broiler). Toast the bread on both sides.

2 Spread thickly on one side with peanut butter.

3 Top with the cheese and grill (broil) until melted and bubbling.

Grilled sardine fingers with chilli relish

SERVES 1

1–2 slices of bread
Butter or margarine
2 tbsp chilli relish
1 × 120 g/4½ oz/small can of sardines
in oil, drained
½ tsp lemon juice
Pepper

1 Preheat the grill (broiler). Toast the bread on both sides. Spread on one side with butter or margarine and chilli relish. See how many sardines there are in the can and cut the toast into the same number of fingers.

2 Put a sardine on each and sprinkle with lemon juice and pepper. Return to the grill until sizzling.

3 Serve hot.

Cheese and pickled onion Ⓥ grill Ⓥ

SERVES 1

1 slice of bread
A good knob of butter or margarine
A handful of grated Cheddar cheese
2 pickled onions, chopped

1 Toast the bread on both sides.

2 Mash the butter or margarine in a bowl with the cheese and pickles.

3 Spread on the toast and grill (broil) until golden and bubbling.

Grilled bacon, tomato, mushroom and lettuce sandwich

SERVES 1

2 rashers (slices) of bacon, rinded
2 tomatoes, halved
4 small mushrooms
Butter or margarine
2 slices of bread
A little mustard
2 tsp mayonnaise
2 crisp lettuce leaves

1 Preheat the grill (broiler). Put the bacon, tomatoes and mushrooms on the grill rack. Dot the mushrooms with tiny pieces of butter or margarine.

2 Grill (broil) for about 4 minutes until the bacon, tomatoes and mushrooms are cooked.

3 Spread the bread with a little butter or margarine. Spread one slice with a scraping of mustard and the other with the mayonnaise.

4 Put the bacon, tomatoes and mushrooms on one slice, top with the lettuce and then the other slice.

Grilled bacon, cheese and tomato sandwich

SERVES 1

2 slices of bread
2–3 rashers (slices) of streaky bacon
2–3 slices of Cheddar cheese,
rind removed
1 tomato, sliced

1 Preheat the grill (broiler). Put the bread on the rack with the bacon and grill (broil) for a few minutes on one side.

2 Remove one slice of bread. Turn the other over and put the bacon on top, then arrange the cheese so the slices fit together to cover the bacon, trimming them if necessary. Top with the tomato slices.

3 Grill (broil) again until the cheese melts and the tomatoes are cooked.

4 Top with the other slice of toast, toasted side out, and cut in half.

Blue cheese and celery Ⓥ toast Ⓥ

SERVES 1

1 finger of soft blue cheese, such as
Dolcelatte, Castello or Cambozola
1 tbsp butter or margarine
1 celery stick, chopped
1 slice of bread

1 Preheat the grill (broiler). Mash the cheese with the butter or margarine and the celery.

2 Toast the bread on both sides.

3 Spread the cheese mixture on the toast and grill (broil) until melted and bubbling.

Sardine special on toast

SERVES 1–2

2 slices of bread
1 tbsp butter or margarine
2 tsp horseradish relish
1 × 120 g/4½ oz/small can of
sardines, drained
Lemon juice
Pepper

1 Preheat the grill (broiler) and toast the bread on both sides.

2 Mash the butter or margarine with the horseradish in a small bowl and spread on the toast.

3 Top the toast with the sardines and return to the grill to heat through. Sprinkle with lemon juice and pepper and serve straight away.

Cheese, ham and pineapple toast

Use the remaining pineapple for a dessert with yoghurt, broken up on your breakfast cereal or for the grilled ham steak recipe on page 248.

SERVES 1

1 thick slice of bread
Butter or margarine
2 tsp tomato purée (paste)
1 slice of ham
1 slice of canned pineapple
1 slice of Cheddar or Emmental
(Swiss) cheese
2.5 ml/½ tsp dried mixed herbs

1 Preheat the grill (broiler) and toast the bread on one side only.

2 Butter the untoasted side.

3 Spread with the tomato purée, then top with the ham, then the cheese.

4 Sprinkle with the dried herbs. Grill (broil) until the cheese melts and bubbles.

Sizzling luncheon meat squares

SERVES 1

2 slices of bread
Butter or margarine
2 slices of luncheon meat
Tomato ketchup (catsup)

1 Preheat the grill (broiler) and toast the bread on one side.

2 Turn over and spread the other sides with butter or margarine.

3 Top each with a slice of luncheon meat and tear at intervals round the edges to prevent them curling up when cooking.

4 Grill (broil) until golden and sizzling. Spread with a little ketchup and eat while hot.

Toasted BLT

SERVES 1

2 rashers (slices) of back bacon
or 4 of streaky bacon, rinded
2 slices of bread
Butter or margarine
2 tsp mayonnaise
1 small tomato, sliced
1–2 crisp lettuce leaves
Pepper

1 Preheat the grill (broiler). Grill (broil) the bacon until cooked to your liking.

2 Lightly toast the bread on one side only. Spread the untoasted sides with a little butter or margarine and spread one slice with the mayonnaise. Top with slices of tomato, then the lettuce.

3 Lay the hot bacon on top, add a good grinding of pepper, then cover with the remaining toast.

James's bacon and Edam toasted munch

SERVES 1

2 slices of bread
Butter or margarine
Tomato ketchup (catsup)
2 rashers (slices) of back bacon, rinded
4 slices of Edam (Dutch) cheese
A few drops of Worcestershire sauce

1 Preheat the grill (broiler). Toast the slices of bread on one side, then spread the other sides with butter or margarine and ketchup.

2 Put the bacon on foil on the grill and grill (broil) until beginning to curl up. Arrange the Edam in the 'bowls' of the curled bacon. Continue to grill until the cheese melts and the edges of the bacon are crisp.

3 Put one slice of toast on a plate, ketchup-side up. Top with the bacon and cheese, then sprinkle with Worcestershire sauce before topping with the other slice of toast.

Melting crescents

SERVES 1

1 large croissant
1 thin slice of smoked cooked ham
1 slice of Gruyère or Emmental (Swiss) cheese
Slices of tomato, to serve

1 Preheat the grill (broiler). Split the croissant open, to form a pocket.
2 Fill with the folded ham and the cheese.
3 Grill (broil) under a moderate heat until the cheese melts, turning once.
4 Serve with slices of tomato.

Ⓥ Golden meltie **Ⓥ**

SERVES 1

1 slice of white bread
Butter or margarine
1 tbsp corn relish
1-2 slices of Cheddar or Gruyère (Swiss) cheese

1 Preheat the grill (broiler). Toast the bread on both sides.

2 Spread with the corn relish, then the cheese.

3 Grill (broil) until the cheese is melting.

Toasted French cheese **Ⓥ** slices **Ⓥ**

SERVES 1

4 slices of French bread
Butter or margarine
2 tsp redcurrant jelly (clear conserve) or raspberry jam (conserve)
1 individual portion of Camembert
Lettuce leaves

1 Preheat the grill (broiler). Toast the French bread on both sides.

2 Spread one side with butter or margarine, then the jelly or jam.

3 Cut the Camembert into four slices and put a slice on each piece of toast. Grill (broil) until the cheese melts and bubbles.

4 Put on lettuce leaves and serve.

Creamy mushroom ⓥ croissants ⓥ

SERVES 1–2

2 large croissants
1 × 215 g/7½ oz/small can of
creamed mushrooms
A good pinch of dried oregano

1 Split the croissants open, to form a pocket in each.

2 Spread the creamed mushrooms inside.

3 Place under a moderate grill (broiler), not too near the heat, for about 2 minutes on one side until piping hot through. Take care not to let the croissants burn.

Cheesy salami and tomato crescents

SERVES 1

1 large croissant
1 small tomato, sliced
2 thin slices of salami, halved
4 basil leaves, torn
2 thin slices of Mozzarella cheese

1 Preheat the grill (broiler). Split the croissant along one edge.

2 Fill with the sliced tomato and salami and add the basil and cheese.

3 Grill (broil) under a moderate heat, turning once, until the cheese has melted and is golden on top. Serve hot.

American-style fish fingers

SERVES 1

4 fish fingers
1 soft bread roll
1 slice of Cheddar cheese
or 1 processed cheese slice
1 tbsp tartare sauce or mayonnaise
A little shredded lettuce

1 Grill (broil) the fish fingers on both sides.

2 Split the rolls, lay the fish fingers on the bottom halves and put on the grill (broiler) rack.

3 Top the fish with the cheese and grill (broil) to melt the cheese.

4 Add the tartare sauce or mayonnaise and a little shredded lettuce, then top with the lids of the rolls.

Fish-finger fingers

SERVES 1

A good knob of butter or margarine
2 tsp tomato ketchup (catsup)
2 gherkins (cornichons), chopped
3 fish fingers
1 slice of bread

1 Preheat the grill (broiler). Mash the butter or margarine in a small bowl with the tomato ketchup and gherkins.

2 Grill (broil) the fish fingers and the bread on both sides until the fish is cooked and the bread is golden. Remove the bread if toasted before the fish.

3 Spread the toast with the butter mixture. Cut each slice into three fingers. Top each with a fish finger and serve.

Parma crescents

There are other brands of raw cured ham, such as Westphalian, that are much cheaper than Parma ham – look out for them in your supermarket.

SERVES 1

1 tbsp grated Parmesan cheese
1 tsp butter or margarine
A good pinch of dried oregano
Pepper
1 large croissant
1 slice of Parma ham
1 small tomato, thinly sliced

1 Preheat the grill (broiler). Mash the cheese with the butter or margarine, oregano and some pepper.

2 Split the croissant and spread inside with the cheese mixture, then top with a slice of ham and the tomato.

3 Grill (broil) under a moderate heat, turning once, until hot through and the croissant is crisp.

Marguerita
🆅 pitta pizza 🆅

SERVES 1

1 pitta bread
Butter or margarine
2 tsp tomato purée (paste)
1 tomato, sliced
A pinch of dried basil
3 slices of Cheddar cheese

1 Preheat the grill (broiler). Toast the pitta bread on one side, then turn it over.

2 Spread the untoasted side with tomato purée, then arrange the tomato slices on top and sprinkle with the basil.

3 Lay the cheese slices on top and grill (broil) until the cheese melts and bubbles.

Fish and chip butties

SERVES 1

1 frozen breaded cod or haddock fillet
A little oil
1 handful of oven chips (fries)
2 slices of white bread
A knob of butter or margarine
Tomato ketchup (catsup)
Vinegar
Salt and pepper

1 Brush the fish fillet with oil. Put on foil on the grill (broiler) rack with the chips to one side.

2 Grill (broil) for 3–4 minutes on each side until golden and cooked through. Turn the chips frequently and remove if cooked before the fish.

3 Spread the bread lightly with butter or margarine. Put one slice on a plate.

4 Spread a little ketchup over.

5 Lay the fish and chips on top and sprinkle with vinegar, salt and pepper to taste.

6 Cover with the remaining slice of bread.

Chilli fingers

SERVES 1

1 small baguette, split
Butter or margarine
1 tbsp tomato ketchup (catsup)
1 tbsp mayonnaise
Hot chilli sauce, to taste
5 fish fingers
Shredded lettuce

1 Split the baguette and spread with butter or margarine.

2 Mix the tomato ketchup in a bowl with the mayonnaise and add chilli sauce to taste.

3 Grill (broil) the fish fingers until golden and cooked through.

4 Put inside the baguette. Top with the spicy mayonnaise and push in some shredded lettuce. Eat while hot.

Hot pastrami on rye

SERVES 1

2 slices of dark rye bread
2 tbsp soft white cheese,
such as Philadelphia
1 tbsp horseradish relish
4 slices of pastrami
A little sunflower oil
Pepper
A few gherkins (cornichons), halved

1 Toast the bread on one side.

2 Mash the cheese and horseradish together and spread over the untoasted side.

3 Place the pastrami on foil on the grill (broil) rack. Brush with oil and grill (broil) until just beginning to sizzle.

4 Quickly place on top of the cheese, sprinkle with pepper and top with halved gherkins. Eat while hot.

Ⓥ Pizza bagel Ⓥ

SERVES 1

1 bagel
2 tsp olive oil
2 tsp tomato purée (paste)
A handful of grated Cheddar
or Mozzarella cheese
2 small tomatoes, sliced
2 good pinches of dried oregano

1 Preheat the grill (broiler). Split the bagel in half. Place on the grill rack and toast until golden on both sides. Trickle a teaspoonful of olive oil over each half and spread out to allow it to soak in.

2 Spread with the tomato purée, then top with the cheese, the sliced tomatoes and a sprinkling of dried oregano.

3 Grill (broil) until the cheese melts and bubbles.

Ⓥ Garlic bread Ⓥ

This would serve four as
an accompaniment.

SERVES 1–2

2 tbsp butter or margarine
1 small garlic clove, peeled and crushed,
or ½ tsp garlic purée (paste)
1½ tsp dried mixed herbs
A pinch of salt
1 sandwich baguette

1 Mash the butter or margarine with the garlic, herbs and salt. Preheat the grill (broiler).

2 Split the baguette and toast on the rounded sides.

3 Turn the bread over and spread the cut sides with the garlic mixture. Grill (broil) until golden and bubbling and the garlic butter has soaked into the bread.

Minted curried lamb naans

SERVES 1

2.5 cm/1 in piece of cucumber,
grated or chopped
2 tbsp thick plain yoghurt
1 tsp dried mint
Salt and pepper
1 frozen minced (ground) lamb steak
2 small naan breads (plain or garlic and
coriander, according to your taste)
2 tsp curry paste

1 Mix the cucumber with the yoghurt, mint and some salt and pepper.

2 Grill (broil) the lamb steak for 4 minutes on each side until cooked.

3 Grill the naan breads briefly to warm, then place one on a plate.

4 Spread the curry paste on one of the naans, then spread the yoghurt and cucumber mixture on top.

5 Top with the lamb steak, then cover with the remaining bread.

Grilled aubergine with Ⓥ tomatoes and cheese Ⓥ

SERVES 1

½ aubergine (eggplant),
cut into slices lengthways
Sunflower or olive oil
2 tomatoes, sliced
A good pinch of dried basil
2–4 slices of Cheddar cheese
Bread

1 Preheat the grill (broiler). Smear the aubergine slices with oil on both sides. Place on foil on the grill rack. Cook for about 3–4 minutes on each side until lightly golden and cooked through.

2 Top with the tomato slices, sprinkle with the basil, then top with the cheese. Return to the grill for 2–3 minutes until the cheese melts and bubbles.

3 Serve hot with bread.

Butter bean salsa Ⓥ grill Ⓥ

SERVES 1

1 × 200 g/7 oz/small can of
butter (lima) beans, drained
1 small garlic clove, peeled and crushed,
or ½ tsp garlic purée (paste)
2 tbsp olive or sunflower oil
1 tbsp tomato ketchup (catsup) or purée
1 small red (bell) pepper, chopped
2–3 stoned (pitted) black olives, sliced
A pinch of dried basil or oregano
Salt and pepper
1 ciabatta or other crusty roll, halved

1 Mash the beans in a bowl with the garlic, half the oil and the tomato ketchup or purée.

2 Stir in the red pepper, olives and herbs and season with salt and pepper.

3 Preheat the grill (broiler). Halve the roll and toast under the grill.

4 Pile the butter bean mixture on top and drizzle with the remaining oil. Grill (broil) under a moderate heat for 3–4 minutes until sizzling and hot through.

Hot salmon special

You can make half the quantity, then store the remainder of the salmon in a covered container in the fridge and use for a sandwich or other recipe the next day.

SERVES 2

1 × 200 g/7 oz/small can of
pink salmon
2 tbsp mayonnaise
2 tsp capers or 1 cornichon, chopped
2.5 cm/1 in piece of cucumber, chopped
4 slices of wholemeal bread
Butter or margarine
A good handful of grated
Mozzarella cheese
Pepper

1 Drain the fish, discard any skin and mash well. Remove the bones if you like but they are very good for you.

2 Mix in the mayonnaise, capers or gherkin and cucumber.

3 Toast the bread on both sides. Spread one side with butter or margarine, then top with the salmon mixture.

4 Sprinkle the cheese over and sprinkle generously with pepper. Grill (broil) under a moderate heat until the cheese melts and bubbles. Eat while hot.

Ham, mushroom and cheese pitta

SERVES 1

1 pitta bread
Butter or margarine
1 mushroom, thinly sliced
1 slice of ham
3 slices of Edam (Dutch) cheese, rinded

1 Preheat the grill (broiler). Put the pitta bread on the grill rack. Put a small piece of foil alongside and lay the mushroom slices on it. Dot them with butter or margarine.

2 Grill (broil) until the pitta bread is toasted on one side and the mushrooms are sizzling.

3 Turn the pitta over and spread with a little butter or margarine. Set the slice of ham on top, then add the mushrooms and any juices. Cover with the cheese slices, fitting them together.

4 Grill until the cheese melts.

Main Courses You Can Do With ... a Grill and One Pan

Grilling (broiling) is a healthy way to cook meat, fish and poultry. Sausages and fatty meats, like bacon or oily fish, can be cooked without any added fat but some food, such as chicken or chops are best with a little extra to prevent them drying out. This may not be very good news for dieters but it does make them taste succulent and delicious.

With the addition of just one ring on the hob, you can prepare everything you need to make a complete meal. The recipes include all the accompaniments, so there is nothing else to do except make a salad where recommended. For grill-only recipes, see pages 221–29.

Stuffed giant mushrooms

SERVES 1

2 large open mushrooms
¹/₄ × 450 g/1 lb packet of pork sausagemeat
or 2 thick sausages, skins removed
2 tbsp soft white cheese, such as Philadelphia
¹/₂ small red or green chilli, seeded and chopped
1 tbsp chopped fresh parsley or 1 tsp dried parsley
Pepper
1 tbsp sunflower oil
Crusty bread and a Green Salad (see page 45), to serve

1 Peel the mushrooms by pulling the skin from the edge to the centre all round with your fingers. Remove the stalks and chop them finely.

2 Dry-fry the sausagemeat with the mushroom stalks in a saucepan for about 3 minutes over a fairly high heat, stirring until cooked through and crumbly. Remove from the heat and stir in the cheese, chilli, parsley and some pepper, using a wooden spoon. Spoon the mixture into the mushroom caps, pressing down well.

3 Heat the oil in a frying pan (skillet) over a moderate heat. Add the mushrooms and fry (sauté) for 5 minutes until golden underneath.

4 Preheat the grill (broiler). Place the pan under the grill and cook for about 5 minutes until bubbling and lightly golden on top.

5 Serve the mushrooms with crusty bread and the salad.

Ⓥ French pea bread Ⓥ

SERVES 1–2

*1 × 200 g/7 oz/small can of
garden peas, drained
1 egg
1 tbsp mayonnaise
3 tbsp butter or margarine
1 small garlic clove, peeled and crushed,
or ½ tsp garlic purée (paste)
1½ tsp dried mixed herbs
A pinch of salt
1 sandwich baguette*

1 Tip the peas into a bowl and mash with a fork. Add the egg and mayonnaise and whisk well with the fork until blended.

2 Heat 1 tbsp of the butter or margarine in a frying pan (skillet). Add the pea mixture and cook, stirring, until scrambled but still creamy. Turn off the heat.

3 Mash the remaining butter or margarine with the garlic, herbs and salt. Preheat the grill (broiler).

4 Split the baguette and toast on the rounded sides.

5 Turn the bread over and spread the cut sides with the garlic mixture. Grill (broil) until golden and bubbling. Meanwhile, reheat the egg mixture.

6 Transfer the baguette to a plate and spoon the pea mixture on top.

Quick butter bean
Ⓥ grill Ⓥ

If this is too much for one meal, eat the remainder cold or reheat in the microwave for 2–3 minutes on High (100 per cent power) the next day. If you don't have a flameproof casserole, heat the bean and ratatouille mixture in a saucepan, then transfer to a flameproof dish for browning.

SERVES 1–2

*1 × 425 g/15 oz/large can of ratatouille
1 × 200 g/7 oz/small can of
butter (lima) beans
½ tsp dried mixed herbs
Salt and pepper
1–2 slices of bread
Butter or margarine
A handful of grated Cheddar cheese*

1 Put the ratatouille and beans in a flameproof casserole (Dutch oven) with the herbs and a little seasoning.

2 Heat fairly gently, stirring occasionally, until piping hot.

3 Preheat the grill (broiler). Spread the bread with the butter or margarine, cut into cubes and sprinkle over the bean mixture. Sprinkle with the cheese and grill (broil) for 3–4 minutes until golden brown and bubbling.

Vegetable satay in salad ⓥ pitta breads ⓥ

SERVES 1

¼ small swede (rutabaga), peeled thickly
and cut into chunks
1 small carrot, peeled and
cut into chunks
1 courgette (zucchini), cut into chunks
A knob of softened butter or margarine
1 tsp clear honey
Salt and pepper
3 tbsp milk
2 tbsp smooth peanut butter
A good pinch of chilli powder
2 pitta breads
A small handful of shredded lettuce
Slices of tomato and cucumber

1 Put a saucepan of lightly salted
water over a high heat. Add the
vegetables, bring to the boil and cook
for 4 minutes until almost tender.
Drain in a colander in the sink.

2 When cool enough to handle,
thread the vegetables on skewers. Lay
on foil on the grill (broiler) rack.

3 Mash the butter or margarine with
the honey and smear all over the
kebabs.

4 Preheat the grill. Cook the kebabs
for 6–8 minutes, turning once or
twice, until golden.

5 While they are cooking, put the
milk, peanut butter and chilli powder
in the vegetable saucepan and heat
gently, stirring until the mixture
forms a thick sauce.

6 Put the pitta breads under the grill
to warm briefly.

7 Split along one edge and fill with
the salad. Slide the kebabs off the
skewers into the pitta breads and
spoon the sauce over so it trickles
down into the salad.

Sweetcorn and banana ⓥ omelette with waffles ⓥ

This is serious energy food to keep
you going through those long
revision sessions.

SERVES 1

2 knobs of butter or margarine
1 unripe banana, thickly sliced
1 tomato, thickly sliced
2 eggs
1 tbsp milk
1 × 200 g/7 oz/small can of sweetcorn
(corn), drained
Salt and pepper
2 waffles

1 Melt a knob of butter or margarine
in a frying pan (skillet). Add the slices
of banana and tomato and fry (sauté)
for 1–2 minutes until cooked but not
completely soft. Remove from the
pan with a fish slice. Wipe out the
pan with a piece of kitchen paper
(paper towel).

2 Beat the eggs and milk together
with a pinch of salt and pepper until
well blended.

3 Add the sweetcorn and stir well.

4 Heat the remaining butter or
margarine in the frying pan. Add the
sweetcorn mixture and fry, gently
lifting and stirring the mixture, until
it is almost set and golden brown
underneath.

5 Preheat the grill (broiler). Spoon
the banana and tomato mixture on
top of the sweetcorn mixture. Put the
waffles and the frying pan on the grill
rack to brown the top and warm the
waffles.

6 Transfer the waffles to a warm
plate. Fold the omelette in half, cut in
two and place a piece of it on top of
each waffle.

Macaroni, egg and spinach Ⓥ grill Ⓥ

SERVES 1

½ mug of macaroni
1 egg, scrubbed under cold
running water
1 mug of frozen spinach
2 tbsp plain (all-purpose) flour
⅔ mug of milk
A knob of butter or margarine
½ tsp made mustard
A good handful of grated
Cheddar cheese
Salt and pepper
A handful of cornflakes or bran flakes
or ½ Weetabix

1 Cook the macaroni according to the packet directions, with the scrubbed egg added to the pan. Drain in a colander in the sink, then tip the macaroni into a flameproof dish. Put the hard-boiled egg in a bowl of cold water.

2 Cook the spinach according to the packet directions in the same pan, then drain in the colander in the sink. Rinse out the pan.

3 Put the flour and milk in the same saucepan and whisk with a balloon whisk or fork until smooth.

4 Add the butter or margarine and cook over a fairly high heat, stirring all the time until boiling, thick and smooth. Continue to stir while it bubbles gently for 2 minutes.

5 Stir in the mustard, about two-thirds of the cheese and salt and pepper to taste.

6 Tip the cooked macaroni into the sauce and stir well over a fairly gentle heat until piping hot.

7 Preheat the grill (broiler). Spoon the spinach into the flameproof dish. Shell the egg, cut up and scatter over the spinach. Top with the macaroni cheese. Crush the cereal and sprinkle over with the remaining cheese. Grill (broil) until golden, bubbling and hot through.

Mackerel with chick peas

SERVES 1

1 cleaned mackerel, head removed
Salt and pepper
1 × 225 g/8 oz/small can of chick peas
(garbanzos), drained
2 tbsp passata (sieved tomatoes)
2 tsp tomato purée (paste)
2 tbsp dry white wine or apple juice
½ tsp caster (superfine) sugar
½ small garlic clove, peeled and crushed,
or ¼ tsp garlic purée
¼ tsp dried thyme or mixed herbs
French bread, to serve

1 Preheat the grill (broiler).

2 Make several slashes on both sides of the mackerel, then season with salt and pepper.

3 Grill (broil) for about 5 minutes on each side until cooked through and golden brown.

4 While the fish is cooking, put the chick peas in a saucepan with the remaining ingredients. Bring to the boil over a high heat and cook for about 4 minutes until the chick peas are bathed in sauce. Season to taste.

5 Spoon the chick peas on to a warm plate and top with the mackerel. Serve with lots of crusty French bread.

ⓥ Special pasta grill ⓥ

Use grated Cheddar cheese if
you prefer.

SERVES 1

½–1 mug of pasta shapes
2 knobs of butter or margarine
½ green (bell) pepper, diced
4 mushrooms, sliced
2 tbsp plain (all-purpose) flour
⅔ mug of milk
Salt and pepper
2.5 cm/1 in finger of blue cheese,
crumbled
2 tomatoes, sliced

1 Cook the pasta according to the
packet directions. Drain in a colander
in the sink.

2 Heat a knob of butter or margarine
in the pasta saucepan. Add the
pepper and mushrooms and cook,
stirring, for 3 minutes until softened.

3 Remove from the pan. Put the flour
and milk in the pan and whisk with a
fork or balloon whisk until smooth.
Add the remaining butter or
margarine and bring to the boil,
stirring until thickened. Cook for
2 minutes, stirring all the time.

4 Add the pepper and mushrooms
and the cheese and stir until melted.
Tip the pasta into the sauce and
season to taste with salt and pepper.
Heat through, stirring.

5 Preheat the grill (broiler). Turn the
mixture into a flameproof dish and
arrange the tomatoes over the top.
Grill (broil) until the tomatoes are soft
and turning lightly golden.

Grilled salmon with tomatoes and crushed potatoes with cheese

Farmed salmon is now very cheap. It
makes a quick, posh supper – great if
you're cooking for friends too. Make
the salad in advance.

SERVES 1

2–3 potatoes, peeled and cut into
small chunks
Salt and pepper
A knob of butter or margarine
A small handful of grated
Cheddar cheese
1 salmon tail fillet, about 150 g/5 oz
2 tomatoes, halved
1 tbsp olive oil
2 tsp balsamic vinegar
A Green Salad (see page 45),
to serve

1 Boil the potatoes in lightly salted
water for about 10 minutes until
tender. Drain in a colander in the
sink and return to the pan. Crush
with a fork – don't make it too
smooth. Stir in the seasoning, butter
or margarine and cheese until
melted.

2 Preheat the grill (broiler). Put the
salmon and tomatoes on foil on the
grill rack. Season lightly, trickle all
over with the olive oil and sprinkle
the tomatoes with the balsamic
vinegar.

3 Grill (broil) for about 5–6 minutes
until the salmon and tomatoes are
cooked through. Do not overcook and
do not turn over.

4 Spoon the crushed potatoes on to a
warm plate. Carefully lay the fish on
top with the tomatoes to one side.

5 Serve with a Green Salad.

Flash-in-the-pan veggie grill

SERVES 1

1 tbsp sunflower oil
A knob of butter or margarine
1 large potato, scrubbed and
thinly sliced
1½ mugs of frozen
mixed vegetables
½ × 295 g/10½ oz/medium can of
condensed mushroom soup
A good handful of grated
Cheddar cheese

1 Heat the oil and butter or margarine in a frying pan (skillet). Add the potatoes and fry (sauté), stirring and turning, for 4 minutes until softened.

2 Add the mixed vegetables and soup. Cook, stirring, until bubbling. Turn down the heat, cover with a lid or foil and cook very gently for about 8 minutes until the vegetables are cooked.

3 Preheat the grill (broiler). Sprinkle the cheese over the surface and flash the pan under the grill for 2–3 minutes until the cheese melts, bubbles and turns lightly golden.

Thai-style fish with sticky rice and peas

You can use ordinary long-grain rice if you haven't any fragrant rice.

SERVES 1

1 white fish fillet, about 150 g/5 oz
Salt
Coarsely grated zest and juice
of ½ lime
Chilli powder
¼ mug of Thai fragrant rice
A handful of peas
A knob of butter or margarine
1 tbsp light brown sugar

1 Sprinkle the fish with salt, the lime juice and a good pinch of chilli powder. Leave to marinate while you prepare the rice.

2 Wash the rice, then cook according to the packet directions, adding the peas for the last 5 minutes' cooking time. Drain in a colander in the sink, return to the pan, add a knob of butter or margarine and a good pinch of chilli powder. Stir to mix.

3 Preheat the grill (broiler). Put the fish on foil on the grill rack. Sprinkle with the sugar and grill (broil) for 5 minutes until cooked through.

4 Spoon the rice and peas on a plate and top with the fish. Sprinkle with the lime zest to garnish.

Spiced mackerel with lemon and coriander on buttered rice and beans

SERVES 1

1 tbsp lemon juice
1 tbsp chopped fresh coriander (cilantro)
½ small green chilli, seeded and finely chopped
1 cleaned mackerel, head removed
Salt and pepper
¼ mug of long-grain rice
A good knob of butter or margarine
A handful of French (green) beans, tops and tails removed
A little sunflower oil

1 Mix the lemon juice with the coriander and chilli.

2 Make several slashes on each side of the fish through to the bone. Lay the fish in a shallow dish and sprinkle with this mixture and some salt and pepper. Leave to marinate for 30 minutes.

3 Put a pan of water with a pinch of salt on to boil. When boiling, add the rice and beans and boil for 10 minutes. Drain in a colander in the sink and return to the pan. Add the butter or margarine and mix thoroughly.

4 While the rice is boiling, preheat the grill (broiler). Lay the fish on foil on the grill rack and smear with oil. Grill (broil) for 5 minutes until the skin is golden and crisp. Turn over, smear with a little more oil and grill for a further 5 minutes or until cooked through.

5 Spoon the rice on to a plate. Put the fish to one side and pour any juices over.

Tuna and vegetable cheese

It's cheaper to buy a 185 g/6½ oz can of tuna. Use half for this dish and half for a sandwich (or any other tuna recipe) the next day. Store it in a covered container in the fridge – not in the can.

SERVES 1–2

2 tbsp plain (all-purpose) flour
½ mug of milk
A knob of butter or margarine
Salt and pepper
A good handful of grated Cheddar cheese
1 × 85 g/3½ oz/very small can of tuna, drained
1 × 225 g/8 oz/small can of diced mixed vegetables, drained
A small handful of cornflakes, crushed
2 tomatoes, sliced

1 Mix the flour and milk together in a saucepan with a wire whisk until smooth. Add the butter or margarine and bring to the boil, stirring all the time with the whisk, until bubbling, thick and smooth. Season with salt and pepper and stir in half the cheese.

2 Mix in the tuna and vegetables and heat through for about 2 minutes until piping hot.

3 Preheat the grill (broiler). Turn the hot mixture into a flameproof serving dish.

4 Sprinkle with the remaining cheese and the crushed cornflakes.

5 Arrange the slices of tomato around the top.

6 Remove the grill (broiler) rack and place the dish in the grill pan. Cook for about 3–4 minutes until golden and bubbling. Serve hot.

Buttered chicken with herbs on crushed sweet potatoes

SERVES 1

1 small sweet potato, peeled and cut into small chunks
1 ordinary potato, peeled and cut into small chunks
Salt and pepper
2 good knobs of butter or margarine
1 skinless chicken breast
½ tsp lemon juice
¼ tsp dried mixed herbs
A Mixed Salad (see page 45), to serve

1 Cook the sweet and ordinary potatoes together in boiling water with a pinch of salt added for about 10 minutes or until tender. Drain thoroughly in a colander in the sink. Return to the pan, crush briefly with a potato masher or fork and add a sprinkling of salt and pepper and good knob of butter or margarine. Mix thoroughly but don't make it too creamy.

2 Preheat the grill (broiler). Place the chicken on foil on the grill rack.

3 Mix the remaining butter or margarine with the lemon juice, herbs and a sprinkling of salt and pepper. Smear all over the chicken.

4 Grill (broil) for about 15 minutes, turning several times, until golden brown and cooked through.

5 Serve on the bed of crushed potatoes with the herby juices poured over, with the salad on the side.

Buttered garlic chicken

SERVES 1

Prepare as for Buttered Chicken with Herbs (left), but add a small crushed garlic clove or ½ tsp garlic purée (paste) to the butter or margarine and herbs.

Chicken teriyaki

You can use white wine or apple juice instead of the sherry.

SERVES 1

2 tbsp soy sauce
½ tbsp medium-dry sherry
½ small garlic clove, peeled and crushed, or ¼ tsp garlic purée (paste)
A good pinch of ground ginger
1 tsp clear honey
1 skinless chicken breast, cut into cubes
¼ × 250 g/9 oz packet of rice noodles
A Beansprout Salad (see page 45), to serve

1 Mix 1 tbsp of the soy sauce with the sherry, garlic, ginger and honey. Add the diced chicken and toss well. Leave in a cool place to marinate for at least 2 hours. Thread on two skewers.

2 Cook the noodles according to the packet directions. Drain in a colander in the sink, then return to the pan and sprinkle with the remaining soy sauce. Lift and stir with a spoon and fork to mix. Preheat the grill (broiler).

3 Put the chicken on foil on the grill rack. Grill (broil) for 8–10 minutes, turning occasionally and spooning over any remaining marinade, until tender and cooked through.

4 Spoon on to the hot noodles and serve with the salad.

Spicy minted chicken with new potatoes and mangetout

SERVES 1

About 6 small new potatoes, scrubbed and halved
A handful of mangetout (snow peas), topped and tailed
2 tbsp butter or margarine
½ tsp dried mint
A good pinch of ground cinnamon
A good pinch of ground cumin
1 tsp lemon juice
½ tsp sugar
1 skinless chicken breast

1 Cook the potatoes in boiling, salted water for about 10 minutes or until tender. After 8 minutes, add the mangetout. Drain in a colander in the sink and return to the pan.

2 Meanwhile, use a fork or knife to mash the butter or margarine on a small plate with the mint, spices, lemon juice and sugar.

3 Preheat the grill (broiler). Place the chicken on foil on a grill (broiler) rack and spread the spice mixture all over.

4 Grill (broil) the chicken for about 15 minutes, turning occasionally, until golden brown and cooked through.

5 Serve with the potatoes and mangetout, with any spicy juices spooned over.

Sweet spiced chicken with mango

SERVES 1

Prepare as for Sweet Spiced Chicken with Mint (left) but omit the mint and add 2 tsp mango chutney to the mixture. Try substituting curry powder for the cinnamon and cumin too.

Cheat's cottage pie

Large cans of corned beef are much better value than small ones. Use the rest over the next few days for any of the other recipes in this book or wrap in foil and freeze for up to 3 months.
Likewise, use half a large can of beans, if you prefer, and use the rest up later.

SERVES 1

½ × 350 g/12 oz/large can of corned beef, cut into small pieces
1 × 225 g/8 oz/small can of baked beans
1 portion of instant mashed potato
A knob of butter or margarine
A small handful of grated Cheddar cheese

1 Put the beef and beans in a saucepan and heat through.

2 Make up the mashed potato according to the packet directions, adding a knob of butter or margarine.

3 Preheat the grill (broiler). Spoon the beef and beans into an individual flameproof dish. Top with the potato, then the cheese. Grill (broil) until the top is golden brown.

Swiss-style chicken with sweetcorn and tomato bread

SERVES 1

1 skinless chicken breast
A knob of butter or margarine
Salt and pepper
1 × 200 g/7 oz/small can of sweetcorn
(corn), drained
1 slice of Emmental (Swiss) or
Leerdammer cheese
For the garlic bread:
1 sandwich baguette or torpedo roll
2 large knobs of butter or margarine
2 tsp tomato purée (paste)
½ tsp dried basil
A Mixed Salad (see page 45), to serve

1 Preheat the grill (broiler). Place the chicken breast in a plastic bag and beat with a rolling pin or meat mallet to flatten.

2 Smear with butter or margarine and place on foil on a grill rack. Season lightly. Grill (broil) for 3 minutes. Turn the chicken over and spoon the buttery juices over. Grill for another 3 minutes.

3 Spoon the sweetcorn over and top with the cheese. Grill until the cheese is melted and golden.

4 While it is cooking, split the baguette or torpedo roll into three pieces lengthways. Mash the large knobs of butter or margarine with the tomato purée, basil and some salt and pepper. Spread over both sides of the slices of bread. Heat a frying pan (skillet). Add the bread and fry (sauté) for about 2 minutes on each side until lightly golden round the edges but still soft in the middle.

5 Serve the chicken with the tomato bread and a salad.

Cheesy chicken, ham and tomato grill with tagliatelle

SERVES 1

3–4 tagliatelle nests
A knob of butter or margarine
Salt and pepper
1 skinless chicken breast
1 tbsp sunflower or olive oil
1 slice of lean ham
1 tomato, sliced
2 fresh basil leaves, chopped,
or a good pinch of dried basil
A handful of grated Mozzarella cheese

1 Cook the pasta according to the packet directions, stirring occasionally to break up the nests. Drain in a colander in the sink and return to the pan. Add the butter or margarine and stir well until every strand is coated. Add a good sprinkling of pepper.

2 Preheat the grill (broiler).

3 Put the chicken breast into a plastic bag and beat with a rolling pin or meat mallet to flatten. Brush with half the oil.

4 Place on foil on the grill rack and cook for 3 minutes. Turn over, brush with the remaining oil and cook for a further 3 minutes.

5 Top with the slice of ham, then tomato slices, then the basil. Cover with the cheese and grill (broil) for about 2 minutes until the cheese is melted and bubbling.

6 Spoon the buttered pasta on a warm plate, add the chicken and serve.

Chicken, mushroom and tomato kebabs with pesto pasta

If you have no balsamic vinegar, use ½ tsp wine vinegar mixed with ½ tsp clear honey or sugar.

SERVES 1

1 skinless chicken breast,
cut into chunks
2 tsp olive oil
½ tsp balsamic vinegar
1 small garlic clove, peeled and crushed,
or ½ tsp garlic purée (paste)
Salt and pepper
4 button mushrooms
2 small tomatoes
2 basil leaves
3–4 tagliatelle nests
1 tbsp pesto, ready-made or see page 418

1 Put the chicken in a shallow dish. Add the oil, vinegar and garlic and season with salt and pepper. Mix well and leave to stand for 30 minutes. Meanwhile, put the mushrooms in a pan with a little water and boil for 1 minute, then drain.

2 Thread the chicken on skewers with the mushrooms, tomatoes and basil.

3 Meanwhile, cook the pasta according to the packet directions, stirring occasionally. Drain in a colander in the sink, return to the pan and stir in the pesto.

4 While the pasta is cooking, preheat the grill (broiler). Put the kebabs on foil on the grill rack and grill (broil) for 8–10 minutes, turning once or twice, until the chicken is cooked through.

5 Spoon the tagliatelle on to a warm plate and lay the kebabs beside.

Spiced chicken kebabs with yellow rice

SERVES 1

1 tbsp plain yoghurt
½ tsp garam masala
or curry powder
1 small garlic clove, peeled and crushed,
or ½ tsp garlic purée (paste)
½ tsp sugar
1 tsp lemon juice
Salt and pepper
1 skinless chicken breast, cut into cubes
4 button mushrooms
¼ mug of long-grain rice
1 yellow (bell) pepper, diced
A good pinch of ground turmeric
½ chicken stock cube
A Mixed Salad (see page 45),
to serve

1 Mix together the yoghurt, spice, garlic, sugar, lemon juice and a pinch of salt and pepper. Add the chicken and mushrooms and toss well. Leave to marinate for up to 2 hours. Thread the chicken and mushrooms on one or two skewers.

2 Preheat the grill (broiler).

3 Cook the rice and pepper for 10 minutes in boiling water to which the turmeric and stock cube have been added. Check they are tender, then drain in a colander in the sink.

4 While the rice is cooking, put the kebabs on foil on the grill rack and grill (broil) for 8–10 minutes, turning frequently until golden and cooked through.

5 Spoon the rice on a plate, top with the kebabs and serve with a Mixed Salad.

Saucy chicken and courgette supper

You can also make this with cooked, leftover chicken or, even better, lamb – add it after cooking the courgettes for 5 minutes. Make the salad before you start cooking the dish so it has time to develop in flavour.

SERVES 1

1 slice of bread
Butter or margarine
1 small skinless chicken breast,
cut into chunks
1 courgette (zucchini), cut into small dice
2 tsp capers
2 tsp liquid from the jar of capers
½ chicken stock cube
½ mug of water
1 tsp cornflour (cornstarch)
Salt and pepper
1 egg
1 tbsp chopped fresh parsley
or 1 tsp dried parsley
French Cabbage Salad (see page 46),
to serve

1 Spread the bread with butter or margarine, then cut into cubes.

2 Heat a knob of butter or margarine in a saucepan, add the chicken and cook, stirring, over a fairly high heat for 4 minutes until almost cooked through.

3 Add the courgette, stir for 1 minute, then turn down the heat, cover with a lid and cook for 3 minutes.

4 Add the capers, caper liquid and stock cube. Stir until the cube dissolves.

5 Blend the water with the cornflour and stir into the pan. Bring to the boil and cook, stirring, for 1 minute. Season to taste with salt and pepper.

6 Break the egg into a mug and whisk with a fork, add to the pan and stir until slightly thickened. Add the parsley.

7 Preheat the grill (broiler). Spoon the mixture into a flameproof dish. Cover with the cubes of bread and grill (broil) for 2–3 minutes until the bread is golden.

8 Serve with the French Cabbage Salad.

Cheat's Kentucky-fried turkey with chips and barbecued beans

SERVES 1

*3 crumb-coated minced (ground)
turkey drumsticks
A little sunflower oil
A good pinch of ground cumin
A good pinch of dried mixed herbs
A good pinch of salt and pepper
2 handfuls of oven chips (fries)
1 × 225 g/8 oz/small can of
baked beans
2 tsp bottled barbecue sauce
or sweet brown table sauce
Lettuce and slices of tomato and
cucumber, to garnish*

1 Preheat the grill (broiler). Brush the turkey drumsticks with a little oil. Sprinkle on both sides with cumin, herbs and a little salt and pepper. Place on foil on the grill rack with the chips.

2 Grill the turkey according to the packet directions until golden brown and cooked through, turning once. Cook the chips until crisp and golden, turning once or twice.

3 Meanwhile, put the beans in a saucepan and stir in the sauce. Heat through thoroughly, stirring occasionally.

4 Transfer the turkey and chips to a plate and add the beans. Garnish with the salad stuffs.

Chicken, bacon and sweetcorn kebabs

SERVES 1

*1 small corn cob, cut into 4 chunks
1 skinless chicken breast,
cut into chunks
2 tsp olive oil
1 tsp lemon juice
¼ tsp dried sage
Salt and pepper
1 rasher (slice) of streaky bacon, rinded
A little butter or soft margarine
Hot Potato Salad (see page 134), to serve*

1 Put the pieces of corn cob in a pan with a little water and boil for 5 minutes, then drain in a colander in the sink.

2 Put the chicken in a dish. Add the oil, lemon juice, sage and a little salt and pepper and mix well. Stretch the bacon with the back of a knife. Cut in half and roll up each half.

3 Thread the chicken on to skewers, interspersed with the bacon rolls and corn. Preheat the grill (broiler).

4 Put the kebabs on foil on the grill rack and smear the corn with a little butter or margarine. Grill (broil) for 8–10 minutes, turning and spooning any melted butter or margarine or remaining marinade over, until golden and cooked through.

5 Serve with the Hot Potato Salad.

Chicken satay

You can use a piece of thick turkey
steak instead of the chicken.

SERVES 1

2 tsp sunflower oil
1 small onion, peeled and
finely chopped
1 small garlic clove, peeled and crushed,
or ½ tsp garlic purée (paste)
2 tsp smooth peanut butter
½ tsp lemon or lime juice
1 tsp clear honey
1 tsp soy sauce
A pinch of chilli powder
2 tbsp milk
1 skinless chicken breast, diced
¼ mug of long-grain rice
A Beansprout Salad (see page 46),
to serve

1 Heat the oil in a saucepan over a
high heat. Add the onion and fry
(sauté) for 2 minutes, stirring. Stir in
all the remaining ingredients except
the milk, chicken and rice. Bring to
the boil, stirring.

2 Stir in 1 tbsp of the milk, reduce
the heat to moderate and cook for
2 minutes.

3 Preheat the grill (broiler). Thread
the chicken on a skewer. Place on foil
on the grill rack. Brush with a little of
the sauce.

4 Grill (broil) for about 8 minutes,
turning occasionally, until tender and
cooked through. Meanwhile, cook the
rice according to the packet directions.
Drain in a colander in the sink.

5 Add the remaining milk to the
sauce and heat through, stirring.
Spoon the rice on to a plate. Top with
the kebab and spoon the remaining
sauce over.

6 Serve with a Beansprout Salad

Chicken breast masala with spinach rice

SERVES 1

3 tbsp plain yoghurt
1 small garlic clove, peeled and crushed,
or ½ tsp garlic purée (paste)
¼ tsp ground ginger
¼ tsp chilli powder
¼ tsp ground cumin
1 tsp garam masala
A good pinch each of salt and pepper
1 skinless chicken breast
¼ mug of long-grain rice
½ tsp ground cinnamon
1 mug of frozen leaf spinach

1 Mix the yoghurt with the garlic,
ginger, chilli, cumin, garam masala,
salt and pepper in a shallow dish. Add
the chicken, turn over to coat
completely, cover and chill to
marinate for several hours or
overnight.

2 Cook under a preheated grill
(broiler) for about 8 minutes on each
side, smearing with any remaining
marinade during cooking.

3 Meanwhile, cook the rice according
to the packet directions with the
cinnamon added to the water. Add the
spinach for the last 5 minutes'
cooking. Drain in a colander in the
sink. Tip back into the pan and add
the remaining garam masala. Heat,
stirring gently for 1 minute to
evaporate any excess moisture.

4 Pile the spinach rice on a plate and
top with the chicken.

Grilled ham steak with mandarins, cheese and sautéed potato slices

You'll find pre-packed round ham steaks next to the bacon in the supermarket. They're much cheaper than gammon steaks, but still very tasty and quick to cook. They're often sold in packs of two, so wrap one in clingfilm or foil and store it in the fridge for up to 3 days. Use the other half of the mandarins with yoghurt or custard for a dessert, for the smoothie on page 69 or for the sandwich on page 52.

SERVES 1

A little sunflower oil
1 large potato, scrubbed and cut into
5 slices lengthways
1 ham steak
¹/₂ × 300 g/11 oz/medium can of broken
mandarin segments, drained well
1–2 slices of Cheddar cheese,
or 1 processed cheese slice
A Green Salad (see page 45), to serve

1 Heat enough oil to cover the base of a frying pan (skillet). When hot but not smoking (see page 35), add the potato slices and fry (sauté) for about 6 minutes, turning once with a fish slice, until golden and cooked through.

2 Meanwhile preheat the grill (broiler). Grill the ham steak on foil on the grill rack for 3 minutes. Turn over and cook for 2 minutes. Top with the mandarins, then the cheese. Grill until the cheese melts and bubbles.

3 Drain the potatoes on kitchen paper (paper towels), then transfer to a plate. Top with the ham steak and serve with a Green Salad.

Lemon chicken with garlic sauté potatoes and green beans

SERVES 1

1 chicken portion
A little sunflower oil
Salt and pepper
¹/₄ tsp dried mixed herbs
1 tbsp lemon juice
1 tsp clear honey
1 large potato, scrubbed or peeled and
cut into dice
A good handful of French (green) beans,
cut into short lengths

1 Preheat the grill (broiler). Rub the chicken with a little oil and sprinkle with a little salt and pepper.

2 Put the chicken on a piece of foil and grill (broil) for 7–8 minutes on each side until golden and almost cooked.

3 Whisk 1 tbsp of oil with the herbs, lemon juice and honey. Spread all over the chicken with a pastry brush or your fingers.

4 Grill again for 3–4 minutes, smearing with any remaining lemon mixture after 2 minutes.

5 While the chicken is cooking, boil the potato and beans in lightly salted water for 4 minutes. Drain in a colander in the sink.

6 Heat 2 tbsp of oil in a frying pan (skillet). When hot but not smoking (see page 35), add the potato and beans and cook, turning every few minutes, for about 6 minutes until the potato pieces are golden and both vegetables are cooked through.

7 Transfer the chicken with any juices, the potato and beans to a plate and serve.

Grilled chicken thighs with garlic and herb sauce and vegetable couscous

SERVES 1

2 chicken thighs
1 tbsp sunflower oil
Salt and pepper
For the couscous:
1 × 200 g/7 oz/small can of mixed
vegetables, drained
½ mug of boiling water
¼ mug of couscous
For the sauce:
1 tsp cornflour (cornstarch)
A small knob of butter or margarine
5 tbsp milk
1 good tbsp garlic-and-herb-flavoured
soft cheese

1 Preheat the grill (broiler). Put the chicken thighs on foil on the grill rack. Rub all over with a little oil, then sprinkle with salt and pepper.

2 Grill (broil) for 20 minutes, turning occasionally, until golden brown, crisp and cooked through.

3 While the chicken is cooking, empty the can of vegetables into a bowl. Add the boiling water and the couscous. Stir gently, then cover with a plate and leave in a warm place while you prepare the sauce.

4 Put the cornflour in a saucepan with the milk and mix with a wooden spoon until blended. Add the butter or margarine and bring to the boil, stirring until thickened. Add the cheese in small pieces and stir over a gentle heat to blend. Season to taste.

5 Stir the couscous lightly with a fork to fluff it up, then spoon it on to a plate. Add the chicken and spoon the sauce over.

Ham, broccoli and tomato gratin

SERVES 1

1 small head of broccoli,
cut into 4 florets
2 thin slices of ham, halved
4 tbsp passata (sieved tomatoes)
A good pinch of dried basil
1 small carton of plain yoghurt
Salt and pepper
A good handful of grated
Cheddar cheese
A small handful of cornflakes, crushed

1 Bring a pan with about 5 cm/2 in lightly salted water in it to the boil over a high heat. Add the broccoli and cook for 4 minutes. Drain in a colander in the sink.

2 Wrap half a slice of ham round each floret and arrange in a flameproof serving dish.

3 Spoon the passata over the broccoli and sprinkle with the basil.

4 Preheat the grill (broiler). Mix the yoghurt with a little salt and pepper and half the cheese. Spoon over and sprinkle with the remaining cheese and the cornflakes.

5 Remove the grill rack and put the dish in the grill pan. Grill (broil) for about 5 minutes until piping hot and the top is golden and bubbling. Serve hot.

Indian-style pork chop with naan

SERVES 1

1 pork shoulder chop
2 tsp sunflower oil
½ tsp garam masala
Salt and pepper
1 × 225 g/8 oz/small can of
pease pudding
2 tsp curry paste
1 tbsp sultanas (golden raisins)
1 individual naan bread
2 tsp desiccated (shredded) coconut
Mango chutney and a Mixed Salad
(see page 45), to serve

1 Rub the chop all over with the oil and sprinkle with garam masala and salt and pepper. Put the chop on foil on the grill (broiler) rack and cook for 8–10 minutes on each side until golden and cooked through.

2 Empty the pease pudding into a saucepan and stir in the curry paste and sultanas. Heat through, stirring gently.

3 Warm the naan bread under the grill (broiler).

4 Place the naan on a warm plate. Spoon the pease pudding mixture on top and then add the pork chop. Pour any juices over.

5 Sprinkle the chops with the coconut and serve straight away with mango chutney and a Mixed Salad.

Bacon, leek and potato pie

SERVES 1

2 knobs of butter or margarine
2 rashers (slices) of streaky bacon,
rinded and diced
1 leek, trimmed, washed well and sliced
1 large potato, peeled and sliced
1 tbsp milk
A good handful of grated
Cheddar cheese
Salt and pepper
A small handful of cornflakes, crushed

1 Melt one knob of butter or margarine in a saucepan. Add the bacon and leek and cook, stirring, for 5 minutes until cooked. Tip out and reserve.

2 Cook the potato in boiling water in the same pan with a pinch of salt added for about 10 minutes or until tender. Drain off the water and mash with the remaining knob of butter or margarine and the milk.

3 Stir in the bacon and leek and half the cheese.

4 Preheat the grill (broiler). Turn the mixture into a flameproof dish, sprinkle with the remaining cheese and the cornflakes. Grill (broil) for 3–4 minutes until golden and piping hot.

Seekh kebabs

SERVES 1

½ small onion, peeled
¼ tsp ground ginger
½ tsp ground cinnamon
¼ tsp ground cumin
A good pinch of chilli powder
A handful of minced (ground) lamb
½ tsp lemon juice
2 tsp plain yoghurt
2 tsp plain (all-purpose) flour,
plus extra for dusting
2 tsp chopped fresh coriander (cilantro)
A pinch each of salt and pepper
1 tbsp sunflower oil
¼ mug of long-grain rice
A squeeze of lemon juice
Shredded lettuce, slices of tomato and
cucumber and mango chutney, to serve

1 Grate the onion into a bowl, add the spices and mix to a paste.

2 Add the lamb, lemon juice, yoghurt, flour, coriander and salt and squeeze together with your hands until well mixed.

3 Preheat the grill (broiler).

4 With floured hands, divide the mixture in half and shape each piece into a sausage shape around a skewer. Lay on foil on a grill rack. Smear with the oil. Grill (broil) for about 10 minutes, turning once or twice, until golden brown and cooked through.

5 Meanwhile, cook the rice according to the packet directions. Drain in a colander in the sink.

6 Pile on a plate and top with the kebabs. Squeeze a little lemon juice over and serve with shredded lettuce, tomatoes, cucumber and mango chutney.

No-effort cottage pie

If you haven't got a flameproof casserole dish, heat the mixture in saucepan, then tip it into a heatproof dish before topping with the potato. If eating alone, when you've mixed all the ingredients together in the casserole or saucepan, before heating, spoon half of it into a covered container and store in the fridge for another day. Make up half the quantity of potato for the first pie, then make another lot when you make the second pie.

SERVES 2

1 × 175 g/6 oz/small can of minced
(ground) steak with onion
1 × 400 g/14 oz/large can of
baked beans
1 × 300 g/11 oz/medim can of sliced
carrots, drained
1 tsp Worcestershire sauce
A good pinch of dried mixed herbs
2 servings of instant mashed potato
2 handfuls of grated Cheddar cheese

1 Mix the minced steak with the beans, carrots, Worcestershire sauce and herbs in a flameproof casserole (Dutch oven). Heat through, stirring occasionally, until piping hot.

2 Preheat the grill (broiler). Reconstitute the potato according to the packet directions. Pile on top of the meat mixture and sprinkle with the cheese. Grill (broil) until golden and bubbling on top.

Alpine ham grill with sauté potatoes

If you have to open a new can of pineapple slices, eat the remainder for pud, or have it for breakfast over cereal or with yoghurt, or use it for any of the other recipes calling for pineapple in this book.

SERVES 1

1 ham steak
1 canned pineapple slice, drained
1 gherkin (cornichon), chopped
½ tsp Dijon mustard
1 slice of Emmental (Swiss) cheese
Sunflower oil
1 large or 2 medium potatoes, scrubbed and diced
2 tomatoes, sliced

1 Preheat the grill (broiler). Snip the edges of the ham steak with scissors to stop it curling up during cooking. Place on foil on a grill rack.

2 Grill (broil) the steak for 3 minutes on each side.

3 Spread the top with Dijon mustard, then top with a slice of pineapple and fill the hole in the centre with the chopped gherkin. Lay a slice of cheese on top.

4 Grill until the cheese melts and bubbles and the fruit is hot.

5 Pour enough oil in a frying pan (skillet) to cover the base. Heat until very hot but not smoking (see page 35). Carefully slide the potatoes into the pan and fry (sauté), stirring occasionally, for 6–8 minutes until golden and cooked through. Lift out of the pan with a fish slice or draining spoon on to kitchen paper (paper towels) to drain.

6 Serve with the ham steak and the sliced tomatoes.

Sausage, sage and apple burgers

SERVES 1

½ eating (dessert) apple, sliced
1 spring onion (scallion), trimmed and finely chopped
¼ tsp dried sage
1 tsp sugar
1 tbsp water
¼ × 450 g/1 lb packet of sausagemeat or 2 thick sausages, skins removed
1 tbsp sunflower oil
1 tbsp mayonnaise
Slices of tomato and cucumber
Shredded lettuce
1 burger bun

1 Put the apple, onion, sage, sugar and water in a small saucepan (non-stick, if you have one). Cook, stirring, over a moderate heat until the apple is pulpy. Leave to cool.

2 Divide the sausagemeat in half. Flatten one piece and spoon the apple mixture into the centre, keeping away from the edges. Top with the remaining sausagemeat and press the edges well together to seal.

3 Preheat the grill (broiler).

4 Smear the burger with oil and grill (broil) for 4–5 minutes on each side until browned and cooked through. Drain on kitchen paper (paper towels).

5 Put the mayonnaise and a little salad in the burger bun and add the burger.

Fast beef in beer

If cooking for two, use the whole can of meat and double the quantity of other ingredients. If eating alone, you can use the other half for the Beef and Carrots in Wine recipe on page 289. Make the salad before you start the rest of the dish.

SERVES 1

3–4 slices of French bread
A good knob of butter or margarine
1 tsp French or English mustard
½ × 440 g/15½ oz/large can of stewed steak in gravy
2 tbsp beer (any sort)
1 tbsp instant mashed potato powder or instant oat cereal
French Bean Salad (see page 55), to serve

1 Preheat the grill (broiler). Toast the slices of bread on one side. Turn them over. Mash the butter or margarine with the mustard and spread on the untoasted sides of the bread.

2 Put the beef in a flameproof dish with the beer and stir well. Heat, stirring, until bubbling. Stir in the mashed potato or oat cereal to thicken the gravy.

3 Arrange the bread on top of the meat. Place under the grill until the bread is golden and bubbling.

4 Serve with the French Bean Salad.

Main Courses You can Do With ... two pans

Most of these recipes make one portion but a few staples – those that reheat well and can be used in different ways – serve four. Each recipe includes everything you need for a complete meal, so you don't have to juggle other pans or think what to have as accompaniments.

Ⓥ Curried potato nests Ⓥ

SERVES 1

2 potatoes, peeled and cut into
small chunks
Salt
A knob of butter or margarine
1/2 tsp curry powder or paste
1/2 tsp tomato purée (paste)
1 tbsp milk
1 1/2 mugs of frozen mixed vegetables
A handful of grated Cheddar cheese

1 Put the potatoes in a pan and cover with water and a pinch of salt. Bring to the boil, cover and boil for about 10 minutes or until tender. Drain in a colander in the sink and return to the pan.

2 Mash the potatoes with the butter or margarine, curry powder or paste, tomato purée and milk, using a potato masher or fork.

3 Cook the frozen vegetables according to the packet directions. Drain in the colander.

4 Spoon the potato into a nest on a plate. Spoon the cooked vegetables in the centre and sprinkle with the grated cheese before serving.

Ⓥ Cuban eggs Ⓥ

SERVES 1

1/4 mug of long-grain rice
2 tbsp sunflower oil
1 small onion, peeled and
finely chopped
1/2 small garlic clove, peeled and crushed,
or 1/4 tsp garlic purée (paste)
1 banana, peeled and cut into chunks
2 eggs

1 Cook the rice according to the packet directions. Drain in a colander in the sink and rinse with boiling water.

2 Heat 1 tbsp of the oil in a frying pan (skillet). Add the onion and garlic and fry (sauté) for 3 minutes until softened and lightly golden. Add the banana and cook, stirring and turning gently, for 2–3 minutes until the banana is just cooked but still holds its shape. Remove from the pan.

3 Heat the remaining oil in the frying pan. Break the eggs one at a time into a mug, then slide into the pan and cook to your liking.

4 Pile the rice on to a plate, top with the banana mixture, then the eggs and serve.

ⓥ Mushroom stroganoff ⓥ

SERVES 1

¼ mug of long-grain rice
A good knob of butter or margarine
1 small onion, peeled and chopped
1 small garlic clove, peeled and crushed,
or ½ tsp garlic purée (paste)
8 medium mushrooms, quartered
3 tbsp white wine or cider
1 tsp cornflour (cornstarch)
1 tbsp water
5 tbsp crème fraîche or plain yoghurt
Salt and pepper
1 tbsp chopped fresh parsley or a few
dried chives (optional)
A Green Salad (see page 45),
to serve

1 Cook the rice according to the packet directions. Drain in a colander in the sink and return the colander to the pan to keep warm.

2 Melt the butter or margarine in a separate pan. Add the onion and garlic and cook, stirring, for 2 minutes.

3 Add the mushrooms, stir, turn down the heat, cover and cook gently for 10 minutes.

4 Remove the lid and continue cooking until any liquid has evaporated, stirring occasionally.

5 Add the wine or cider and simmer for 2 minutes.

6 Blend the cornflour with the water and stir into the pan with the crème fraîche or yoghurt. Turn up the heat and cook, stirring, until bubbling, then cook for a further 1 minute.

7 Season to taste. Spoon the rice on to a plate, top with the mushrooms and sprinkle with parsley or chives, if liked, before serving with a Green Salad.

Spaghetti with fresh tomato ⓥ and basil sauce ⓥ

To make this even tastier, chop a small disc of goat's cheese and add it to the sauce when you toss in the spaghetti.

SERVES 1

1 tbsp olive or sunflower oil
1 small onion, peeled and chopped
2 ripe tomatoes, chopped
2 tsp tomato purée (paste)
A good pinch of sugar
Salt and pepper
3 fresh basil leaves, chopped
¼ × 450 g/1 lb packet of spaghetti
Grated cheese and a Green Salad
(see page 45), to serve

1 Heat the oil in a saucepan and add the onion. Cook, stirring, for 2 minutes. Add the tomatoes, purée, sugar and seasoning, cover and cook over a low heat for 5 minutes. Remove the lid and cook for 5 minutes until pulpy. Stir in the basil.

2 Meanwhile, cook the spaghetti according to the packet directions. Drain in a colander in the sink and return to the pan.

3 Add the tomato sauce and lift and stir to coat each strand in the sauce. Tip into a bowl and serve with grated cheese and a Green Salad.

Warm mushroom and Ⓥ butter bean salad Ⓥ

SERVES 1

2 flat mushrooms
3 tbsp olive oil
1 slice of bread, cut into cubes
1 small garlic clove, peeled and chopped
or ½ tsp garlic purée (paste)
¼ tsp dried thyme
or mixed herbs
2 tsp chopped fresh parsley
or ½ tsp dried parsley
Salt and pepper
1 × 225 g/8 oz/small can of
butter (lima) beans
½ tsp lemon juice
Lettuce leaves

1 Peel the mushrooms by gently pulling the outer layer away from the edge all round.

2 Remove any stalks and chop. Slice the caps.

3 Heat 1 tbsp of the oil in a frying pan (skillet). Add the bread cubes and fry (sauté), stirring, until golden brown all over. Drain on kitchen paper (paper towels).

4 Heat a further 1 tbsp of the oil in the frying pan. Add the mushrooms and cook, stirring gently, for 2 minutes. Cover with a lid, turn down the heat to low and cook for a further 5 minutes, stirring occasionally.

5 Add the garlic, herbs, parsley and a little salt and pepper.

6 Heat the beans in a separate saucepan, then drain and tip into a salad bowl. Add the remaining oil, the lemon juice and the contents of the mushroom pan. Lift and stir gently.

7 Put lettuce leaves on a plate. Mix the croûtons into the salad, spoon on to the lettuce and serve straight away.

Ⓥ Oriental tofu Ⓥ

If eating alone, reheat the rest the next day for 2–3 minutes in the microwave on High (100 per cent power) or in a saucepan.

SERVES 2

½ mug of long-grain rice
A knob of butter or margarine
1 tbsp sunflower oil
1 × 250 g/9 oz block of firm tofu, cubed
1 × 300 g/11 oz/medium can of broken
mandarin orange segments
1 carrot, peeled and coarsely grated
A handful of frozen peas
½ tsp ground ginger
1 tbsp clear honey
1 tbsp soy sauce
1 tbsp vinegar
1 tbsp tomato purée (paste)
½ garlic clove, peeled and crushed,
or ½ tsp garlic purée
1 tbsp cornflour (cornstarch)
1 tbsp water

1 Cook the rice according to the packet directions. Drain in a colander in the sink.

2 Meanwhile, melt the butter or margarine and oil in a frying pan (skillet). When hot but not smoking (see page 35) add the tofu and fry (sauté), stirring and turning, for 3–4 minutes until turning golden.

3 Add the oranges and half a can of water. Stir in everything else except the cornflour and water. Bring to the boil, turn down the heat and cook for 3 minutes.

4 Mix the cornflour with the water and stir into the pan. Bring back to the boil and boil for 1 minute, stirring until thickened.

5 Spoon the rice on to a plate or into a bowl and top with the tofu mixture.

Vegetarian dolmas with 🅥 cheese mash 🅥

SERVES 1

2 large outer green cabbage leaves
1 tbsp sunflower oil
1 small onion, peeled and finely chopped
½ × 100 g/4 oz/small packet of vegetarian burger mix
2 tsp tomato purée (paste)
½ mug boiling water
½ vegetable stock cube
2 potatoes, peeled and cut into fairly small chunks
A knob of butter or margarine
A handful of grated Cheddar cheese
Pepper

1 Trim off any thick central stalk from the cabbage leaves. Rinse well.

2 Heat the oil in a frying pan (skillet) and, when hot but not smoking (see page 35), fry (sauté) the onion for 2 minutes to soften.

3 Make up the burger mix according to the packet directions. Add the softened onion in its oil and the tomato purée. Mix well.

4 Put the water and stock cube in the frying pan. Bring to the boil, add the cabbage leaves, cover with a lid or foil and cook for 3 minutes. Lift the cabbage out of the stock and put the leaves side by side on a board.

5 Divide the burger mix between the cabbage leaves. Fold in two sides, then roll up to form parcels – a bit like spring rolls. Put back in the stock in the frying pan.

6 Bring to the boil, cover, turn down the heat and cook for 5–10 minutes until cooked through.

7 While the cabbage rolls are cooking, put the potatoes in a saucepan and cover with water. Add a pinch of salt. Cover, bring to the boil and boil for about 10 minutes or until the potatoes are soft.

8 Drain in a colander in the sink and return to the pan. Add the butter or margarine, cheese and a sprinkling of pepper and mash well with a potato masher or fork.

9 Pile the cheese mash on a plate and top with the cabbage rolls. Spoon any cooking stock over.

Sausage and chestnut dolmas with leek mash

SERVES 1

2 large outer green cabbage leaves
1 tbsp sunflower oil
1 onion, peeled and finely chopped
½ mug of boiling water
½ vegetable stock cube
½ × 85 g/3½ oz/small packet of
sausagemeat and chestnut stuffing mix
2 potatoes, peeled and cut into fairly
small chunks
1 leek, trimmed, washed well and sliced
Salt and pepper
A knob of butter or margarine
1 tbsp milk
Redcurrant jelly (clear conserve)
or cranberry sauce (optional), to serve

1 Trim off any thick central stalk from the cabbage leaves. Rinse well.

2 Heat the oil in a frying pan (skillet) and fry (sauté) the onion for 2 minutes to soften.

3 Make up the stuffing according to the packet directions. Add the softened onion in its oil. Mix well.

4 Put the water and stock cube in the frying pan. Bring to the boil, add the cabbage leaves, cover with a lid or foil and cook for 3 minutes. Lift the cabbage out of the stock and put the leaves side by side on a board.

5 Divide the stuffing mix between the cabbage leaves. Fold in two sides, then roll up to form parcels – a bit like spring rolls. Put back in the stock in the frying pan. Bring to the boil, cover, turn down the heat and cook for 5–10 minutes until cooked through.

6 While the cabbage rolls are cooking, put the potatoes and leek in a saucepan and cover with water. Add a pinch of salt. Cover, bring to the boil and boil for about 10 minutes or until soft.

7 Drain in a colander in the sink and return to the pan. Heat for 1 minute to evaporate any moisture. Add the butter or margarine, milk and a sprinkling of pepper and mash well with a potato masher or fork.

8 Pile the leek mash on a plate and top with the cabbage rolls. Spoon any cooking stock over.

Sausage-stuffed cabbage leaves with tomato sauce and noodles

SERVES 1

2 large green cabbage leaves
A knob of butter or margarine,
plus extra for greasing
2 tsp sunflower oil
1 smallish leek, trimmed, washed well
and thinly sliced
¼ × 450 g/1 lb packet of sausagemeat
or 2 thick sausages, skins removed
2 tsp tomato purée (paste)
¼ tsp dried sage or dried mixed herbs
½ mug of passata (sieved tomatoes)
2 tbsp water
Salt and pepper
3–4 tagliatelle nests

1 Cut out any thick stalk at the ends of the cabbage leaves. Bring a pan of water to the boil with a pinch of salt added and cook the cabbage leaves for 2 minutes. Tip into a colander over a bowl to catch the water. Rinse with cold water and dry on kitchen paper (paper towels). Reserve the cabbage water to cook the tagliatelle.

2 Heat the butter or margarine and oil in a small saucepan.

3 Add the sliced leek and cook, stirring, for 2 minutes until softened. Remove from the heat and tip the leek into a bowl. Mash in the sausagemeat, tomato purée and sage or mixed herbs with a fork.

4 Add a little extra butter or margarine to the leek saucepan and smear it round the base.

5 Put the two cabbage leaves on a board. Divide the sausage mixture between them, fold in two sides and roll up. Place, folded sides down, in the pan.

6 Pour the passata over and add the water and a sprinkling of salt and pepper. Heat until boiling, turn down the heat until just bubbling round the edges, cover with a lid and cook gently for 20 minutes. Remove the lid and boil more rapidly for 5–10 minutes or until the cabbage is cooked and the sauce has thickened.

7 While the cabbage rolls are cooking, bring the cabbage water to the boil again, add the tagliatelle and cook according to the packet directions, stirring occasionally to break up the nests. Drain in a colander in the sink.

8 Tip on to a plate and top with the cabbage rolls and their sauce.

Corn fritters with
Ⓥ satay sauce Ⓥ

The sauce will serve 3–4 people but it keeps for ages in the fridge and can be used with plain grilled or fried chicken or pork.

SERVES 1

For the satay sauce:

1 × 300 g/11 oz/medium can of coconut milk
5 tbsp crunchy peanut butter
2 tsp sugar
¼ tsp chilli powder
1 tsp wine vinegar or lemon juice
1 small garlic clove, peeled and crushed, or ½ tsp garlic purée (paste)
For the fritters:
3 tbsp plain (all-purpose) flour
Salt and pepper
1 egg
2 tbsp milk
1 × 200 g/7 oz/small can of sweetcorn (corn), drained
Oil, for cooking
Raw vegetables, such as carrots, cucumber, (bell) peppers, etc., cut into strips, for dipping

1 Put all the sauce ingredients in a pan and cook, stirring, over a moderate heat until the mixture boils. Remove from the heat.

2 Make the fritters. Put the flour with a sprinkling of salt and pepper in a bowl. Add the egg and milk and whisk with a hand blender, fork or balloon whisk until thick and smooth.

3 Stir in the sweetcorn.

4 Heat about 5 mm/¼ in of oil in a frying pan (skillet). When hot but not smoking (see page 35), add spoonfuls of the sweetcorn batter and cook for about 2 minutes until golden underneath. Turn over with a fish slice and cook the other sides. Drain on kitchen paper (paper towels).

5 Spoon about a quarter of the sauce into a small pot and put on a plate. Surround with the fritters and vegetable sticks to dip in the sauce.

Dhal with mushroom ⓥ rice ⓥ

This goes well with Cucumber Raita
(see page 43).

SERVES 1

For the rice:
1 tbsp sunflower oil
½ small onion, peeled and chopped
4-6 mushrooms, chopped
¼ mug of long-grain rice
⅔ mug of water
½ vegetable stock cube
Salt and pepper
For the dhal:
½ mug of red lentils
½ small onion, peeled and chopped
½ garlic clove, peeled and crushed,
or ¼ tsp garlic purée (paste)
1 tbsp curry powder or paste
1½ mugs of water
1 vegetable stock cube
Chutney and slices of cucumber,
to serve

1 First, make the rice. Heat the oil in
a saucepan. Add the onion and
mushrooms and cook, stirring, for
2 minutes. Add the rice and cook for
1 minute until every grain is
glistening in the oil.

2 Add the water, stock cube and a
sprinkling of salt and pepper. Bring to
the boil, stirring until the stock cube
has dissolved.

3 Turn down the heat very low, cover
with a lid and simmer for 20 minutes.
Remove from the heat, leave to stand
covered for 5 minutes, stir with a fork
to fluff up the grains.

4 While the rice is cooking, put all
the dhal ingredients in a saucepan.
Bring to the boil over a high heat, stir,
turn down the heat to moderately low
and allow to bubble gently for

15–20 minutes until thick and soft,
stirring frequently to prevent sticking.
Season to taste with salt and pepper.

5 Spoon the rice into a large bowl.
Add the dhal and serve with lots of
sliced cucumber and chutney.

Bacon and egg pancakes

SERVES 1

1 quantity of pancakes (see page 258)
2-3 rashers (slices) of streaky bacon,
rinded and cut into pieces
A knob of butter or margarine
2 eggs
4 tbsp milk
Salt and pepper
Brown table sauce
or tomato ketchup (catsup)
Slices of tomato, to serve

1 Make the pancakes. Place them on
a plate, cover and keep them warm
over a pan of gently bubbling water
while you make the filling.

2 Put the bacon and butter or
margarine in a saucepan and cook,
stirring, over a moderate heat, until
the bacon in lightly golden but not
crisp.

3 Beat the eggs with the milk and add
to the pan. Turn down the heat and
cook gently, stirring all the time until
softly scrambled. Do not boil. Season
to taste.

4 Spread the pancakes with a little
brown sauce or ketchup. Divide the
scrambled mixture between them and
roll up. Serve with slices of tomato.

Beefy stuffed pancakes

If you have a grill, you can flash the stuffed pancakes under it to brown and bubble before you serve. If you're short of milk, use a mixture of milk and water for the pancakes.

SERVES 1

For the pancakes:
8 tbsp plain (all-purpose) flour
A pinch of salt
1 egg
½ mug of milk
Oil, for cooking
For the filling:
*½ × 350 g/12 oz/large can of
corned beef, chopped*
1 tbsp tomato ketchup (catsup)
1 tbsp sweet pickle
A handful of grated Cheddar cheese
A Mixed Salad (see page 45), to serve

1 Mix the flour and salt in a bowl.

2 Make a hollow in the centre and add the egg and half the milk. Mix briskly with a hand blender, whisk or wooden spoon until thick and smooth. Stir in the remaining milk.

3 Heat a little oil in a frying pan (skillet) and pour off the excess into a small bowl to use for the next pancake. When very hot, pour in just enough batter to coat the base of the pan when tipped and swirled gently. Cook until set and the base of the pancake is golden brown.

4 Toss or flip over with a fish slice or knife. Cook the other side. Slide out on to a plate, then cover and keep warm over a pan of gently bubbling water while cooking the remainder.

5 Make the filling. Heat the corned beef with the ketchup and pickle in a saucepan, stirring.

6 Spoon over the pancakes and roll up. Place on a plate and sprinkle with grated cheese before serving with a Mixed Salad.

Crab-stuffed pancakes

SERVES 1

1 quantity of pancakes (left)
4 button mushrooms, sliced
½ mug of milk
2 tbsp plain (all-purpose) flour
A knob of butter or margarine
4 crabsticks, cut into small pieces
½ tsp lemon juice
2 tsp chopped fresh parsley
Salt and pepper
A Mixed Salad (see page 45), to serve

1 Make the pancakes. Place them on a plate, cover and keep them warm over a pan of gently bubbling water while you make the filling.

2 Put the mushrooms with all but about 3 tbsp of the milk in a saucepan. Cook over a high heat until the milk bubbles. Turn down the heat and cook for 2 minutes.

3 Blend the flour with the remaining milk in a small bowl, using a wire whisk. Stir into the mushrooms and milk in the saucepan.

4 Add the butter or margarine. Cook over a high heat, stirring all the time with the whisk, until the mixture thickens and bubbles. Turn down the heat and continue to cook, stirring, for 2 minutes. Add the crabsticks, lemon juice, parsley and salt and pepper to taste. Heat through for a further 2 minutes.

5 Divide the mixture among the pancakes, roll up and arrange on a plate. Serve with a salad.

Tuna and mexicorn pancakes

The canned filling makes enough for two servings. If eating alone, cool the remainder and store in the fridge on a plate wrapped in clingfilm to eat the next day. To reheat, roll back the clingfilm at one edge and reheat in the microwave for 2–3 minutes on High (100 per cent power) until the base of the plate feels really hot in the middle. Alternatively, remove the clingfilm and put the plate of pancakes over a pan of boiling water. Cover the pancakes with the saucepan lid and cook over a gentle heat for about 10 minutes until piping hot through.

SERVES 2

2 quantities of pancakes (see page 258)
For the filling:
1 × 185 g/6½ oz/small can of tuna, drained
1 × 295 g/10½ oz/medium can of condensed mushroom soup
1 × 200 g/7 oz/small can of sweetcorn (corn) with (bell) peppers, drained
Salt and pepper
A good handful of grated Cheddar cheese
Slices of cucumber, to garnish

1 Make the pancakes. Place them on a plate, cover and keep them warm over a pan of gently bubbling water while you make the filling.

2 Put the tuna, soup and sweetcorn in a pan. Heat through until bubbling. Season to taste.

3 Use the mixture to fill the pancakes, roll up and place on plates. Sprinkle with the cheese, then garnish with cucumber slices before serving.

French ham and cheese crêpes

If your frying pan is small, make four pancakes and divide the filling amongst them.

SERVES 1

1 quantity of pancakes (see page 258)
A large knob of butter or margarine
2 slices of ham
2 slices of Emmental (Swiss) or Leerdammer cheese
A Mixed Salad (see page 45), to serve

1 Make the pancakes, using a large frying pan (skillet) – the quantity of batter should make two large pancakes. Place them on a plate, cover and keep them warm over a pan of gently bubbling water.

2 Quickly spread a little butter or margarine over each. Put a slice of ham and cheese in the centre of each one. Fold in the edges to make flat parcels and place, folded side down, on a warm plate.

3 Serve with a Mixed Salad.

Quick beef and tomato pancakes

SERVES 1

1 quantity of pancakes (see page 258)
1 × 225 g/8 oz/small can of minced
(ground) beef with onion
1 tbsp tomato purée (paste)
A good pinch of dried mixed herbs
2 tomatoes, sliced
A good handful of grated
Cheddar cheese

1 Make the pancakes. Place them on a plate, cover and keep them warm over a pan of gently bubbling water while you make the filling.

2 Put the meat in a saucepan with the tomato purée and herbs. Heat through, stirring, until piping hot.

3 Divide between the pancakes, top with the slices of tomato and the cheese and roll up.

Ratatouille and Mozzarella Ⓥ pancakes Ⓥ

SERVES 1

1 quantity of pancakes (see page 258)
1 × 425 g/15 oz/large can of ratatouille
A good handful of grated
Mozzarella cheese
A few fresh basil leaves, torn,
or ½ tsp dried basil

1 Make the pancakes. Place them on a plate, cover and keep them warm over a pan of gently bubbling water while you make the filling.

2 Put the ratatouille in a saucepan and heat through until piping hot, stirring occasionally.

3 Divide the cheese between the pancakes, add the ratatouille, then sprinkle with the basil leaves or dried basil. Roll up and serve.

Egg foo yung with rice

SERVES 1

¼ mug of long-grain rice
3 eggs
1 tsp soy sauce, plus extra for serving
Pepper
2 spring onions (scallions), trimmed,
or 1 small onion, peeled and
finely chopped
2 tbsp frozen peas, thawed
4 crabsticks, thawed if frozen and cut
into chunks
A pinch of Chinese five-spice powder
1 tbsp sunflower oil

1 Cook the rice according to the packet directions. Drain in a colander or sieve (strainer) in the sink, then put the colander or sieve over the saucepan.

2 While the rice is cooking, use a fork or wire whisk to mix the eggs in a bowl with the soy sauce and a little pepper. Stir in the onions, peas, crabsticks and spice.

3 Heat the oil in a frying pan (skillet) over a moderate heat. Add the egg mixture and cook, lifting and stirring, until golden brown underneath and almost set.

4 Turn the omelette over with a fish slice and cook the other side.

5 Roll up and transfer to a warm plate with the rice. Sprinkle with soy sauce and serve.

Mushrooms and sweetcorn in rich tomato sauce with  cheese and egg bread Ⓥ

SERVES 1

A knob of butter or margarine
1 small onion, peeled and sliced
8 button mushrooms, left whole
or halved
½ × 400 g/14 oz/large can of
chopped tomatoes
½ tsp sugar
¼ tsp dried oregano
2 tsp tomato purée (paste)
1 × 200 g/7 oz/small can of
sweetcorn (corn)
Salt and pepper
1 slice of bread
2–3 slices of Cheddar cheese
1 egg
1–2 tbsp sunflower oil

1 Melt the butter or margarine in a saucepan. Add the onion and cook, stirring, for 3 minutes until softened. Add the mushrooms and cook, stirring, for 2 minutes.

2 Add the tomatoes, sugar, oregano, tomato purée and sweetcorn and season well. Bring to the boil, then reduce the heat until gently bubbling round the edges and cook for 10 minutes until the mushrooms are bathed in a rich sauce.

3 While the sauce is cooking, cut the bread in half and make a sandwich with the cheese. Cut in half. Break the egg on to a plate and beat with a fork until completely blended. Season the egg lightly. Dip the cheese sandwiches in the egg on both sides to coat completely.

4 Heat the oil in a frying pan (skillet) until hot but not smoking (see page 35). Add the sandwiches and fry (sauté) on both sides until golden and the cheese has melted. Drain on kitchen paper (paper towels).

5 Tip the mushroom and sweetcorn mixture into a bowl and arrange the cheese and egg bread to one side.

Spaghetti Bolognese

Prepare the salad when the sauce is cooking. It's worth making enough sauce for four people as it keeps for several days (in fact it improves in flavour!) in the fridge.

SERVES 4

3–4 good handfuls of
minced (ground) beef
1 large onion, peeled and finely chopped
1 carrot, peeled and finely chopped
1 garlic clove, peeled and crushed,
or 1 tsp garlic purée (paste)
1 × 400 g/14 oz/large can of
chopped tomatoes
2 tbsp tomato purée
3 tbsp red wine or water
1 tsp sugar
1 bay leaf
1 slice of lemon (optional)
Salt and pepper
1 × 450 g/1 lb packet of spaghetti
Grated Parmesan cheese
A Green Salad (see page 45), to serve

1 Put the beef, onion, carrot and garlic in a saucepan and cook over a fairly high heat, stirring for about 5 minutes until the meat is brown and all the grains are separate.

2 Add the tomatoes, tomato purée, wine or water, the sugar, bay leaf and lemon, if using. Season well. Bring to the boil, stirring. Part-cover, reduce the heat and simmer gently for 30 minutes until tender and the meat is bathed in a rich sauce. Remove the bay leaf and lemon, if used.

3 While the sauce is simmering, cook the spaghetti according to the packet directions. Drain in a colander in the sink.

4 Pile the spaghetti on plates. Top with the Bolognese sauce and sprinkle with Parmesan before serving with a Green Salad.

Spaghetti with
Ⓥ bean sauce Ⓥ

SERVES 4

Make as for Spaghetti Bolognese (left) but add 2 × 425 g/15 oz/large cans of red kidney beans, drained, instead of the beef. Brown the onion, carrot and garlic, then add the lentils with the tomatoes. Flavour the mixture with 1 tsp of ground cumin and 1 tsp of dried oregano and omit the bay leaf and the lemon.

Fiery mushroom
Ⓥ spaghetti Ⓥ

You can stretch this to enough for two by cooking extra spaghetti – you'll just have a bit less sauce to pasta!

SERVES 1

1 tbsp olive oil
1 small onion, peeled and
finely chopped
1 small garlic clove, peeled and crushed,
or ½ tsp garlic purée (paste)
1 small red chilli, seeded and chopped
1 canned pimiento,
drained and chopped (optional)
½ × 400 g/14 oz/large can of
chopped tomatoes
2 tsp tomato purée
6–8 mushrooms, sliced
Salt and pepper
¼ × 450 g/1 lb packet of spaghetti
A Green Salad (see page 45), to serve

1 Heat the oil in a saucepan. Add the onion and garlic and cook over a moderate heat for 2 minutes, stirring until softened but not browned.

2 Add the chilli, pimiento, if using, the tomatoes and tomato purée. Bring to the boil, reduce the heat until gently bubbling round the edges and cook for 5 minutes until pulpy.

3 Stir in the mushrooms. Season to taste and cook for 2 minutes.

4 Meanwhile, cook the spaghetti according to the packet directions. Drain in a colander and return to the pan.

5 Add the mushroom mixture and lift and stir gently over a low heat until well mixed.

6 Serve with a Green Salad.

Spaghetti with green lentil
Ⓥ and tomato sauce Ⓥ

Put the ingredients in a saucepan early in the morning, then it's ready to cook quickly at lunchtime or in the evening.

SERVES 1

⅓ mug of green lentils
½ × 400 g/14 oz large can of
chopped tomatoes
½ mug of vegetable stock,
made with ½ stock cube
1 small onion, peeled and chopped
½ small green (bell) pepper, chopped
¼ tsp dried basil
Salt and pepper
1 tsp chopped fresh parsley
or ¼ tsp dried parsley
¼ × 450 g/1 lb packet of spaghetti
1 tbsp grated Parmesan cheese

1 Put all the ingredients except the spaghetti and cheese in a saucepan and leave to stand for several hours.

2 Cook over a high heat until the mixture is boiling, stirring occasionally, then turn down the heat so it is bubbling gently round the edges, cover and cook for 30 minutes, stirring occasionally. Taste and add more seasoning if necessary.

3 Meanwhile, cook the spaghetti according to the packet directions. Drain in a colander in the sink and return to the pan. Add the lentil sauce and lift and stir with a spoon and fork until every strand is coated in the sauce.

4 Pile on a plate and sprinkle with cheese before serving.

Vegetable pasta with Ⓥ cheese sauce Ⓥ

If cooking for one, put the leftover pasta in a non-metallic dish with the cheese sauce spooned over. Reheat the next day in the microwave for 3–4 minutes on High (100 per cent power) or put it in any heatproof dish in a steamer or in a colander over a pan of boiling water. Turn the heat to moderate, cover and steam for about 10–15 minutes until hot through.

SERVES 2

1 mug of small pasta shapes
1 × 400 g/14 oz/large can of
chopped tomatoes
1 × 200 g/7 oz/small can of
sweetcorn (corn)
1 mug of frozen chopped spinach
¼ tsp dried oregano
Salt and pepper
2 tbsp plain (all-purpose) flour
1 mug of milk
A knob of butter or margarine
A good handful of grated
Cheddar cheese

1 Cook the pasta according to the packet directions. Drain in a colander in the sink.

2 Empty the tomatoes into the pan. Add the sweetcorn and spinach and boil rapidly, stirring, for 3–4 minutes until the spinach is thawed and the sauce is pulpy.

3 Stir in the pasta, the oregano and salt and pepper to taste.

4 In a separate pan, whisk the flour and milk together with a fork or balloon whisk until smooth. Add the butter or margarine and bring to the boil, stirring all the time with a wooden spoon or the whisk, until smooth and thickened. Cook for

2 minutes. Add the cheese and season to taste.

5 Reheat the pasta. Spoon on to plates and pour the cheese sauce over.

Tagliatelle alla rustica

If cooking for one, use half the sauce one day and store the rest in the fridge for another meal. You can cook all the pasta in one go and store the rest in a plastic bag in the fridge. To reheat it simply pour boiling water over it in a colander over the sink.

SERVES 2

1 small garlic clove, peeled and crushed,
or ½ tsp garlic purée (paste)
3 tbsp olive oil
1 × 50 g/2 oz/small can of anchovies,
chopped, reserving the oil
½ tsp dried oregano
2 tbsp roughly chopped fresh parsley
Pepper, preferably black
6–8 tagliatelle nests
Grated Parmesan cheese
A Green Salad (see page 45),
to serve

1 Fry (sauté) the garlic in the oil until golden brown. Remove from the heat and add the anchovies together with their oil. Return to the heat and cook gently, stirring, until the anchovies form a paste.

2 Stir in the oregano, parsley and some pepper.

3 Meanwhile, cook the tagliatelle according to the packet directions. Drain and return to the pan.

4 Add the sauce and, over a gentle heat, lift and stir gently to coat well. Spoon into bowls, sprinkle with Parmesan and serve with a Green Salad.

Vegetable and lentil curry ⓥ with rice ⓥ

The rest of the cauliflower will keep for several days in the fridge. Use it to make Creamy Cauliflower Cheese (see page 298), eat it with any of the dips on pages 43–4 or cook as a vegetable to serve with any meat or chicken. The creamed coconut will keep for ages in the fridge.

SERVES 1

*1 potato, peeled and cut into
small chunks
1 carrot, peeled and sliced
¼ small cauliflower, cut into
small florets
¼ mug of long-grain rice
1 tbsp sunflower oil
1 small onion, peeled and chopped
2 tsp curry powder or paste
2 tsp tomato purée (paste)
2 tbsp red lentils
A handful of frozen peas
⅙ block of creamed coconut,
cut into pieces
A handful of sultanas (golden raisins)
Salt and pepper*

1 Put about 10 cm/4 in water in a saucepan. Add a pinch of salt. Bring to the boil, add the potato, carrot and cauliflower, cover and boil for 5 minutes. Drain in a colander over a bowl to reserve the cooking water.

2 Bring a second saucepan of water to the boil and cook the rice according to the packet directions. Drain in a colander in the sink.

3 Heat the oil in the vegetable saucepan, add the onion and fry (sauté), stirring, for 2 minutes. Stir in the curry powder or paste, tomato purée, lentils, peas, coconut, sultanas, the partially cooked vegetables and 1 mug of the cooking water. Bring to the boil, reduce the heat and simmer for 15 minutes, adding a little more liquid if too thick. Season to taste.

4 Spoon the cooked rice on to a plate and add the curry.

ⓥ Curried eggs ⓥ

SERVES 1

A knob of butter or margarine
1 small onion, peeled and chopped
1 tsp plain (all-purpose) flour
1 tsp curry powder or paste
½ mug of vegetable stock,
made with ½ stock cube
1 tsp sweet pickle or mango chutney
5 mm/¼ in slice of creamed coconut,
cut from a block
A squeeze of lemon juice
Salt and pepper
¼ mug of long-grain rice
2 eggs, scrubbed under cold
running water
Cucumber Raita (see page 43) and a
Mixed Salad (see page 45),
to serve

1 Heat the butter or margarine in a saucepan. Add the onion and cook, stirring, for 3 minutes until lightly golden.

2 Add the flour and curry powder or paste and cook, stirring, for 1 minute.

3 Blend in the stock, add the pickle or chutney and crumble in the coconut. Cook, stirring, until thickened and the coconut has melted.

4 Turn down the heat until gently bubbling and cook for a further 15 minutes. Add lemon juice and salt and pepper to taste.

5 Cook the rice in plenty of boiling water according to the packet directions, adding the eggs to the water at the same time as the rice.

6 Lift the eggs out of the pan and put immediately into a bowl of cold water. Drain the rice in a colander in the sink.

7 Shell the eggs and cut into halves.

8 Spoon the rice on to a warm plate. Top with the egg halves, then spoon the curry sauce over. Serve with raita and a Mixed Salad.

Quick vegetable curry with ⓥ pilau rice ⓥ

SERVES 1

1 small onion, peeled and chopped
1 tbsp sunflower oil
1–2 tsp curry powder or paste
¾ mug of water
¼ block of creamed coconut
1 tsp tomato purée (paste)
1½ mugs of country-style frozen mixed
vegetables
Salt and pepper
¼ mug of long-grain rice
½ tsp ground turmeric
½ tsp garam masala
A small handful of raisins

1 Fry (sauté) the onion in the oil for 2 minutes, stirring. Stir in the curry powder or paste and cook for 1 minute.

2 Add the water, coconut and tomato purée and cook, stirring, until the coconut dissolves.

3 Add the vegetables, bring back to the boil, turn down the heat until gently bubbling round the edges and cook for 15 minutes until the vegetables are cooked and bathed in sauce.

4 While the vegetables are cooking, cook the rice according to the packet directions with the turmeric added to the water. Drain in a colander in the sink, then return to the saucepan and stir in the garam masala and raisins.

5 Pile the rice on a plate, top with the vegetable curry and serve.

ⓥ Vegetable curry cake ⓥ

SERVES 1

1 potato, scrubbed
1 small sweet potato, peeled
1 small carrot, peeled
1 small onion, peeled
1 tsp garam masala
A pinch of chilli powder
Salt and pepper
2 tsp sunflower oil
1 × 225 g/8 oz/small can of
pease pudding
1 tsp curry paste or powder
1 tsp mango chutney
5 tbsp water
5 mm/¼ in slice of creamed coconut,
cut from a block
1 tbsp chopped fresh coriander (cilantro)
A little lemon juice
Lettuce and slices of tomato and
cucumber, to garnish

1 Grate all the vegetables into a bowl. Squeeze them thoroughly and drain off the excess moisture.

2 Stir in the spices and season well.

3 Heat the oil in a frying pan (skillet). Add the grated vegetable mixture and press down well. Cover and cook over a gentle heat for 15 minutes. Remove the lid, turn up the heat to moderate and cook for a further 15 minutes until the cake is tender and the base golden brown.

4 Empty the pease pudding into a saucepan and stir in the curry paste or powder, mango chutney, water and coconut. Cook, stirring, until blended and bubbling. Season to taste and add half the coriander.

5 Transfer the cake to a warm plate. Spoon the sauce partially over the cake, sprinkle with a little lemon juice and the remaining coriander. Garnish with the salad stuffs.

Eggs and golden scallops ⓥ with peas ⓥ

SERVES 1

1–2 large potatoes, peeled
Sunflower or corn oil, for shallow-frying
Salt
Frozen or canned peas
2 eggs

1 Cut the potatoes into 5 mm/¼ in thick slices. Drop into a bowl of iced water and leave to stand for 15 minutes.

2 Heat about 5 mm/¼ in of oil on a large frying pan (skillet) until hot but not smoking (see page 35). Drain the potatoes and dry thoroughly on kitchen paper (paper towels).

3 Hold a fish slice at the side of the frying pan and slide the slices down into the pan (this will stop them from splashing into the hot oil). Cook for about 5 minutes, turning once or twice if necessary, until golden brown and cooked through.

4 Remove from the pan with the fish slice and drain on kitchen paper. Sprinkle with salt and keep warm.

5 Meanwhile, heat or cook the peas according to the directions. Drain in a colander in the sink.

6 Break the eggs one at a time into a cup, then slide into the pan. Fry (sauté) until cooked to your liking, then remove from the pan with the fish slice.

7 Serve with the potatoes and peas.

Chick peas and spinach in Ⓥ creamy paprika sauce Ⓥ

You can use 1 mug of frozen spinach – just cook it according to the packet directions.

SERVES 1

$^1/_2$ × 350 g/12 oz packet of fresh spinach
Salt and pepper
1 tsp sunflower oil
1 small onion, peeled and chopped
1 tsp paprika
$^1/_2$ × 400 g/14 oz/large can of
chopped tomatoes
1 tsp tomato purée (paste)
2 tbsp crème fraîche
$^1/_4$ tsp sugar
1 × 425 g/15 oz/large can of chick peas
(garbanzos), drained
Chopped fresh parsley or a little dried
parsley, to garnish
Pan Garlic Bread (see page 145),
to serve

1 Wash the spinach well and shake off the excess water. Tear into pieces, discarding any thick stalks. Place in saucepan and sprinkle lightly with salt and pepper.

2 Cover and cook over a moderate heat, stirring frequently for 4–5 minutes until tender and wilted. Drain in a colander in the sink, pressing out all the excess moisture.

3 Heat the oil in a separate pan. Fry (sauté) the onion gently for 3 minutes, stirring, until softened but not browned.

4 Add the tomatoes and tomato purée and cook, stirring, for 5 minutes until pulpy. Stir in half of the crème fraîche, the sugar, spinach and drained chick peas. Heat through, stirring. Taste and re-season, if necessary.

5 Spoon the mixture into a warm bowl. Add the remaining spoonful of crème fraîche and a sprinkling of parsley and serve hot with Pan Garlic Bread.

Chilli cod with spring onion mash

SERVES 1

2 good-sized potatoes, peeled
2 knobs of butter or margarine
1 frozen cod or coley steak
$^1/_2$ × 400 g/14 oz/large can of
chopped tomatoes
1 × 275 g/10 oz/medium can of green
beans, drained
A good pinch of chilli powder
or a dash of chilli sauce
A good pinch of sugar
Salt and pepper
A splash of milk
2 spring onions (scallions), trimmed
and finely chopped

1 Cut the potatoes into walnut-sized pieces. Put in a saucepan, cover with water and add a good pinch of salt. Cover, bring to the boil, turn down the heat slightly and boil for about 10 minutes or until the potatoes are tender.

2 While the potatoes are cooking, melt a knob of butter or margarine in a frying pan (skillet). When sizzling, add the frozen fish steak. Fry (sauté) for 5 minutes. Turn the fish over and add the tomatoes, then add the drained beans, the chilli powder or sauce, the sugar and a sprinkling of salt and pepper.

3 Cover the pan with a lid or foil and cook for 5 minutes.

4 When the potatoes are cooked, tip them into a colander in the sink to drain, then return the potatoes to the pan. Add the remaining butter or margarine and the milk and mash well with a fork or potato masher. Add the spring onions and a little salt and pepper to taste and mix in thoroughly.

5 Spoon the potato mixture on to a plate and put the fish and tomato mixture to one side.

Chick pea goulash with ⓥ buttered noodles ⓥ

If serving for one, store the leftover rice or pasta and goulash in separate containers in the fridge. You can reheat the remaining rice or pasta by pouring boiling water over it the following day. Heat the goulash in a saucepan until piping hot, adding extra water, if necessary.

SERVES 2

1 tbsp olive or sunflower oil
1 onion, peeled and chopped
1 carrot, peeled and sliced
1 garlic clove, peeled and crushed,
or 1 tsp garlic purée (paste)
1 × 425 g/15 oz/large can of chick peas
(garbanzos), drained
1 mug of boiling water
½ vegetable stock cube
4 button mushrooms, sliced
2 tsp paprika
A good pinch of dried oregano
A squeeze of tomato purée (paste)
½ tsp sugar
Salt and pepper
6–8 tagliatelle nests
2 knobs of butter or margarine
Crème fraîche or plain yoghurt and
caraway seeds (optional), to garnish

1 Heat the oil in a saucepan. Fry (sauté) the onion, carrot and garlic for 2 minutes, stirring.

2 Add all the remaining ingredients except the tagliatelle and butter or margarine. Bring to the boil, stirring. Turn down the heat until gently bubbling round the edges and cook for 10–15 minutes, stirring occasionally, until the chick peas are bathed in a rich sauce.

3 Meanwhile, cook the pasta according to the packet directions, stirring occasionally to separate the strands. Drain in a colander in the sink, then return to the pan. Add the butter or margarine and lift and stir until coated.

4 Pile the noodles into bowls. Top with the goulash and add a spoonful of crème fraîche or yoghurt and a sprinkling of caraway seeds, if liked.

Fish ragu

Use any white fish fillets – choose the cheapest, such as pollack or coley.

SERVES 1

1 small onion, peeled and chopped
1 small garlic clove, peeled and crushed,
or ½ tsp garlic purée (paste)
1 tbsp olive oil
½ × 400 g/14 oz/large can of
chopped tomatoes
2 tsp tomato purée (paste)
A handful of frozen peas
¼ tsp dried mixed herbs
Salt and pepper
1 piece of white fish fillet, about
150 g/5 oz, skinned and cubed
3–4 tagliatelle nests
A few basil leaves
A small handful of grated
Cheddar cheese

1 Fry (sauté) the onion and garlic in the oil in a saucepan over a moderate heat for 2 minutes until softened but not browned.

2 Add the remaining ingredients except the fish, pasta, basil and cheese. Bring to the boil over a high heat, reduce the heat to moderate until gently bubbling and cook for 5 minutes until pulpy, stirring occasionally.

3 Add the fish and cook for a further 5 minutes, stirring gently occasionally, until the fish is cooked.

4 While the sauce is cooking, cook the tagliatelle according to the packet directions, stirring occasionally to separate the strands. Drain in a colander in the sink.

5 Pile on to a plate and spoon the fish mixture over. Scatter the basil over and sprinkle with the grated cheese.

Creamy lemon chicken

If you haven't got a grater, just use 1 tbsp bottled lemon juice instead of the fresh zest and juice. You can use ordinary long-grain rice if you haven't any wild rice mix.

SERVES 1

1 skinless chicken breast
5 tbsp water
¼ chicken stock cube
1 tsp finely grated lemon zest
2 tsp lemon juice
2 tsp clear honey
1 bay leaf
Salt and pepper
½ mug of wild rice mix
1 tsp cornflour (cornstarch)
2 tsp cold water
1 tbsp double (heavy) cream
A good handful of frozen peas

1 Put the chicken breast in a saucepan. Add the water, stock cube, lemon zest and juice, honey, bay leaf, salt and pepper. Bring to the boil over a high heat, reduce the heat to fairly low, cover and cook very gently for 15 minutes.

2 While the chicken is cooking, cook the wild rice mix in boiling water according to the packet directions, adding the peas for the last 5 minutes. Drain in a colander in the sink.

3 Remove the bay leaf from the pan, then carefully lift out the chicken.

4 Mix the cornflour with the water in a cup or small bowl. Stir into the cooking juices. Bring to the boil over a high heat and cook for 1 minute, stirring all the time.

5 Stir in the cream. Return the chicken to the sauce and heat through.

6 Serve with wild rice mix and peas.

Fish and potato fry with mushy peas

If you don't like mushy peas, you can use ordinary frozen or canned ones instead but they won't make the lovely saucy base for the meal. If your fillet of fish is frozen, it will be easier to pull off the skin.

SERVES 1

1 large potato, scrubbed
1 tbsp sunflower oil
1 small onion, peeled and sliced
1 fillet of white fish, about 150 g/5 oz
Salt and pepper
1 × 300 g/11 oz/medium can of mushy peas
Tomato ketchup (catsup), to serve

1 Cut the potato into small dice.

2 Heat the oil in a frying pan (skillet) fry (sauté) the potato and onion for 5 minutes, stirring occasionally, until golden and the potato is almost cooked.

3 Meanwhile, loosen the skin from one end of the fish fillet and pull off the skin, using a knife to help ease the flesh away, if necessary. Cut the fish into bite-sized chunks.

4 Add the fish to the pan and sprinkle with salt and pepper. Turn down the heat to moderate and cook, stirring and turning over, for a further 3–4 minutes until everything is cooked and golden.

5 Empty the peas into a small saucepan and heat through.

6 Spoon the mushy peas on to a plate and pile the fish and potato mixture on top.

7 Serve with ketchup.

Chicken bites with satay sauce and couscous

Spice this up with a pinch of chilli powder mixed into the flour, if you like.

SERVES 1

¼ mug of couscous
½ mug of boiling water
1 tbsp plain (all-purpose) flour
Salt and pepper
1–2 tbsp milk
½ × small packet of plain or cheese-and-onion-flavoured crisps (potato chips), crushed
1 skinless chicken breast, cut into chunks
¼ portion of Satay Sauce (see page 256)
A Green Salad (see page 45), to serve

1 Put the couscous in a bowl and pour the boiling water over. Stir, cover with a plate and leave to stand while cooking the chicken and sauce (if you don't have any already made).

2 Mix the flour with a sprinkling of salt and pepper on a plate. Put the milk on a separate plate and the crushed crisps on a third.

3 Dip the chicken in the flour, then the milk, then the crisps.

4 Heat about 5 mm/¼ in oil in a frying pan (skillet). When hot but not smoking (see page 35), add the chicken and cook for about 3 minutes on each side until crisp, golden and cooked through. Remove with a fish slice and drain on kitchen paper (paper towels).

5 Stir the couscous with a fork to fluff up, and put on a plate. Add the chicken and the satay sauce and serve with a Green Salad.

Quick Italian chicken casserole

To use up the rest of the soup, have it for a quick lunch with some grated cheese. You could also make another meal by thinning it slightly with water and adding it to cooked dried stuffed pasta shapes (like tortellini or ravioli) with a sprinkling of grated Parmesan and dried oregano or basil.

SERVES 1

1 skinless chicken breast
1 tomato, sliced
¼ × 295 g/10½ oz/medium can of
condensed cream of tomato soup
3 tbsp water
A good pinch of dried basil
Salt and pepper
3–4 tagliatelle nests
2 tsp olive oil
A Green Salad (page 45), to serve

1 Put the chicken breast in a saucepan or flameproof casserole (Dutch oven). Lay the slices of tomato on top and spoon over the soup. Add the water, basil and a sprinkling of salt and pepper.

2 Bring to the boil over a high heat, turn down the heat until just gently bubbling round the edges, cover and cook for 20 minutes, moving the chicken around occasionally until cooked through and bathed in a rich tomato sauce.

3 While the chicken is cooking, cook the tagliatelle according to the packet directions, stirring occasionally to separate the strands. Drain the pasta in a colander in the sink and return to the pan. Add the olive oil and plenty of pepper and stir gently until every strand is coated in oil.

4 Pile the pasta on a plate. Top with the chicken and sauce and serve with a Green Salad.

Quick French chicken casserole

SERVES 1

Prepare as for Quick Italian Chicken Casserole (left) but use 3 sliced button mushrooms instead of the tomato, and condensed mushroom soup instead of the tomato soup. Use white wine instead of water, if liked, and add dried mixed herbs instead of basil.

Chinese lemon chicken with rice

If you haven't got a grater, just use 1 tbsp bottled lemon juice instead of the fresh zest and juice.

SERVES 1

¼ mug of long-grain rice
Salt
1 tbsp sunflower oil
1 skinless chicken breast, cut into thin strips
2 spring onions (scallions), trimmed and cut into short lengths
3 mushrooms, sliced
2 tsp soy sauce
1 tbsp water
Finely grated zest and juice of ½ lemon
2 tsp clear honey
A Beansprout Salad (see page 45), to serve

1 Cook the rice according to the packet directions. Drain in a colander in the sink. Rinse with boiling water and drain again.

2 Meanwhile, heat the oil in a frying pan (skillet) or wok. Add the chicken, spring onions and mushrooms and stir-fry for 6 minutes until the chicken is cooked through.

3 Add the remaining ingredients to the pan and stir-fry for a further 2 minutes.

4 Pile the rice on a warm plate with the chicken to one side. Serve with a Beansprout Salad.

Cheat's chicken Maryland with buttered sweetcorn rice

SERVES 1

¼ mug of long-grain rice
A large knob of butter or margarine
1 × 200 g/7 oz/small can of sweetcorn (corn)
Salt and pepper
2 rashers (slices) of streaky bacon, rinded and cut in half
6 chicken nuggets
1 small banana, cut into 4 chunks
2 tbsp sunflower oil
2 tomatoes, quartered

1 Cook the rice according to the packet directions. Drain in a colander in the sink. Rinse with boiling water, then drain again. Return to the pan and stir in the butter or margarine, sweetcorn and a good sprinkling of pepper. Cover with a lid and leave to one side.

2 Roll up each half rasher of bacon.

3 Heat enough oil to cover the base of a frying pan (skillet). Add the nuggets, and fry (sauté) for 3 minutes. Turn over and add the bacon and banana chunks. Fry for a further 3 minutes, turning the bacon and banana once, until golden and cooked but the banana pieces are still holding their shape.

4 Heat the rice mixture for a minute or two, stirring. Pile on to a plate, arrange the chicken, bacon and banana to one side and add the wedges of tomato.

Chicken paprika

SERVES 1

A good knob of butter or margarine
1 small onion, peeled and sliced
1 chicken portion
2 tsp paprika
½ × 400 g/14 oz/large can of
chopped tomatoes
1 small red (bell) pepper, thinly sliced
Salt and pepper
3–4 tagliatelle nests
1 tsp caraway seeds (optional)
1 tbsp plain yoghurt
A little chopped fresh parsley or a little
dried parsley, to garnish
A Green Salad (see page 45), to serve

1 Melt half the butter or margarine over a high heat in a small flameproof casserole dish (Dutch oven) or a saucepan. Fry (sauté) the onion, stirring, for 2 minutes.

2 Add the chicken and fry, turning, until browned all over. Add all the remaining ingredients except the caraway seeds and yoghurt. Bring to the boil, reduce the heat until just bubbling around the edges, part-cover and cook for 20 minutes. Remove the lid after 10 minutes.

3 While the chicken is cooking, cook the tagliatelle according to the packet directions, stirring once or twice to separate the strands. Drain in a colander in the sink and return to the pan. Add the remaining butter or margarine, the caraway seeds, if using, and a good sprinkling of pepper. Heat gently, stirring until every strand is coated.

4 Remove the chicken from the sauce and transfer to a plate. Stir the yoghurt into the sauce. Taste and re-season, if necessary. Do not re-boil.

5 Spoon over the chicken, garnish with parsley and serve with the noodles and a Green Salad.

Oriental chicken curry

SERVES 1

5 mm/¼ in slice of creamed coconut,
cut from a block
½ mug of boiling water
1 tbsp curry powder
¼ tsp Chinese five-spice powder
1 skinless chicken breast, diced
1 tbsp sunflower oil
1 small garlic clove, peeled and crushed,
or ½ tsp garlic purée (paste)
Salt
2 tsp chopped fresh coriander (cilantro)
¼ mug of long-grain rice
½ bunch of spring onions (scallions),
trimmed and cut into short lengths
A Beansprout Salad (see page 45),
to serve

1 Crumble the coconut into a bowl and stir in the boiling water. When dissolved, stir in the curry and five-spice powders. Leave to cool, then add the chicken and leave to marinate for 1 hour.

2 Heat the oil in a frying pan (skillet) or wok over a fairly high heat. Add the garlic and stir-fry for 30 seconds.

3 Lift the chicken out of the marinade, add to the pan and stir-fry for 5 minutes. Pour in the marinade and cook over a moderate heat for a further 15–20 minutes, stirring. Season with salt to taste and stir in the coriander.

4 While the chicken is cooking, cook the rice according to the packet directions, adding the spring onions for the last 5 minutes' cooking time. Drain in a colander in the sink.

5 Spoon the rice on to a plate, top with the curry and serve.

Chicken and coconut masala with pilau rice

If you are into spices and authentic cooking, add a couple of cardamom pods and a piece of cinnamon stick to the water when cooking the rice. To avoid using a third pan when you are preparing the accompaniment, grate the carrots in advance, then heat the mustard seeds in the oil in the rinsed-out rice pan when it is draining in the colander.

SERVES 1

¼ tsp ground turmeric
1 chicken stock cube
¼ mug of long-grain rice
¼ tsp garam masala
1 tbsp sunflower oil
1 skinless chicken breast, diced,
or a handful of diced chicken meat
1 small onion, peeled and chopped
1–2 tsp curry powder or paste
½ mug of water
5 mm/¼ in of creamed coconut,
cut from a block
A small handful of raisins
A small handful of fresh coriander
(cilantro), chopped

1 Put a pan half-full of water on to boil. Add the turmeric and half the stock cube. When boiling, add the rice. Stir, bring to the boil and allow to boil for 10 minutes or until the rice is tender but still has some 'bite'. Drain in a colander in the sink. Stir in the garam masala.

2 While the rice is cooking, heat the oil in a separate saucepan. Add the chicken and onion and stir-fry for 3 minutes. Stir in the curry powder or paste and cook for 1 further minute.

3 Add the water, coconut and raisins. Crumble in the other half of the stock cube. Bring to the boil, stirring, turn down the heat, cover and cook gently, stirring occasionally, for about 6 minutes until the chicken is cooked and bathed in a rich sauce. Season to taste. Stir in the coriander.

4 Pile the rice on a plate and top with the curry.

Shanghai rice

If you have any cooked chicken left over from another meal, you can use it instead of (or in addition to) the ham.

SERVES 1

⅓ mug of long-grain rice
2 handfuls of frozen mixed vegetables
2 tsp sunflower oil
1 egg, beaten
1–2 slices of ham, diced
2.5 cm/1 in piece of cucumber, diced
1 spring onion (scallion),
trimmed and chopped
1 tsp soy sauce
Salt and pepper

1 Cook the rice according to the packet directions. Add the vegetables for the last 5 minutes' cooking. Drain in a colander in the sink, rinse with boiling water and drain again.

2 Heat half the oil in a frying pan (skillet) or wok. Add the egg and fry (sauté), stirring, until just beginning to set. Add the rice, ham, cucumber and onion and cook, stirring, for about 3 minutes until piping hot.

3 Sprinkle with the soy sauce and stir gently, then serve.

Simple fried chicken and chips

SERVES 1

1 large potato, scrubbed or peeled
1 chicken portion
1 tbsp milk
2 tsp plain (all-purpose) flour
Salt and pepper
2 tbsp butter or margarine
2 tsp olive oil
Sunflower or corn oil, for cooking
1 tsp lemon juice
1 tsp chopped fresh parsley
or ½ tsp dried parsley
A Green Salad (see page 45), to serve

1 Cut the potato into thick slices, then into thick chips (fries). Place in a bowl of cold water.

2 Dip the chicken in the milk, turning to coat completely. Mix the flour with a little salt and pepper and sprinkle it all over the chicken to coat completely.

3 Melt half the butter or margarine and the olive oil in a frying pan (skillet) over a high heat. Fry (sauté) the chicken, turning, to brown on all sides. With the skin-side up, cover the pan, reduce the heat to fairly low and cook gently for about 20 minutes until the chicken is tender and cooked through.

4 While the chicken is cooking, heat about 2.5 cm/1 in of sunflower or corn oil in a separate pan. Drain the raw chips and dry on kitchen paper (paper towels). When the oil is very hot (see page 35), carefully slide in the chips (I slide them down a fish slice, so they don't splash into the hot oil). They will bubble furiously. Cook, turning if necessary, until golden brown – it should take about

6 minutes. Do not leave them unattended. Lift out of the oil with a draining spoon and drain on kitchen paper.

5 Transfer the chicken to a plate. Add the remaining butter or margarine, lemon juice and parsley to the frying pan, turn up the heat and stir until melted. Season lightly.

6 Spoon over the chicken and serve straight away with the chips and a Green Salad.

Garlic-fried chicken and chips

SERVES 1

Prepare as for Simple Fried Chicken and Chips (left) but add a small finely chopped garlic clove to the browned chicken before covering and finishing cooking (Step 3).

Spicy fried chicken and chips

SERVES 1

Prepare as for Simple Fried Chicken and Chips (left) but add a good pinch of chilli powder to the seasoned flour and add a few drops of Tabasco sauce or other chilli sauce with the lemon juice (Step 5). Serve with tomato or chilli relish on the side.

Fragrant fried chicken and chips

SERVES 1

Prepare as for Simple Fried Chicken and Chips (left) but add 1 tsp of chopped fresh basil or sage, or ¼ tsp dried, with the parsley (Step 5).

Savoury herb-crumbed turkey steak with carrot mash

You can use any flavour of stuffing mix. If you have a lemon, squeeze a wedge of it over the fried turkey for extra zing.

SERVES 1

2 potatoes, peeled and cut into small chunks
1–2 carrots, peeled and sliced
Salt and pepper
A knob of butter or margarine
1 turkey breast steak
2 tbsp milk
2 tbsp sage and onion stuffing mix
Sunflower oil, for cooking
Redcurrant jelly (clear conserve)
or cranberry sauce, to serve

1 Put the potatoes and carrots in a pan and cover with water. Add a pinch of salt, bring to the boil, part-cover and boil for about 10 minutes or until very tender.

2 Drain in a colander in the sink and return to the pan. Mash with the butter or margarine and a sprinkling of salt and pepper, using a fork or potato masher.

3 Put the turkey steak in a plastic bag and beat with a rolling pin or bottle until flattened.

4 Put the milk on one plate and the stuffing on another. Dip the steak in the milk, then stuffing mix, to coat completely. If necessary, repeat the process to coat thoroughly.

5 Heat enough oil to coat the base of a frying pan (skillet). When hot but not smoking (see page 35), add the turkey steak and fry (sauté) over a fairly high heat for 3 minutes on each side until golden brown and cooked through.

6 Transfer the turkey and the carrot mash to a plate and serve with redcurrant jelly or cranberry sauce.

American fried chicken with rice, peas and sweetcorn

SERVES 1

2 tbsp milk
1 tbsp plain (all-purpose) flour
Salt and pepper
1 chicken portion
1 small knob of butter or margarine
1 tbsp sunflower oil
¼ mug of long-grain rice
A small handful of frozen peas
1 × 200 g/7 oz/small can of sweetcorn (corn)
1 banana

1 Put the milk on a small plate. Put the flour with a sprinkling of salt and pepper on another one. Turn the chicken portion over in the milk until it is wet all over. Put it on the flour plate and turn it over, using your hands to help coat the portion completely in the flour.

2 Heat the butter or margarine and oil in a frying pan (skillet) until sizzling. Add the chicken, skin-side down, and fry (sauté) for about 3 minutes until the skin is golden brown. Turn the chicken over and turn down the heat and continue to fry the chicken for about 20 minutes until cooked through, moving it in the pan from time to time so it doesn't burn.

3 While the chicken is cooking, cook the rice according to the packet directions, adding the peas for the last 5 minutes. Drain in a colander in the sink and return to the pan.

4 Add the can of sweetcorn, heat through for 1 minute, stirring, then turn off the heat and cover the pan with a lid.

5 When the chicken is almost cooked, peel and cut the banana into three or four pieces. Add to the chicken and cook, turning the pieces over for a few minutes until they are slightly softened and lightly browned.

6 Spoon the rice, peas and sweetcorn on to a plate. Add the chicken and banana and serve.

Chicken with peppers and pasta

SERVES 1

½–1 mug of pasta shapes
1 tbsp olive or sunflower oil
1 small onion, peeled and thinly sliced
1 small yellow (bell) pepper, cut into strips
1 skinless chicken breast
½ × 400 g/14 oz/large can of chopped tomatoes
A pinch of sugar
A pinch of dried oregano
Salt and pepper

1 Cook the pasta according to the packet directions. Drain in a colander in the sink.

2 While it is cooking, heat the oil in a frying pan (skillet) and fry (sauté) the onion and pepper for 2 minutes, stirring. Add the chicken and cook for 1 minute on each side to seal.

3 Add the remaining ingredients, with salt and pepper. Cover with a lid and turn down the heat to fairly low. Cook for 20 minutes.

4 Stir in the pasta until coated in sauce.

5 Heat for 1 minute, then serve.

Cidered turkey rice with sweetcorn and cheese

SERVES 1

¼ mug of long-grain rice
1 × 200 g/7 oz/small can of sweetcorn
(corn), drained
A handful of grated Cheddar cheese
A knob of butter or margarine
1 small turkey steak
4 tbsp cider or apple juice
5 tbsp water
½ chicken stock cube
4 button mushrooms, sliced
A good pinch of dried thyme
or dried mixed herbs
Pepper
1 tsp cornflour (cornstarch)
1 tbsp crème fraîche
A pinch of dried parsley
or chopped fresh parsley, to garnish

1 Cook the rice according to the packet directions. Drain in a colander in the sink, return to the pan and add the corn and cheese and cover with the lid.

2 Meanwhile, melt the butter or margarine in a frying pan (skillet) over a fairly high heat. Add the turkey and brown on both sides.

3 Add the cider or apple juice, 4 tbsp of the water, the crumbled stock cube and mushrooms and season with the thyme or mixed herbs and pepper.

4 Bring to the boil, stirring to dissolve the stock cube, then turn down the heat until just gently bubbling round the edges, cover and cook for about 8 minutes or until tender and cooked through.

5 Remove the turkey steak and keep warm.

6 Mix the cornflour with the remaining water and stir in. Bring to the boil, stirring, and boil for 1 minute.

7 Stir the crème fraîche into the sauce and heat through. Taste and re-season.

8 Stir the rice to mix thoroughly and spoon on to a plate. Top with the turkey and spoon the sauce over. Sprinkle with the parsley.

Crunchy pork steak with cheese and chive mash

SERVES 1

1 large potato, peeled and cut into
small chunks
1 small pork shoulder steak
1 tbsp plain (all-purpose) flour
Salt and pepper
2–3 tbsp sage and onion stuffing mix
4–5 tbsp milk
Sunflower oil, for shallow-frying
A knob of butter or margarine
A handful of grated Red Leicester or
Cheddar cheese
1 tsp dried chives
Slices of tomato, to serve

1 Boil the potato pieces in plenty of boiling water with a pinch of salt added for about 10 minutes until tender.

2 While they are cooking, put the pork steak in a plastic bag and beat with a rolling pin or bottle until flattened and fairly thin. Coat in the flour and sprinkle lightly with salt and pepper.

3 Put the stuffing mix in a shallow dish and about half the milk in a separate dish.

4 Dip the pork in the milk, then stuffing, to coat well. Repeat the coating to cover thoroughly.

5 Heat the oil in a frying pan (skillet) and fry (sauté) the pork for 4–5 minutes until golden brown underneath.

6 Turn over and fry the other side for 4–5 minutes until cooked through and golden. Drain on kitchen paper (paper towels).

7 When the potato pieces are cooked, drain in a colander in the sink and return to the pan. Mash well with the butter or margarine and the remaining milk, using a fork or potato masher, then beat in the cheese and chives and season to taste with salt and pepper.

8 Spoon the mash on to a plate and add the pork to one side. Serve with slices of tomato.

Mock Peking duck

This is so much cheaper than the real thing but equally tasty! It's not worth making it for just one person, so share it with friends.

SERVES 4

1 bunch of spring onions (scallions),
trimmed
1/4 cucumber, cut into thin strips
4 good handfuls of turkey stir-fry pieces
1 tbsp sunflower oil
4 tbsp soy sauce
1 1/2 tsp ground ginger
1 garlic clove, peeled and crushed,
or 1 tsp garlic purée (paste)
1 tbsp vinegar
4 tbsp plum jam (conserve)
1 tsp lemon juice
12 small flour tortillas

1 Cut the spring onions into short lengths, then shred finely. Put into a bowl, cover with clingfilm (plastic wrap) and put them in the fridge to get really cold. Put the cucumber in a separate bowl and also chill.

2 Cut any thick pieces of turkey into thinner strips. Mix half the soy sauce, ½ tsp of the ginger, the garlic and vinegar in a container with a sealable lid and add the turkey. Stir well to coat completely, seal with the lid and leave in the fridge to marinate for at least 1 hour or up to 6 hours if necessary.

3 Mix the plum jam and lemon juice in a small bowl with the remaining soy sauce and ginger.

4 When nearly ready to eat, put the tortillas on a plate over a pan of simmering water Cover with another plate or the saucepan lid and warm through.

5 Heat the oil in a large frying pan (skillet) or wok. Stir-fry the turkey for about 5 minutes until cooked through.

6 Spread each tortilla with a little of the plum sauce. Add a few strips of spring onion, cucumber and turkey, then roll up.

Turkey stroganoff with tagliatelle

You can use beer, cider or apple juice instead of the wine – whatever comes to hand!

SERVES 1

3–4 tagliatelle nests
A good knob of butter or margarine
1 small onion, peeled and sliced
4 button mushrooms, sliced
1 small turkey breast steak,
cut into strips
1 tbsp white wine
5 tbsp crème fraîche
Salt and pepper
A little chopped fresh or dried parsley
A Green Salad (see page 45), to serve

1 Cook the tagliatelle according to the packet directions, stirring occasionally to separate the strands. Drain in a colander in the sink.

2 While the pasta is cooking, melt the butter or margarine in a saucepan. Add the onion, mushrooms and turkey and stir-fry for 6–8 minutes until everything is cooked.

3 Add the wine and let it bubble briefly. Stir in the crème fraîche and season to taste. Heat through briefly. Don't let the mixture boil, especially if you use low-fat crème fraîche, or the mixture will curdle.

4 Pile the tagliatelle on to a plate, spoon the stroganoff to one side and sprinkle with the parsley, if using. Serve with a Green Salad.

Frankfurters with sauerkraut and mustard potatoes

This is so tasty and dead easy! If cooking for one, cook half the quantity of potatoes and mustard mixture and heat half the frankfurters and sauerkraut. Store the rest in covered containers in the fridge for up to 5 days. If making the same dish again, to heat the remaining frankfurters, wrap them in foil and add them to the pan of potatoes after 10 minutes' cooking. Alternatively, use the frankfurters for another recipe. Sauerkraut goes well with grilled or fried sausages or a pork shoulder chop.

SERVES 2

8 even-sized potatoes, peeled but left whole
1 × 410 g/15 oz/large can of frankfurters
1 × 450 g/1 lb jar of sauerkraut
2 tsp caraway seeds
2 tbsp butter or margarine
1 tbsp German, French or grainy mustard
A pinch of sugar
Salt and pepper
1 tbsp chopped fresh parsley or 1 tsp dried parsley

1 Put the potatoes in a pan and cover with water. Add a pinch of salt.

2 Peel the label off the can of frankfurters. Wash the outside of the can with hot water. Open the can and pour off about half of the liquid. Stand the can of frankfurters in the pan with the potatoes. Bring to the boil, part-cover and boil for 15–20 minutes or until the potatoes are tender but still holding their shape.

3 While the potatoes are cooking, empty the sauerkraut into a separate pan. Sprinkle with the caraway seeds and heat through.

4 When the potatoes are cooked, lift the can of frankfurters out of the pan. Drain the potatoes in a colander in the sink.

5 Melt the butter or margarine in the potato pan with the mustard, sugar, salt and pepper. Stir to blend. Return the potatoes to the pan and turn gently in the mustard mixture to coat.

6 Serve the sauerkraut with the frankfurters on top with the potatoes to one side.

Sausage sauté

SERVES 1

1 large potato, peeled and cut into small
even-sized pieces
1 large carrot, peeled and sliced
4 chipolata sausages,
each cut into 3 pieces
1 onion, peeled and chopped
A good pinch of dried sage
or mixed herbs
A good knob of butter or margarine
Salt and pepper
A splash of milk

1 Cook the potatoes and carrots
together in boiling, lightly salted
water for about 10 minutes until
tender. Drain in a colander in the
sink.

2 Fry (sauté) the sausage pieces,
onion and herbs in half the butter or
margarine for about 4 minutes,
stirring all the time, until browned
and cooked through.

3 Using a fork or potato masher, mash
the potatoes and carrots with the
remaining butter or margarine and a
splash of milk. Season to taste. Spoon
the mash on to a warm plate and
shape into a 'nest'.

4 Spoon the sausages and onions into
the centre and serve straight away.

Barbecued bangers and pea mash

SERVES 1

2 good-sized potatoes, peeled
4 chipolata sausages
2 tsp vinegar
2 tsp tomato purée (paste)
1 tsp brown table sauce
2 tsp golden (light corn) syrup
or clear honey
A knob of butter or margarine
1 × 275 g/10 oz/medium can of
garden peas, drained

1 Cut the potatoes into walnut-sized
pieces. Put in a saucepan, cover with
water and add a pinch of salt. Cover
with a lid, bring to the boil, turn
down the heat slightly and boil for
about 10 minutes until tender.

2 While the potatoes are cooking,
heat a frying pan (skillet) and add the
sausages, separating them first if
necessary. Fry (sauté), turning
occasionally, for 8 minutes until
brown all over.

3 Add the vinegar, tomato purée,
brown sauce and syrup or honey to
the pan and stir until blended. Turn
the sausages over in the mixture to
coat completely and cook for a
minute or two until stickily glazed.

4 Drain the potatoes in a colander or
sieve (strainer) in the sink. Return to
the pan over a low heat and add the
butter or margarine and drained peas.
Mash with a potato masher or fork
until blended. Give the mixture a
vigorous stir after mashing to make it
more fluffy. Heat, stirring, for
1 minute.

5 Pile the pea and potato mash on to
a plate and top with the bangers in
their sticky glaze.

Rustic pan pork steak

SERVES 1

A knob of butter or margarine
1 large potato, peeled and
cut into small chunks
1 pork shoulder steak
Salt and pepper
A good pinch of dried oregano
4 mushrooms, sliced
½ mug of water
½ chicken stock cube
A handful of French (green) beans,
topped and tailed
1 small garlic clove, peeled
and finely chopped
1 tbsp chopped fresh parsley

1 Melt the butter or margarine in a
frying pan (skillet) over a high heat.
Add the potatoes and pork and brown
the pork for 2 minutes on each side,
turning the potatoes frequently to
brown slightly all over. Season and
sprinkle with the oregano.

2 Add the mushrooms, the water and
stock cube, then turn up the heat and
bring to the boil, stirring to dissolve
the stock cube. Turn down the heat,
cover with a lid, plate or foil and cook
gently for 15 minutes until tender.

3 Sprinkle the garlic and parsley over,
cover and cook gently for 5 minutes.

4 While the pork mixture is cooking,
cook the beans in boiling, salted
water for about 6 minutes or until just
tender but still with some 'bite'. Drain
in a colander in the sink.

5 Transfer the pork and potatoes to a
plate. If the liquid left in the pan is
rather thin, boil it quickly, stirring,
until it thickens slightly.

6 Pour the liquid over the pork. Add
the beans and serve.

Pork and green pepper stir-fry with oyster sauce

A jar of oyster sauce will last ages
and is great for loads of
Chinese-style meals.

SERVES 1

A good handful of pork stir-fry meat
2 tsp cornflour (cornstarch)
Salt and pepper
1 tbsp sunflower oil
3 spring onions (scallions),
trimmed and chopped
1 small green (bell) pepper, cut into
narrow strips
½ mug of pork or chicken stock, made
with ½ stock cube
2 tsp oyster sauce
A pinch of dried sage
½–1 slab of Chinese egg noodles

1 Toss the pork in the cornflour,
seasoned with a little salt and pepper.

2 Heat the oil in a frying pan (skillet)
over a high heat. Add the spring
onions and pepper and stir-fry for
3 minutes. Remove from the pan with
a draining spoon.

3 Add the pork and stir-fry until
browned.

4 Return the vegetables to the pan
and add all the remaining ingredients
except the noodles. Bring to the boil,
turn down the heat to fairly low and
cook for about 8 minutes, stirring
occasionally, until the pork is tender
and bathed in sauce.

5 Meanwhile, cook the noodles
according to the packet directions,
stirring occasionally to separate the
strands.

6 Drain and pile into a bowl. Spoon
the stir-fry on top and serve.

Sticky ham steak with sautéed vegetable medley

SERVES 1

2 tbsp sunflower oil
1 potato, scrubbed and cut into
small dice
1 carrot, peeled and thinly sliced
1 × 200 g/7 oz/small can of sweetcorn
(corn), drained
Salt and pepper
A pinch of dried mixed herbs
A knob of butter or margarine
1 round ham steak
2 tsp orange marmalade
A pinch of ground ginger
¼ tsp lemon juice

1 Heat the oil in a saucepan. Add the diced potato and sliced carrot and fry (sauté), stirring, for 5 minutes until the potatoes are turning golden. Turn down the heat, cover with a lid and cook gently for a further 5 minutes.

2 Add the sweetcorn, a sprinkling of salt and pepper and the herbs. Stir, re-cover and leave over a very low heat while you cook the ham steak.

3 Heat the butter or margarine in a frying pan (skillet). Snip the edges of the ham steak to prevent it curling up. Add to the pan and fry for 2 minutes. Turn the steak over and smear with half the marmalade and all the ginger, and sprinkle with the lemon juice. Cook for 2 minutes.

4 Turn the steak over and add the remaining marmalade. Cook for 2 minutes. Turn the steak over briefly again to brown the underside.

5 Transfer to a plate and spoon any sticky glaze over. Serve with the vegetable medley.

Pytt i panna

This was originally a Swedish dish made with leftover cooked meat. I prefer to make it with sausages. If you like, cook the potato in a microwave for about 4 minutes instead of boiling it in a pan.

SERVES 1

1 large potato, scrubbed
A knob of butter or margarine
1 tbsp olive or sunflower oil
1 small onion, peeled and thinly sliced
3–4 pork sausages, cut into chunks
1–2 rashers (slices) of streaky bacon,
rinded and diced
1 tsp Worcestershire sauce
Salt and pepper
1 egg

1 Prick the potato and boil in water for about 20 minutes until tender. Cut into dice.

2 Heat half the butter or margarine and half the oil in the same pan over a high heat. Add the onion, sausage chunks and bacon pieces and fry (sauté) for 5–6 minutes, stirring, until golden brown and cooked through. Remove from the pan with a draining spoon.

3 Put the potatoes in the pan. Fry, stirring, for about 5 minutes until golden brown. Return the sausage mixture to the pan and sprinkle over the Worcestershire sauce and some salt and pepper.

4 In a frying pan (skillet), heat the remaining oil and butter or margarine over a fairly high heat. Break the egg into a mug and slide the egg into the pan. Cook to your liking.

5 Spoon the potato mixture on to a plate and top with the egg.

Pork and water chestnut stir-fry with fried egg noodles

The leftover water chestnuts can be frozen in their liquid in a covered container for up to 3 months. When thawed, they lose a bit of their crunchiness but you won't really notice in cooked dishes.

SERVES 1

½ slab of Chinese egg noodles
1 tbsp sunflower oil
1 small onion, peeled, cut into wedges
and separated into layers
A good handful of pork stir-fry meat
1 head of pak choi, shredded,
or a wedge of green cabbage
1 small garlic clove, peeled and crushed,
or ½ tsp garlic purée (paste)
½ × 225 g/8 oz/small can of water
chestnuts, drained and sliced
A good pinch of Chinese
five-spice powder
2 tsp soy sauce

1 Put the noodles in a bowl and cover with boiling water. Leave to soak for 5 minutes. Drain thoroughly in a colander in the sink.

2 Heat half the oil in a frying pan (skillet). Add the onion and stir-fry for 2 minutes. Add the pork and stir-fry for 3 minutes.

3 Add the pak choi or cabbage, the garlic, water chestnuts and five-spice powder. Stir-fry for a further 2–3 minutes until cooked to your liking. Stir in the soy sauce.

4 Quickly heat the remaining oil in a separate frying pan and, when very hot, add the noodles. Fry, lifting and stirring with a spoon and fork, for 2–3 minutes until crisp and golden.

5 Tip on to a plate and serve with the pork stir-fry.

Pork and spring onion stir-fry with rice

SERVES 1

½ bunch of spring onions (scallions),
trimmed
2 tsp cornflour (cornstarch)
Salt and pepper
A good handful of pork stir-fry meat
¼ mug of long-grain rice
A good knob of butter or margarine
2–3 mushrooms, sliced
6 tbsp apple juice
1 tsp tomato purée (paste)

1 Cut the spring onions diagonally into short lengths.

2 Mix the cornflour with a sprinkling of salt and pepper and stir in the pork.

3 Cook the rice according to the packet directions.

4 While the rice is cooking, melt the butter or margarine in a frying pan (skillet). Add the spring onions, pork and mushrooms and stir-fry for 4 minutes.

5 Add the juice and tomato purée, bring to the boil, stirring, then turn down the heat and cook gently for 5 minutes, stirring occasionally, until the pork is cooked through and bathed in a thick sauce. Season to taste with salt and pepper.

6 Drain the rice in a colander in the sink. Rinse with boiling water and drain again.

7 Spoon the rice on to a plate and top with the pork mixture.

Sweet and sour pork with vegetable rice

You can use pineapple instead of orange juice, if you prefer.

SERVES 1

¼ mug of long-grain rice
1½ mugs of frozen mixed vegetables
1 eating (dessert) apple
2 belly pork slices
½ mug of water
2 tsp sugar
2 tsp vinegar
1 tbsp tomato ketchup (catsup)
2 tsp soy sauce
1 tbsp raisins
3 tbsp pure orange juice

1 Put at least 3 mugs of water in a saucepan with a pinch of salt. Bring to the boil and add the rice and vegetables. Bring back to the boil, stir well and cook for 10 minutes, then drain in a colander in the sink and return to the saucepan. Cover with a lid to keep warm.

2 While the rice is cooking, cut the apple into quarters, then peel and cut out the core. Cut the apple into small chunks.

3 Cut the rind off the slices of pork, then cut them into chunks, discarding any bones. Heat a frying pan (skillet). Add the pork and fry (sauté), stirring, for 10 minutes until brown and cooked through.

4 Add the remaining ingredients to the pan, bring back to the boil and cook, stirring, for 2 minutes until the pork is coated in the sauce.

5 Spoon the rice on to a plate, top with the pork and serve.

Meatballs with spaghetti

The rest of the stuffing mix can be kept for crumb-coating chicken, meat or fish (see Crunchy Pork with Cheese and Olive Mash, page 280).

SERVES 1

A good handful of minced (ground) beef
½ small garlic clove, peeled and crushed, or ¼ tsp garlic purée (paste)
2 tbsp sage and onion stuffing mix
2 tsp grated Parmesan cheese
Salt and pepper
¼ × 450 g/1 lb packet of spaghetti
2 tbsp sunflower oil
½ mug of passata (sieved tomatoes)
¼ tsp dried basil or dried oregano
½ tsp sugar
Grated Parmesan cheese and a Green Salad (see page 45), to serve

1 Mix the meat with the garlic, stuffing mix, cheese and a sprinkling of salt and pepper.

2 Squeeze the mixture well together with your hands and shape into small balls.

3 Cook the spaghetti according to the packet directions.

4 While the spaghetti is cooking, heat the oil in a frying pan (skillet) and fry (sauté) the meatballs for about 3 minutes, turning until brown all over. Pour off the oil.

5 Add the passata to the frying pan with the herbs and sugar. Cover with a lid, plate or foil, and cook over a gentle heat for about 7 minutes while the spaghetti finishes cooking.

6 Drain the spaghetti in a colander in the sink. Pile on to a plate and lift the meatballs on to the spaghetti. Spoon the sauce over.

7 Sprinkle with Parmesan and serve with the salad.

Fried piquant steak and sautéed potatoes with sweetcorn

SERVES 1

3 tbsp sunflower oil
2 knobs of butter or margarine
1 large potato, scrubbed and
cut into cubes
1 × 200 g/7 oz/small can of
sweetcorn (corn)
1 thin frying steak
½ tsp lemon juice
Pepper
1 small onion, peeled and
finely chopped
1 tbsp chopped fresh parsley
or 1 tsp dried parsley
1 tsp soy sauce
1 tbsp Worcestershire sauce

1 Heat 2 tbsp of the oil and 1 knob of the butter or margarine in a frying pan (skillet) or saucepan. Add the potatoes and stir until coated in the fat. Continue to fry (sauté), stirring and turning occasionally, for about 10 minutes until golden and cooked through.

2 Drain the can of sweetcorn, add to the pan and heat through, stirring.

3 Put the steak in a plastic bag and beat with a rolling pin or bottle to tenderise and flatten it. Sprinkle generously with the lemon juice and pepper.

4 Melt the remaining butter or margarine in a separate frying pan (skillet) over a high heat. Add the steak and cook for about 2 minutes on each side until just cooked through. Remove from the pan and put on a plate.

5 Put the onion in the frying pan and cook, stirring, for 1 minute. Add the parsley, soy and Worcestershire sauces and allow to bubble for 1 minute.

6 Spoon over the steak and serve with the potatoes and sweetcorn.

Simple beef curry

Share this with friends or store the leftovers in a covered container in the fridge for up to 3 days. The flavour actually improves with keeping.

SERVES 4

2 tbsp plain (all-purpose) flour
Salt and pepper
4–6 handfuls of diced braising steak,
about 700 g/1½ lb
3 tbsp sunflower oil
2 large onions, peeled and chopped
1 garlic clove, peeled and crushed,
or 1 tsp garlic purée (paste)
2 tbsp mild curry paste or powder
3 tbsp mango chutney
2 mugs of beef stock,
made with 1 stock cube
1 tbsp tomato purée (paste)
2 tbsp fresh chopped coriander (cilantro)
1 mug of long-grain rice
2 tbsp desiccated (shredded) coconut,
to garnish

1 Mix the flour with a little salt and pepper in a plastic bag. Add the meat, hold the bag ends firmly and shake the bag to coat the meat in the flour.

2 Heat 2 tbsp of the oil in a flameproof casserole dish (Dutch oven) or saucepan. Add the meat and cook over a high heat until no longer pink, stirring frequently. Remove from the pan with a draining spoon.

3 Add the remaining oil and fry (sauté) the onions and garlic, stirring, for 2 minutes until lightly golden.

4 Add the curry paste or powder and stir over the heat for 1 minute.

5 Add the chutney, stock and tomato purée. Bring to the boil, stirring all the time. Turn down the heat very low so the liquid is just bubbling very gently around the edges. Cover and cook for 2½ hours, stirring occasionally and adding a little water if drying out.

6 About 15 minutes before the curry will be ready, cook the rice according to the packet directions. Drain in a colander in the sink, then spoon on to plates.

7 Season the curry and stir in the coriander. Spoon the curry on top of the rice and sprinkle with coconut.

Beef and carrots in wine

If cooking for two, use more potatoes (obviously!), the whole can of meat, a medium-sized onion and add a drained 300 g/11 oz/medium can of button mushrooms. If eating alone, use the rest of the meat for the Fast Beef in Beer recipe on page 249.

SERVES 1

1 large or 2 medium potatoes, peeled and cut into small chunks
Salt and pepper
A knob of butter or margarine
1 tbsp milk
1 small onion, peeled and finely chopped
1 tbsp sunflower oil
½ × 420 g/15 oz/large can of stewed steak in gravy
5 tbsp red wine
1 tsp tomato purée (paste)
A pinch of sugar
¼ tsp dried mixed herbs
1 × 275 g/10 oz/medium can of carrots, drained
2 tsp cornflour (cornstarch)
4 tsp water

1 Put the potatoes in a pan with enough water to cover. Add a pinch of salt. Bring to the boil, part-cover and boil for about 10 minutes or until tender (the exact time will depend on the size of the chunks of potato). Drain the potatoes in a colander in the sink. Return to the pan and mash with a potato masher or fork with the butter or margarine and milk. Season to taste with pepper.

2 While the potatoes are cooking, fry (sauté) the onion in the oil in a separate pan for 3 minutes, stirring until lightly golden.

3 Add the meat, wine, tomato purée, sugar, herbs and a sprinkling of pepper. Stir gently to combine and heat until bubbling, stirring gently occasionally.

4 Add the carrots, stir gently again and heat until bubbling, stirring gently occasionally, taking care not to break up the pieces of meat and the carrots.

5 Blend the cornflour with the water. Stir into the pan and cook, stirring gently, until thickened. Cook for 1 minute.

6 Spoon the mashed potatoes into a large nest on a plate and spoon the beef in wine into the centre.

Traditional keema curry with rice

Make the salad in advance to allow the flavours to develop.

SERVES 1

2 tsp sunflower oil
1 small onion, peeled and chopped
A good handful of minced (ground) beef
2 tsp curry powder
1 small garlic clove, peeled and crushed, or ½ tsp garlic purée (paste)
¼ tsp ground ginger
5 tbsp water
1 tsp tomato purée
Salt
¼ mug of long-grain rice
Eastern Tomato Salad (see page 46), to serve

1 Heat the oil in a frying pan (skillet). Add the onions and fry (sauté) gently, stirring, for 2 minutes until softened but not browned.

2 Add the meat and fry until browned and all the grains are separate.

3 Add the curry powder and fry for a further 3 minutes, stirring.

4 Add the garlic, ginger, water, tomato purée and salt to taste. Bring to the boil, stirring, reduce the heat and simmer gently for 15–20 minutes, stirring from time to time, until everything is cooked. Taste and add more salt, if necessary.

5 Meanwhile, cook the rice according to the packet directions. Drain in a colander in the sink.

6 Spoon the rice on to a plate and spoon the keema to one side. Serve with Eastern Tomato Salad.

Chilli con carne

If cooking for one, store the leftover chilli in a covered container in the fridge for up to 3 days. Use it for tacos (see page 203), enchiladas (see page 326) or to top jacket potatoes.

SERVES 4

4 handfuls of minced (ground) lamb or beef
1 large onion, peeled and chopped
1 tsp chilli powder
1 tsp ground cumin
1 tsp dried oregano
2 mugs of passata (sieved tomatoes)
2 × 425 g/15 oz/large cans of red kidney beans, drained
1 tbsp tomato purée (paste)
Salt and pepper
1 mug of long-grain rice
Shredded lettuce and grated Cheddar cheese, to serve

1 Put the mince and onion in a saucepan and dry-fry, stirring, over a high heat for 5 minutes until the meat is no longer pink and all the grains are separate.

2 Stir the chilli powder (add more if you like your chilli hot), cumin and oregano into the meat and cook for 1 minute.

3 Stir in the passata, beans, tomato purée and a little salt and pepper.

4 Bring to the boil and when bubbling, turn down the heat until just bubbling round the edges and simmer for 20 minutes, stirring occasionally.

5 While the sauce is cooking, cook the rice according to the packet directions. Drain in a colander in the sink and spoon into bowls. Top with the chilli and serve with shredded lettuce and grated Cheddar cheese.

Kidneys in rich tomato and broccoli sauce with eggy bread

SERVES 1

2 lamb's kidneys
A knob of butter or margarine
1 small onion, peeled and sliced
½ × 400 g/14 oz/large can of
chopped tomatoes
½ tsp sugar
¼ tsp dried mixed herbs
½ tsp vinegar
1 small head of broccoli,
cut into very small florets
Salt and pepper
1 slice of bread
1 egg
1–2 tbsp sunflower oil

1 Cut the kidneys in half. Using scissors (or a sharp knife if you don't have any scissors), snip out the central cores, then cut the kidneys into bite-sized pieces.

2 Melt the butter or margarine in a saucepan. Add the onion and cook, stirring for 3 minutes until softened. Add the kidneys and cook, stirring, for 2 minutes until brown all over.

3 Add the tomatoes, sugar, herbs, vinegar and broccoli and season well. Bring to the boil, then reduce the heat until gently bubbling round the edges and cook for 10 minutes, stirring occasionally, until the kidneys are tender and the tomato mixture is pulpy.

4 While the kidneys are cooking, cut the bread into four triangles. Break the egg on to a plate and beat with a fork until completely blended. Season the egg lightly. Dip the bread in the egg on both sides to coat completely.

5 Heat the oil in a frying pan (skillet) until hot but not smoking (see page 35). Add the bread and fry (sauté) on both sides until golden, then drain on kitchen paper (paper towels).

6 Tip the kidney and broccoli mixture into a bowl and arrange the eggy bread around the edges.

Corned beef fritters with tomato mash and peas

If you've got a big appetite, double the quantity of batter and corned beef. Wrap the rest of the corned beef in clingfilm and store in the fridge for up to 3 days.

SERVES 1

1 large potato, peeled and cut into smallish chunks
½ mug of frozen peas
4 tbsp plain (all-purpose) flour
1 tsp baking powder
Salt and pepper
About 5 tbsp water
¼ × 350 g/12 oz/large can of corned beef, cut into slices
Oil, for shallow-frying
A knob of butter or margarine
1–2 tbsp tomato ketchup (catsup)

1 Put the potato pieces in a pan. Stand the mug of peas in the pan too. Pour cold water on to the potatoes, around the mug. Add a pinch of salt to the potatoes and peas. Bring to the boil, cover with a lid, reduce the heat and cook for about 10 minutes until the potatoes and peas are cooked.

2 While the potatoes are cooking, put the flour in a bowl and stir in the baking powder and a little salt and pepper. Mix with enough water to form a thick creamy batter.

3 Dip the slices of corned beef in the batter.

4 Heat about 5 mm/¼ in oil in a frying pan (skillet) until hot but not smoking (see page 35) and fry (sauté) the fritters for about 3 minutes on each side until golden brown.

5 Drain on kitchen paper (paper towels).

6 Lift the mug of peas out of the saucepan. Drain the potatoes in a colander in the sink and return to the pan. Add the butter or margarine and mash well with a fork or potato masher. Work in tomato ketchup to taste. Drain off any water from the peas.

7 Spoon the tomato mash on to a plate. Add the fritters and peas and serve.

Main Courses You can Do With ... an electric Steamer (or a Colander and a Saucepan)

My daughter discovered that many students have an electric steamer – and steaming is a very healthy and easy way to cook. But you don't have to have a special gadget as all these recipes can be cooked equally well in a metal colander over a saucepan of gently bubbling water.

A word of warning: You **must not** let the pan boil dry when steaming. Top it up from time to time with boiling water from the kettle but don't let the water come into contact with the food. An electric steamer usually has a gauge to show you the water level. If it does run dry, it will switch off – which is very safe but really annoying if you are timing a recipe, so look out!

Melting cheese, mushroom ⓥ and chutney rolls ⓥ

Use the soft bread for breadcrumbs for another recipe. Store the rest of the mushrooms in a covered container in the fridge for a toasted sandwich (see page 83) or for the quick pasta recipe on page 300.

SERVES 1–2

2 soft round rolls
½ × 170 g/6 oz/small can of creamed mushrooms
½ tsp dried oregano
2 tsp tomato chutney
A good handful of grated Cheddar cheese
A selection of salad stuffs, to serve

1 Cut the top off each roll and pull out most of the soft bread, leaving a thick wall all round.

2 Spoon the mushrooms into the rolls and sprinkle with the oregano. Top each with a spoonful of chutney.

3 Pack the cheese into the rolls. Cover with the 'lids'. Wrap each one in foil.

4 Place in an electric steamer or in a colander over a saucepan of simmering water. Cover and steam for 10 minutes until the cheese has melted.

5 Unwrap and serve straight away with a selection of salad stuffs.

✔ Pizza rolls ✔

Spread the soft bread you've pulled out on a plate or baking (cookie) sheet and leave to dry for a few hours, then crumble and store in a plastic bag to make breadcrumbs. If not intending to use for a while, pop the tied bag in the freezer or ice box of the fridge.

SERVES 1-2

2 soft rolls
2 tomatoes, chopped
2 tsp tomato purée (paste)
A good sprinkling of dried oregano
2 handfuls of grated Mozzarella
or Cheddar cheese

1 Cut a slit across the top of each roll, not quite cutting the slice off the top.

2 Gently pull out some of the soft bread inside, leaving a thick wall.

3 Mix the chopped tomatoes with the tomato purée and spoon into the rolls. Sprinkle with the oregano and top with the cheese.

4 Wrap each roll in foil and place in an electric steamer or a colander over a pan of simmering water. Cover and steam for 10 minutes until the cheese has melted and they are hot through.

Cheesy rice and carrot ✔ pudding ✔

If you like more sauce, heat some passata in a saucepan or put in a small bowl in the electric steamer while cooking the beans and tomatoes.

SERVES 1

2 tbsp risotto rice
1 carrot, peeled and chopped
3 tbsp milk
1 tbsp double (heavy) cream
A handful of grated Cheddar cheese
¼ tsp dried mixed herbs
2 tomatoes
A good handful of French (green) beans,
topped and tailed

1 Mix together all the ingredients except the tomatoes and beans and spoon into an individual dish (a cereal bowl will do).

2 Cover the bowl securely with foil and place in an electric steamer or in a colander over a pan of simmering water. Cover and steam for 45 minutes.

3 Put the tomatoes in a fairly large piece of foil, sprinkle with the sugar and a pinch of salt and pepper and wrap loosely but securely. Put beside the cheese pudding with the beans (if in an electric steamer, you can use a separate tier). Steam for a further 15 minutes or until the rice is soft and has absorbed all the liquid.

4 Leave the rice pudding to cool for 3 minutes, then loosen the edges and turn out on to a plate. Add the tomatoes and beans and serve.

Cheese fondue with 🆅 crudités 🆅

This is a party dish, rather than dinner for one. You can also serve chunks of French bread to dip in.

SERVES 4

*2 large handfuls of grated
Cheddar cheese
2 large handfuls of grated Emmental
(Swiss) cheese
2 tsp cornflour (cornstarch)
6 tbsp fruity dry white wine,
such as Chardonnay
1 tbsp kirsch or vodka
4 tbsp crème fraîche
A pinch of cayenne or chilli powder
Pepper, preferably black
1 large carrot, peeled and
cut into matchsticks
2 celery sticks, cut into matchsticks
5 cm/2 in piece of cucumber,
cut into matchsticks
1 red (bell) pepper, cut into slices*

1 Put the cheeses in a bowl over a pan of simmering water or in the rice bowl of an electric steamer and mix with the cornflour. Add the wine and kirsch or vodka.

2 Steam, stirring, for about 10 minutes until the mixture is melted and creamy. Stir in the crème fraîche and season the fondue with the cayenne or chilli powder and pepper to taste.

3 Arrange the vegetables on four plates. Spoon the fondue into small bowls or pots, place on the plates with the vegetable sticks and serve straight away.

Cheese and broad bean 🆅 mash with parsley 🆅

SERVES 1

*1 large potato, peeled and cut into
walnut-sized pieces
½ mug of frozen
baby broad (fava) beans
Salt and pepper
A knob of butter or margarine
1 tbsp milk
2 tsp chopped fresh parsley
1 cm/½ in finger of Edam (Dutch)
cheese, cut into small cubes*

1 Spread the potatoes and beans out in a steamer tier or in a colander over a pan of simmering water. Sprinkle with salt, then cover and steam for 25 minutes or until really tender.

2 Tip the cooked vegetables into a bowl. Add the butter or margarine and milk and mash thoroughly with a potato masher or fork. Season to taste and add the parsley and cheese. Stir until the cheese is beginning to melt, then serve.

Scalloped potatoes with  onion

These potatoes will sit quite happily in the steamer for longer than their cooking time, so don't worry if other foods take slightly longer to cook. These taste good on their own for lunch, or as an accompaniment to meat, chicken or fish.

SERVES 1

A good knob of butter or margarine
1 large potato, peeled and thinly sliced
1 small onion, peeled and thinly sliced
Salt and pepper
2 tbsp milk
Tomato ketchup (catsup) and
a Green Salad (see page 45), to serve

1 Grease a large sheet of foil with the butter or margarine.

2 Put the potatoes in a layer on the centre of the foil. Separate the onion slices into rings and scatter over the top, then sprinkle with salt and pepper.

3 Spoon over the milk, then fold the foil up over the potatoes, sealing the edges well together. Transfer to an electric steamer or a colander over a pan of simmering water.

4 Cover and steam for 20–30 minutes until cooked through (the time will depend on how thickly you cut the potatoes).

5 Transfer to a plate. Open up and eat with ketchup and salad.

Scalloped potatoes with cheese

SERVES 1

Prepare as for Scalloped Potatoes with Onion (left) but add a good handful of grated Cheddar cheese over the potatoes before adding the onion.

Scalloped potatoes with ham and tomatoes

SERVES 1

Prepare as for Scalloped Potatoes with Onions (left) but add a chopped slice of ham and a sliced tomato to the layer of potatoes before adding the onion, and sprinkle the whole thing with $\frac{1}{4}$ tsp dried basil.

Ⓥ Spiced potato cakes Ⓥ

These are like Rosti (see page 133) but not fried. They make a good snack with some pickles, and a more substantial meal with a steam-cooked egg on top. You can also eat them with meat or fish or with a curry as a change from rice.

SERVES 1–2

2 large potatoes, scrubbed
1 small onion, peeled
½ tsp ground cumin
¼ tsp ground coriander (cilantro)
A good pinch of salt
A pinch of pepper
1 tbsp plain (all-purpose) flour
1 tbsp fresh chopped coriander
or parsley
1 small egg, beaten
A little sunflower oil, for greasing

1 Grate the potatoes coarsely into a colander. Squeeze thoroughly to remove excess liquid. Tip into a bowl.

2 Grate the onion into the bowl and stir in the cumin, ground coriander, salt, pepper, flour and herbs. Mix with the beaten egg.

3 Lightly oil two squares of foil. Shape the mixture into two flat cakes and place one on each piece of foil. Fold the foil over and seal the edges all round. Place in an electric steamer or in a colander over a pan of simmering water and steam for 30 minutes until tender.

4 Slide on to warm plates and serve.

Puy lentil and vegetable Ⓥ pot Ⓥ

This is also delicious served cold, sprinkled with a little balsamic vinegar to taste.

SERVES 2

½ mug of Puy lentils
1 carrot, peeled and chopped
1 red (bell) pepper, cut into small dice
1 courgette (zucchini), cut into small dice
2 spring onions (scallions),
trimmed and chopped
½ mug of hot vegetable stock,
made with ½ stock cube
1 small bay leaf
Salt and pepper
A little chopped fresh parsley,
to garnish
Crusty bread, to serve

1 Rinse the lentils and place in a bowl that will fit in your steamer. Add the remaining ingredients. Cover with foil.

2 Place in the electric steamer or in a colander over a pan of simmering water. Cover and steam for 45 minutes until the lentils and vegetables are tender and most of the liquid is absorbed.

3 Discard the bay leaf, garnish with the chopped parsley and serve with crusty bread.

Creamy cauliflower ⓥ cheese ⓥ

This version of cauliflower cheese omits the necessity for making cheese sauce in a saucepan. To turn it into a lunch dish, open a large can of chopped tomatoes and stand it in the steamer at the same time as cooking the cauliflower. Spoon them over the vegetable before adding the cheese sauce.

SERVES 1–2

½ small cauliflower, cut into small florets
Salt and pepper
A good handful of grated Cheddar cheese
5 tbsp milk
¼ tsp English mustard
2 tsp cornflour (cornstarch)
1 tbsp crushed cornflakes, to garnish

1 Put the cauliflower in an electric steamer or in a colander over a saucepan of simmering water. Sprinkle with salt.

2 Mix the cheese, milk, mustard and cornflour together in a small bowl. Add a little salt and pepper. Place either in the colander with the cauliflower or in a separate tier if using an electric steamer.

3 Cover and steam for 10 minutes. Stir the sauce and rearrange the florets. Cook for a further 10 minutes until the cauliflower is tender and the sauce is thick.

4 Transfer the cauliflower to a serving dish. Stir the sauce well and spoon over the cauliflower. Sprinkle with crushed cornflakes and serve.

Creamy mushrooms with ⓥ wine and garlic ⓥ

This will also make a delicious starter for four people, to impress your friends.

SERVES 1–2

8 medium mushrooms
A good knob of butter or margarine
1 garlic clove, peeled and crushed, or 1 tsp garlic purée (paste)
6 tbsp dry white wine
Salt and pepper
6 tbsp single (light) cream
1 tbsp chopped fresh parsley
French bread, to serve

1 Trim and cut the mushrooms into thick slices.

2 Melt the butter or margarine in the rice bowl of an electric steamer or in a shallow dish in a colander over a pan of simmering water. Stir in the garlic.

3 Add the mushrooms and stir gently. Pour over the wine and sprinkle with salt and pepper. Cover the dish with foil, then cover and steam for 25 minutes. Remove the foil but leave the dish in the steamer.

4 Stir in the cream. Taste and re-season, if necessary. Leave in the steamer, uncovered, for 2 minutes to heat through without boiling at all.

5 Spoon into warm dishes. Sprinkle with the parsley and serve with lots of crusty bread to mop up the juices.

All-in-one risotto
ⓥ Milanese ⓥ

Risottos are made normally by adding a little stock at a time. This version bypasses all that effort, but still creates a creamy, glorious risotto. Saffron is expensive, so look out for saffron stock cubes for rice, which will give you the flavour you want without costing you a fortune. If you do happen to have some saffron (maybe brought back from holiday abroad), stir a good pinch into the boiling water and add half a vegetable or chicken stock cube.

SERVES 1

*1 small onion, peeled and
finely chopped
1 tbsp olive oil
½ mug of risotto rice
½ saffron rice stock cube
1¼ mugs of boiling water
Salt and pepper
1 tbsp butter or margarine
1 tbsp grated Parmesan cheese
1 tbsp chopped fresh parsley,
to garnish*

1 Fry (sauté) the onion in the oil in a small frying pan (skillet) for 2 minutes to soften. Stir in the rice until glistening. Tip into the rice bowl of an electric steamer or a bowl that will fit in a colander over a pan of simmering water.

2 Stir the stock cube into the boiling water and add to the rice with a little salt and pepper.

3 Cover with foil, then a lid and steam for 30 minutes until most (but not all) of the liquid has been absorbed and the rice is tender but still has some 'bite'.

4 Stir in the butter or margarine and the Parmesan to form a creamy risotto and serve garnished with chopped parsley.

Bulghar salad in crisp
ⓥ lettuce ⓥ

SERVES 1

*¼ mug of bulghar (cracked wheat)
¼ mug of boiling water
Salt and pepper
2 tbsp olive oil
1 tbsp lemon juice
1 small garlic clove, peeled and crushed,
or 1 tsp garlic purée (paste)
1 ripe tomato, chopped
½ green (bell) pepper, chopped
2 tsp dried mint
4–5 round lettuce leaves*

1 Put the bulghar in the rice bowl of an electric steamer or a bowl that will fit in a colander over a saucepan of simmering water. Stir in the boiling water and a good pinch of salt. Cover with foil, then the lid, and steam for 20 minutes.

2 Remove from the steamer and stir in plenty of pepper, the oil and lemon juice. Leave to cool.

3 Stir in all the remaining ingredients except the lettuce.

4 Spoon the mixture into the lettuce leaves, roll up and eat.

Saucy mushroom
Ⓥ pasta Ⓥ

Serve this as a side dish with steamed or grilled meat or chicken. It is also delicious on its own, sprinkled with grated Parmesan cheese. You can add any ingredients you like, from cooked, peeled prawns, to diced, cooked chicken, spicy chorizo sausage, cooked, diced vegetables or drained sweetcorn and tuna. You can also vary the flavours with other canned soups to complement the rest of the meal, such as creamed vegetable with vegetables, or cream of chicken with cooked chicken or tuna.

SERVES 1–2

1 mug of large pasta shapes
A knob of butter or margarine,
for greasing
1 × 200 g/7 oz/small can of cream of
mushroom soup (not condensed)
½ mug of milk
Salt and pepper
¼ tsp dried oregano
1 tbsp chopped fresh parsley
or 1 tsp dried parsley

1 Put the pasta shapes into a greased shallow heatproof dish that will fit in a colander over a pan of simmering water or into the rice bowl of an electric steamer.

2 Blend the soup with the milk and stir in. Season well and stir in the oregano. Cover the dish with foil.

3 Place in the steamer, cover and steam for 20 minutes. Stir well, re-cover and steam for a further 20 minutes until the pasta is cooked through and bathed in sauce. Stir again, taste and re-season, if necessary. Sprinkle with the parsley and serve.

Ⓥ Steam-boiled eggs Ⓥ

Serve these with toast or bread in your normal way. They are cooked so gently that the results are perfect every time.

COOK UP TO 8 EGGS

1 Place the eggs either in the special holder in the rice bowl of an electric steamer or in a bowl that will fit in a colander over a saucepan. You can put them in a polystyrene or cardboard egg box to hold them in the steamer tier but take care when removing it – if it's cardboard, it will be very hot and soggy!

2 Cover and steam for 8–10 minutes for soft-boiled; 15–20 minutes for hard-boiled (hard-cooked).

Ⓥ Creamy scrambled eggs Ⓥ
COOK UP TO 8 EGGS

1 Melt a knob of butter or margarine either in the rice bowl of an electric steamer or in a bowl standing in a colander over a pan of gently simmering water. Do not let the water come in contact with the bowl.

2 Whisk in the eggs and 1 tbsp milk for each egg. Add seasoning to taste.

3 Cook, stirring all the time, until the eggs softly scramble but are still creamy (the time will depend on the number of eggs). Serve straight away.

ⓥ Warm vegetable salad ⓥ

You can use whatever vegetables you have to hand. Add a little cooked diced meat or chicken or tuna to this just before serving, if liked.

SERVES 1–2

1 carrot, peeled and diced
1 potato, peeled and diced
¼ small cauliflower, cut into tiny florets
1 courgette (zucchini), diced
A handful of frozen peas
or broad (fava) beans
1 tbsp olive or sunflower oil
1 tsp lemon juice
A good pinch of dried mixed herbs
Salt and pepper
French bread, to serve

1 Put all the vegetables in an electric steamer or in a colander over a pan of simmering water. Spread them out evenly. Cover and steam for 15–20 minutes until tender.

2 Tip into a bowl, sprinkle with the oil, lemon juice, herbs and a little salt and pepper. Lift and stir with a spoon and fork to blend and serve warm with French bread.

Easy-does-it macaroni ⓥ cheese ⓥ

SERVES 1

½ mug of macaroni
1 mug of water
Salt and pepper
¼ × 200 g/7 oz tub of cheese spread
1 tbsp milk
2 tomatoes, sliced

1 Put the pasta in the rice bowl of an electric steamer or in a bowl that will fit in a colander over a pan of simmering water. Add the water and a good pinch of salt and stir well.

2 Cover loosely with foil, then the lid. Steam for 15 minutes. Stir well, re-cover and steam for a further 15 minutes until tender. Stir, then drain and return to the dish or turn into a serving dish if you used the rice bowl.

3 Stir in the cheese spread until melted, then thin with the milk.

4 Arrange the sliced tomatoes over the top. Cover the dish with foil again and either return to the steamer for 2–3 minutes to heat through or flash under a preheated grill (broiler) to heat through and lightly cook the tomatoes.

ⓥ Chakchouka ⓥ

SERVES 1

½ green (bell) pepper, thinly sliced
1 tomato, chopped
½ small garlic clove, peeled and crushed,
or ¼ tsp garlic purée (paste)
2 tsp olive oil
1 tsp tomato purée
Salt and pepper
A good pinch of sugar
1–2 eggs
Pitta breads, to serve

1 Put the pepper, tomato, garlic, oil, tomato purée, a little salt and pepper and the sugar in the rice bowl of an electric steamer or in a bowl that will fit in a colander over a pan of simmering water. Stir well. Cover with a lid and steam for 20 minutes, stirring once, until tender.

2 Make a well for each egg in the mixture and break an egg in. Re-cover and steam for a further 6–10 minutes or until the eggs are cooked to your liking.

3 Serve with pitta breads.

Greek-style lamb-stuffed aubergine

Use the remaining half of the aubergine in a ratatouille (see page 219) or for the Cheese-topped Aubergine Layer on page 212.

SERVES 1

1 large aubergine (eggplant)
1 small onion, peeled and
finely chopped
1 small garlic clove, peeled and crushed,
or ½ tsp garlic purée (paste)
A handful of minced (ground) lamb
2 tsp tomato purée
A pinch of ground cinnamon
A pinch of dried oregano
2 tsp water
A pinch of sugar
Salt and pepper
1 cm/½ in finger of feta cheese
A Village Salad (see page 45)
and pitta bread, to serve

1 Halve the aubergine lengthways. Place one half in an electric steamer or in a colander over a pan of simmering water, then cover and steam for 10 minutes. Lift out and leave to cool.

2 Scoop out most of the aubergine with a teaspoon, leaving a wall all round. Chop the scooped-out flesh.

3 Put the onion, garlic and meat in a saucepan and cook, stirring all the time until the lamb is no longer pink and all the grains are separate. Stir in the chopped aubergine, the tomato purée, cinnamon, oregano, water, sugar and salt and pepper to taste.

4 Put the aubergine shell in a small shallow dish. Pack the meat mixture into the shell and crumble the feta cheese over. Cover the dish with foil. Steam for 30 minutes.

5 Serve with salad and pitta bread.

Neapolitan-style ham and eggs

You can buy other dry-cured raw hams that are cheaper than the traditional Parma – look out for them in your supermarket. The Pan Garlic Bread on page 145 goes really well with this, or you could eat it with some crusty bread and, maybe, a salad too.

SERVES 1

A little olive oil, for greasing
1 slice of Parma ham, finely chopped
2 tomatoes, chopped
2 fresh basil leaves, chopped
2 eggs
2 tbsp single (light) cream
Salt and pepper

1 Lightly oil a small dish (a cereal bowl will do).

2 Put the ham in the base and top with the tomato and the basil.

3 Break the eggs in.

4 Spoon the cream over and season with salt and pepper.

5 Place in the steamer or in a colander over a pan of simmering water, then cover and steam for 10–15 minutes or until the eggs are cooked to your liking.

Sweet and sour pork medley

If you're eating alone, cook half the
noodles the first day. Cool the
remaining sweet and sour mixture
and reheat either in the steamer for
about 10 minutes or in a saucepan the
following day. Cook the remaining
noodles fresh.

SERVES 2

A good handful of pork stir-fry meat
2 spring onions (scallions), trimmed and
cut into short lengths
2 carrots, peeled and
cut into matchsticks
¼ cucumber, cut into matchsticks
2 celery sticks, cut into matchsticks
1 red (bell) pepper, cut into thin strips
2 tsp cornflour (cornstarch)
2 tbsp wine vinegar
2 tbsp water
A good pinch of ground ginger
½ mug of chicken or vegetable stock,
made with ½ stock cube
1 tbsp sugar
2 tbsp soy sauce
1 slab of Chinese egg noodles

1 Put the pork in an even layer in the
rice bowl of an electric steamer, or in
a shallow heatproof dish that will fit
in a colander over a pan of
simmering water.

2 Cover and steam for 10 minutes.

3 Add all the vegetables. Blend the
cornflour in a small bowl with the
vinegar and water, then stir in all the
remaining ingredients except the
noodles. Pour over the pork and
vegetables.

4 Cover with foil and steam for
15 minutes. Stir well, re-cover and
steam for a further 15 minutes until
the vegetables are just cooked but still
have some 'bite', and the pork is
tender.

5 Meanwhile, put the noodles in a
bowl and cover with boiling water.
Stir, then leave to stand for at least
5 minutes to soften.

6 Stir the cooked sweet and sour
mixture. Remove from the colander, if
necessary. Drain the noodles in the
colander in the sink. Spoon into
bowls and top with the pork mixture.

Ⓥ Cheese soufflé Ⓥ

A light-as-air dish, that needs
absolutely no skill at all!

SERVES 1

4 tbsp cheese spread
1 tbsp milk
1 tbsp plain (all-purpose) flour
¼ tsp made English or Dijon mustard
Salt and pepper
1 egg, separated
1 tbsp crushed cornflakes
A Green Salad (see page 45) and crusty
bread, to serve

1 Put the cheese, milk, flour and
mustard in a bowl and season with a
little salt and pepper. Stir in the egg
yolk and mix vigorously until smooth.

2 Whisk the egg white until stiff, then
stir gently into the mixture with a
metal spoon.

3 Grease an individual dish (a cereal
bowl will do). Spoon the mixture into
the dish and sprinkle with the
cornflakes. Place in an electric
steamer or in a colander over a pan
of simmering water. Cover and steam
for 15 minutes until risen and set.

4 Serve with a Green Salad and crusty
bread. Don't hang around or it will
sink!

Blue cheese and walnut pot

This is a delicious light meal, served with crusty bread and a salad. A slice of bread, crust removed, pulled into small pieces, will do if you haven't any proper breadcrumbs.

SERVES 1

A knob of butter or margarine,
for greasing
1 egg, separated
3 tbsp crème fraîche
3 tbsp milk
1 tbsp chopped walnut pieces
A good handful of fresh
white breadcrumbs
A handful of crumbled blue cheese
1 tbsp snipped fresh chives
or 1 tsp dried chives
Salt and pepper
1 tbsp tomato ketchup (catsup)
2 tsp tomato purée (paste)
½ tsp Worcestershire sauce

1 Grease an individual heatproof dish (a cereal bowl will do).

2 Beat the egg yolk with 2 tbsp of the crème fraîche and 2 tbsp of the milk in another bowl. Mix in the nuts, breadcrumbs and cheese. Stir in the chives and some salt and pepper.

3 Whisk the egg white until stiff with a hand blender or balloon whisk and stir in gently, cutting and turning the mixture over gently with a metal spoon. Turn into the greased dish.

4 Place in an electric steamer, or in a colander over a pan of simmering water. Cover and steam for 20 minutes until set.

5 Meanwhile, mix the remaining crème fraîche with the tomato ketchup, purée and Worcestershire sauce. Thin to a pouring consistency with the remaining milk.

6 Loosen the steamed mixture all round the edges with a round-bladed knife and turn it out on to a plate, then spoon the sauce around.

Minted lamb and peas with couscous

SERVES 1

A knob of butter or margarine
1 onion, peeled and very finely chopped
A good handful of frozen minced
(ground) lamb
1 mug of frozen peas
½ round lettuce, finely shredded
1 tsp dried mint
Salt and pepper
¼ mug of couscous
½ mug of boiling water
Crusty bread, to serve

1 Melt the butter or margarine in the rice bowl of an electric steamer or in a bowl that will fit in a colander over a pan of simmering water. Add the onion and lamb and steam until the mince is cooked and all the grains are separate. Add the peas, lettuce, mint and a little salt and pepper. Stir well.

2 Put the couscous in a separate bowl that will fit in a steamer tier or in a saucepan with a colander on top. Stir in the boiling water and a pinch of salt. Either put in a separate tier in the electric steamer or cover the bowl securely with foil and stand the bowl in the pan of simmering water (the water should come halfway up the sides of the bowl). Put the colander with the bowl of lamb mixture on top. Cover and steam for 15–20 minutes, stirring once.

3 Stir the couscous with a fork to fluff up the grains. Spoon on to a plate and top with the lamb mixture.

Cheesy cod and tomatoes with potatoes and broccoli

Use other white fish, such as coley, if you like.

SERVES 1

1 piece of cod fillet,
about 175 g/6 oz
Salt and pepper
¹/₄ tsp dried oregano
1 tomato, thickly sliced
A handful of grated Cheddar cheese
1 medium potato, scrubbed or peeled
and cut into bite-sized chunks
1 small head of broccoli, cut into florets

1 Wipe the fish and place in a small dish that will fit in an electric steamer or in a colander over a pan of simmering water.

2 Season lightly, then sprinkle with the oregano. Top with the slices of tomato, then the cheese.

3 Either put the potatoes in the bottom tier of an electric steamer and sprinkle lightly with salt or put in the simmering water in a saucepan and add a pinch of salt.

4 Put the fish in the top tier or in the colander with the broccoli alongside.

5 Cover and steam for 15 minutes until everything is cooked through and the cheese has melted.

6 Remove the fish and broccoli from the colander, if using, then drain the potatoes in the colander in the sink.

7 Transfer the fish, potatoes and broccoli to a plate and serve.

Chicken with baby new potatoes with mint and garlic butter

SERVES 1

1 chicken breast
A large knob of butter or margarine
For the potatoes:
Salt and pepper
4–6 baby new potatoes,
scrubbed or scraped
1 sprig of fresh mint
or ¹/₂ tsp dried mint
¹/₂ small garlic clove, peeled and crushed,
or ¹/₄ tsp garlic purée (paste)
A Mixed Salad (see page 45), to serve

1 Smear a square of foil with a little of the butter or margarine. Add the chicken breast and sprinkle lightly with salt and pepper. Wrap tightly.

2 Place the potatoes in the electric steamer or in a colander over a pan of simmering water with a little of the mint and a sprinkling of salt. Put the chicken parcel in as well. Cover and steam for 15 minutes.

3 If using fresh mint, pull the rest of the leaves off and chop. Add the mint, fresh or dried, to the bowl with the garlic, the remaining butter or margarine and a good grinding of pepper.

4 Put in the steamer with the potatoes and chicken, pushing the potatoes up the sides of the colander a bit, if necessary, to accommodate the bowl. Re-cover and steam for a further 5 minutes or until the potatoes and chicken are tender and the butter or margarine has melted.

5 Tip the potatoes into a bowl. Stir the melted mixture and pour over. Toss gently and serve with the chicken and salad.

Smoked haddock with potatoes, spinach and egg

SERVES 1

A knob of butter or margarine
½ × 350 g/12 oz bag of fresh spinach,
washed well and dried
Salt and pepper
1 piece of smoked haddock fillet,
about 150 g/5 oz
1 tbsp milk
1 egg, scrubbed
1 large potato, peeled, if liked, and cut
into bite-sized chunks
Chilli powder or paprika (optional)

1 Lightly grease a large square of foil with the butter or margarine. Pile the spinach in the centre and sprinkle very lightly with salt.

2 Rinse the fish, pat dry on kitchen paper (paper towels) and lay on the top of the spinach.

3 Add the milk and a sprinkling of pepper. Fold over the foil securely to form a parcel.

4 Put the potatoes either in the bottom tier of an electric steamer and sprinkle with salt or in a saucepan of simmering water with a colander over the top.

5 Put the fish in the tier above the potatoes or in the colander. Cover and steam for 5 minutes. Put the egg beside the fish and continue to steam for a further 10 minutes until the potatoes and fish are cooked.

6 Lift the fish and egg out of the steamer. Run the egg quickly under cold water to cool slightly and to prevent further cooking.

7 Drain the potatoes, if necessary, in the colander in the sink. Shell the egg (take care as it will still be quite hot).

8 Put the spinach and fish on a plate with the potatoes beside them. Put the egg on the fish and cut open to allow the yolk to trickle out. Sprinkle with a little chilli powder or paprika, if liked, and serve.

Mackerel with red curry rub and coconut rice

For the best flavour, leave the rubbed fish to marinate for a while before cooking.

SERVES 1

1 medium mackerel, cleaned
A little oil
For the rub:
1 tsp curry powder
1 tsp ground cumin
1 tsp paprika
¼ tsp sugar
A good pinch of salt
A good pinch of pepper
For the rice:
¼ mug of long-grain rice
1 spring onion (scallion), trimmed and
finely chopped
1 cm/½ in slice of creamed coconut
from a block, finely chopped
5 tbsp boiling water
¼ vegetable stock cube
½ tsp garam masala
½ tsp sunflower oil
Mango chutney and a Tomato and
Onion Salad (see page 46), to serve

1 Rinse the fish inside and out and wipe dry with kitchen paper (paper towels). Make several slashes on each side of the fish. Remove the head, if preferred. Place the fish on a large square of oiled foil.

2 Mix the spices, sugar, salt and pepper together and rub all over the mackerel, in the slits and body cavity.

3 Wrap up the fish in the foil, folding the ends securely to seal. If time allows, place in the fridge to marinate for 1–4 hours.

4 When ready to cook the fish, prepare the rice. Put the rice in the rice bowl of an electric steamer or a dish that will stand in the saucepan with the colander over the top. Add the remaining ingredients and stir well. Cover tightly with foil. Either put the fish in the steamer tier with the rice in the rice bowl or stand the dish of rice in a saucepan with enough boiling water to come halfway up the sides of the dish. Put the colander on top and add the fish. Cover and steam for 25 minutes.

5 Remove from the heat and leave to stand for 5 minutes. Unwrap the fish and transfer to a plate. Stir the rice, taste and add more salt, if necessary. Spoon beside the fish and serve with mango chutney and salad.

Salmon steak with orange and courgettes with herby new potatoes

SERVES 1

2 good knobs of butter or margarine
1 courgette (zucchini), sliced
Salt and pepper
1 salmon steak,
about 175 g/6 oz
1 small orange
4–6 small new potatoes, scrubbed and
cut in half
1 tbsp chopped fresh parsley
¼ tsp dried basil
Mayonnaise, to serve

1 Grease a large square of foil with a little of the butter or margarine.

2 Put the slices of courgette in an even layer in the centre of the foil. Sprinkle with salt and pepper.

3 Sit the fish on top. Cut a slice off the orange and reserve to garnish. Grate the zest off half of the orange and squeeze all the juice.

4 Scatter the orange zest and juice over the fish and dot with half the remaining butter or margarine. Top with the slice of orange. Wrap up securely in the foil to form a parcel.

5 Put the potatoes in the bottom tier of an electric steamer and sprinkle with salt. Alternatively, put them in simmering water in a saucepan with a pinch of salt and put the colander on top. Put the fish in the top tier of the steamer or in the colander. Cover and steam for 15–20 minutes until the potatoes are tender.

6 Remove the fish parcel from the steamer. Drain the potatoes, if necessary, in the colander in the sink. Return to the pan. Add the remaining butter or margarine to the potatoes with the parsley and basil. Stir gently to coat in melted butter or margarine and herbs.

7 Slide the fish, courgettes and juices on to a plate. Spoon the potatoes to one side and serve with mayonnaise.

Lemon chicken with pesto sauce and rice

If you're feeling flash, wild rice mix looks and tastes great with this and makes a nice change.

SERVES 1

1 tsp water
1 tsp cornflour (cornstarch)
1 tbsp pesto sauce, ready-made
or see page 418
2 tsp medium-dry white wine
or apple juice
Salt and pepper
2 chicken thighs, skinned
2 slices of lemon
¼ mug of long-grain rice
6 tbsp water
A Tomato and Onion Salad
(see page 46), to serve

1 Mix the water and cornflour together in shallow dish that will hold the chicken. Stir in the pesto, wine or apple juice and some salt and pepper.

2 Make a few slashes in the flesh of the chicken, add the chicken to the pesto mixture and turn over to coat completely. Cover and leave to marinate in the fridge for at least 30 minutes – or even overnight.

3 Cut the slices of lemon into quarters, then tuck them in around the chicken. Cover tightly with foil.

4 Place in a steamer or in a colander over a pan of simmering water. Cover and steam for 20 minutes. Turn the chicken over in the marinade.

5 If using an electric steamer, put the rice and measured water with a pinch of salt in the rice bowl over the chicken. Re-cover the steamer and cook for a further 25 minutes or until the chicken is cooked through and tender and the rice has absorbed the liquid and is tender. If using a colander over a saucepan, continue to cook the chicken for a further 15 minutes, then add the rice to the boiling water in the saucepan with a pinch of salt (make sure there is plenty). Cook for a further 10 minutes, then remove the chicken and drain the rice in the colander in the sink, rinse with boiling water, then drain again.

6 Spoon the rice on to a plate, add the chicken and sauce, discarding the lemon slices, and serve with salad.

Spanish-style yellow rice and chicken

SERVES 1

2 chicken thighs
Salt and pepper
¼ mug of long-grain rice
2 tomatoes, cut into wedges
1 courgette (zucchini), cut into chunks
½ red (bell) pepper, cut into strips
A good pinch of ground turmeric
½ mug of chicken stock,
made with ½ stock cube
1 small bay leaf
2 stuffed green olives, sliced (optional)

1 Put the chicken in the rice bowl of an electric steamer or in a dish that will fit in a colander over a saucepan of simmering water. Season with salt and pepper.

2 Rinse the rice with cold water, then put in the dish with the chicken. Put the prepared vegetables on top.

3 Mix the turmeric into the stock and pour over the chicken. Add the bay leaf and olives, if using. Cover and steam for 50 minutes.

4 Remove the bay leaf and serve.

Chicken parcels with rosemary, garlic and Mediterranean vegetables

If you use a red onion for this, it looks and tastes even better.

SERVES 1

1 tbsp olive oil

1 tsp lemon juice

1 tsp clear honey

¼ tsp dried rosemary

½ small garlic clove, peeled and crushed, or ¼ tsp garlic purée (paste)

Salt and pepper

1 skinless chicken breast

4 baby new potatoes, scrubbed and sliced thinly

1 small onion, peeled and quartered

1 small yellow (bell) pepper, cut into quarters

1 small courgette (zucchini), cut diagonally into slices

1 tomato, quartered

Salt and pepper

2 tsp water

1 Put half of the oil in a small shallow dish and stir in the lemon juice, honey, rosemary, garlic and a little salt and pepper.

2 Make several diagonal slashes in the chicken breast, not right through. Lay slashed side down in the marinade, then turn over so it is coated completely. Cover and leave to marinate for 1 hour.

3 Smear a little of the marinade over a large square of foil.

4 Lay the potatoes in a single layer over one half of the foil, not right to the edges. Sprinkle lightly with salt. Top with a chicken breast and spoon any marinade over. Fold the foil over the top and twist and fold all round to make a secure parcel.

5 Smear another large square of foil with a little of the remaining oil. Separate the layers of onion and arrange on one half of the foil with the pieces of pepper and courgette. Trickle the remaining oil over. Sprinkle with salt and pepper and add the water. Fold the foil over and twist and fold to seal all round.

6 Put the vegetable parcel in an electric steamer or in a colander over a pan of simmering water. Cover and steam for 15 minutes.

7 Add the chicken parcel. Cover and steam for 25 minutes or until the chicken and vegetables are cooked.

8 Open up the chicken parcel and carefully slide on to a plate. Tip the vegetables on to the plate and serve.

Paprika chicken with vegetables

SERVES 4

1.5 kg/3 lb oven-ready chicken
1 bay leaf
1 tbsp paprika
Salt
8 small potatoes, scrubbed
3 large carrots, peeled and thickly sliced
2 onions, peeled and quartered
1 corn cob, cut into 4 pieces
1 chicken stock cube
1 tbsp cornflour (cornstarch)
1 mug of boiling water
A little chopped fresh parsley

1 Wipe the chicken inside and out with kitchen paper (paper towels). Pull out any fat from just inside the body cavity opening. Push the bay leaf inside.

2 Sprinkle the paprika and some salt all over the skin.

3 If using an electric steamer, put the chicken in the steamer with the juice collector underneath. If using a colander over a saucepan of simmering water, place the chicken in a shallow dish in the colander. Cover and steam for 45 minutes.

4 If using an electric steamer, arrange the vegetables in the tier above the chicken. Sprinkle with salt. If using a colander over a pan of simmering water, put the potatoes and carrots in the water in the saucepan and add a pinch of salt. Cover again and steam for 20 minutes. Arrange the onions and corn pieces around the chicken. Cover again and steam for a further 25 minutes or until the chicken and all the vegetables are tender.

5 Transfer the chicken to a carving dish or large plate and the vegetables to a serving dish. Keep warm.

6 Pour the cooking juices into a small saucepan. Whisk in the stock cube, then the cornflour. Gradually add the water, bring to the boil and cook for 1 minute, stirring until thickened. Stir in the parsley.

7 Carve the chicken on to plates. Spoon the sauce over the chicken and serve with the vegetables.

Warm Russian pilchard salad

If you prefer a cold version, leave the vegetables until completely cold before adding to the dressing.

SERVES 2

¼ small swede (rutabaga), peeled and cut into small dice
1 potato, peeled and cut into small dice
1 carrot, peeled and cut into small dice
1 small turnip, peeled and cut into small dice
Salt and pepper
1 tbsp mayonnaise
1 tbsp crème fraîche
1 × 155 g/5¼ oz/small can of pilchards in tomato sauce
½ tsp dried chives

1 Spread the vegetables out in an electric steamer or a colander over a pan of simmering water. Sprinkle with salt. Cover and steam for 20 minutes until really tender.

2 Mix the mayonnaise with the crème fraîche and season with a little salt and pepper. Add the vegetables and toss to coat completely.

3 Turn into dishes, top with the fish and sprinkle with the chives. Eat warm or cold.

Turkey and ham roll with leek mash

If you like more sauce, heat a little passata in a small pan, or put some in a small bowl in the electric steamer at the same time as cooking the meal. Pour it around the base of the mash before serving.

SERVES 1

2 knobs of butter or margarine
1 turkey breast escalope
1 slice of cooked ham
½ tsp Dijon mustard
A good pinch of dried sage
or dried mixed herbs
Salt and pepper
1 large potato, peeled
1 leek, trimmed and washed well

1 Grease a large square of foil with a little of the butter or margarine.

2 Put the escalope in a polythene bag and beat with a rolling pin (or a can of beans etc.) to flatten.

3 Lay a slice of ham on top and trim to fit, if necessary. Spread with the mustard and sprinkle with the sage or mixed herbs. Roll up.

4 Put on the foil, add 1 tbsp water, sprinkle with salt and pepper and wrap it up, sealing the ends well so the juices can't escape.

5 If using an electric steamer, cut the potato into small pieces and slice the leek thinly. Put them with the turkey parcel in the steamer tier and sprinkle the vegetables lightly with salt. If using a colander over a saucepan, cut the potato and leek into chunks and put in the boiling water in the saucepan and add a pinch of salt. Put the turkey parcel in the colander over the pan. Cover and steam for 20 minutes.

6 When everything is cooked, remove the turkey parcel and leave wrapped. Drain the potato and leek (if necessary) and return to the pan or tip them from the steamer tier into a bowl. Using a potato masher or fork, mash well with the remaining butter or margarine.

7 Unwrap the turkey roll, taking care to keep the juices. Put on a plate and cut into four slices. Spoon the cooking juices over, pile the leek mash to one side and serve.

Main Courses You can Do with ... an oven

Most of the recipes in this chapter serve two or four people. It's not worth putting on the oven to cook enough for one person – unless you're cooking a pizza or something that can't be cooked another way. However, if you are eating alone or with just one mate, most of the recipes can easily be reheated (or eaten cold) the following day.

If you are lucky enough to live in a classy joint with a fan-assisted oven, there are two things to remember. First, you don't have to bother to preheat it before starting to cook. Secondly, it's hotter than a conventional oven so you need to reduce the heat by around 20°C from that given in recipes for conventional ovens. I have given cooking temperatures for fan ovens throughout this chapter.

Ⓥ Hot ploughman's Ⓥ

SERVES 1

1 sandwich baguette
Butter or margarine
4–6 slices of Cheddar cheese
2 tbsp sweet pickle
1–2 tomatoes, sliced
A Green Salad (see page 45), to serve

1 Preheat the oven to 200°C/400°F/ gas 6/fan oven 180°C.

2 Split the baguette down one edge. Spread inside and out with butter or margarine. Fill with cheese, pickle and tomatoes.

3 Wrap in foil.

4 Bake in the oven for 15–20 minutes until the crust feels crisp when squeezed (protect your hand with an oven glove or cloth).

5 Serve hot with the salad.

Ⓥ Potato pudding Ⓥ

You need a large ovenproof dish that will hold 5 mugs of water.

SERVES 4

A little butter or margarine, for greasing
4 large potatoes, peeled and grated
1 egg, beaten
Salt and pepper
2 tbsp snipped fresh chives
1 × 400 g/14 oz/large can of tomatoes

1 Preheat the oven to 190°C/375°F/ gas 5/fan oven 170°C.

2 Grease a large ovenproof dish, mix all the ingredients, except the tomatoes, together and spoon into the dish.

3 Bake in the oven for about 1 hour until the potatoes are cooked and the top is golden brown.

4 Open the can of tomatoes and place in the oven, to heat for the last 30 minutes. Serve with the pudding.

Jacket potatoes

I have put the recipes for ordinary jacket bakes in the microwave chapter, as they take so much less time and fuel. But if you want to bake potatoes for several people – or because you like the crisp skin you get with oven-baked ones – it is better to do them in a conventional oven, using the method below, and add any of the fillings from the microwave chapter. They can be cooked for longer in a slower oven if you're cooking other foods too. To shorten the cooking time, thread the potatoes on metal skewers. The heat will then be conducted through the potatoes to the centres and can reduce the cooking time by about a third.

1 Preheat the oven to 200°C/400°F/gas 6/fan oven 180°C.

2 Scrub as many large potatoes as you need.

3 Prick all over with a fork.

4 Rub the skins with a little sunflower oil and a sprinkling of salt.

5 Place on the centre oven shelf and bake for 1½ hours or until the potatoes feel soft when squeezed (wear an oven glove or cover your hand with a cloth when you do this). Use as required.

Cheese and potato
ⓥ bake ⓥ

SERVES 4

A knob of butter or margarine,
for greasing
3 large potatoes, peeled and sliced
1 bunch of spring onions (scallions),
trimmed and chopped
1 tbsp chopped fresh parsley
½ tsp dried sage
3 good handfuls of grated
Cheddar cheese
Salt and pepper
1 mug of milk
2 eggs, beaten
A Mixed Salad (see page 45),
to serve

1 Preheat the oven to 180°C/350°F/gas 4/fan oven 160°C.

2 Grease a medium-sized ovenproof dish with the butter or margarine.

3 Layer the potatoes with the spring onions, herbs and cheese, sprinkling each layer of potatoes with a little salt and pepper and finishing with a layer of cheese.

4 Whisk the milk and eggs together in a bowl with a wire whisk and pour into the dish.

5 Cover the dish with foil and bake in the oven for 1 hour. Remove the foil and continue cooking for about 15 minutes until golden and the potatoes are tender. While it is cooking, make the salad.

6 Serve the potato bake hot with the salad.

ⓥ Egg and potato nests ⓥ

You can't justify making this delicious dish just for one person, but for two or four of you this is a great, easy meal. For an extra accompaniment, open a can of baked beans. Leave the beans in the can, cover the top with foil and stand on the lower shelf of the oven when you add the eggs to the potatoes.

You can fry (sauté) the leftover potato for breakfast with some bacon, or make it into Bubble and Squeak (see page 136) or Hash Browns (see page 141).

SERVES 2

2 large potatoes, scrubbed
A little sunflower oil
Salt and pepper
A good knob of butter or margarine
2 tsp milk
2 slices of cooked ham, diced
2 eggs
A Green Salad (see page 45), to serve

1 Preheat the oven to 200°C/400°F/ gas 6/fan oven 180°C.

2 Prick the potatoes all over with a fork.

3 Rub the skins with a little oil and a sprinkling of salt.

4 Place on the centre oven shelf and bake for 1½ hours or until the potatoes feel soft when squeezed.

5 Cut a slice lengthways off the top of each potato. Scoop out most of the potato into a bowl. Put about a third of the potato into a clean container to store in the fridge (see note above).

6 Mash the remainder with half the butter or margarine and all the milk and stir in the ham.

7 Pack this mixture back into the potatoes, and make a deep hollow in the centre of each.

8 Break an egg into each hollow and dot the tops with the rest of the butter or margarine.

9 Return to the oven for 20–25 minutes until the eggs are cooked to your liking. Serve hot.

Potato, beetroot and cheese ⓥ bake ⓥ

The best beetroot for this are those sold in a vacuum pack without vinegar.

SERVES 4

A large knob of butter or margarine
1 bunch of spring onions (scallions), trimmed and chopped
4 small cooked beetroot (red beets), peeled and cut into small dice
1 × 300 g/11 oz/medium can of new potatoes, drained and cut into small dice
2 good handfuls of grated Cheddar cheese
4 eggs
1 mug of milk
1 tsp dried sage or dried mixed herbs
Salt and pepper
A Green Salad (see page 45), to serve

1 Preheat the oven to 190°C/375°F/ gas 5/fan oven 170°C.

2 Put the butter or margarine in a medium-sized ovenproof dish and add the spring onions. Cook in the oven for 5 minutes.

3 Remove from the oven and add the beetroot and potatoes and stir well. Cover with the cheese.

4 Break the eggs into a bowl, add the milk, herbs and some salt and pepper and beat well. Pour into the dish.

5 Bake in the oven for about 40 minutes until set and golden brown.

6 Serve with a Green Salad.

ⓥ Baked eggs ⓥ

If cooking more eggs to cater for more than one person, it's better to cook them, two at a time, in separate dishes rather than all in one large one, or it takes too long to set the whites.

SERVES 1

Butter or margarine, for greasing
2 eggs
Salt and pepper
1–2 tbsp double (heavy) cream
Crusty bread and a Green Salad (see page 45), to serve

1 Preheat the oven to 180°C/350°F/ gas 4/fan oven 160°C.

2 Lightly grease a small, shallow ovenproof dish.

3 Break in the eggs. Season lightly and add the cream.

4 Stand the dish in a shallow baking tin (pan) with enough boiling water to come halfway up the sides.

5 Cook in the oven for 10–15 minutes until cooked to your liking.

6 Serve with bread and salad.

Baked eggs with ham

SERVES 1

Prepare as for Baked Eggs (left) but chop 1–2 slices of ham and put in the base of the dish before adding the eggs.

Baked eggs with ⓥ beans ⓥ

SERVES 1

Prepare as for Baked Eggs (left) but put a 225 g/8 oz/small can of baked beans in the base of the dish before adding the eggs.

Baked eggs with ⓥ tomatoes ⓥ

SERVES 1

Prepare as for Baked Eggs (left) but put a skinned, chopped tomato in the base of the dish and sprinkle with 2 chopped fresh basil leaves before adding the eggs.

ⓥ Cheesy baked eggs ⓥ

SERVES 1

Prepare as for Baked Eggs (left) but put a small handful of grated Cheddar Emmental (Swiss) cheese in the base of the dish before adding the eggs.

Bean and ratatouille
ⓥ lasagne ⓥ

SERVES 4

1 × 425 g/15 oz/large can of ratatouille
1 × 425 g/15 oz/large can of cannellini
beans, drained
5 ml/1 tsp dried oregano
Salt and pepper
8 sheets of no-need-to-precook lasagne
1 mug of crème fraîche
or thick plain yoghurt
1 egg
2–3 tbsp grated Parmesan cheese
Garlic Bread (see page 439) and a Green
Salad (see page 45), to serve

1 Preheat the oven to 190°C/375°F/
gas 5/fan oven 170°C.

2 Mix the ratatouille with the beans,
oregano and plenty of pepper. Spoon
a little of the ratatouille mixture in
the base of a shallow, rectangular
ovenproof dish, big enough to take
two sheets of lasagne side by side.

3 Top with a layer of two lasagne
sheets.

4 Spread about one-third of the
remaining mixture over the lasagne.
Repeat the layers, finishing with a
layer of lasagne.

5 Whisk the crème fraîche or yoghurt
with the egg and a little salt and
pepper, spoon over and sprinkle with
the Parmesan. Bake in the oven for
about 35 minutes or until golden and
the lasagne feels tender when a knife
is inserted down through the centre.

6 While the lasagne is cooking, make
the garlic bread. Bake towards the top
of the oven for the last 15 minutes of
the lasagne cooking time until the
crust feels crisp when squeezed
(protect your hand with an oven
glove or cloth).

7 Serve the lasagne with the garlic
bread and salad.

Herby baked mushroom
ⓥ and cheese omelette ⓥ

You could make Garlic Bread (see
page 439) to serve with this.

SERVES 1

2 eggs, beaten
1 small carton of cottage cheese
2 tbsp milk
4–6 button mushrooms, sliced
1 tbsp chopped fresh parsley
1 small garlic clove, peeled and crushed,
or ½ tsp garlic purée (paste)
A pinch of dried mixed herbs
Salt and pepper
A good knob of butter or margarine,
for greasing
A Green Salad (see page 45), to serve

1 Preheat the oven to 200°C/400°F/
gas 6/fan oven 180°C.

2 Place all the ingredients except the
butter or margarine in a bowl and
mix well.

3 Grease a smallish ovenproof dish.
Pour in the egg mixture and bake in
the oven for about 15–20 minutes
until set and golden.

4 Cut into pieces and serve with
salad.

ⓥ Italian vegetable pie ⓥ

You can buy ready-made shortcrust pastry if you like, but making your own is easy and cheaper! If you don't have a pie dish, use a large ovenproof dinner plate.

SERVES 4

For the pastry (paste):
*2 mugs of plain (all-purpose) flour,
plus extra for sprinkling
A good pinch of salt
¹/₂ × 250 g/9 oz tub of soft margarine
About 6 tbsp cold water
For the filling:
1 × 425 g/15 oz/large can of cannellini
beans, drained
1¹/₂ mugs of frozen mixed vegetables
1 × 400 g/14 oz/large can of
cream of tomato soup
¹/₂ tsp dried basil
Pepper
A little milk
A Green Salad (see page 45), to serve*

1 Put the flour and salt into a bowl. Add the butter or margarine and, using a fork, 'mash' the fat into the flour until the mixture looks like breadcrumbs.

2 Stir in the water, a little at a time, using enough of it to make a firm dough.

3 Sprinkle a little flour on to a work surface or board. Squeeze the dough gently together to form a ball, then cut it in half. Roll out one half with a rolling pin or a clean bottle to a round large enough to line a shallow pie dish.

4 Spoon the beans and vegetables into the centre. Pour the soup over and sprinkle with the basil and some pepper. Dampen the pastry edges with water.

5 Roll out the other half of the pastry to a round large enough to cover the pie. Carefully put the pastry 'lid' in position and press down the edges all round. Trim all round with a knife, then press round the edge with the prongs of a fork to seal the two layers of pastry together.

6 Make a small slit in the centre of the top to allow steam to escape, then brush or smear a little milk all over the top to glaze.

7 Preheat the oven to 200°C/400°F/ gas 6/fan oven 180°C. If you have a baking (cookie) sheet, put the pie on this (it helps to cook the bottom layer of pastry); if not, put the pie directly on the centre shelf of the oven.

8 Bake for about 30 minutes until golden brown.

9 Serve with the salad.

Baked bean loaf with oven wedges and ❿ baked tomatoes ❿

If you're eating this on your own, you'll find it's just as good cold. If you like food in sauces, heat a can of mushroom soup to serve with the loaf.

SERVES 4

1 × 400 g/14 oz/large can of baked beans
1 small onion, peeled and chopped
1 slice of bread, crumbled
2 tbsp tomato ketchup (catsup)
1 egg, beaten
1 tsp Marmite or other yeast extract
1 tsp dried mixed herbs
Salt and pepper
A pinch of chilli powder (optional)
4 large potatoes, scrubbed
3 tbsp sunflower oil,
plus extra for greasing
8 tomatoes
1 tbsp balsamic vinegar (optional)
1 tsp sugar

1 Grease a 450 g/1 lb loaf tin (pan) or similar-sized ovenproof dish with a little oil. Preheat the oven to 190°C/ 375°F/gas 5/fan oven 170°C.

2 Mix the beans with the onion, bread, ketchup, egg, Marmite, herbs and a sprinkling of salt and pepper. Add the chilli powder, if using. Turn into the greased container and level the surface.

3 Cut the potatoes in half, then each half into about five wedges. Place in a bowl and add 2 tbsp of the oil. Mix well. Spread out on a baking (cookie) sheet or a shallow baking tin (pan).

4 Put the potatoes at the top of the oven and the loaf on the middle shelf. Bake for 20 minutes.

5 Meanwhile, put the tomatoes in a shallow dish, stalk-ends down. Using a sharp knife, make a 'cross' cut into the top of each. Trickle the remaining oil and the balsamic vinegar, if using, over the tomatoes and sprinkle with the sugar.

6 After 20 minutes' cooking, turn the potato wedges over with a fish slice. Put the tomatoes beside the loaf and bake everything for a further 10 minutes until the loaf is set and the potato wedges are golden and cooked.

7 Loosen the loaf in its container and turn out. Cut into slices and serve with the potato wedges and the tomatoes.

Marmite, cheese and ⓥ tomato slices ⓥ

Eat one hot and the other cold for lunch the next day.

SERVES 2

¹/₂ × 350 g/12 oz packet of frozen puff pastry (paste), thawed
2 tbsp Marmite or other yeast extract
2 good handfuls of grated Cheddar cheese
2 tomatoes, sliced
A little milk
A Mixed Salad (see page 45), to serve

1 Using a rolling pin (or a clean bottle), roll out the pastry on a lightly floured surface to about a 30 cm/ 12 in square. Cut into quarters. Rinse a baking (cookie) sheet with water and place two of the squares on it.

2 Spread these two squares with Marmite, not quite to the edges.

3 Scatter the cheese over, then top with the tomato slices. Smear the edges with water.

4 Lightly fold the other squares in half and make a series of cuts at regular intervals through the fold to within 1 cm/¹/₂ in of the open edges (like making a child's paper lantern). Gently open out and place the squares of pastry over the filling. Press the edges well together to seal. Pinch the edges all round between your finger and thumb, to decorate and help the pastry to stick together.

5 Preheat the oven to 220°C/425°F/ gas 7/fan oven 200°C. Gently smear a little milk over the top of the pastry to glaze it as it cooks.

6 Bake in the oven for about 15–20 minutes until golden and puffy.

7 Serve warm or cold with a mixed salad.

Baked chick peas with tomatoes in ⓥ minted yoghurt ⓥ

If you don't have a food processor, you can make crumbs by simply crumbling stale bread, grating it on a cheese grater or chopping it.

SERVES 2

A good knob of butter or margarine
2 handfuls of breadcrumbs
1 × 425 g/15 oz/large can of chick peas (garbanzos), drained
4 tomatoes, sliced
¹/₂ tsp sugar
Salt and pepper
1 small carton of plain yoghurt
¹/₂ tsp dried mint
Crusty bread and a Green Salad (see page 45), to serve

1 Preheat the oven to 200°C/400°F/ gas 6/fan oven 180°C. Put the butter or margarine in a fairly shallow ovenproof dish and put in the oven to melt.

2 Add the breadcrumbs and stir until coated, then tip out on to a plate.

3 Tip the chick peas into the dish. Arrange the tomato slices over the top and sprinkle with the sugar and a good sprinkling of salt and pepper.

4 Mix the yoghurt with the mint and spoon over. Scatter the buttered crumbs on top.

5 Bake in the oven for about 25 minutes until golden and hot through.

6 Serve with crusty bread and a green salad.

Baked courgette chilli dogs

This is a great meal to eat in front of the TV! You can prepare them in advance, then bake them just before you want to eat. If you don't like chilli, use plain ketchup instead.

MAKES 8

4 large finger rolls
Butter or margarine
4 even-sized courgettes (zucchini)
8 canned hot dog sausages, drained
4 tbsp tomato ketchup (catsup)
¼ tsp chilli powder
½ tsp Worcestershire sauce
4 tomatoes, cut into wedges, and pickled onions, to serve

1 Preheat the oven to 190°C/375°F/gas 5/fan oven 170°C.

2 Cut the bread rolls in half lengthways. Pull out some of the soft bread, leaving a wall all round. Spread liberally with butter or margarine and place on a baking (cookie) sheet.

3 Cut the courgettes in half lengthways and scoop out the seeds with a small spoon.

4 Place in a baking tin (pan) and cover with boiling water. Cover the tin with foil and bake in the oven for 5 minutes.

5 Drain off nearly all the water, leaving just enough to cover the base. Put a hot dog in each courgette half and re-cover with foil.

6 Mix the ketchup with the chilli powder and the Worcestershire sauce.

7 Put the bread on the top shelf and the courgettes just below. Bake for about 20 minutes until the bread is crisp and golden and the courgettes are cooked through.

8 Spread the bread 'boats' with the chilli ketchup. Put a courgette dog in each and serve with tomatoes and pickled onions.

Ⓥ Rich cheese pudding Ⓥ

You will need an ovenproof dish that holds 5 mugs of water.

SERVES 4

1 × 170 g/6 oz/small can of evaporated milk
2 eggs, beaten
4 slices of bread, crusts removed, broken into small pieces
2 good handfuls of grated Cheddar cheese
½ tsp dried oregano
Salt and pepper
A little butter or margarine, for greasing
1 mug of passata (sieved tomatoes)
A Green Salad (see page 45), to serve

1 Pour the milk into a bowl and add a canful of water.

2 Mix with the eggs, breadcrumbs, one-third of the cheese, the oregano and a little salt and pepper.

3 Lightly grease a large ovenproof dish (see note above).

4 Turn the mixture into the dish and leave to stand for 15 minutes. Sprinkle with the remaining cheese. Meanwhile, preheat the oven to 190°C/ 375°F/gas 5/fan oven 170°C.

5 Bake in the oven for about 45 minutes until golden brown, risen and set. Put the passata in the oven for the last 15 minutes to warm.

6 Serve the cheese pudding hot, with the passata and salad served separately.

Ⓥ Basic nut roast Ⓥ

You will need an ovenproof dish that holds 5 mugs of water for this.

SERVES 4

4 large potatoes, scrubbed and
cut into small chunks
30 ml/2 tbsp sunflower oil
1 mug of chopped mixed nuts
3 slices of wholemeal bread, crusts
removed, broken into very small pieces
1 small onion, peeled and
finely chopped
1 tbsp soy sauce
½ tsp dried oregano
1 tsp lemon juice
2 tbsp butter or margarine,
plus a little for greasing
1 tsp Marmite or other yeast extract
⅔ mug of hot water
2 mugs of passata (sieved tomatoes)
A Green Salad (see page 45), to serve

1 Preheat the oven to 190°C/375°F/ gas 5/fan oven 170°C. Lightly grease a large ovenproof dish with a little butter or margarine.

2 Put the potatoes in a roasting tin (pan). Add the oil and turn to coat. Sprinkle with salt. Put in the oven near the top.

3 Mix together everything except the yeast extract and water.

4 Blend the yeast extract and water together and stir in thoroughly. Spoon into the prepared dish.

5 Bake in the centre of the oven for 30–40 minutes until golden brown and hot through.

6 Put the passata in a bowl. Cover with foil and place near the bottom of the oven for the last 10–15 minutes of cooking time.

7 Serve the nut roast with the potatoes, hot passata and salad.

Ⓥ Nachos Ⓥ

This is more filling than it seems and is fun to share with someone else. The nachos are also good with a pile of grated carrot.

SERVES 2

1 × 425 g/15 oz/large can of red kidney
beans, drained
1 small onion, peeled and
finely chopped
1 tbsp sunflower oil
1 large tomato, finely chopped
1 tsp chilli powder
1 × 200 g/7 oz/large packet of
tortilla chips
2 good handfuls of grated
Cheddar cheese

A Mixed Salad (see page 45), to serve

1 Preheat the oven to 200°C/400°F/ gas 6/fan oven 180°C.

2 Put the beans in bowl. Mash thoroughly with a potato masher or fork, then work in the chopped onion, oil, tomato and chilli powder with a wooden spoon.

3 Spread about 30 tortilla chips with a little of the mixture. Place on a baking (cookie) sheet or in a shallow baking tin (pan).

4 Sprinkle with the cheese.

5 Bake in the oven for about 8 minutes until the cheese melts and bubbles.

6 Serve straight away with a Mixed Salad.

ⓥ Creamy cheese flan ⓥ

SERVES 4

*²/₃ × 350 g/12 oz packet of puff pastry
(paste), thawed if frozen
3 good handfuls of grated
Cheddar cheese
4 spring onions (scallions), trimmed and
finely chopped
2 eggs
1 medium carton of double
(heavy) cream
¹/₂ tsp grated nutmeg
Salt and pepper
A Mixed Salad (see page 45), to serve*

1 Preheat the oven to 200°C/400°F/
gas 6/fan oven 180°C.

2 Roll out the pastry and use to line a
20 cm/8 in flan dish (pie pan) or
similar-sized, shallow ovenproof dish.
Prick the base with a fork in several
places.

3 Put the cheese in the pastry-lined
dish and scatter the onions over.

4 Break the eggs in a bowl and whisk
in the cream, the nutmeg and a little
salt and pepper, using a wire whisk.
Pour into the dish.

5 Bake in the oven for about
30 minutes until golden and set.

6 Serve warm with a Mixed Salad.

The easiest ⓥ cheese soufflé ⓥ

So you thought soufflés were for
experienced cooks only? Not any
more – this absolutely-no-skill version
is light and delicious. Make it to eat
with a friend you want to impress (it
won't reheat well – though you could
eat it cold at a push).

SERVES 2

*A little butter or margarine, for greasing
2 good handfuls of grated
Cheddar cheese
2 tbsp milk
2 tbsp plain (all-purpose) flour
¹/₄ tsp made English mustard
2 tbsp grated Parmesan cheese
Salt and pepper
2 eggs, separated
Crusty bread and a Mixed Salad
(see page 45), to serve*

1 Preheat the oven to 190°C/375°F/
gas 5/fan oven 170°C. Grease a
15 cm/6 in deep, round ovenproof
dish.

2 Put all the ingredients except the
egg whites in a bowl and mix with a
wooden spoon until well blended.

3 Using a balloon whisk or hand
blender, whisk the egg whites in a
separate bowl until stiff and fold
gently into the mixture with a metal
spoon.

4 Turn into the prepared dish and
bake in the oven for 25 minutes until
well risen, golden and just set.

5 Serve straight away with crusty
bread and salad.

Cheese and carrot bread ⓥ and butter pudding ⓥ

You will need a large ovenproof dish
that holds 6 mugs of water.

SERVES 4

6 medium slices of white bread
Butter or margarine, for spreading
1 tsp Marmite or other yeast extract
2 carrots, peeled and coarsely grated
4 good handfuls of grated
Cheddar cheese
2 eggs
1 mug of milk
¼ tsp made English mustard
Salt and pepper
2 tbsp chopped fresh parsley
A Green Salad (see page 45), to serve

1 Spread the bread thinly with butter
or margarine. Spread four of the slices
with a scraping of yeast extract. Cut
all the slices into triangles.

2 Line a large, lightly buttered
ovenproof dish (see note above) with
some of the yeast extract triangles.
Sprinkle with half the carrots and half
the cheese.

3 Cover with the other yeast extract
triangles and then the remaining
carrot and cheese. Arrange the plain
buttered triangles attractively over
the top.

4 Whisk the eggs and milk together
with the mustard and a little salt and
pepper.

5 Pour over the bread and leave to
soak for 30 minutes. Meanwhile,
preheat the oven to 190°C/375°F/gas
5/fan oven 170°C.

6 Bake the pudding in the oven for 45
minutes until golden and set.

7 Serve warm with the salad.

ⓥ Savoury soufflé ⓥ

Ring the changes with different
canned soups and appropriate
vegetables

SERVES 2–4

1 × 295 g/10½ oz/medium can of
condensed mushroom soup
4 eggs, separated
2 good handfuls of grated
Cheddar cheese
1 × 300 g/11 oz/medium can of sliced
carrots, drained
A little butter or margarine, for greasing
Crusty bread and a Mixed Salad (see
page 45), to serve

1 Preheat the oven to 200°C/400°F/
gas 6/fan oven 180°C. Empty the
soup into a bowl. Beat in the egg
yolks and cheese.

2 In a separate bowl, whisk the egg
whites until stiff with a balloon whisk
or hand blender, then fold into the
mixture with a metal spoon.

3 Put the carrots in a lightly greased
18 cm/7 in round, deep dish. Spoon
the egg mixture on top.

4 Bake in the oven for about
25 minutes or until risen, golden and
just set.

5 Serve the soufflé straight from the
oven with crusty bread and the salad.

Blue cheese, egg and Ⓥ broccoli saucers Ⓥ

SERVES 4

²/₃ × 350 g/12 oz packet of
frozen shortcrust pastry
(basic pie crust), thawed
1 medium head of broccoli, cut into
tiny florets
2 cm/³/₄ in wedge of blue cheese,
crumbled
3 eggs
3 tbsp milk, plus extra for glazing
Salt and pepper
Pickles, to serve

1 Preheat the oven to 200°C/400°F/
gas 6/fan oven 180°C. Cut the pastry
(paste) into eight equal pieces. Roll
out each piece to a round the size of a
saucer. Use four of the rounds to line
four saucers.

2 Put about 5 mm/2 in water in a
medium saucepan and add a pinch of
salt. Bring to the boil and cook the
broccoli for 3 minutes. Drain in a
colander, rinse with cold water and
drain again.

3 Divide the broccoli and cheese
among the pastry-lined saucers.

4 Whisk the eggs and milk with a
little salt and pepper and pour over.

5 Smear the edges with water and
place the other pastry rounds on top,
pressing the edges with the prongs of
a fork all round to seal them together
and decorate.

6 Smear with a little milk to glaze.

7 Bake in the oven for 15 minutes,
then turn down the oven to 160°C/
325°F/gas 3/fan oven 145°C and
continue cooking for a further
10–15 minutes until golden and the
filling is set.

8 Serve with pickles.

Speedy seaside crumble

SERVES 4

³/₄ mug of plain (all-purpose) flour
A pinch of salt
3 tbsp soft tub margarine
A good handful of Cheddar
cheese, grated
4 white fish fillets, about 175 g/6 oz
each, skinned and diced
1 mug of diced frozen mixed vegetables
1 × 295 g/10¹/₂ oz/medium can of
condensed celery soup
1 tsp dried chives
or 1 tbsp fresh snipped chives

1 Preheat the oven to 200°C/400°F/
gas 6/fan oven 180°C.

2 Put the flour and salt in a bowl and
mash in the margarine with a fork
until crumbly. Stir in the cheese.

3 Put the fish in an ovenproof dish.
Add the vegetables, then spoon the
soup over.

4 Sprinkle with the chives, then the
cheese crumble. Bake in the oven for
30 minutes or until golden and
cooked through.

5 Serve hot.

Salmon, cucumber and tomato parcels

These are quite filling, so one should be enough for a meal. They are also good cold. For an extra accompaniment serve some canned new potatoes. Just open the can and place it in the oven at the same time as the parcels. They will heat through beautifully and you'll have no extra washing-up. See the note about filo pastry on page 326.

MAKES 4

1 × 425 g/15 oz/large can of pink salmon
4 sheets of filo pastry (paste)
Sunflower oil
1 tomato, chopped
2.5 cm/1 in piece of cucumber, finely chopped
½ tsp dried mixed herbs
Pepper
A Mixed Salad (see page 45) and mayonnaise or tartare sauce, to serve

1 Open the can of salmon, drain off the liquid and discard the skin. Ideally, keep the bones as they are very good for you. Divide the fish into four equal portions.

2 Lay the sheets of filo pastry on a work surface. Smear each one gently with a very little oil and fold in half to form four squares in all. Smear with a little more oil.

3 Put a small pile of tomato and cucumber in the centre of each pastry square and sprinkle with the herbs.

4 Top each pile with a piece of salmon and sprinkle with pepper.

5 Fold the pastry over the salmon to form parcels.

6 Preheat the oven to 190°C/375°F/gas 5/fan oven 170°C. Smear a baking (cookie) sheet with a little oil and transfer the parcels to it, folds down. Smear them with a little more oil.

7 Bake in the oven for about 20 minutes until crisp and golden.

8 Serve warm with the salad and mayonnaise or tartare sauce.

Golden-topped ratatouille with cod

You can use other white fish, such as coley or pollack, if you prefer.

SERVES 4

4 fillets of cod, about 175 g/6 oz each
1 × 425 g/15 oz/large can of ratatouille
1 tbsp red wine
2 handfuls of grated Cheddar cheese
Crusty bread, to serve

1 Preheat the oven to 190°C/375°F/gas 5/fan oven 170°C.

2 Lay the cod in a large, shallow ovenproof dish in a single layer.

3 Mix the ratatouille with the wine and spoon over. Top with the cheese and bake in the oven for 20 minutes or until golden and bubbling and the fish is cooked through.

4 Serve straight away with crusty bread.

Greek spinach and cheese Ⓥ parcels Ⓥ

Filo pastry is one of the few foods that you can re-freeze after thawing, which is a good thing as you will have to thaw the roll to remove the number of sheets you need. Don't leave the whole roll lying around, getting warm – re-wrap and return to the freezer as soon as you can. Keep the sheets you've removed covered with clingfilm or a damp piece of kitchen paper to prevent them drying out.

One or two parcels will be enough for a meal for most people, so have the remainder cold the next day.

SERVES 2

2 mugs of frozen chopped spinach, thawed
2 large tomatoes, chopped
1 mug of crumbled feta cheese
½ tsp dried oregano
1 small garlic clove, peeled and crushed, or ½ tsp garlic purée (paste)
6 stoned (pitted) black olives, sliced (optional)
Pepper
4 sheets of filo pastry (paste)
Olive or sunflower oil
A Village Salad (see page 45), to serve

1 Put the spinach in a bowl and squeeze thoroughly to remove excess moisture, tipping the bowl over the sink to drain it off.

2 Add the tomatoes, cheese, oregano, garlic, olives (if using) and a good sprinkling of pepper. Mix together thoroughly.

3 Lay the sheets of filo on a work surface. Smear gently with a very little oil. Fold the sheets in half to make double-thickness squares.

4 Spoon some of the filling into the centre of each square. Fold the sides over the filling to form parcels.

5 Preheat the oven to 190°C/375°F/ gas 5/fan oven 170°C. Smear a baking (cookie) sheet with a little oil. Put the parcels, folds down, on the sheet. Smear with a little more oil and bake in the oven for about 20 minutes until golden and crisp.

6 Serve warm with a Village Salad.

Enchiladas

SERVES 1

2 flour tortillas
Chilli relish
¼ quantity of Chilli con Carne (see page 290)
A good handful of grated Cheddar cheese
A Green Salad (see page 45), to serve

1 Spread the tortillas with a little chilli relish. Divide the chilli between them and roll up.

2 Lay them in an ovenproof dish. Sprinkle liberally with the cheese. Cover with foil and bake in a preheated oven at 190°C/ 375°F/ gas 5/fan oven 170°C for 20 minutes.

3 Serve with a Green Salad.

Tuna and pea gnocchi

If eating on your own, reheat the second portion in a microwave on High (100 per cent power) for 2–3 minutes or place the mixture on a plate over a pan of boiling water. Cover the plate with the saucepan lid, turn down the heat and simmer it for 10–15 minutes until piping hot.

SERVES 2

1 × 185 g/6½ oz/small can of tuna, drained
1 × 295 g/10½ oz/medium can of condensed mushroom soup
½ mug of frozen peas
1 packet of ready-made gnocchi
A knob of butter or margarine
A small handful of grated Cheddar or Parmesan cheese
A Tomato and Onion Salad (see page 46), to serve

1 Preheat the oven to 200°C/400°F/ gas 6/fan oven 180°C. Mix the can of tuna with the soup and the peas in a fairly shallow ovenproof dish.

2 Arrange the gnocchi over the top.

3 Put tiny pieces of the butter or margarine over the surface and sprinkle with the cheese.

4 Bake in the oven for 30 minutes until golden brown and hot through.

5 Serve with the salad.

Oven-baked chicken risotto

SERVES 4

4 tbsp olive oil
1 small onion, peeled and finely chopped
2 large boneless chicken breasts, cut into chunks
2 mugs of risotto or long-grain rice
5 mugs of chicken stock, made with 2 stock cubes
Salt and pepper
1 × 400 g/14 oz/large can of chopped tomatoes
1 tbsp butter or margarine
4 tbsp grated Parmesan cheese

1 Preheat the oven to 180°C/350°F/ gas 4/fan oven 160°C.

2 Heat the oil in a flameproof casserole dish (Dutch oven) over a fairly high heat. Add the onion and chicken and fry (sauté) for 2 minutes.

3 Stir the rice into the casserole and cook for 1 minute.

4 Stir in the stock, season well and bring to the boil. Cover tightly and bake in the oven for 1 hour.

5 Put the tomatoes in a small bowl, cover with foil and heat in the oven for the last 15 minutes..

6 Stir the butter or margarine into the casserole and re-season if necessary. Sprinkle with the grated Parmesan cheese and serve with the hot tomatoes spooned over.

Oven-fried chicken and potatoes with sour chive dip

SERVES 4

4 chicken portions
3 tbsp plain (all-purpose) flour
1 tsp curry powder
Salt and pepper
¹/₃ × 250 g/9 oz block or tub of butter
or soft margarine
5 tbsp sunflower oil
4 potatoes, peeled, halved and
cut into wedges
¹/₄ tsp chilli powder
1 small carton of plain yoghurt
2 tbsp snipped fresh chives
A pinch of garlic salt
A Mixed Salad (see page 45), to serve

1 Preheat the oven to 180°C/350°F/ gas 4/fan oven 160°C.

2 Mix the flour with the curry powder and a little salt and pepper in a shallow dish. Add the chicken and turn over in the mixture to coat.

3 Melt two-thirds of the butter or margarine with 4 tbsp of the oil in a large roasting tin (pan) in the oven.

4 Add the chicken, skin-sides down.

5 Melt the remaining butter or margarine and oil in a separate shallow baking tin. Add the potato wedges, season with salt, pepper and the chilli powder and turn in the fat.

6 Put the potatoes on the top shelf of the oven and the chicken just above the middle. Bake for 25 minutes.

7 Turn the potatoes and chicken over and return to the oven for a further 25–30 minutes until golden brown and cooked through.

8 Meanwhile, mix the yoghurt with the chives, garlic salt and a little pepper. Chill until ready to serve.

9 Drain the chicken and potatoes on kitchen paper (paper towels) and serve with the yoghurt and a Mixed Salad.

Baked paprika chicken with courgette rice

This tastes really good hot or cold.

SERVES 2

2 chicken portions
1 tbsp paprika
A good pinch of salt and pepper
¹/₂ mug of long-grain rice
2 courgettes (zucchini), diced
1 small garlic clove, peeled and crushed,
or ¹/₂ tsp garlic purée (paste)
1 chicken stock cube
1 mug of boiling water
1 small bay leaf

1 Preheat the oven to 180°C/350°F/ gas 4/fan oven 160°C. Wipe the chicken with kitchen paper (paper towels). Rub all over with the paprika and sprinkle with salt and pepper.

2 Mix the rice with the courgettes and garlic in a casserole dish (Dutch oven).

3 Crumble the chicken stock cube into the boiling water and stir until dissolved. Pour into the rice and stir well.

4 Add the chicken portions, skin-sides up, to the dish and tuck the bay leaf in at one side.

5 Cover and cook in the oven for 1 hour until the chicken is cooked through and the rice is tender and has absorbed the liquid.

6 Taste and re-season the rice, if necessary. Discard the bay leaf before serving.

Braised turkey with red cabbage

SERVES 4

2 large knobs of butter or margarine
4 turkey steaks
1 onion, peeled and finely chopped
1 eating (dessert) apple, peeled, cored
and chopped
1 garlic clove, peeled and crushed,
or 1 tsp garlic purée (paste)
1 small red cabbage, finely shredded
2 tbsp raisins
Salt and pepper
2 large potatoes, thinly sliced
1 mug of chicken stock,
made with 1 stock cube

1 Preheat the oven to 160°C/325°F/ gas 3/fan oven 145°F.

2 Melt the butter or margarine in a flameproof casserole dish (Dutch oven) over a high heat. Add the turkey and brown quickly on both sides. Remove from the pan.

3 Add the onion, apple and garlic and fry (sauté) stirring for 1 minute. Add the cabbage and cook, stirring, for 2 minutes until the cabbage begins to soften slightly.

4 Sprinkle with the raisins and a little salt and pepper. Return the turkey to the pan and top with the potato slices. Pour over the stock and season again lightly with salt and pepper. Cover with a lid or foil and bake in the oven for 1 hour.

5 Remove the lid or foil, turn up the heat to 190°C/375°F/gas 5/fan oven 170°C and cook for a further 30 minutes until the potatoes are turning golden brown.

6 Serve hot.

Tandoori chicken

Lemon wedges are good to squeeze over this. Warm the naan, wrapped in foil, in the base of the oven for 5 minutes before serving.

SERVES 4

4 large chicken portions
1 mug of plain yoghurt
1 small garlic clove, peeled and crushed,
or ½ tsp garlic purée (paste)
1 tbsp tandoori powder
Salt and pepper
Naan breads, mango chutney or sweet
pickle, Cucumber Raita (see page 43)
and a little lettuce, tomato and
cucumber, to serve

1 Pull off as much skin as possible from the chicken. Make several slashes in the flesh.

2 Mix together the yoghurt, garlic, tandoori powder and a little salt and pepper in a large baking tin (pan). Add the chicken and turn to coat completely in the yoghurt mixture, rubbing it into the slits. Cover the tin with foil and leave in the fridge to marinate for at least 3 hours.

3 Preheat the oven to 200°C/400°F/ gas 6/fan oven 180°C. Cook the chicken in the oven for 45 minutes. Remove the foil and cook, uncovered, for a further 15 minutes until well browned and cooked through.

4 Lift out of the liquid in the pan and serve with naan bread, mango chutney or sweet pickle, raita and a little lettuce, tomato and cucumber.

Chinese chicken with water chestnuts

SERVES 4

4 skinless chicken breasts,
cut into chunks
1 tbsp dry sherry
1 tsp light brown sugar
2 tbsp sunflower oil
1 bunch of spring onions (scallions),
trimmed and cut diagonally into pieces
12 button mushrooms, quartered
1 × 225 g/8 oz/small can of water
chestnuts, quartered
2 mugs of chicken stock,
made with 1 stock cube
1 tbsp soy sauce
1 slab of Chinese egg noodles
1 tbsp cornflour (cornstarch)
2 tbsp water

1 Place the chicken in a shallow dish. Add the sherry and sugar. Mix with your hands until well coated, then cover and leave to marinate for 2 hours.

2 Preheat the oven to 180°C/350°F/gas 4/fan oven 160°C.

3 Heat the oil in a flameproof casserole dish (Dutch oven) over a high heat. Add the chicken and brown on all sides. Remove from the pan with a draining spoon.

4 Add the spring onions and mushrooms and cook, stirring, for 2 minutes. Add the water chestnuts, stock and soy sauce. Return the chicken to the pan and bring to the boil. Cover and cook in the oven for 45 minutes until the chicken is tender.

5 Meanwhile, put the noodles in a bowl. Cover with boiling water and leave to stand for 5 minutes. Drain in a colander in the sink.

6 Mix the cornflour with the water in a small cup and stir into the casserole until it thickens. Return to the oven for 5 minutes. Stir in the noodles.

7 Spoon into warm bowls and serve.

Crunchy beef pot meal

This is ideal when you have very little time. It's a complete meal in one dish.

SERVES 4

3 large potatoes, scrubbed and sliced
2 × 420 g/15 oz/large cans of stewed
steak in gravy
1 × 225 g/8 oz/small can of water
chestnuts, drained and sliced
1 × 400 g/14 oz/large can of baby
carrots, drained
Salt and pepper
1 × 295 g/10½ oz/medium can of
condensed mushroom soup

1 Preheat the oven to 190°C/375°F/gas 5/fan oven 170°C.

2 Put the potato slices in a saucepan with enough lightly salted water to cover. Bring to the boil over a high heat and cook for 3–4 minutes until almost tender but still holding their shape. Drain in a colander in the sink.

3 Spoon the stewed steak and its gravy into an ovenproof dish. Gently stir in the water chestnuts. Scatter the carrots over. Season with salt and pepper.

4 Spoon half the soup over and spread out gently.

5 Arrange the potatoes in overlapping slices on top.

6 Mix the remaining soup with 3 tbsp of water to make it just pourable. Spread over the potato.

7 Bake in the oven for about 45 minutes until golden brown on top and piping hot.

Rich weekday mince with potatoes

This makes enough for two meals, so you can reheat the remainder in the microwave or in a saucepan the next day. Make sure it is piping hot before eating.

SERVES 2

1 large onion, peeled and chopped
2 handfuls of minced (ground) beef
1 carrot, peeled and chopped
1 tbsp sunflower oil
1½ tbsp plain (all-purpose) flour
1½ mugs of beef stock,
made with 1 stock cube
1 bay leaf
Salt and pepper
8–10 baby new potatoes, scrubbed but left whole
¾ mug of frozen peas

1 Preheat the oven to 160°C/325°F/ gas 3/fan oven 145°C.

2 Fry (sauté) the onion, beef and carrot in the oil in a flameproof casserole dish (Dutch oven), stirring over a fairly high heat for about 5 minutes until the meat is no longer pink and all the grains are separate.

3 Stir in the flour and cook for 1 minute.

4 Blend in the stock and bring to the boil, stirring.

5 Add the bay leaf, seasoning and the vegetables. Cover with the lid and cook in the oven for 2 hours.

6 Discard the bay leaf, stir in the peas and return to the oven for 15 minutes. Taste and re-season, if necessary.

7 Ladle into warm bowls and serve.

Pork and bean hotpot

You can make this without browning the ingredients in a frying pan first (in which case, omit the oil) but the flavour isn't quite so good. If eating alone, have half one night, then reheat the remainder in a pan or in the microwave on High (100 per cent power) for 3 minutes the next day.

SERVES 2

1 tbsp sunflower oil
1 onion, peeled and thinly sliced
¼ small white cabbage, thinly shredded, discarding any thick stalk
2 pork shoulder chops
Salt and pepper
3 tbsp water
1 × 400 g/14 oz/large can of baked beans
2 potatoes, scrubbed and thinly sliced
A knob of butter or margarine

1 Preheat the oven to 190°C/375°F/ gas 5/fan oven 170°C. Heat the oil in a frying pan (skillet). Add the onion and cabbage and cook, stirring, for 2 minutes. Lift out of the pan with a fish slice and transfer to an ovenproof dish.

2 Brown the pork chops in the frying pan quickly on both sides. Put on top of the onion and cabbage and sprinkle lightly with salt and pepper. Add the water.

3 Spoon the baked beans over, then arrange the potatoes in an even layer over the top and sprinkle with salt and pepper. Put tiny pieces of butter or margarine over the surface.

4 Cover the dish with foil and bake in the oven for 1 hour. Remove the foil and bake for a further 30 minutes until golden on top and cooked through.

Beef pot with braised sweet and sour cabbage

You can usually buy half a small cabbage. The rest will keep well in the fridge to use as salad or to make this cabbage dish again in up to a week's time.

SERVES 2

For the braised cabbage:
¼ small white or red cabbage
1 small onion, peeled and thinly sliced
1 eating (dessert) apple, peeled,
quartered, cored and sliced
1 small handful of raisins or sultanas
(golden raisins)
1 tbsp vinegar
1 tbsp water
1 tbsp sugar
Salt and pepper
A knob of butter or margarine
For the beef pot:
1 × 440 g/15½ oz/large can of stewed
steak in gravy
1 celery stick, chopped
1 × 295 g/10½ oz/medium can of
condensed celery soup
2 potatoes, scrubbed or peeled and
very thinly sliced

1 Preheat the oven to 200°C/400°F/ gas 6/fan oven 180°C. Shred the cabbage finely, discarding any thick central core. Mix with the onion, apple and raisins or sultanas in a small casserole dish (Dutch oven).

2 Pour the vinegar and water over and sprinkle with the sugar and a little salt and pepper. Dot the top with tiny bits of the butter or margarine. Cover with a lid or foil and put on the bottom shelf of the oven to start cooking.

3 Empty the beef into a separate ovenproof dish.

4 Stir the celery into the beef. Spoon half the soup over and spread out gently.

5 Arrange the potato slices, overlapping, on top.

6 Mix the remaining soup with 3 tbsp of water to make it just pourable. Spread over the surface of the potato.

7 Bake in the oven on the shelf above the middle for about 45 minutes to 1 hour until golden brown on top and the potatoes are cooked.

8 Stir the cabbage and serve with the beef.

Rich baked tomato chicken with roast potatoes and root vegetables

SERVES 2

2 potatoes, peeled and halved
2 carrots, peeled and cut into
thick wedges
1 parsnip, peeled and cut into wedges
Salt and pepper
2 tbsp sunflower oil
2 chicken portions
1 × 295 g/10½ oz/medium can of
condensed tomato soup
2 tbsp water
½ tsp dried basil
A Green Salad (see page 45), to serve

1 Preheat the oven to 180°C/350°F/gas 4/fan oven 160°C. Put all the prepared vegetables in a roasting tin (pan). Sprinkle with salt and pepper and trickle the oil over. Toss with your hands to coat each piece in oil.

2 Put the vegetables at the top of the oven to start cooking.

3 Put the chicken in a casserole dish. Spoon the soup over the chicken, add the water and sprinkle with the basil and a little salt and pepper. Cover with a lid and place in the centre of the oven. Cook for 1¼ hours.

4 Serve the chicken and sauce with the roast vegetables and salad.

Swiss baked ham and potato cake

You can buy ham pieces very cheaply at your supermarket deli counter. You will need an ovenproof dish large enough to hold 5 mugs of water.

SERVES 4

¼ × 250 g/9 oz block or tub of butter
or soft margarine
4 potatoes, scrubbed and
very thinly sliced
3 good handfuls of grated Gruyére
or Emmental (Swiss) cheese
2 handfuls of diced cooked ham pieces
1 garlic clove, peeled and crushed,
or 1 tsp garlic purée (paste)
1 tbsp chopped fresh parsley
½ tsp dried sage
Salt and pepper
1 mug of plain yoghurt
1 egg, beaten
A Green Salad (see page 45), to serve

1 Preheat the oven to 190°C/375°F/gas 5/fan oven 170°C. Grease a large ovenproof dish (see note above) with a little of the butter or margarine.

2 Layer the potatoes, cheese, ham, garlic, parsley, sage and a little salt and pepper in the dish, putting small pieces of the remaining butter or margarine over each layer, then finish with a layer of cheese.

3 Whisk the yoghurt and egg together and pour over the potatoes. Cover with foil.

4 Bake in the oven for 30 minutes, then remove the foil and bake for a further 30 minutes or until the potatoes feel tender when a knife is inserted down through the centre and the top is golden.

5 Serve with the salad.

Boston baked beans

SERVES 4

1½ mugs of dried haricot (navy) beans,
soaked overnight in cold water
2 mugs of water
1 beef stock cube
4 lean belly pork slices, rinded and
diced, discarding any bones
1 large onion, peeled and finely chopped
1 carrot, peeled and finely diced
1 tbsp sunflower oil
4 tomatoes, chopped
1 tbsp black treacle (molasses)
½ tsp dried mixed herbs
A few drops of Tabasco sauce
1 tsp light brown sugar
Salt and pepper
A little chopped fresh or dried parsley,
to garnish
Crusty bread and a Green Salad
(see page 45), to serve

1 Drain the beans and place in a flameproof casserole dish (Dutch oven) with the measured water. Bring to the boil over a high heat and boil rapidly for 10 minutes. Stir in the stock cube until dissolved. Preheat the oven to 150°C/300°F/gas 2/fan oven 135°C.

2 Meanwhile, heat the oil in a frying pan (skillet) over a high heat. Add the meat, onion and carrot and fry (sauté), stirring, for 3 minutes until browned.

3 Tip into the casserole dish with the beans and add all the remaining ingredients. Stir well.

4 Cover and cook in the oven for 4 hours or until the beans are soft and bathed in a rich sauce.

5 Taste and re-season the beans, if necessary. Sprinkle with the parsley and serve with crusty bread and the salad.

No-effort Italian lamb with herby potatoes

Look out for lamb shoulder chops – they tend to be cheaper than loin chops or cutlets.

SERVES 4

4 large potatoes, scrubbed and cut into
large chunks
3 tbsp olive or sunflower oil
Salt and pepper
2 tsp dried mixed herbs
4 large or 8 small lamb chops
1 onion, peeled and finely chopped
1 × 295 g/10½ oz/medium can of
condensed tomato soup
½ tsp dried basil
A Green Salad (see page 45), to serve

1 Preheat the oven to 160°C/325°F/ gas 3/fan oven 145°C.

2 Put the potatoes in a baking tin (pan). Add 2 tbsp of the oil and stir well with your hands to coat, then sprinkle with salt and the mixed herbs. Put on the shelf near the top of the oven to start cooking.

3 Brown the chops and onion in the remaining oil in a flameproof casserole dish (Dutch oven) over a high heat for 2–3 minutes, turning the chops once.

4 Spoon the soup over and sprinkle with the basil and a little salt and pepper. When bubbling, cover and cook in the oven for 1–1¼ hours or until the chops are tender and bathed in sauce.

5 Serve the lamb with the potatoes and salad.

Greek-style lamb

If you're eating on your own, this can be reheated the following day. Simply put just enough water in a saucepan to cover the base, then add the potatoes and pieces of lamb, with any leftover stock. Cover and heat fairly gently for 10 minutes until piping hot. Alternatively, microwave on a plate, covered with another plate, for 3–4 minutes on High (100 per cent power).

SERVES 2-3

½ shoulder of lamb, about 750 g/¾ lb
1 garlic clove, peeled and cut into thin slivers, or 1 tsp garlic purée (paste)
2–3 large potatoes, peeled and halved
½ chicken stock cube
½ mug of water
½ tsp dried oregano
Salt and pepper
A small handful of chopped fresh parsley
A Village Salad (see page 45), to serve

1 Preheat the oven to 160°C/325°F/ gas 3/fan oven 145°C. Cut any visible thick white fat off the lamb.

2 Pierce the meat in several places with the sharp point of a knife.

3 Push a garlic sliver in each hole or smear the surface with the garlic purée.

4 Put the lamb in a large casserole dish (Dutch oven) or a roasting tin (pan).

5 Put the potatoes all round the meat. Crumble the stock cube around and add the water.

6 Sprinkle the oregano over the meat and season everything with salt and pepper.

7 Cover tightly with a lid or foil, tucking it firmly under the rim of the container all round.

8 Cook in the oven for 3½ hours until the meat is meltingly tender.

9 Cut the meat off the bones (it will probably fall off in chunks). Put on plates with the potatoes. Spoon the cooking liquid over and sprinkle with parsley.

10 Serve with a Village Salad.

Mix-it-up meat loaf

You can serve this in all sorts of ways – as a hot main meal with tomatoes (as in the recipe), cold with salad and pickles or in baguettes or rolls. Make sure any leftovers are completely cold before wrapping in foil and storing in the fridge.

SERVES 4

A little oil, for greasing
4 good handfuls of minced (ground) beef
or lamb
1 onion, peeled and finely chopped
1 tsp dried mixed herbs
1 tbsp Worcestershire sauce
3 tbsp red wine or cranberry juice
1 tbsp tomato purée (paste)
A good pinch each of salt and pepper
1 egg, beaten
1 × 400 g/14 oz/large can of tomatoes
Crusty bread, to serve

1 Preheat the oven to 180°C/350°F/ gas 4/fan oven 160°C.

2 Grease a 450 g/1 lb loaf tin (pan) or deep, smallish ovenproof dish. Alternatively, grease a large square of foil.

3 Put everything except the canned tomatoes in a bowl and mix together (with your hands, or with a wooden spoon) until thoroughly blended.

4 Press the mixture into the prepared tin or dish. Alternatively, shape the mixture into a thick, fat, oblong cake on the foil and wrap up securely. If in a container, cover it with greased foil, twisting and folding under the rim to secure. If in foil, put it on a baking (cookie) sheet or in a shallow baking tin.

5 Bake in the oven for 1 hour.

6 Remove the paper from the can of tomatoes. Open the can, leaving the lid resting on top of the tomatoes. Place on the shelf beside the meat loaf for 15 minutes to heat through.

7 When cooked, unwrap the loaf, loosen the edges if in a container, then turn out on to a plate. Slice as much as you need and serve hot with the tomatoes and crusty bread.

Cornish-style pasties

To make your own pastry, use the quick method given for Apple Pie (see page 389), making up 1½ quantites. For big appetites, double the quantity of baked beans. Leftover pasties can be eaten cold over the next few days. They can also be reheated in the microwave on High (100 per cent power) for 1–2 minutes but the pastry will go a bit soft.

SERVES 4

1 carrot, peeled and finely chopped
¼ small swede (rutabaga), peeled and
finely chopped
1 potato, peeled and finely chopped
1 small onion, peeled and
finely chopped
2 handfuls of minced (ground) lamb
Salt and pepper
½ tsp dried mixed herbs
1 × 350 g/12 oz packet of frozen
shortcrust pastry (basic pie crust),
thawed
A little oil, for greasing
A little milk
1 × 400 g/14 oz/large can of
baked beans
Brown table sauce, to serve

1 Mix the prepared vegetables with the meat, some salt and pepper and the herbs.

2 Preheat the oven to 200°C/400°F/ gas 6/fan oven 180°C. Lightly grease a baking (cookie) sheet.

3 Roll out the pastry (paste) using a rolling pin (or a clean bottle) on a lightly floured surface and cut into four circles, approximately 18 cm/ 7 in in diameter.

4 Spoon the filling into the centre of each. Add 2 tsp of water to each. Dampen the edges with water and draw up over the filling. Press the edges well together to seal and crimp the edge between your finger and thumb, by squeezing it across the fold at regular intervals.

5 Transfer the pasties to the baking sheet with the help of a fish slice. Using a pastry brush or the tips of your fingers, smear with a little milk to glaze.

6 Bake in the oven for 15 minutes, then reduce the heat to 180°C/350°F/ gas 4/fan oven 160°C and continue cooking for 30 minutes until the vegetables are tender and the pastry is golden brown.

7 Open the can of baked beans, leave the lid on and put the can on the lowest shelf in the oven to heat for the last 15 minutes of cooking.

8 Serve the pasties hot with the baked beans and brown table sauce.

Ham pudding

You will need an ovenproof dish large enough to hold 5 mugs of water. Don't cut the jelly off the ham – it adds extra flavour.

SERVES 4

A little butter or margarine, for greasing
4 slices of bread
1 × 225 g/8 oz/small can of ham,
cut into small dice
1 small onion, peeled
A good pinch of dried mixed herbs
2 eggs
1½ mugs of milk
Salt and pepper
1 large handful of grated Cheddar
or Red Leicester cheese
A Mixed Salad (see page 45), to serve

1 Grease a fairly large ovenproof dish (see note above).

2 Tear the bread into smallish pieces and place in the dish. Add the diced ham and any jelly.

3 Grate the onion into the dish and sprinkle the herbs over.

4 Break the eggs into a bowl and whisk in the milk and a good pinch of salt and pepper. Pour into the dish and stir well. Leave to stand for 15 minutes, then stir well with a fork to break up the bread. Meanwhile, preheat the oven to 190°C/ 375°F/ gas 5/fan oven 170°C.

5 Sprinkle the cheese over the surface of the pudding and bake in the oven for about 45 minutes until golden and set.

6 Serve with a Mixed Salad.

Corned beef Wellington

The size of the packet of pastry may vary, but you can use it all. Cook as many potatoes as you and your friends can eat.

SERVES UP TO 4

4 medium potatoes, scrubbed
6–8 mushrooms, sliced
1 tbsp sweet pickle
1 × 350 g/12 oz packet of frozen puff pastry (paste), thawed
1 × 350 g/12 oz/large can of corned beef
A little milk
1 mug of passata (sieved tomatoes)
A Green Salad (see page 45), to serve

1 Preheat the oven to 220°C/425°F/ gas 7/fan oven 200°C. Prick the potatoes with a fork and place on the top shelf of the oven to start cooking.

2 Mix the mushrooms with the sweet pickle.

3 Roll out the pastry on a floured surface to about 25 cm × 18 cm/ 10 in × 7 in.

4 Spoon the mushroom mixture in the centre. Remove the corned beef from the can and place on top.

5 Gently smear a little water round the edges of the pastry, then fold the edges over the filling to make a sealed parcel.

6 Turn over and place, sealed side down, on a baking (cookie) sheet. Using a knife, mark a criss-cross pattern in the top of the pastry. Smear a little milk gently over the surface to glaze the pastry as it cooks.

7 Bake in the oven for about 30 minutes until puffy and golden brown.

8 Meanwhile, put the passata in an ovenproof dish. Cover with foil and put in the oven to heat through.

9 Cut the parcel into four slices, put on plates with the passata poured round and serve with the jacket potatoes and a green salad.

Main Courses You Can Do With ... a Whole Kitchen

If you have a whole kitchen with all the gadgets and utensils you need, you really have the opportunity to cook some great meals. Just be careful you don't end up doing all the cooking!

Like the main meal recipes in the Oven chapter, most of these aren't worth making just for one person. The minimum is for two (or you can eat half one day, half the next, if you're eating alone) but many serve four people – ideal if you're cooking with or for others. Don't be daunted by them: they are all easy, economical and impressive!

Stuffed pizzas

Anything that goes on an ordinary pizza is good in these pizza footballs. You can use a handful of thawed frozen peas instead of the beans, if you prefer.

SERVES 2

1 packet of pizza base mix
2 tomatoes, chopped
1 canned pimiento cap, chopped,
or ¹/₂ red (bell) pepper, finely diced
A few cooked French (green) beans,
cut into small pieces
1 slice of ham, diced
2 mushrooms, sliced
1 tsp capers or a chopped gherkin
(cornichon)
¹/₄ tsp dried oregano
2 handfuls of grated Mozzarella cheese
Salt and pepper
A little olive oil
¹/₂ mug of passata (sieved tomatoes)
A good pinch of dried basil
2 tbsp grated Parmesan cheese
A Green Salad (see page 45), to serve

1 Preheat the oven to 200°C/400°F/ gas 6/fan oven 180°C. Make up the pizza base mix and squeeze it together into a ball.

2 Cut it in half and roll out each half to a fairly thin round.

3 Divide the tomatoes, pimiento or pepper, beans, ham, mushrooms, capers or gherkin, oregano and Mozzarella between the centres of the rounds. Season lightly.

4 Smear the edges with water and draw the dough up over the filling to cover completely. Press the edges together to seal.

5 Place, sealed sides down, on a lightly oiled baking (cookie) sheet.

6 Smear with olive oil. Bake in the oven for about 20 minutes until golden brown and cooked through.

7 Meanwhile, warm the passata with the basil. Transfer the stuffed pizzas to warm plates. Spoon the sauce over the centre and sprinkle with Parmesan cheese before serving with the salad.

Cottage cheese lasagne with ⓥ broccoli and tomatoes ⓥ

You can get away with one quantity
of sauce, but I prefer to make double
the quantity for a really
moist topping.

SERVES 4

*1 or 2 quantities of Cheese Sauce
(see page 428)
1 medium head of broccoli,
cut into tiny florets
1 large tub of cottage cheese with chives
Salt and pepper
1 × 400 g/14 oz/large can of
chopped tomatoes
½ tsp dried basil
8 sheets of no-need-to-precook lasagne
2 tbsp grated Parmesan cheese
Garlic Bread (see page 439), to serve*

1 Make the cheese sauce.

2 Cook the broccoli in boiling, lightly
salted water for 3–4 minutes until just
tender. Drain thoroughly in a
colander in the sink.

3 Preheat the oven to 190°C/375°F/
gas 5/fan oven 170°C. Mix the cottage
cheese with a little salt and pepper.

4 Spread 2 tbsp of the cheese sauce in
a fairly shallow dish ovenproof dish,
large enough to hold two sheets of
lasagne side by side.

5 Put two sheets of lasagne on top.

6 Top with half the broccoli and half
the tomatoes. Sprinkle with half the
basil and a little salt and pepper. Top
with two more sheets of lasagne and
press down fairly firmly. Spread all
the cottage cheese over, then add two
more sheets of lasagne, the remaining
broccoli, tomatoes, basil and some
salt and pepper, then the last two
sheets of lasagne and finally the

cheese sauce. Sprinkle liberally with
the Parmesan.

7 Bake in the oven for 35 minutes
until golden brown and the lasagne
feels soft when a knife is pushed
down through the centre.

8 Serve with garlic bread.

ⓥ Vegetarian cottage pie ⓥ

If you haven't any leftover cooked
veg, cook some frozen ones instead.

SERVES 4

*4 medium potatoes, peeled and
cut into chunks
A knob of butter or margarine
1 tbsp milk
3 mugs of leftover cooked vegetables,
finely chopped
2 slices of bread, chopped
1 × 400 g/14 oz/large can of
baked beans
2 tsp Marmite or other yeast extract
2 tbsp boiling water
½ tsp dried mixed herbs
Salt and pepper
A good handful of grated
Cheddar cheese
3 tomatoes, sliced*

1 Preheat the oven to 200°C/400°F/
gas 6/fan oven 180°C.

2 Put the potatoes in a pan of lightly
salted water. Bring to the boil, cover
and cook for 10–15 minutes until
tender. Drain in a colander in the
sink and return to the pan. Mash,
using a potato masher or fork, with
the butter or margarine and milk.

3 Mix the vegetables with the bread
and beans in a medium-sized
ovenproof serving dish.

4 Blend the yeast extract with the
water and stir in with the herbs and

seasoning to taste. Stir into the dish until thoroughly mixed.

5 Top with the mashed potato, then the cheese. Arrange the tomatoes round the edge.

6 Bake in the oven for about 35 minutes until golden brown and piping hot. Serve hot.

Lasagne with spinach and Ⓥ soft cheese Ⓥ

Traditionally this is made with ricotta cheese, but supermarket own-brand soft white cheese is much cheaper. Make the double quantity of sauce if you like a really moist lasagne.

SERVES 4

1 or 2 quantities of Cheese Sauce (see page 428)
1 × 250 g/9 oz bag of fresh spinach
1 × 400 g/14 oz/large can of chopped tomatoes
1 garlic clove, peeled and crushed, or 1 tsp garlic purée (paste)
1 tbsp tomato purée
¹/₂ tsp sugar
¹/₂ tsp dried oregano
Salt and pepper
1 small carton of soft cheese with chives
4 tbsp milk
8 sheets of no-need-to-precook lasagne
2 tbsp grated Parmesan cheese
Garlic Bread (see page 439), to serve

1 Make the cheese sauce.

2 Wash the spinach well. Put in a saucepan with no extra water and cook for 5 minutes until wilted. Drain in a colander in the sink and snip well with scissors. Return to the pan and add the tomatoes, garlic, tomato purée, sugar, oregano and a little salt and pepper. Bring to the boil and boil for 3–4 minutes until rich and pulpy.

3 Preheat the oven to 190°C/375°F/ gas 5/fan oven 170°C.

4 Spread 2 tbsp of the cheese sauce in a fairly shallow dish ovenproof dish, large enough to hold two sheets of lasagne side by side.

5 Put two sheets of lasagne on top, then spread with half the spinach mixture.

6 Top with two more sheets of lasagne. Mix the cheese with the milk and a little seasoning and spread over. Add two more sheets of lasagne, the remaining spinach mixture, then the last two sheets of lasagne. Spoon the cheese sauce over. Sprinkle liberally with the Parmesan.

7 Bake in the oven for 35 minutes until golden brown and the lasagne feels soft when a knife is pushed down through the centre.

8 Serve with garlic bread.

ⓥ Savoury egg pasta ⓥ

For a delicious variation, use a drained 425 g/15 oz/large can of chick peas instead of the eggs.

SERVES 4

2 mugs of small pasta shapes
3 eggs, scrubbed under cold running water
2 good knobs of butter or margarine
1 large onion, peeled and finely chopped
1 garlic clove, peeled and crushed, or 1 tsp garlic purée (paste)
1 small head of spring (collard) greens, shredded
1 × 400 g/14 oz/large can of chopped tomatoes
1 tsp caster (superfine) sugar
A good pinch of dried basil
Salt and pepper
1 quantity of Basic White Sauce (see page 427)
1 small packet of cheese and onion crisps (potato chips)

1 Preheat the oven to 190°C/375°F/gas 5/fan oven 170°C.

2 Cook the pasta according to the packet directions, with the eggs in the pan at the same time. Lift the eggs out of the pan and place in a bowl of cold water. Drain the pasta in a colander in the sink.

3 Melt a good knob of butter or margarine in the pasta saucepan over a fairly high heat and cook the onion and garlic for 2 minutes, stirring.

4 Add the greens, tomatoes, sugar, basil and a little salt and pepper. Cover, turn down the heat to moderate and cook for 5 minutes, stirring occasionally. Stir in the drained pasta.

5 Use a little of the remaining butter or margarine to grease a medium-sized ovenproof dish.

6 Spoon half the pasta into the dish. Shell the eggs, slice and put in a layer over the pasta. Add the remaining pasta.

7 Make the white sauce and spoon over.

8 Sprinkle with the crushed crisps. Bake in the oven for about 25 minutes until hot through and turning golden on top.

Creamed baked rice ⓥ with cheese ⓥ

SERVES 2

1 mug of risotto rice
5 cm/2 in chunk of Cheddar cheese, thinly sliced
A large knob of butter or margarine
2 tbsp double (heavy) cream
Salt and pepper
A handful of grated Parmesan cheese
A Green Salad (see page 45), to serve

1 Cook the rice according to the packet directions. Drain thoroughly in a colander in the sink.

2 Preheat the oven to 180°C/350°F/gas 4/fan oven 160°C. Spread half the rice in a shallow ovenproof dish. Cover with half the Cheddar cheese and tiny pieces of butter or margarine. Sprinkle with salt and pepper and trickle over half the cream.

3 Repeat the layers and top it all with the grated Parmesan. Bake for about 20 minutes until golden on top. While it is cooking, make the Green Salad.

4 Serve the rice hot with the salad.

🅥 Mushroom and veg pie 🅥

SERVES 4

*²/₃ × 350 g/12 oz packet of frozen
shortcrust pastry (basic pie crust),
thawed
2 mugs of frozen mixed vegetables
1 × 400 g/14 oz/large can of
mushroom soup
1 tsp dried oregano
A little milk
Baked beans, to serve*

1 Preheat the oven to 200°C/400°F/
gas 6/fan oven 180°C.

2 Cut the pastry (paste) in half. Roll
out one half with a rolling pin (or
clean bottle) and place in a 20 cm/
8 in pie dish. Press gently in position
and trim the edges. Put the dish on a
baking (cookie) sheet. Roll out the
other half as a lid.

3 Put a pan of water over a high heat.
When bubbling, add the vegetables
and cook for 3 minutes. Drain in a
colander in the sink, rinse under cold
running water, then drain well again.

4 Tip into the pastry-lined dish and
spoon the soup over. Sprinkle with
the oregano.

5 Smear the edges of the pastry with
water and put the pastry 'lid' on top.
Trim the edges and press them well
together to seal.

6 Make a small hole in the centre to
allow steam to escape and smear all
over with a little milk.

7 Bake in the oven for about
30 minutes until golden brown and
cooked through.

8 Heat the baked beans in a saucepan
and serve with the pie.

Fast stuffed 🅥 courgettes 🅥

SERVES 4

*4 large courgettes (zucchini)
1 × 120 g/4½ oz packet of mushroom
or vegetable savoury rice
3 tbsp olive oil
2 good handfuls of grated
Cheddar cheese
½ mug of water
Crusty bread, to serve*

1 Preheat the oven at 200°C/400°F/
gas 6/fan oven 180°C.

2 Cut the ends off the courgettes and
cut in half lengthways. Scoop out the
seeds with a teaspoon.

3 Put a large saucepan of water over
a high heat. When boiling, add the
courgettes, bring back to the boil and
cook for 3 minutes. Tip into a
colander in the sink to drain. Rinse
with cold water, then drain again.
Place the courgettes in a baking tin
(pan).

4 Cook the rice according to the
packet directions. Spoon into the
courgettes and trickle the oil over the
tops. Cover with the cheese.

5 Pour the water around the
courgettes.

6 Bake in the oven for about
20 minutes or until tender and the
cheese has melted.

7 Serve hot with crusty bread.

Potato moussaka

SERVES 4

2–3 large potatoes, peeled and sliced
1 onion, peeled and chopped
1 garlic clove, peeled and crushed,
or 1 tsp garlic purée (paste)
3–4 good handfuls of minced (ground)
lamb or beef
½ mug of water
½ beef stock cube
2 tbsp tomato purée
½ tsp ground cinnamon
½ tsp dried oregano
Salt and pepper
1 small carton of plain yoghurt
1 egg
½ mug of crumbled feta cheese
A Village Salad (see page 45), to serve

1 Preheat the oven to 190°C/375°F/ gas 5/fan oven 170°C.

2 Put the potatoes in a pan. Cover with water and add a pinch of salt. Bring to the boil and cook for about 5 minutes until the slices are just tender but still hold their shape. Drain in a colander in the sink, rinse with cold water and drain again.

3 Meanwhile, put the onion, garlic and minced meat in a separate saucepan and fry (sauté) for 4–5 minutes, stirring until the meat is no longer pink and all the grains are separate.

4 Add the water, stock cube, tomato purée, cinnamon, oregano and seasoning and simmer, stirring occasionally, for about 8 minutes until the meat is tender and coated in the tomato sauce but most of the liquid has evaporated. Season to taste.

5 Layer the meat and potatoes in an ovenproof dish, finishing with a layer of potatoes.

6 Empty the yoghurt into a bowl and whisk in the egg. Add some pepper and the feta cheese. Spoon over the potatoes. Bake in the oven for 35 minutes until the top is set and golden.

7 Serve with a Village Salad.

Ⓥ Nutty stuffed peppers Ⓥ

SERVES 4

4 red (bell) peppers, halved
2 mugs of frozen mixed vegetables
1 tsp dried minced (ground) onion
1 slice of bread, finely chopped
3 tbsp pine nuts
A large handful of grated
Cheddar cheese
1 tbsp soy sauce
1 egg
½ mug of water

1 Preheat the oven to 190°C/375°F/ gas 5/fan oven 170°C.

2 Put a large saucepan of salted water over a high heat. When boiling, add the peppers and vegetables and cook for 5 minutes.

3 Drain in a colander in the sink. Rinse under cold water, then drain again. Place the peppers in a baking tin (pan). Tip the mixed vegetables into a bowl.

4 Add the dried minced onion, the bread, pine nuts and cheese to the mixed vegetables.

5 Whisk the soy sauce and egg together in a small bowl with a wire whisk or fork and stir into the mixture to bind.

6 Spoon the mixture into the peppers. Pour the water around.

7 Bake in the oven for 20 minutes until golden and cooked through.

8 Serve hot.

Salmon and cucumber puffs

SERVES 4

7.5 cm/3 in piece of cucumber,
finely chopped
Salt
1 × 425 g/15 oz/large can of pink or red
salmon, drained
1 × 350 g/12 oz packet of frozen puff
pastry (paste), thawed
1 tsp dried dill (dill weed)
Pepper
A little milk
16 fairly small new potatoes, scrubbed
or scraped and halved
2 mugs of frozen peas
1 × 170 g/6 oz/small can of
creamed mushrooms
Wedges of lemon and sprigs of fresh
parsley, to garnish

1 Put the cucumber in a colander and sprinkle with salt. Leave to stand for 15 minutes. Rinse under cold running water, then pat dry on kitchen paper (paper towels).

2 Preheat the oven to 200°C/400°F/ gas 6/fan oven 180°C. Rinse a baking (cookie) sheet with cold water and leave damp.

3 Empty the fish into a shallow dish. Carefully split into four portions, discarding the black skin and bones, if liked – but they are very good for you.

4 Cut the pastry into quarters and roll out each to a thin square, using a rolling pin (or a clean bottle). Trim. Divide the cucumber between the centres of the pastry and sprinkle with the dill. Top with the fish. Smear the edges with water and fold over the fish to cover completely. Set on the dampened baking (cookie) sheet, folded sides down. Cut leaves out of the trimmings, to decorate. Smear the parcels with milk, put the leaves in place and smear again.

5 Cook in the oven for about 15 minutes until puffy and golden brown.

6 While the parcels are cooking, cook the potatoes in boiling, salted water for 10–15 minutes until tender. Put the peas in a colander over the pan of potatoes and steam them for 8–10 minutes. Alternatively, cook them in a separate pan of salted water according to the packet directions.

7 Put the mushrooms and 15 ml/ 1 tbsp of the milk in a saucepan. Heat, stirring, until smooth and bubbling.

8 Using a fish slice, transfer the puffs to warm plates and put a spoonful of the mushroom mixture to one side of each. Garnish with wedges of lemon and sprigs of parsley, and serve with the new potatoes and peas.

Stuffed pot-roast chicken

This is great if you're cooking for friends but it's even worth cooking it on your own, then eating it over a few days. Take care to reheat it thoroughly though.

SERVES 4–6

1.5 kg/3 lb oven-ready chicken
1 × 85 g/3½ oz/small packet of parsley
and thyme stuffing mix
3 good knobs of butter or margarine
3 carrots, peeled and sliced
3 leeks, trimmed, washed well and sliced
4–6 medium potatoes,
scrubbed and halved
1 tbsp cornflour (cornstarch)
1½ mugs of chicken stock,
made with 1 stock cube

1 Wipe the chicken inside and out with kitchen paper (paper towels) and pull off any fat just inside the body cavity.

2 Make up the stuffing according to the packet directions. Push the stuffing into the neck end of the bird and secure the flap of skin to the back (not the breast) of the bird with cocktail sticks (toothpicks).

3 Preheat the oven to 180°C/350°F/ gas 4/fan oven 160°C.

4 Melt the butter or margarine in a flameproof casserole dish (Dutch oven) and brown the chicken all over. Remove from the pan.

5 Add the carrots, leeks and potatoes and turn over in the fat. Spread the vegetables out and put the chicken back on top of the vegetables. Cover and cook in the oven for 1½ hours.

6 Transfer the chicken and vegetables to a carving dish or large plate.

7 Stir the cornflour into any cooking juices, then gradually add the stock, stirring all the time to remove any lumps. Bring to the boil and cook for 1 minute, stirring. Taste and re-season if necessary.

8 Cut up the chicken and serve with the vegetables and gravy.

Curried chicken casserole with rice and peas

SERVES 4

A good knob of butter or margarine
4 chicken portions
1 onion, peeled and finely chopped
1 tbsp mild curry paste or powder
1 × 295 g/10½ oz/medium can of
condensed mushroom or celery soup
1 mug of long-grain rice
1 mug of frozen peas

1 Preheat the oven to 180°C/350°F/ gas 4/fan oven 160°C.

2 Melt the butter or margarine in a flameproof casserole dish (Dutch oven) over a high heat.

3 Add the chicken and fry (sauté), turning, until browned all over. Remove with a draining spoon.

4 Add the onion and fry for 3 minutes to soften.

5 Add the curry paste or powder and cook for 30 seconds, stirring.

6 Stir in the soup until well blended. Return the chicken to the casserole and spoon the soup mixture over.

7 Cover the casserole with a lid and cook in the oven for 1¼ hours until tender and bathed in a rich sauce.

8 Cook the rice according to the packet directions. Add the peas for the last 5 minutes' cooking time. Drain in a colander in the sink.

9 Spoon the rice on to plates and top with the chicken and sauce.

Cheat's chicken Maryland

If your oven has only two shelves, put an upturned baking tin in the base and stand the pan of bananas on it. The number of chicken pieces will depend on their size.

SERVES 4

2 bananas, halved widthways, then lengthways
4 good handfuls of oven chips (fries)
4–8 crumb-coated chicken breast pieces
A good knob of butter or margarine
4–8 rashers (slices) of streaky bacon, rinded
1 × 320 g/12 oz/medium can of sweetcorn (corn)
Watercress, to garnish

1 Preheat the oven to 200°C/400°F/ gas 6/fan oven 180°C (or according to the chip and chicken manufacturers' directions). Spread out the oven chips on a baking (cookie) sheet. Spread out the chicken on another sheet.

2 Put the two sheets one above the other on shelves towards the top of the oven. Cook for about 30 minutes, turning once or twice and swapping the two baking sheets over halfway through cooking.

3 Put the bananas in a small roasting tin (pan) and cover with tiny pieces of butter or margarine. Cook on the bottom shelf of the oven for 10–15 minutes.

4 Stretch the bacon rashers with the back of a knife. Cut into halves and roll up. Grill (broil), turning once, for about 4 minutes until cooked through. Place on a plate, cover with foil and keep warm on the bottom shelf of the oven.

5 Heat the sweetcorn in a saucepan.

6 Put the chicken, bacon and bananas on warm plates, garnish with the watercress and serve with the oven chips and the sweetcorn.

Ⓥ Vegetable crumble Ⓥ

SERVES 3–4

2 tbsp sunflower oil
1 red (bell) pepper, cut into thin strips
2 courgettes (zucchini), sliced
8 mushrooms, sliced
400 g/14 oz/large can of chopped tomatoes
425 g/15 oz/large can of chick peas (garbanzos)
1 garlic clove, peeled and crushed, or 1 tsp garlic purée (paste)
Salt and pepper
½ tsp dried basil
2 Weetabix, crushed
¾ mug of grated Cheddar cheese

1 Heat the oil in a flameproof casserole dish (Dutch oven). Add the pepper, courgettes and mushrooms and fry (sauté), stirring, for 2 minutes until slightly softened.

2 Add the can of tomatoes, stir in the chick peas, garlic, a sprinkling of salt and pepper and the basil. Bring to the boil over a high heat, then turn down the heat to moderate and allow to bubble for about 8 minutes until the vegetables are bathed in a rich sauce.

3 Mix the Weetabix with the cheese and sprinkle over the surface. Bake in a preheated oven at 200°C/400°F/ gas 6/fan oven 180°C for about 25 minutes until golden brown.

Easy chicken casserole with jackets and peas

You can use white wine or apple juice instead of the sherry.

SERVES 4

4 large potatoes, scrubbed
2 tbsp sunflower oil
4 chicken portions
1 large onion, peeled and finely chopped
2 carrots, peeled and thinly sliced
6 button mushrooms, quartered
1 tbsp cornflour (cornstarch)
1 × 400 g/14 oz/large can of chopped tomatoes
2 tbsp sherry
½ tsp dried mixed herbs
Salt and pepper
2 mugs of frozen peas

1 Preheat the oven to 180°C/350°F/ gas 4/fan oven 160°C. Prick the potatoes all over with a fork and place towards the top of the oven to start cooking while you prepare the casserole.

2 Heat the oil in a flameproof casserole dish (Dutch oven) over a fairly high heat. Add the chicken portions and cook for about 5 minutes until browned all over. Remove from the pan with a draining spoon.

3 Add the onion and carrots and fry (sauté) for 2 minutes, stirring. Add the mushrooms and cook for 1 minute. Remove from the heat.

4 Sprinkle in the cornflour and stir well. Add the can of tomatoes and the sherry, wine or juice and stir in. Bring back to the boil over a high heat, stirring.

5 Return the chicken to the casserole. Add the herbs and some salt and pepper.

6 Cover and cook in the oven for 1½ hours or until the chicken is really tender.

7 Cook the peas in a little boiling, salted water in a saucepan for 4–5 minutes. Alternatively, put in a bowl with 1 tbsp water and microwave on High (100 per cent power) for 3–4 minutes, stirring once. Drain a colander in the sink.

8 Stir the cooked casserole gently. Taste and re-season, if necessary. Serve with the jacket-baked potatoes and peas.

One-step roast chicken

You can use more vegetables if everyone is very hungry.

SERVES 4

*1 small frozen roasting chicken,
about 1.2 kg/2¾ lb, thawed
1 tsp dried mixed herbs
Oil
Salt and pepper
4 potatoes, scrubbed
4 carrots, peeled
4 parsnips, peeled
8 small onions, peeled
1 tbsp plain (all-purpose) flour
1 chicken or vegetable stock cube
1 mug of frozen peas*

1 Remove the giblets from inside the bird if there are any. Wipe inside and out with kitchen paper (paper towels). Feel around just inside the body cavity and if there is any excess fat, pull it out.

2 Put the herbs in the body cavity, then place the bird in a large roasting tin (pan). Rub all over with oil and a little salt.

3 Preheat the oven to 190°C/375°F/ gas 5/fan oven 170°C.

4 Cut the scrubbed potatoes into even-sized pieces. Cut the carrots and parsnips into chunky fingers. Put the potato, carrot and parsnip pieces into a pan, cover with water and bring to the boil. Cook for 3 minutes, then drain in a colander over a bowl. Reserve 1½ mugfuls of the cooking water.

5 Arrange the vegetable pieces and the onions all round the chicken and trickle 2–3 tbsp oil over, then turn them over to coat completely. Sprinkle with a little salt.

6 Roast in the oven for 1½ hours, turning the vegetables once, until the chicken and vegetables are golden and cooked through.

7 Transfer the chicken and vegetables to serving dishes and keep warm.

8 Stir the flour with a little cold water until smooth, then blend in the reserved vegetable water. Stir into the juices in the roasting tin and crumble in the stock cube. Bring to the boil on the hob, stirring all the time, until thickened. Season to taste.

9 Put the peas in a small saucepan with a little salted water, bring to the boil and cook for 4–5 minutes until tender. Alternatively, put in a bowl with 1 tbsp water and microwave on High (100 per cent power) for 3–4 minutes, stirring once. Drain in the colander in the sink.

10 Carve the chicken and serve with the roasted vegetables, peas and the gravy.

Roast joints and poultry

Large joints and birds are a good idea if you're cooking for a large number, and they're not difficult to roast. The instructions here are suitable for all normal roasting joints – which can be expensive – but also for cheaper, fattier cuts, such as belly pork slices or breast of lamb.

1 Preheat the oven to 220°C/425°F/gas 7/fan oven 200°C.

2 Weigh the joint or bird and calculate the cooking time:

- For rare meat (beef only) allow 15 minutes per 450 g/1 lb, plus 15 minutes over.

- For medium, i.e. slightly pink in the centre (for beef or lamb), allow 20 minutes per 450 g/1 lb, plus 20 minutes over.

- For well-done meat (beef, lamb or pork), allow 30 minutes per 450 g/1 lb, plus 30 minutes over.

- For chicken, allow 20 minutes per 450 g/1 lb, plus 20 minutes over.

3 Place the joint in a roasting tin (pan). For pork, stand it on a rack in the tin.

4 Smear beef or lamb with a little oil. Season lightly. Rub the skin of poultry with a little oil and sprinkle with salt. For pork, score the rind by slashing it with a sharp knife at regular intervals all over. Rub the rind with oil and salt. This will help it 'crackle' as it cooks.

5 Roast in the preheated oven for 10 minutes, then reduce the heat to 190°C/375°F/gas 5/fan oven 170°C for the remaining cooking time.

Traditional Sunday lunch

Despite what lots of people think, there's nothing really hard about making a Sunday roast lunch – it's just a matter of getting the timing right. Here is the perfect guide to getting everything on the table hot and at the same moment.

When cooking a roast, decide what time you want to eat. Work out how long the meat (or chicken) will take (see Roast Joints and Poultry, left), then add on an extra 45 minutes to allow for preparing the vegetables, making the gravy and so on.

Work out how many vegetables you need – for each person, I usually allow 4 pieces of potatoes and 2 pieces of parsnip, an average-sized carrot and a handful of green vegetable.

Make sure you have the right accompaniments and condiments. Beef is traditionally served with Yorkshire puddings, horseradish sauce or mustard. Pork is served with sage and onion stuffing and apple sauce. Lamb is served with redcurrant jelly (clear conserve) and mint sauce. Chicken is served with bread sauce and a herb stuffing, such as parsley and thyme. I would suggest that you buy all these ready-prepared. Yorkshire puddings can be bought ready-cooked, so all you have to do is reheat them while you make the gravy and dish up the vegetables. Mixes for bread sauce and stuffings can be bought in packets – just follow the directions for preparation and cooking – and apple sauce, redcurrant jelly and mint sauce are all available in jars.

1 Preheat the oven, check the weight of the meat and calculate the cooking time, then prepare the meat for the oven (see left).

2 Put the meat on the centre shelf and note the time it will be cooked.

3 About 1¼ hours before the meat will be ready, put 30 ml/2 tbsp of oil in a roasting tin (pan) and put on a shelf near the top of the oven.

4 Peel the potatoes and parsnips and cut into large pieces. Put in a saucepan, cover with water, add a pinch of salt and boil together for 3 minutes only. Don't prepare the carrots or greens yet.

5 Strain the potatoes and parsnips in a colander over a bowl, reserving the cooking water for gravy. Remove the roasting tin of hot oil from the oven and add the part-cooked potatoes and parsnips. Turn over in the oil, then return to the shelf near the top of the oven.

6 Check the potatoes and parsnips after 30 minutes and turn over in the oil to brown the other sides.

7 Prepare any packet mixes of stuffing, bread sauce, etc., and place in the oven.

8 Peel the carrots and cut into slices. Put in a pan, cover with water and add a pinch of salt. Cover with a lid, bring to the boil, reduce the heat slightly and boil them for about 10 minutes or until cooked to your liking.

9 Wash and cut cabbage into shreds or separate broccoli or cauliflower into florets. Bring a pan of water to the boil, add a pinch of salt, then the prepared veg. Cook for about 5 minutes, depending on the vegetable, until just tender. Cook frozen peas according to the packet directions. Drain all the boiled vegetables in a colander over the bowl to reserve their cooking water.

10 Put plates, a carving dish and serving dishes, if using, in the oven to warm.

11 When the meat is cooked, remove from the oven and transfer to a carving dish. Leave to rest while making the gravy. Put the bought Yorkshire puds in to heat now, if using.

12 Sprinkle about 3 tbsp of flour into the meat roasting tin and stir into the fat and juices with a whisk. Add more flour if necessary to soak up all the fat.

13 Measure about 2 mugs of the vegetable cooking water and gradually add to the roasting tin, stirring all the time. Put over a fairly high heat and cook, still stirring all the time with the whisk, until bubbling, thickened and smooth. Add gravy block or browning and salt and pepper to taste. Alternatively, crumble in a suitable flavoured stock cube. If the gravy seems a little thick for your liking, add a little more vegetable water, or ordinary water or wine.

14 Carve the meat and serve with the vegetables, gravy and chosen condiments.

Chicken and mushroom casserole

SERVES 4

A good knob of butter or margarine
4 chicken portions
1 onion, peeled and finely chopped
8 button mushrooms, sliced
1 × 295 g/10½ oz/medium can of
condensed mushroom soup
½ tsp dried mixed herbs
1 mug of long-grain rice
½ small head of green cabbage, shredded

1 Preheat the oven to 180°C/350°F/ gas 4/fan oven 160°C.

2 Melt the butter or margarine in a flameproof casserole dish (Dutch oven) over a high heat.

3 Add the chicken and fry (sauté), turning, until browned all over. Remove with a draining spoon.

4 Add the onion and mushrooms and fry for 3 minutes to soften.

5 Stir in the soup and herbs until well blended. Return the chicken to the pan and spoon the soup mixture over them.

6 Cover the casserole with a lid and cook in the oven for 1¼ hours until tender and bathed in a rich sauce.

7 Meanwhile, cook the rice according to the packet directions, adding the cabbage after 5 minutes. Drain in a colander in the sink.

8 Serve the casserole with the rice and cabbage.

Lasagne al forno

If, like me, you prefer a really moist top, use double the quantity of cheese sauce.

SERVES 4

1 quantity of Bolognese Sauce
(see page 262)
1 quantity of Cheese Sauce
(see page 428)
8 sheets of no-need-to-precook lasagne
1–2 tbsp grated Parmesan cheese
A Green Salad (see page 45), to serve

1 Make the Bolognese and cheese sauces.

2 Preheat the oven to 190°C/375°F/ gas 5/fan oven 170°C. Spread a spoonful of the cheese sauce in the base of a fairly shallow ovenproof dish that will hold two sheets of lasagne side by side.

3 Spread with a third of the Bolognese sauce.

4 Put on two more sheets of lasagne and repeat the layers, finishing with the last sheets of lasagne.

5 Spoon the cheese sauce over. Sprinkle with the Parmesan, if using.

6 Bake in the oven for 35–40 minutes until golden on top and the lasagne feels soft when a knife is inserted down through the centre.

7 Serve with a Green Salad.

Very slow-cooked braised beef in cider with jacket potatoes

The potatoes are delicious if you cook them in the oven for the same time as the casserole. You can use red wine or beer instead of cider if you like.

SERVES 4

6 handfuls of diced stewing steak,
about 700 g/1½ lb, trimmed of
excess fat or gristle
3 tbsp plain (all-purpose) flour
Salt and pepper
3 tbsp sunflower oil
1 large onion, peeled and thinly sliced
2 carrots, peeled and cut into small dice
1 mug of cider
2 mugs of beef stock,
made with 1 stock cube
1 tbsp tomato purée (paste)
½ tsp Dijon mustard
1 tsp sugar
½ tsp dried mixed herbs
or 1 bay leaf
12 button mushrooms
4 large potatoes, scrubbed
1 medium head of broccoli

1 Preheat the oven to 150°C/300°F/ gas 2/fan oven 135°C.

2 Mix the flour with a little salt and pepper in a plastic bag. Add the meat and shake the bag well to coat the meat in the flour.

3 Heat 1 tbsp of the oil in a flameproof casserole dish (Dutch oven) over a fairly high heat and fry (sauté) the onion and carrots for 2 minutes, stirring until browning. Remove from the pan with a draining spoon.

4 Add the remaining oil and brown the meat on all sides. Remove from the pan.

5 Add any remaining flour to the pan, then blend in the cider, stock, tomato purée, mustard and sugar, scraping up any sediment from the base of the pan. Season well and return the carrots and onion to the liquid, followed by the meat. Bring to the boil and add the herbs and mushrooms.

6 Cover and place in the oven. Prick the potatoes all over and place on the shelf beside the casserole.

7 Cook for 4 hours or until the meat is really tender and bathed in a rich sauce.

8 About 10 minutes before the casserole is ready, cook the broccoli in boiling water with a pinch of salt added for about 4 minutes or until just tender but not soggy. Drain in a colander in the sink. Discard the bay leaf, if used, taste and re-season the casserole, if necessary.

9 Serve hot with the jacket potatoes and broccoli.

Rich country beef casserole with roast potatoes and beans

SERVES 4

*4 large potatoes, peeled and
cut into quarters
6 handfuls of diced stewing steak,
about 700 g/1½ lb, trimmed of
any fat or gristle
4 tbsp plain (all-purpose) flour
Salt and pepper
5 tbsp sunflower oil
2 onions, peeled and sliced
2 carrots, peeled and diced
2 mugs of beef stock,
made with 1 stock cube
1 bay leaf
2 good handfuls of French (green) beans,
topped and tailed*

1 Preheat the oven to 160°C/325°F/
gas 3/fan oven 145°C. Cook the
potatoes in boiling, salted water for
3 minutes only. Drain in a colander
in the sink.

2 Put the meat in a plastic bag with
the flour and a little salt and pepper.
Shake well to coat.

3 Heat 3 tbsp of the oil in a
flameproof casserole dish (Dutch
oven) over a fairly high heat. Add the
onions and carrots and fry (sauté),
stirring, for 2 minutes. Remove from
the pan with a draining spoon.

4 Add the beef and fry, stirring, until
browned on all sides.

5 Add any flour left in the bag and
stir in with the onions and carrots.
Pour on the stock, stirring, and bring
to the boil. Add a little more
seasoning and the bay leaf.

6 Cover and cook in the oven for
2–2½ hours until the meat is really
tender.

7 When the casserole has been in the
oven for about 1 hour, pour the rest of
the oil into a roasting tin (pan) and
put on the shelf near the top of the
oven for 5 minutes until hot. Remove
and add the part-cooked potatoes.
Turn over in the oil, then put back in
the oven to roast. Turn them once
during cooking. If the potatoes are
brown before the meat is cooked, put
them down on the bottom shelf of the
oven and lay a sheet of foil loosely
over the top.

8 About 10 minutes before everything
is ready, put a pan of water on to boil
with a pinch of salt. Cook the beans
for about 6 minutes or until just
tender. Drain in a colander in the
sink.

9 Remove the bay leaf from the
casserole. Serve the meat and gravy
with the roast potatoes and beans.

Beef in beer

SERVES 4

Prepare as for Rich Beef Casserole
(left) but use a 330 ml can of brown
ale or bitter beer and 1 mug of beef
stock, made with 1 stock cube, instead
of the stock in the recipe. To garnish
the dish, cut 8 slices of French bread.
Toast under the grill (broiler), then
spread them with butter or margarine
and a little grainy mustard and return
to the grill until bubbling. Arrange
around the top of the dish just before
serving.

Steak and tomato casserole with sweetcorn mash

SERVES 4

4 tbsp plain (all-purpose) flour
Salt and pepper
6 handfuls of diced stewing steak,
about 700 g/1½ lb, trimmed of
any excess fat or gristle
3 tbsp sunflower oil
1 large onion, peeled and chopped
1 garlic clove, peeled and crushed,
or 1 tsp garlic purée (paste)
1 × 400 g/14 oz/large can of
chopped tomatoes
1 tbsp tomato purée
1 tsp dried basil
4 large potatoes, peeled and cut into
small chunks
A good knob of butter or margarine
1 tbsp milk
1 × 350 g/12 oz/medium can of
sweetcorn (corn)
2 tbsp crème fraîche or plain yoghurt
and 1 tsp dried parsley,
to garnish

1 Preheat the oven to 160°C/325°F/ gas 3/fan oven 145°C. Put the flour with a little salt and pepper in a plastic bag with the meat. Hold the ends of the bag firmly and shake to coat the meat in the flour.

2 Heat 1 tbsp of the oil in a flameproof casserole dish (Dutch oven). Add the onion and garlic and fry (sauté) for 2 minutes, stirring. Remove from the pan.

3 Add the remaining oil and then fry the steak on all sides to brown. Tip any remaining flour from the bag into the pan and stir, then add the tomatoes, tomato purée, basil and the onion and garlic. Stir well until bubbling and season again with a little salt and pepper.

4 Cover and cook in the oven for 2 hours until the meat is really tender.

5 About 25 minutes before the casserole will be ready, cook the potatoes in boiling, salted water for about 10 minutes or until tender. Drain in a colander in the sink and return to the pan. Mash well with the butter or margarine and milk, using a potato masher or fork, then stir in the contents of the can of sweetcorn, including any liquid. Mix well and season to taste. Heat through for 1 minute.

6 Spoon the mash on to warm plates. Spoon the casserole alongside and garnish each with a spoonful of crème fraîche or yoghurt and a sprinkling of parsley.

Traditional moussaka

There are many variations of this famous dish, but this is the simplest I know. For a richer dish, fry the aubergine slices in sunflower oil for about 2 minutes on each side to brown, instead of boiling them in water. Be warned, they soak up oil like a sponge so you'll need quite a lot! You will need an ovenproof dish large enough to hold 6 mugs of water for this recipe.

SERVES 4

2 aubergines (eggplants), sliced
3–4 handfuls of minced (ground) lamb
1 onion, peeled and finely chopped
1 garlic clove, peeled and crushed,
or 1 tsp garlic purée (paste)
1 × 400 g/14 oz/large can of
chopped tomatoes
½ tsp ground cinnamon
½ tsp dried oregano
2 tbsp chopped fresh parsley
or 2 tsp dried parsley
Salt and pepper
1 egg
1 small carton of plain yoghurt
A good handful of grated
Cheddar cheese
A Village Salad (see page 45), to serve

1 Bring a saucepan of water to the boil and add a good pinch of salt. Add the aubergine slices and when the water is bubbling again, cook for 4 minutes. Drain in a colander.

2 Put the meat, onion and garlic in a saucepan and cook over a high heat, stirring, until the meat is no longer pink and all the grains are separate.

3 Add the tomatoes, cinnamon, herbs and some salt and pepper and cook over a high heat until boiling. Turn down the heat until the mixture is just bubbling round the edges and continue to cook, stirring occasionally, for 15 minutes. Taste and re-season, if necessary.

4 Preheat the oven to 190°C/375°F/ gas 5/fan oven 170°C.

5 Put about one-third of the aubergine slices in a layer in a large ovenproof dish (see note, left). Spoon half the meat over. Repeat the layers, finishing with a layer of aubergine slices.

6 Break the eggs into a bowl and add the yoghurt and little salt and pepper. Stir briskly with a fork or whisk until blended. Pour over the top of the aubergines and sprinkle with the cheese.

7 Bake in the oven for about 40 minutes until the top is set and golden.

8 Serve the moussaka hot with the salad.

Plain sausage toad with onion gravy and mixed vegetables

SERVES 2

8 chipolata sausages
2 tbsp sunflower oil
½ mug of plain (all-purpose) flour
Salt and pepper
1 egg
¼ mug milk and ¼ mug of water, mixed
2 potatoes, scrubbed and cut into small chunks
2 carrots, peeled and fairly thinly sliced
A handful of French (green) beans, topped and tailed and cut into short lengths
A knob of butter or margarine
1 onion, peeled and sliced
1 tsp sugar
1 tbsp cornflour (cornstarch)
2 tbsp cold water
1 beef or chicken stock cube

1 Preheat the oven to 200°C/400°F/gas 6/fan oven 180°C.

2 Put the chipolatas in a small, shallow baking tin (pan) with the oil. Put on the shelf towards the top of the oven for about 5 minutes until sizzling.

3 Meanwhile, put the flour in a bowl with the salt. Make a well in the centre and break in the egg. Add half the milk and water and mix briskly with a balloon whisk, hand blender or wooden spoon until smooth. Stir in the remaining milk and water.

4 Pour the batter into the tin and bake for about 35 minutes until risen, crisp and golden.

5 Meanwhile, bring a pan of salted water to the boil. Add the potatoes, carrots and beans and cook for about 10 minutes until tender. Drain, reserving a mugful of the cooking water.

6 While everything is cooking, melt the butter or margarine in a small pan. Add the onion and cook, stirring, for 3 minutes until turning golden. Sprinkle on the sugar and continue to cook, stirring, for 3–4 minutes until richly browned.

7 Blend the cornflour with the measured cold water until smooth.

8 Pour the reserved cooking water into the onions. Add the stock cube and stir until dissolved. Stir in the blended cornflour and bring to the boil, stirring until thickened. Cook for 1 minute.

9 Cut the toad in half and serve with the mixed vegetables and the onion gravy.

Sausage-stuffed aubergines with seeded roast potatoes

If you are eating alone, cook only half the amount of potatoes and seeds (they aren't very nice when reheated). You can reheat the remaining portion of aubergine in a covered dish in the microwave for 2–3 minutes on High (100 per cent power). Alternatively, reheat it, covered, in a saucepan with just enough water to cover the base until piping hot through.

SERVES 2

1 large aubergine (eggplant)
Salt
4 small potatoes, scrubbed and halved
3 tbsp sunflower oil,
plus a little for greasing
1 tsp sesame or poppy seeds
1 small onion, peeled and chopped
1 small garlic clove, peeled and crushed,
or ½ tsp garlic purée (paste)
½ × 450 g/1 lb packet of
pork sausagemeat
or 4 thick sausages, skin removed
1 tbsp tomato purée
½ tsp dried basil
Pepper
2 good handfuls of grated
Cheddar cheese
1 small carton of plain yoghurt
Crusty bread and a Green Salad
(see page 45), to serve

1 Preheat the oven to 190°C/375°F/gas 5/fan oven 170°C.

2 Cut the stalk off the aubergine, then cut it in half lengthways. Scoop out most of the flesh with a spoon, leaving a border about 5 mm/¼ in thick all round.

3 Chop the scooped-out flesh. Sprinkle the shells with salt and leave to stand for 15 minutes (this will draw out any bitter juices). Drain, rinse with cold water and pat dry on kitchen paper (paper towels).

4 Put the potatoes in a small baking tin (pan). Add 1 tbsp of the oil and turn the pieces over until completely coated. Sprinkle with salt and the sesame or poppy seeds. Place on the shelf near the top of the oven to start cooking.

5 Heat the remaining oil in a saucepan. Add the onion, garlic and chopped aubergine and cook, stirring, for 5 minutes. Remove from the heat and work in the sausagemeat, tomato purée and basil, then season lightly with salt and pepper.

6 Lightly oil an ovenproof dish just large enough to take the aubergine shells side by side. Put in the shells and spoon in the filling. Add 2 tbsp of water to the dish.

7 Cover the dish with foil and bake in the centre of the oven for 40 minutes.

8 Mix the cheese and yoghurt together with a little salt and pepper. Remove the foil from the aubergines and spoon the yoghurt mixture over them. Return to the oven and bake for a further 20 minutes until the cheese melts and the tops are slightly golden. Transfer the aubergines to plates and spoon any cooking juices over.

9 Serve with the potatoes and a Green Salad.

The easiest Chinese pork ribs

SERVES 4

½ mug of soy sauce
1 tsp ground ginger
2 large garlic cloves, peeled and crushed,
or 2 tsp garlic purée (paste)
¼ tsp chilli powder
2 tsp Chinese five-spice powder
6 tbsp sunflower oil
1 kg/2¼ lb Chinese pork spare ribs
4 tbsp clear honey
2 tbsp water
Prawn crackers and a Beansprout Salad
(see page 45), to serve

1 Mix together the soy sauce, ginger, garlic and spice powders in a large container with a lid. Add the ribs and turn over to coat completely. Seal the lid and leave to marinate for several hours or preferably overnight in the fridge.

2 Preheat the oven to 180°C/350°F/ gas 4/fan oven 160°C.

3 Heat the oil in a large flameproof casserole dish (Dutch oven) over a high heat. Lift the ribs out of the marinade and fry (sauté) a few at a time until browned on all sides.

4 Put them all back in the casserole with the remaining marinade, the honey and water. Cover with a lid and cook in the oven for 2 hours, turning occasionally, until really tender.

5 Serve the ribs hot with lots of prawn crackers and a Beansprout Salad.

Chinese red-cooked lamb

SERVES 4

6 handfuls of diced lamb,
about 700 g/1½ lb
2 large garlic cloves, peeled and chopped,
or 2 good tsp garlic purée (paste)
1 bunch of spring onions (scallions),
trimmed and cut into short lengths
1 × 200 g/7 oz/small can of pimientos,
drained and chopped
½ tsp ground ginger
1 tsp Chinese five-spice powder
1 tbsp tomato purée
3 tbsp dry sherry or apple juice
5 tbsp soy sauce
2 mugs of beef stock,
made with 1 stock cube
3 tbsp clear honey
1 mug of Thai fragrant rice, rinsed well

1 Preheat the oven to 160°C/325°F/ gas 3/fan oven 145°C.

2 Put the lamb, garlic, half the spring onions and the pimientos in a flameproof casserole dish (Dutch oven).

3 Mix together all the remaining ingredients except the rice and the remaining spring onions and pour over. Stir well.

4 Cook over a high heat until boiling. Cover and cook in the oven for 1½–2 hours until the sauce is rich and thick and the lamb really tender. If there is too much liquid, put the casserole back on the hob and boil for a few minutes to evaporate a little of the liquid, stirring all the time.

5 Cook the rice according to the packet directions. Drain in a colander in the sink.

6 Spoon the rice on to warm plates, top with the lamb and scatter the remaining spring onions over before serving.

Baked tuna and potato cake with broccoli

SERVES 4

2 large knobs of butter or margarine
4 large potatoes, scrubbed and very
thinly sliced
3 good handfuls of grated
Cheddar cheese
2 × 185 g/6½ oz/small cans of tuna,
drained
1 × 200 g/7 oz/small can of sweetcorn
(corn)
1 garlic clove, peeled and crushed,
or 1 tsp garlic purée (paste)
1 tbsp chopped fresh parsley
or 1 tsp dried parsley
½ tsp dried oregano
Salt and pepper
1 mug of plain yoghurt
1 egg, beaten
1 medium head of broccoli,
cut into florets

1 Preheat the oven to 190°C/375°F/ gas 5/fan oven 170°C. Grease a medium-sized ovenproof dish with a little of the butter or margarine.

2 Layer the potatoes, cheese, tuna, corn, garlic, parsley, oregano and a little salt and pepper in the dish, putting small flakes of butter or margarine over each layer. Finish with a layer of potatoes, covered with cheese.

3 Whisk the yoghurt and egg together and pour over the potatoes. Cover with foil.

4 Bake in the oven for 30 minutes, then remove the foil and bake for a further 30 minutes or until the potatoes feel tender when a knife is inserted down through the centre and the top is golden.

5 Cook the broccoli in a pan of boiling water with a pinch of salt added for 3–4 minutes until just tender but not soggy. Drain in a colander in the sink.

6 Serve the cake hot with the broccoli.

WHaT YOU can DO ...
on a BaRBecue

Now that you can buy disposable barbecues really cheaply at the supermarket, you can cook out of doors in the summer even if you don't have a proper barbecue in the garden of your halls or house. They are easy to light, don't take long to reach the right temperature and you can easily cook enough food for four people on just one of them.

Here's a guide to cooking simple barbecue meals. Obviously times given below are approximate and will depend on the thickness and shape of the food and the heat of the fire. You can marinate the meat first (see pages 371–72), or simply smear with oil and seasoning.

Words of warning

Do make sure you are safe and sensible when you are barbecuing!

Place any barbecue on a firm, heat-proof surface, well away from plants, washing or anything that could catch fire or distract you while you are cooking.

Throw-away barbecues get very hot underneath so must be placed on a metal or stone base. Never stand them on a chair, on the grass or on any kind of garden table. The charcoal may stay safely in the aluminium tray, but the heat will burn the surface beneath.

When you have finished, wait for any remaining charcoal to cool completely, then put the whole thing into the dustbin.

Cooking times

It is essential that barbecued food is cooked through completely. It's okay for beef steaks or lamb to be pink but chicken, pork and meat products, like sausages or burgers, must be thoroughly cooked through or you could get a nasty dose of food poisoning.

Allow time for your barbecue to reach the right temperature for cooking. You don't want the food to be burned on the outside and still raw in the middle. For best results, there should be no flames and the charcoal should be white-hot. You'll then be able to cook your food not cremate it!

Remember that it will be cooler at the edges of the barbecue rack. Move foods to the outside if they are cooking too quickly.

Don't keep prodding food with a fork or skewer during cooking to test if it's done, or all the juices will run out and the results will be dry and disappointing. Use the table below to check your cooking times.

Food	Size	Cooking time per side
Bacon rashers (slices)	Medium	2 minutes
Beef steaks	Thin (frying steaks)	2 minutes
	Thick (1 cm/½ in)	3 minutes (pink)
		5 minutes (well-done)
Burgers	Small	2–3 minutes
	Quarter-pounders	3–4 minutes
	Thick home-made	6 minutes
Chicken/turkey breasts	Thick	8–10 minutes
	Beaten flat (5 mm/¼ in)	2–3 minutes
Chicken drumstick		10–15 minutes
Chicken portion (with bone)		15–20 minutes
Fish, whole	Average (e.g. mackerel)	10 minutes
	Small (e.g. sardine)	2–4 minutes
Fish fillets	All	2–4 minutes
Fish steaks	Thick (2 cm/¾ in)	3–5 minutes
Ham/gammon steaks	Thick (1 cm/½ in)	6–8 minutes
	Thin, round, prepacked	2–3 minutes
Kebabs:		
Chicken/turkey		4–5 minutes
Meat		3–5 minutes
Seafood		2–3 minutes
Vegetable		2–5 minutes
Lamb chops/cutlets/steaks	Thick (2 cm/¾ in)	6–8 minutes
	Thin (1 cm/½ in)	3–4 minutes
Pork chops	Thick (2 cm/¾ in)	10 minutes
Pork steaks	Thick (2 cm/¾ in)	10 minutes
	Beaten flat (5 mm/¼ in)	2–3 minutes
Sausages	Thick	6–8 minutes
	Chipolatas	4–5 minutes
	Frankfurters	2–3 minutes

Home-made beefburgers

These are bigger and better than bought ones! They are more crumbly too, so turn them over only once during cooking. Prepare them in advance so you have time to chill them thoroughly – that will help them to firm up.

Makes 4

4 handfuls of minced (ground) beef or
lamb, about 450 g/1 lb
1 small onion, peeled and grated
1 garlic clove, peeled and crushed,
or 1 tsp garlic purée (paste)
2 tsp tomato purée
2 tsp Worcestershire sauce
¹/₂ tsp salt
Pepper
1 tbsp plain (all-purpose) flour
1 egg, beaten
Burger buns, ketchup (catsup) and
mustard, to serve

1 Mix the mince with the onion, garlic, tomato purée and Worcestershire sauce. Add the salt and a good shake of pepper. Stir in the flour, then the egg. If the mixture seems a bit wet, add another tablespoon of flour. Squeeze the mixture together with your hands to mix everything thoroughly.

2 Divide the mixture into quarters and shape each piece firmly into a flattish cake. Chill until ready to cook.

3 Barbecue for about 6 minutes on each side until cooked through.

4 Serve in buns with ketchup and mustard.

Chilli pork burgers

MAKES 4

4 handfuls of minced (ground)
pork, about 450 g/1 lb
1 small onion, peeled and grated
1 garlic clove, peeled and crushed,
or 1 tsp garlic purée (paste)
¹/₂ tsp chilli powder
1 tbsp tomato purée
¹/₂ tsp dried sage
¹/₂ tsp salt
1 tbsp plain (all-purpose) flour
1 egg, beaten
Burger buns, shredded lettuce and
chilli relish, to serve

1 Mix the mince with the onion, garlic, chilli powder, tomato purée, sage and salt. Stir in the flour, then the egg. If the mixture seems a bit wet, add another tablespoon of flour. Squeeze the mixture together with your hands to mix everything thoroughly.

2 Divide the mixture into quarters and shape each piece firmly into a flattish cake. Chill until ready to cook.

3 Barbecue for about 6 minutes on each side until cooked through.

4 Serve in buns with shredded lettuce and chilli relish.

Lamb spare ribs

You can use ready-cut ribs for this recipe but they're quite expensive to buy and it is really very easy to cut the meat into ribs yourself. Boiling them first means you end up with melt-in-the mouth tender meat that just falls off the bones. You can do up to Step 4 well in advance.

SERVES 4

1 whole breast of lamb,
about 1.25 kg/2½ lb
4 tbsp vinegar
3 tbsp clear honey
2 tbsp tomato ketchup (catsup)
1 tbsp tomato purée (paste)
1 tbsp Worcestershire sauce
1 tbsp soy sauce
A pinch of chilli powder
or a few drops of Tabasco sauce
1 garlic clove, peeled and crushed,
or 1 tsp garlic purée

1 Using a sharp knife, cut most of the visible fat off the lamb.

2 Lay the lamb skin-side down on a board and cut between the bones with a large sharp knife to separate into ribs.

3 Put the ribs in a saucepan and cover with water. Add half the vinegar. Bring to the boil, turn down the heat until bubbling round the edges, cover and cook for 1 hour. Drain in a colander in the sink.

4 Mix the remaining vinegar with the rest of the ingredients in a large, shallow dish. Add the lamb ribs and turn over in the marinade to coat completely.

5 Barbecue for about 15–20 minutes, turning occasionally until richly glazed.

Tex-mex ribs

For more tender ribs, boil them as for Lamb Spare Ribs (left) before marinating.

SERVES 4

2 tbsp butter or margarine
1 tbsp sugar
3 tbsp brown table sauce
2 tbsp tomato ketchup (catsup)
2 tbsp Worcestershire sauce
¼ tsp chilli powder
1.25 kg/2½ lb pork spare ribs

1 Melt the butter or margarine and sugar in a large saucepan, stirring. Stir in all the remaining ingredients except the ribs.

2 Add the ribs and turn them over in the marinade to coat completely. Ideally, leave to marinate for several hours, turning once or twice.

3 Barbecue for 30 minutes, turning occasionally until richly browned and cooked through, spooning (or preferably brushing) any remaining marinade over them during cooking.

Pineapple pork steaks

SERVES 4

1 × 300 g/11 oz/medium can of
crushed pineapple
1 garlic clove, peeled and crushed,
or 1 tsp garlic purée (paste)
A good pinch of chilli powder
1 tsp ground cumin
Salt and pepper
4 pork shoulder steaks
2 tbsp sunflower oil
2 tbsp double (heavy) cream

1 Mix the pineapple with the garlic, chilli powder and cumin in a large shallow dish. Season well with salt and pepper, then add the steaks and turn over in the marinade to cover completely. Leave to marinate for 2 hours.

2 Lift the meat out of the marinade and wipe off any excess. Smear with the oil on both sides.

3 Barbecue, turning occasionally, for 8 minutes on each side until cooked through and golden.

4 Meanwhile, tip the marinade into a saucepan and bring to the boil, stirring. Stir in the cream, taste and season, if necessary.

5 Serve the steaks with the pineapple sauce.

Sticky ham steaks in beer with onions

SERVES 4

4 round ham steaks
½ mug of beer
4 onions, peeled and sliced
1 bay leaf
Salt and pepper
4 tbsp golden (light corn) syrup
1 tbsp lemon juice
2 tbsp sunflower oil

1 Snip the edges of the steaks with scissors to prevent curling when cooking.

2 Mix the beer in a large, shallow dish with all the remaining ingredients except the oil.

3 Add the steaks and turn over to coat completely. Leave to marinade for 2 hours.

4 Lift the steaks out of the marinade. Lift out the onions with a draining spoon.

5 Heat the oil in a frying pan (skillet) and fry (sauté) the onions, stirring, for about 4 minutes until softened and richly browned. Tip into a piece of foil, wrap up and keep warm at the side of the barbecue.

6 Barbecue the steaks for about 10 minutes, turning once or twice, spooning or brushing with any remaining marinade during cooking.

7 Transfer to plates and top with the onions.

Chicken with orange and rosemary

SERVES 4

4 chicken portions
4 tbsp sunflower oil
Salt and pepper
1 tbsp dried rosemary
2 tbsp pure orange juice

1 Smear the chicken all over with half the oil and sprinkle with salt and pepper.

2 Barbecue for 10 minutes, turning occasionally, until golden and partly cooked.

3 Mix the remaining oil with the rosemary, orange juice and a little more salt and pepper. If you have a brush, brush it all over the chicken and continue to cook, brushing from time to time. If you don't have a brush, take the chicken off the barbecue and put in the bowl of marinade. Turn each piece over to coat completely, then return to the barbecue.

4 Cook for a further 15 minutes until cooked through and richly browned.

Turkey envelopes

Soak wooden cocktail sticks in water for a while before use to prevent them burning on the barbecue. These are good served with any chilli relish or salsa.

SERVES 4

4 even-sized turkey steaks,
about 150 g/5 oz each
Sunflower oil
Salt and pepper
4 slices of ham
4 slices of Cheddar cheese
8 fresh basil leaves,
torn into small pieces,
or ¹/₂ tsp dried basil

1 Put the steaks one at a time in a polythene bag and beat flat with a rolling pin or can of beans. Smear with a little oil, then season them with salt and pepper.

2 Lay a slice of ham over one half of each flattened steak. Top with the cheese and basil.

3 Fold the turkey over and secure the 'envelopes' with soaked wooden cocktail sticks (toothpicks). Smear all over with more oil.

4 Barbecue for about 8 minutes on each side until cooked through and golden, smearing or brushing with a little more oil during cooking.

Ⓥ Pizza on the coals Ⓥ

SERVES 4

2 mugs of self-raising (self-rising) flour
A pinch of salt
¼ × 250 g/9 oz tub of soft margarine
Cold water, for mixing
Sunflower oil
4–6 tbsp tomato purée (paste)
3 tomatoes, thinly sliced
2 mugs of grated Mozzarella
or Cheddar cheese
1 tsp dried oregano
A few black olives (optional)

1 Put the flour and salt in a bowl and mash in the butter or margarine with a fork until the mixture resembles breadcrumbs. Using a knife, stir in cold water, a tablespoonful at a time, to form a soft but not sticky dough that you can squeeze together with your hands.

2 Using a rolling pin (or a clean bottle), roll out the dough on a lightly floured surface to a rectangle or round that will just fit your portable barbecue. Oil a sheet of foil large enough to hold the dough. Carefully transfer the dough to the foil, then press out to its original shape again.

3 Transfer to the barbecue and cook for 3 minutes. Smear the top with oil.

4 Oil another sheet of foil. Lay over the pizza, then lift up using both sheets of foil, turn it over and put back down on the barbecue. Remove the top sheet of foil.

5 Spread the dough with the tomato purée, then the tomatoes, then scatter the cheese over and sprinkle with the oregano. Add the olives, if using. Cover loosely with the other sheet of foil and barbecue for 10 minutes until the cheese has melted.

6 Serve cut into wedges.

Thai lemon chilli fish

SERVES 4

5 tbsp sunflower oil
3 tbsp lemon juice
1 tsp chilli powder
A good pinch of salt
4 pieces of white fish fillet,
about 150 g/5 oz each
1 bunch of spring onions (scallions),
trimmed

1 Mix the oil with the lemon juice, chilli powder and salt in a large, shallow dish. Add the fish and turn over in the mixture to coat. Lay the whole spring onions on top and leave to marinate for 1 hour.

2 Remove the fish from the marinade, lay on the barbecue, skin-sides up, and cook for 2 minutes only, then carefully turn over.

3 Turn the onions over in the remaining marinade, then lay on the barbecue with the fish. Cook, turning the spring onions over once and spooning or brushing any remaining marinade over the fish, for 4–6 minutes, depending on the thickness of the fish, until cooked through.

Cheese and bacon frankfurters

The cocktail sticks can be soaked, if you wish, but as this is cooked on foil, they are unlikely to burn.

MAKES 8

8 canned hot dog sausages
or frankfurters
4 slices of Cheddar cheese
or processed cheese slices
8 rashers (slices) of streaky bacon,
rinded

1 Make a slit in each sausage. Cut the cheese slices in half and push a slice of cheese inside each sausage.

2 Coil a piece of bacon round each frankfurter. Secure with wooden cocktail sticks (toothpicks).

3 Place a sheet of foil on the barbecue and lay the wrapped frankfurters on the foil. Cook, turning occasionally, for about 10 minutes until the bacon is sizzling and golden.

Barbecued peppers with Ⓥ garlic herb cheese Ⓥ

MAKES 4

2 red (bell) peppers, halved, stalk and
seeds removed
Olive oil
Salt and pepper
4 tbsp garlic and herb soft cheese

1 Smear a little oil over the peppers and sprinkle lightly with salt and pepper. Lay on the barbecue rack, rounded side down.

2 Barbecue for 10 minutes, pressing down lightly with a fish slice until slightly blackened underneath. Turn over and barbecue for 2 minutes only.

3 Turn back the other way and put a spoonful of the cheese in each pepper. Spread out slightly and barbecue for 1 minute more.

4 Put on plates and trickle with a little more olive oil.

Kebabs

You can make kebabs with meat, poultry, vegetables, even firm, meaty fish.

If you are using wooden skewers, soak them in cold water for about an hour beforehand. This will stop them from burning during cooking.

Sesame beef kebabs

SERVES 4

350 g/12 oz frying steak, in a slab
2 tbsp sesame seeds
1 garlic clove, peeled and crushed,
or 1 tsp garlic purée (paste)
6 tbsp white wine or apple juice
4 tbsp soy sauce
2 tbsp sunflower oil

1 Put the steak in a polythene bag and beat flat.

2 Cut into 2.5 cm/1 in ribbons.

3 Put the sesame seeds in a frying pan (skillet) and heat, stirring, until the seeds are golden brown. Tip into a shallow dish.

4 Add the garlic, wine or apple juice, soy sauce and oil and mix well. Add the beef strips, turn over to coat in the marinade and leave to marinate for 2 hours.

5 Thread the strips, 'concertina-style', on skewers. Barbecue for about 5 minutes, turning frequently.

Grilled chicken with banana, mushroom and sweetcorn kebabs

SERVES 4

4 chicken portions
Sunflower oil
Salt and pepper
1 corn cob, cut into 4 pieces
8 small mushrooms
1 large unripe banana
2 tbsp butter or margarine
¼ tsp mixed (apple-pie) spice
or ground cinnamon

1 Smear the chicken all over with oil and season with salt and pepper.

2 Boil the corn cob pieces in a small pan of boiling water for 3 minutes to soften. Add the mushrooms and leave to stand for 1 minute, then drain them all. Peel the banana and cut into eight chunks.

3 Thread the banana, sweetcorn and mushrooms on four skewers.

4 Mash the butter or margarine and stir in the spice with a pinch of salt and pepper. Smear all over the kebabs.

5 Barbecue the chicken for 25 minutes, turning occasionally, until golden and cooked through, smearing (using the back of a spoon) or brushing with more oil during cooking.

6 After 10 minutes, lay the kebabs on foil and barbecue, turning occasionally, for 15 minutes, spooning or brushing any buttery juices over during cooking.

7 Serve the chicken with the kebabs and any juices.

Sweet and sour chicken kebabs

SERVES 4

4 tbsp clear honey
2 tbsp lemon juice
1 tbsp soy sauce
1 tbsp tomato ketchup (catsup)
2 large skinless chicken breasts
1 onion, cut into quarters, then
separated into layers
3 courgettes (zucchini), cut into chunks

1 Mix the honey, lemon juice, soy sauce and ketchup together in a shallow dish. Add the chicken, onion and courgettes. Stir well to coat and leave to marinate for at least 30 minutes.

2 Thread the chicken, onion and courgettes alternately on skewers.

3 Barbecue for 10–15 minutes, turning occasionally and spooning or brushing frequently with any remaining marinade.

Onion and smoked bacon kebabs with paprika

These are great on their own or served with barbecued chicken or the barbecued peppers on page 368.

SERVES 4

4 even-sized onions, peeled and cut into quarters
3 tbsp sunflower oil
1 tbsp paprika
Salt and pepper
8 rashers (slices) of streaky bacon, rinded and halved

1 Separate the onions into layers (chop the tiny inner bits and use in another recipe, or add to any marinade to flavour it).

2 Mix the oil with the paprika and a sprinkling of salt and pepper. Add the onions and bacon and mix to coat completely.

3 Roll up the pieces of bacon and thread on skewers with the onions.

4 Barbecue for about 10 minutes, turning frequently and spooning (or preferably brushing) with any remaining paprika oil during cooking.

Spiced sausage and potato kebabs

If you can find speciality spicy sausages going cheap, use them.

MAKES 8

16 small new potatoes, scrubbed and halved
8 thick pork sausages
1 garlic clove, peeled and crushed, or 1 tsp garlic purée (paste)
½ tsp chilli powder
½ tsp ground cumin
1 tbsp lemon juice
3 tbsp sunflower oil
Salt and pepper

1 Cook the potatoes in plenty of boiling, salted water for 10 minutes until just tender. Drain in a colander in the sink.

2 Cut each sausage into three pieces.

3 Mix the remaining ingredients in a large, shallow dish. Add the potatoes and sausages and turn over in the marinade to coat. Leave to marinate for 2 hours.

4 Thread the sausages and potato pieces on skewers.

5 Barbecue for 15 minutes, turning occasionally and spooning (or preferably brushing) with any remaining marinade during cooking.

Marinades, rubs and bastes

You can make simple foods much more exciting and flavoursome with a simple marinade.

Basic barbecue marinade, baste or dipping sauce

Use with chicken, turkey, or any meat or sausages.

SUFFICIENT FOR 4 PORTIONS

2 tbsp wine or malt vinegar
2 tbsp tomato ketchup (catsup)
2 tbsp golden (light corn) syrup
1 tbsp Worcestershire sauce
Salt and pepper
1 small garlic clove, peeled and crushed, or ½ tsp garlic purée (paste)

1 Whisk everything together in a bowl, using a wire whisk.

2 Spread over the raw meat or poultry and leave to marinate for up to 2 hours or spread over the food just before barbecuing. Alternatively, serve the mixture in a bowl as a dipping sauce with plain barbecued food.

Red wine and oregano marinade

Use this for lamb, beef or sausages.

SUFFICIENT FOR 4 PORTIONS

1 garlic clove, peeled and crushed, or 1 tsp garlic purée (paste)
1 tbsp tomato purée or ketchup (catsup)
½ mug of red wine
2 tbsp sunflower oil
1 tsp dried oregano
1–2 tsp sugar
A good sprinkling of salt and pepper

Whisk all the ingredients together until thoroughly blended, then use to marinate foods for up to 3 hours.

Yoghurt and horseradish marinade

This is great with beef or oily fish, such as mackerel or salmon (which is not expensive now it's farmed). Try it with fillets of smoked mackerel, too. Just smear it over before grilling for 2 minutes on each side.

SUFFICIENT FOR 4 PORTIONS

1 small carton of plain yoghurt
1 tbsp horseradish sauce
1 tbsp French or grainy mustard
1 tbsp wine vinegar
1 tsp sugar
2 tbsp sunflower oil

Whisk all the ingredients together. Use to marinate fish for up to 1 hour, beef for 2 hours.

White wine and herb marinade

Use this for chicken, pork, fish or vegetables. You can substitute cider or apple juice for the white wine, if you like.

SUFFICIENT FOR 4 PORTIONS

1 onion, peeled and chopped
½ mug of white wine
2 tbsp sunflower oil
1 tsp dried mixed herbs
1–2 tsp clear honey
A good sprinkling of salt and pepper

Mix all the ingredients together and use to marinate food for anything from 30 minutes to 2 hours.

Thai-style marinade

Use with chicken, pork or seafood.

SUFFICIENT FOR 4 PORTIONS

2 tbsp sesame seeds
½ mug of sunflower oil
Finely grated zest and juice of
1 small lemon or 1 lime
2 tbsp Thai fish sauce
or ½ fish stock cube, crumbled
1 garlic clove, peeled and crushed,
or 1 tsp garlic purée (paste)
1 tbsp sugar
½ tsp dried chilli flakes or chilli powder
2 tbsp chopped fresh coriander (cilantro)

1 Put the sesame seeds in a dry frying pan (skillet) and heat, stirring, until lightly golden. Tip them into a bowl.

2 Add the remaining ingredients and whisk together with a wire whisk. Use to marinate foods for up to 2 hours before cooking.

Hot chilli marinade

This is great with any meat, fish or poultry.

SUFFICIENT FOR 4 PORTIONS

4 tbsp sunflower oil
2 tbsp lemon juice
2 tbsp tomato purée (paste)
¼ mug of water
½–1 tsp chilli powder
or dried chilli flakes
½ tsp ground cumin
2 tsp clear honey
A good pinch of salt

Whisk all the ingredients together and use to marinate for up to 1 hour for fish, 2 hours for chicken, 3 hours for meat.

Sweet and sour marinade

Use this with pork, beef, chicken or fish.

SUFFICIENT FOR 4 PORTIONS

3 tbsp sunflower oil
1 tbsp tomato ketchup (catsup)
1 tbsp wine or malt vinegar
1 tbsp clear honey
or golden (light corn) syrup
2 tbsp soy sauce
1 garlic clove, peeled and crushed,
or 1 tsp garlic purée (paste)

Whisk all the ingredients together and use to marinate fish for up to 1 hour, chicken for up to 2 hours and meat for up to 3 hours.

Peanut marinade

This is also good as a dipping sauce or to make satay dishes with pork, chicken or beef.

SUFFICIENT FOR 4 PORTIONS

½ mug of water
2 spring onions (scallions), trimmed and
finely chopped
4 good tbsp crunchy peanut butter
1 tbsp clear honey
2 tbsp light soy sauce
A few drops of Tabasco sauce

1 Put the water in a small saucepan with the spring onions. Bring to the boil over a high heat, turn down to fairly low and cook for 1 minute.

2 Stir in the peanut butter, honey, soy sauce and Tabasco sauce to taste. Stir until smooth. Thin with a little more water, if necessary.

3 Add cubes of meat or poultry and marinate for up to 2 hours, then thread on skewers and barbecue.

Rosemary and garlic rub

Use for lamb or pork steaks or chops
or chicken pieces.

SUFFICIENT FOR 4 PORTIONS

2 tsp dried rosemary
1 garlic clove, peeled and crushed,
or 1 tsp garlic purée (paste)
or 1 tsp dried onion granules
¼ tsp salt
¼ tsp pepper
1–2 tbsp sunflower oil

1 Put the rosemary in a small bowl
and crush as finely as possible with
the end of a rolling pin or clean bottle
(better still, use a pestle and mortar).

2 Mix in the garlic or onion granules
and the salt and pepper.

3 Rub oil on each side of your pieces
of meat, then rub in this flavouring
mixture.

Hot Cajun rub

Use for any meat, fish or chicken.

SUFFICIENT FOR 4 PORTIONS

1 garlic clove, peeled and crushed,
or 1 tsp garlic purée (paste)
1 tbsp paprika
2 tsp chilli powder
1 tsp dried oregano
½ tsp salt
1 tbsp sugar
2 tbsp sunflower oil

1 Mix all the ingredients together
except the oil together. Rub the oil all
over the meat or fish of your choice.

2 Rub the spiced mixture well into
the surface all over and leave to stand
for up to 2 hours before cooking.

Chilli rub

Use for meat, fish or poultry.

SUFFICIENT FOR 4 PORTIONS

1 garlic clove, peeled and crushed,
or 1 tsp garlic purée (paste)
1 small onion, peeled and grated
1 tsp chilli powder
¼ tsp salt
¼ tsp pepper, preferably black
2 tbsp sunflower oil

1 Mix the garlic, onion, chilli powder,
salt and pepper together and use to
rub all over meat, fish or poultry.
Leave to stand for at least 2 hours
before cooking.

2 Smear (or preferably brush) with a
little sunflower oil before cooking.

Dry onion rub

Use for meat, fish, poultry or game.

SUFFICIENT FOR 4 PORTIONS

2 tsp dried onion granules
1 tsp garlic salt
1 tsp celery salt
1 tbsp pepper, preferably black
½ tsp dried basil
2 tsp paprika
2 tbsp sunflower oil

1 Mix all the ingredients except the
oil together and rub all over the food
to be barbecued. Leave to stand for at
least 2 hours.

2 Smear (or preferably brush) with a
little sunflower oil before cooking.

Simple herb baste

This stops any meat, chicken or fish from drying out whilst it is being cooked, and adds a delicate flavour too. It's worth having a long-handled basting brush so you don't burn your fingers.

SUFFICIENT FOR 4 PORTIONS

2 tbsp sunflower or olive oil
1 tsp dried mixed herbs
1 tbsp lemon juice
A good pinch each of salt and pepper

1 Whisk all the ingredients together.

2 Brush or smear over the meat before cooking and repeat several times during barbecuing – especially just before and after you turn the meat over.

Worcestershire baste

This adds a more robust flavour to meat or chicken and prevents drying during cooking.

SUFFICIENT FOR 4 PORTIONS

2 tbsp Worcestershire sauce
2 tbsp sunflower oil
1 tsp paprika
1 tsp sugar
A good pinch each of salt and pepper

1 Whisk the ingredients together.

2 Brush or smear over the meat before cooking and repeat several times during barbecuing – especially just before and just after you turn the meat over.

Cheat's jerk baste

Use for any meat or poultry – it's particularly good with chicken or sausages.

SUFFICIENT FOR 4 PORTIONS

3 tbsp brown table sauce
½ tsp chilli powder
1 tsp sugar
1 tbsp wine or malt vinegar

1 Mix the ingredients together.

2 Brush or smear over the meat before cooking. Continue to brush frequently with the baste during barbecuing – especially just before and after you turn the meat over.

Getting Flash ... Cold Desserts

You are not going to bother with desserts every day. If you do want something to round off your meal, a pot of yoghurt or a piece of fresh fruit makes an easy and healthy option. But now and then it's fun to have something sweet and delicious. Many of these only take seconds to make, others need a bit more forward planning. The recipes in this section mostly serve four people, but some are for one or can easily be reduced in quantity if you want to give yourself a treat!

Ⓥ Greek figs Ⓥ

This recipe works just as well with drained, canned figs instead of fresh ones.

SERVES 4

4 fresh figs, trimmed and cut into bite-sized pieces
2 tbsp brandy (preferably Greek or Spanish) or orange juice
2 medium cartons of Greek-style yoghurt with honey
4 small sprigs of fresh mint

1 Put the figs in the base of four glass dishes and spoon the brandy or orange juice over.

2 Spoon the yoghurt on top and decorate each with a small sprig of mint. Chill, if time allows, before serving.

Ⓥ Fresh fruit salad Ⓥ

Make the fruit salad at least 1 hour in advance to give the flavours time to develop. You will need enough fresh fruit to make about 3 good serving-spoonfuls of prepared fruit per person.

SERVES 4-6

A mixture of fresh fruits
1 × 300 g/11 oz/small can of mandarin oranges in natural juice
½ mug of pure apple or orange juice
1 tsp lemon juice

1 Prepare the fresh fruits. Discard any stones (pits). Leave on any edible peel (for example, on apples, peaches, nectarines or plums) for colour and texture. Chop or slice as appropriate into bite-sized pieces.

2 Put the mandarins and juice in a glass bowl. Stir in the fruit juices.

3 Add the prepared fruits. If using juicy berries such as raspberries or blueberries, add these at the last moment so the colour does not run too much. Chill until ready to serve.

Greek yoghurt Ⓥ pleasure Ⓥ

SERVES 1

3–4 dried apricots, chopped
1 tbsp raisins
1 small carton of Greek-style yoghurt
2 tsp clear honey

1 Mix the apricots and raisins with the yoghurt.

2 Spoon into a dish and trickle the honey over.

3 Chill if possible before serving, to allow the flavours to develop.

Anytime blackcurrant Ⓥ mousse Ⓥ

Try this with other well-flavoured canned fruits with matching jellies.

SERVES 4

1 packet of blackcurrant-flavoured jelly (jello)
1 × 300 g/11 oz/medium can of blackcurrants
1 × 170 g/6 oz/small can of evaporated milk, chilled
1 × 170 g/6 oz/small can of cream or cream from an aerosol can

1 Dissolve the jelly in ²/₃ mug of boiling water in a bowl.

2 Stir in the juice from the can of blackcurrants and chill until on the point of setting.

3 Meanwhile, whisk the chilled evaporated milk until thick and fluffy.

4 When the jelly is the consistency of egg white, whisk it into the fluffy milk.

5 Spoon it into four glasses and chill until set.

6 Spread or squirt the cream over and top with the blackcurrants.

Strawberry meringue Ⓥ surprise Ⓥ

You can use cream from an aerosol can, if you prefer.

SERVES 4

4 meringue nests
4 tbsp chocolate and hazelnut (filbert) spread
1 tbsp orange juice
1 small carton of double (heavy) or whipping cream
3 tbsp sugar
1 small punnet of small strawberries
Shavings of plain (semi-sweet) chocolate, pared off a block with a potato peeler

1 Put the nests on a board. Mix the chocolate spread with the orange juice in a small bowl.

2 Spread the chocolate mixture in the centre of each nest.

3 Pour the cream into a bowl and add half the sugar. Whip with a hand blender or balloon whisk until standing in peaks.

4 Set aside four of the nicest strawberries for decoration. Slice the remainder, discarding the green calyxes. Add to the cream and stir in gently with a metal spoon.

5 Put the meringue nests on four plates. Pile the cream and strawberries on top. Put a reserved strawberry on the top of each.

6 Sprinkle a few chocolate shavings over each nest and serve.

Rich chocolate
Ⓥ mousse Ⓥ

You can decorate the tops of these little puds with sliced fresh fruits, crumbled chocolate Flake bar, some chopped nuts or chocolate shavings pared from a bar with a potato peeler. If you have any spirits – like whisky or vodka or coffee liqueur – you can add 1–2 tbsp to the chocolate spread before folding it into the cream for a really luxurious mousse. To make it look really special, add one or two chocolate mint or orange sticks to each glass before serving.

SERVES 4

1 medium carton of double (heavy)
or whipping cream
4 tbsp chocolate spread
Cream from an aerosol can (optional),
to serve

1 Pour the cream into a bowl and whip with a balloon whisk or hand blender until it stands in soft peaks.
2 Add the chocolate spread and gently whisk again until thoroughly mixed.
3 Spoon the mousse into small glasses and chill until set. Decorate each with a 'squirt' of cream, if liked, just before serving.

Ⓥ Coffee cream cheese Ⓥ

SERVES 1

½ tsp instant coffee granules
½ tsp water
¼ × 200 g/7 oz carton of soft white
cheese, such as Philadelphia
2 tbsp icing (confectioners') sugar
A few chopped walnut pieces
Thin sweet biscuits (cookies), to serve

1 Mix the coffee and water together until dissolved. Stir in the cheese and sugar.
2 Tip the mixture into a small pot and sprinkle with the nuts. Chill until very cold before serving with biscuits.

Ⓥ Mock rum babas Ⓥ

You could treat yourself to one of these when you're eating alone, but I expect you're more likely to keep them for impressing your mates. If you want to toast the nuts, put them in a dry frying pan and heat over a moderate heat, stirring until they turn brown, then tip out of the pan immediately so they don't continue to cook and burn.

SERVES 4

6 tbsp sugar
⅓ mug of water
About 1 tsp rum essence (extract)
4 ring doughnuts
Cream from an aerosol can
2 tbsp chopped mixed nuts (optional)

1 Put the sugar and water in a small saucepan. Heat gently, stirring, until the sugar dissolves, then turn up the heat and boil rapidly for 3 minutes until syrupy. Cool slightly, then add rum essence to taste.
2 Prick the doughnuts in several places with a skewer or cocktail stick (toothpick). Place in a shallow dish.
3 Spoon the syrup over the doughnuts to coat completely, then leave to soak.
4 When ready to serve, squirt cream into the centres and sprinkle with chopped nuts, if liked.

Simple lemon
ⓥ cheesecake ⓥ

SERVES 4-6

1 packet of lemon-flavoured jelly (jello)
Boiling water
1 × 200 g/7 oz/small packet of digestive
biscuits (graham crackers), crushed
¹/₃ × 250 g/9 oz block or tub of butter
or margarine, melted
2 tbsp soft brown sugar
1 × 200 g/7 oz carton of soft white
cheese, such as Philadelphia
4 tbsp caster (superfine) sugar
Finely grated zest and juice of
1 small lemon
or 2 tbsp bottled lemon juice
1 small carton of double (heavy) cream
Ground cinnamon, to decorate (optional)

1 Break up the jelly in a mug and make up to 1 mug with boiling water. Tip into a bowl and add ¹/₄ mug of boiling water. Stir until dissolved, then leave to cool.

2 Mix the biscuits with the melted butter or margarine and brown sugar. Turn into a 20 cm/8 in flan tin (pie pan) or other shallow dish of about the same size and press into the sides and base to form a case (shell).

3 Mix the cheese and caster sugar together with the lemon zest and juice with a wire whisk. Whisk in the cold but not set jelly.

4 Whip the cream with the same whisk and gently stir into the lemon mixture.

5 Tip the mixture into the flan case (pie shell) and chill until set. Decorate with a dusting of ground cinnamon, if liked.

ⓥ Banoffee brûlée ⓥ

SERVES 1

1 banana
1 small carton of
toffee-flavoured yoghurt
2 tsp white or light brown sugar

1 Preheat the grill (boiler).

2 Slice the banana and place in a flameproof serving dish.

3 Spoon the yoghurt over.

4 Sprinkle liberally with the sugar to cover the top completely.

5 Remove the grill rack and place the dish in the pan. Grill (broil) until the sugar melts, bubbles and caramelises.

6 Serve straight away or leave to cool, then chill before serving.

ⓥ Strawberry cheesecake ⓥ

SERVES 6

1 × 200 g/7 oz carton of soft white
cheese, such as Philadelphia
4 tbsp sugar
¹/₂ tsp vanilla essence (extract)
1 small carton of double (heavy) or
whipping cream, whipped
1 × 23 cm/9 in sponge flan case
(pie shell), bought ready-made
1 × 400 g/14 oz/large can of
strawberry pie filling

1 Mix the cheese with the sugar and vanilla essence until well blended, using a wooden spoon. Stir in the whipped cream gently, using a metal spoon.

2 Spoon into the flan case and chill until fairly firm.

3 Spread the strawberry pie filling over before serving.

ⓥ Nectarine brûlée ⓥ

SERVES 1

1 nectarine, stoned (pitted) and sliced
1 small carton of peach-flavoured
yoghurt
2 tsp white or light brown sugar

1 Preheat the grill (broiler).

2 Put the nectarine in a flameproof serving dish.

3 Spoon the yoghurt over.

4 Sprinkle with the sugar to cover the top completely.

5 Remove the grill rack and place the dish in the pan. Grill (broil) until the sugar melts, bubbles and caramelises.

6 Serve straight away or leave to cool, then chill before serving.

ⓥ Trifle ⓥ

This is traditionally made with sherry but you can use any leftover wine, vermouth or spirit in it – but not beer! – or just use fruit juice.

SERVES 4

4 trifle sponges
1 × 300 g/11 oz/medium can
of strawberries
2 tbsp sherry
1 × 425 g/15 oz/large can of custard
1 medium carton of whipping cream,
whipped until softly peaking
1 tbsp toasted flaked (slivered) almonds

1 Crumble the sponges into the base of a glass serving dish.

2 Empty the can of strawberries over and gently mash into the sponges.

3 Sprinkle the sherry over, then cover with the custard. Gently spread the cream over.

4 Sprinkle the surface with toasted almonds and chill until ready to serve.

Cherry and ⓥ custard flan ⓥ

SERVES 4

1 sachet of instant custard powder
1½ mugs of boiling water
1 × 400 g/14 oz/large can of
cherry pie filling
1 × 18 cm/7 in pastry (paste) or sponge
flan case (pie shell), bought ready-made
Cream from an aerosol can (optional)

1 Empty the sachet of custard powder into a bowl.

2 Whisk in the boiling water until very thick and smooth – it should be much thicker than 'pouring' custard but not solid!

3 Spoon in a quarter of the cherry pie filling and mix in well.

4 Spoon the custard mixture into the flan case. Spread out evenly and leave until cold.

5 Spread the remaining pie filling over the surface and chill until ready to serve. If liked, squirt swirls of cream over the surface just before serving (don't do it too soon or it will lose its fluffiness).

ⓥ Mocha ripple bombe ⓥ

This looks impressive but it's so easy and you can use any economy soft ice cream. You need a basin that holds almost exactly 4 mugs of water. If you don't have a suitable basin, use any similar-sized container or pack the mixture into individual cups or thick glasses and serve them either just as they are or turned out in the same way as the bombe.

SERVES UP TO 6

2 tsp instant coffee granules
2 tbsp water
3 tbsp chocolate spread
1 × 1 litre/1¾ pt tub of soft-scoop vanilla or chocolate ice cream
1 chocolate Flake bar, to decorate (optional)

1 Blend the coffee with the water in a mug until dissolved. Mix in the chocolate spread until well blended.

2 Tip the ice cream into a mixing bowl and mash with a fork quickly to break up. Immediately add the chocolate mixture and stir and turn the mixture briefly to form ripples but don't allow the ice cream to melt much.

3 Quickly pack the mixture into a medium-sized basin (see note above). Wrap in foil or clingfilm (plastic wrap) and freeze for at least 3 hours or preferably overnight until firm.

4 When ready to serve, dip the base of the basin briefly in hot water, loosen the edge with a knife and invert on to a serving plate. Holding the plate and basin firmly, give it a good shake to release the ice cream, then lift off the basin.

5 Crumble the Flake bar over the top, if liked, and serve straight away.

ⓥ Lemon yoghurt ice ⓥ

This is so easy and it's full of goodness too!

SERVES ABOUT 6

1 large carton of plain yoghurt
1 × 450 g/1 lb/large jar of lemon curd

1 Spoon the yoghurt and the lemon curd into a large plastic container with a sealable lid. Mix with a balloon whisk or hand blender until completely blended.

2 Put in the freezer or freezing compartment of the fridge for 2 hours. Whisk with a fork to break up the ice crystals, then freeze again until firm. It will keep for a month or two.

3 About 10 minutes before you want to serve it, take it out of the freezer to soften it slightly.

Banana and toffee ⓥ ice cream ⓥ

SERVES UP TO 6

12 soft toffees or squares of fudge
2 ripe bananas
2 tsp lemon juice
1 × 1 litre/1¾ pt tub of soft-scoop ice cream

1 Using wet scissors or a knife, cut the toffees or fudge into tiny pieces.

2 Mash the bananas with the lemon juice.

3 Tip the ice cream into a large bowl and mash quickly. Add the bananas and toffee or fudge and mix quickly together. Tip back into the ice cream container, pressing down well. Cover with the lid (or wrap in foil if the lid won't quite fit back on) and freeze for at least 3 hours or preferably overnight.

4 Serve with a scoop or large spoon.

🅥 Apricot rice layer 🅥

If you want to toast the almonds before using them to decorate the desserts, put them in a dry frying pan and cook, stirring all the time, until they turn golden, then tip out of the pan straight away so they don't burn.

SERVES 4

1 × 400 g/14 oz/large can of apricot pie filling
1 × 425 g/15 oz/large can of creamed rice pudding
Cream from an aerosol can
A few flaked (slivered) almonds, to decorate

1 Spoon half the contents of the pie filling into the base of four glasses. Top with half the rice, then repeat the layers.

2 Chill until ready to serve. Just before serving, squirt a swirl of cream on top of each and scatter with a few flaked almonds.

🅥 Peach yoghurt fool 🅥

SERVES 4

1 × 410 g/14½ oz/large can of peach slices
1 × 425 g/15 oz/large can of custard
1 small carton of plain yoghurt

1 Drain the juice from the peaches and reserve.

2 Tip the fruit into a bowl and either purée it with a hand blender or mash thoroughly with a fork.

3 Add the custard and stir in thoroughly. Add the yoghurt and stir it in gently until it gives a marbled effect – don't blend it completely.

4 Spoon the dessert into glasses and pour a little of the reserved juice over the top.

🅥 Lemon velvet 🅥

SERVES 4

1 packet of lemon meringue pie filling
1 mug of water
1 tbsp bottled lemon juice
½ mug of cold milk
1 packet of Dream Topping
Cream from an aerosol can, to decorate (optional)

1 Put the lemon pie mix in a saucepan and blend in the water. Bring to the boil, stirring all the time, until thick and clear. Stir in the lemon juice. Leave to cool.

2 Pour the milk in a bowl. Add the Dream Topping and whisk with a balloon whisk or electric hand blender until thick and fluffy.

3 Add the Dream Topping mixture to the lemon mixture and stir in gently. Spoon into glasses and chill until ready to serve.

4 Decorate with cream just before serving, if liked.

ⓥ Banoffee pie ⓥ

If this is popular, it's a good idea to boil two or three cans of milk at the same time (to save fuel), then store them in the fridge. They'll keep for months and you'll have the toffee part all ready for whenever you want to make the pud.

SERVES 6

1 × 350 g/12 oz/large can of sweetened condensed milk, label removed
1 × 200 g/7 oz small packet of plain biscuits (cookies)
¼ × 250 g/9 oz block or tub of butter or margarine
2 bananas
1 small carton of double (heavy) or whipping cream
Drinking (sweetened) chocolate powder or grated chocolate, to decorate

1 Put the unopened can of condensed milk just as it is (don't pierce it) in a saucepan of water. Bring to the boil, part-cover with a lid and simmer for 2 hours, topping up with boiling water as necessary to keep the can covered. Pour off the boiling water and fill the pan with cold water. Leave to cool.

2 Put the biscuits in a plastic bag. Bash with a rolling pin until crushed.

3 Melt the butter or margarine in a saucepan. Stir in the biscuit crumbs and press into the base and sides of a 20 cm/8 in flan tin (pie pan) or shallow dish. Chill until firm.

4 Spread the cold caramelised milk on the base. Top with sliced bananas.

5 Whip the cream in a bowl with a hand blender or balloon whisk, and spread over the bananas.

6 Sprinkle with chocolate powder or grated chocolate and chill until ready to serve.

ⓥ Black Forest rice ⓥ

SERVES 4

1 × 425 g/15 oz/large can of creamed rice pudding
2–3 tbsp drinking (sweetened) chocolate powder
A few drops of vanilla essence (extract)
1 × 400 g/14 oz/large can of cherry pie filling
1 chocolate Flake bar, crumbled
Cream from an aerosol can

1 Mix the rice with the chocolate powder and the vanilla until thoroughly blended.

2 Put a layer of half the cherry pie filling in the base of four glasses. Top with half the chocolate rice. Sprinkle on half the Flake bar, then repeat the layers of cherry pie filling and rice.

3 Chill until ready to serve. Just before serving, top each with a squirt of cream, then add the remaining Flake.

Banana, custard and ⓥ strawberry pancakes ⓥ

I think strawberry jam tastes the best with bananas, but use any other flavour you like.

MAKES ABOUT 4

1 quantity of pancakes (see page 258)
2 tbsp strawberry jam (conserve)
2 bananas, peeled and sliced
1 × 425 g/15 oz/large can of custard

1 Cook the pancakes and leave to cool.

2 Spread each with about ½ tbsp jam, then add the sliced banana. Roll up and place on plates.

3 Spoon the custard over and serve.

🕑 Orange yoghurt cones 🕑

MAKES ABOUT 4

1 quantity of pancakes (see page 258)
1 × 300 g/11 oz/medium can of broken
mandarin orange segments, drained
1 small carton of apricot-flavoured
yoghurt
1 chocolate Flake bar

1 Make the pancakes and leave to cool.

2 Mix most of the oranges with the yoghurt.

3 Fold each pancake into quarters. Open up one flap of each and spoon in the orange mixture. Place on plates.

4 Scatter the remaining mandarin pieces over and crumble the Flake bar on top.

Strawberry mousse 🕑 meringues 🕑

SERVES 4

1½ mugs of cold milk
1 sachet of strawberry Instant Whip
4 meringue nests
1 × 300 g/11 oz/medium can of
strawberries, drained, reserving the juice

1 Pour the milk into a bowl. Add the dessert powder and whip with a hand blender or balloon whisk until thick.

2 Put the nests on plates. Reserve four strawberries for decoration. Drain the rest on kitchen paper (paper towels) and place in the nests.

3 Spoon the whipped dessert on top and decorate each with a strawberry. Trickle a little of the syrup around the plates and serve.

🕑 Mocha sponge dream 🕑

SERVES 4

1 chocolate Swiss (jelly) roll,
cut into slices
1½ mugs of cold milk
2 tsp instant coffee granules
1 sachet of chocolate Instant Whip
3 tbsp crème fraîche
A few chopped nuts
or 2 tsp drinking (sweetened) chocolate
powder, to decorate

1 Arrange the slices of cake in four individual dishes.

2 Pour the milk into a bowl and stir in the coffee until dissolved.

3 Whisk in the Instant Whip powder, using a hand blender or balloon whisk.

4 Add 2 tbsp of the crème fraîche and stir gently through the dessert to give a marbled effect.

5 Spoon on top of the sponge slices and chill to set. Top each with a little dollop of crème fraîche and sprinkle with nuts or a little drinking chocolate powder to decorate.

ⓥ Lemon and pear nests ⓥ

SERVES 4

4 meringue nests
1 × 410 g/14¹/₂ oz/large can of pear
quarters, drained and chopped
4 tbsp lemon curd
Cream from an aerosol can

1 Put the meringue nests on plates.

2 Put the pears in the nests and top with a spoonful of lemon curd.

3 Add a squirt of cream on top and serve.

Honey and peanut ⓥ ice nests ⓥ

SERVES 4

3 tbsp clear honey
1 tbsp chopped roasted peanuts
1 tsp lemon juice
4 meringue nests
4 scoops of vanilla ice cream

1 Put the honey, nuts and lemon juice in a pan and heat, stirring, until blended.

2 Put the nests on plates and add a scoop of ice cream to each. Spoon the honey nut sauce over and serve.

ⓥ Peach Melba ⓥ

SERVES 4

4 tbsp raspberry jam (conserve)
2 tbsp sugar
5 tbsp water
1 tsp lemon juice
2 peaches, halved and stoned (pitted)
or 4 canned peach halves
4 scoops of vanilla ice cream

1 Mix the jam with the sugar, water and lemon juice in a saucepan and heat, stirring, until well blended. Boil for 1 minute, then remove from the heat and leave to cool.

2 Put the peaches in small dishes or in wine goblets.

3 Top each with a scoop of ice cream, then trickle the raspberry sauce over.

ⓥ Banana split ⓥ

SERVES 1

3 tbsp instant drinking (sweetened)
chocolate powder
Boiling water
1 banana, peeled and
halved lengthways
2 scoops of vanilla or chocolate
ice cream
A glacé (candied) cherry, to decorate

1 Put the chocolate powder in a small bowl. Add boiling water 1 tsp at a time, stirring with a fork or wire whisk to form a smooth paste. Stop when you have a thick, pouring consistency.

2 Put the banana halves side by side in a shallow dish. Add the scoops of ice cream between the banana halves.

3 Trickle the chocolate sauce over the ice cream and top with a cherry.

Pears with chocolate mousse and rough Ⓥ raspberry sauce Ⓥ

Use any economy chocolate mousse.

SERVES 4

*1 × 300 g/11 oz/medium can
of raspberries
2 tsp cornflour (cornstarch)
2 fresh ripe pears
2 individual pots of chocolate mousse*

1 Drain the raspberry juice from the can into a saucepan. Stir in the cornflour until dissolved. Cook over a high heat, stirring until thickened and clear. Cook for 1 minute more.

2 Tip in the raspberries and mash with a fork, then stir well to form a chunky sauce. Leave to cool.

3 Cut the pears in half and peel off the skin. Scoop out the cores with a teaspoon. Cut a tiny slice off the rounded side of each pear so it won't roll about. Reserve the slices and put each pear on a plate.

4 Spoon the chocolate mousse into the pear cavities. Cut the reserved pear slices in half and stick two halves in the top of each mound of mousse.

5 Spoon the raspberry sauce around the base on the plates and serve.

Ⓥ Caribbean slice Ⓥ

If you like, you can use a small carton of double or whipping cream instead of the aerosol cream. Simply whip it with a hand blender or balloon whisk, then spoon it on and decorate the top with the prongs of a fork before adding the nuts. If you use real whipped cream, you can make it in advance and chill it in the fridge.

SERVES 4

*1 Jamaican ginger cake
1 tbsp pure orange juice
2 large bananas
1 tsp lemon juice
Cream from an aerosol can
2 tbsp toasted chopped nuts*

1 Cut the cake into three slices lengthways. Sprinkle each with 1 tsp of the orange juice.

2 Peel the bananas, then mash with the lemon juice, using a fork.

3 Put the bottom slice of cake on a large plate and spread with half the bananas and a swirl of cream. Add another layer of cake, then the remaining bananas and a bit more cream.

4 Top with the top layer of cake, decorate with more cream and sprinkle with the nuts.

5 Serve within 30 minutes (or the cream will collapse).

🅥 Chocolate cookie log 🅥

This really does need some booze –
vodka, gin, brandy, tequila, rum,
Archers – whatever spirit you have
available. If you don't drink alcohol,
substitute pure orange juice.

SERVES 4

2 tbsp apple juice
4 tbsp any spirit of your choice
1 medium carton of double
(heavy) cream
1 × 200 g/7 oz/small packet of
chocolate chip cookies
1 chocolate Flake bar, crumbled

1 Mix the apple juice with the alcohol
in a shallow dish.

2 Whip the cream with a hand
blender or balloon whisk until
standing in soft peaks.

3 One at a time, dip each cookie in
the liquid, then spread with cream.
Sandwich them all together into a
long roll on a plate. You should use
about half the cream.

4 Spread the rest of the cream all
over the top. Sprinkle with the
crumbled Flake and chill for at least
3 hours so the cookies soften and the
cream starts to absorb the boozy
chocolatey flavour.

Chocolate cherry
🅥 bombe 🅥

For this you need a pudding basin –
or other deep container – that will
hold about 4 mugs of water.

SERVES UP TO 6

1 small tub of glacé (candied) cherries
8 squares of plain (semi-sweet)
or milk chocolate
1 × 1 litre/1¾ pt tub of soft-scoop
vanilla or strawberry ice cream

1 Reserve one cherry for decoration
and chop the remainder and the
chocolate into small pieces.

2 Tip the ice cream into a large bowl
and mash quickly with a fork.
Quickly mix in the cherries and
chocolate.

3 Working fast, so it doesn't melt too
much, pack the ice cream into a
pudding basin (see note above). Press
down firmly, then wrap in foil or
clingfilm (plastic wrap) and freeze for
at least 3 hours or preferably
overnight until firm.

4 To turn out, stand the base of the
basin briefly in hot water, then loosen
the edge with a knife. Invert on to a
plate. Hold the basin and plate firmly
and give it a good shake to release the
ice cream. Remove the basin, top
with the reserved cherry and serve
straight away.

Getting even More Flash ... Hot Desserts

Yes, this chapter is full of reminders of home, sweet home – nursery puds, like crumbles and pies, bread and butter pudding and even a rice pudding. There are also some seriously impressive ones, like Sticky Toffee and Banana Pudding or Peaches Wrapped in Filo Pastry. I promise you though, they are all really easy to make.

Most of the recipes serve four people.

ⓥ Rhubarb Charlotte ⓥ

SERVES 4–5

4–6 sticks of rhubarb,
cut into short lengths
¹/₂ mug of sugar
5 slices of bread
Butter or margarine, for spreading

1 Preheat the oven to 180°C/350°F/ gas 4/fan oven 160°C.

2 Mix the rhubarb with three-quarters of the sugar.

3 Spread the slices of bread generously with butter or margarine. Cut four of the slices into triangles and use to line a medium-sized ovenproof dish.

4 Fill with the rhubarb and sugar. Dice the remaining bread and scatter over the top. Sprinkle with the remaining sugar.

5 Cook in the oven for about 40 minutes until golden brown and cooked through.

ⓥ Apple Charlotte ⓥ

SERVES 4

Prepare as for Rhubarb Charlotte (left), but use 2 cooking (tart) apples, peeled, cored and sliced, instead of the rhubarb. Add a pinch of ground cloves or cinnamon to the apple with the sugar.

ⓥ Apple crumble ⓥ

SERVES 4

3 large cooking (tart) apples, peeled,
cored and sliced
6 tbsp sugar
A good pinch of ground cloves (optional)
1 mug of plain (all-purpose) flour
¼ × 250 g/9 oz block or tub of butter
or margarine

1 Preheat the oven to 190°C/375°F/
gas 5/fan oven 170°C.

2 Put the apples in a medium-sized
ovenproof serving dish.

3 Sprinkle with 2 tbsp of the sugar
and the spice, if using, then add
2 tbsp of water.

4 Put the flour in a bowl. Add the
butter or margarine and mash the fat
into the flour with a fork until the
mixture resembles breadcrumbs.

5 Stir in the remaining sugar. Spoon
over the apples and press down lightly.

6 Bake in the oven for about
45 minutes or until golden and the
apple is cooked through.

ⓥ Rhubarb crumble ⓥ

SERVES 4

Prepare as for Apple Crumble (above)
but use 4–6 sticks of rhubarb, cut into
short lengths, instead of the apple.
Add an extra 1 tbsp of sugar to
sweeten the rhubarb and use ground
ginger instead of cloves.

Apple and blackberry ⓥ crumble ⓥ

SERVES 4

Prepare as for Apple Crumble (above)
but use only 2 apples and add
2–3 good handfuls of blackberries to
the mixture. Omit the spice.

Apple and raisin ⓥ crumble ⓥ

SERVES 4

Prepare as for Apple Crumble (left),
but add 3 tbsp of raisins and use
ground cinnamon instead of cloves.

ⓥ Creamy rice pudding ⓥ

You can cook this more slowly for a
longer time if necessary. For example,
if you are cooking a casserole at
160°C/325°F/gas 3/fan oven 145°C,
cook both for about 2½ hours or as
long as it takes to cook the casserole.
However, don't cook for less than the
time given and don't try to cook it at
a higher temperature.

SERVES 4

¼ mug of round-grain (pudding) rice
2 tbsp caster (superfine) sugar
1 × 400 g/14 oz/large can of
evaporated milk
A little grated nutmeg
or ground cinnamon (optional)
A knob of butter or margarine

1 Preheat the oven to 180°C/350°F/
gas 4/fan oven 160°C.

2 Put the rice and sugar in a medium-
sized ovenproof serving dish.

3 Stir in the milk.

4 Half-fill the can with water and stir
into the milk and rice until
completely blended.

5 Dust the top with grated nutmeg or
ground cinnamon, if liked. Cut the
knob of butter or margarine into tiny
pieces and scatter over the surface.

6 Bake in the oven for about
1½ hours until golden on top and the
rice is tender and creamy.

ⓥ Apple pie ⓥ

Use bought shortcrust pastry if you don't want to make your own, but this version is foolproof and dead easy! You can also ring the changes by using a 425 g/15 oz/large can of any pie filling.

If you don't have a proper pie plate, any medium-sized heatproof dinner plate will do.

SERVES 6

For the pastry:
²/₃ × 250 g/9 oz tub of soft margarine
2 tbsp water
2 mugs of plain (all-purpose) flour
A pinch of salt
For the filling:
4 large cooking (tart) apples
3 tbsp sugar, plus extra for sprinkling
A good pinch of mixed (apple-pie) spice
A little milk

1 Put the margarine in a bowl. Add the water and ½ mug of the flour. Mix with a fork to a smooth paste.

2 Work in the remaining flour and salt to form a soft dough. Wrap in a plastic bag or foil and chill for 30 minutes to make it easier to handle.

3 Preheat the oven to 200°C/400°F/ gas 6/fan oven 180°C.

4 Cut the dough in half. Dust the surface with a little more flour. Roll out one half with a rolling pin (or a clean bottle) to the size of your pie plate. Gently fold the pastry into three and lift on to the plate. Unfold and press gently into place. Roll out the other half of the pastry in the same way and set aside.

5 Peel the apples, cut into quarters, cut out the cores and cut the apples into slices. Place them in the centre of the pastry-lined plate, leaving a rim all round. Sprinkle with the sugar and spice, if using.

6 Brush the edge of the pastry with water or dab all round with your fingers dipped in water.

7 Fold the remaining rolled pastry as before and lift on top of the pie. Unfold and press the edges well together to seal. Trim the edges with a sharp knife all round, then press them together with the prongs of a fork. If the fork sticks to the pastry, dip it in flour first.

8 Make a small hole in the centre to allow steam to escape. Make leaves out of pastry trimmings and use to decorate the pie, if liked. Using a pastry brush, or the tips of your fingers, smear the surface gently with a little milk and sprinkle with a little extra sugar. Place on a baking (cookie) sheet. Bake in the oven for about 40 minutes until golden and cooked through.

9 Serve warm or cold.

Baked apples
v with syrup v

SERVES 4

4 even-sized cooking (tart) apples
4 tbsp golden (light corn) syrup
Cream or custard, to serve

1 Preheat the oven to 180°C/350°F/ gas 4/fan oven 160°C.

2 Cut the cores out of the apples but leave them whole. Using a sharp knife, cut a line round the circumference of the apples (like the equator), just cutting through the skin. This will prevent them from bursting during cooking.

3 Place them in a baking tin (pan) or ovenproof dish and pour about 5 mm/¼ in water around.

4 Spoon the syrup into the centres. Bake in the oven for 50 minutes to 1 hour until just tender.

5 Transfer to bowls and spoon the juices over.

Baked apples
v with fruit v

SERVES 4

Prepare as for Baked Apples with Syrup (above), but fill the centres with mixed dried fruit (fruit cake mix) instead of syrup and sprinkle each apple with 1–2 tsp sugar.

Baked apples
v with jam v

SERVES 4

Prepare as for Baked Apples with Syrup (above), but fill the centres with any flavoured jam (conserve) of your choice instead of the syrup, and sprinkle each apple with 1 tsp sugar.

Baked apples with walnuts
v and honey v

SERVES 4

Prepare as for Baked Apples with Syrup (left) but mix 2 tbsp of clear honey with 2 tbsp of chopped walnuts and spoon this into the apples instead of the syrup. Spoon another 2 tbsp of honey over the apples, then bake as above.

The easiest
v custard tart v

SERVES 4

1 × 18 cm/7 in pastry case (pie shell),
bought ready-made
2 eggs
½ mug of milk
1 × 425 g/15 oz/large can of custard
2 tbsp sugar
Ground nutmeg or cinnamon (optional)

1 Preheat the oven to 190°C/375°F/ gas 5/fan oven 170°C.

2 Put the pastry case on a baking (cookie) sheet or ovenproof plate.

3 Break the eggs into a bowl and whisk in the milk until blended, then whisk in the custard and sugar.

4 Tip the mixture into the pastry case and sprinkle with a little nutmeg or cinnamon, if liked. Bake in the oven for about 40 minutes, until set.

5 Serve warm or cold.

Peach and cheese
♥ parcels ♥

The number you can make depends on the number of peach halves in the can. You can, of course, just make two or four, then eat any remaining fruit with yoghurt, custard, ice cream or with breakfast cereal.

MAKES ABOUT 6

1 small carton of cottage cheese
4 tsp sugar
2 tbsp raisins
About 6 sheets of filo pastry (paste)
¹/₄ × 250 g/9 oz block or tub of butter or margarine, melted
1 × 410 g/14¹/₂ oz/large can of peach halves, drained

1 Preheat the oven to 200°C/400°F/gas 6/fan oven 180°C.

2 Mix the cheese with the sugar and raisins.

3 For each parcel, smear a little melted butter or margarine over a sheet of filo pastry. Fold in half to form a square and smear again.

4 Top with a peach half, then fill the cavity with a portion of the cheese mixture (the exact amount will depend on how many peaches you have to fill).

5 Draw the pastry over the filling and pinch it together to form a pouch. Smear a little of the melted butter or margarine on a baking (cookie) sheet and place the parcel on the sheet. Repeat with the remaining fruit. Smear any remaining melted butter or margarine over the parcels. Bake in the oven for about 15 minutes until golden.

6 Serve warm or cold.

Sticky toffee banana
♥ pudding ♥

SERVES 4

¹/₄ × 250 g/9 oz block or tub of butter or margarine
1 mug of light brown sugar
1 tbsp lemon juice
4 thick slices of wholemeal bread, crusts removed, cubed
4 slightly unripe bananas, cut into chunks
Crème fraîche, to serve

1 Melt the butter or margarine in a large frying pan (skillet) over a moderate heat.

2 Add the sugar and lemon juice and stir until the sugar has melted. Turn down the heat to fairly low.

3 Stir the bread gently through the toffee mixture until evenly coated.

4 Add the bananas, stir gently, then cover and cook for about 4 minutes until the bananas are soft but still hold their shape.

5 Serve hot, or cool, then chill before serving with crème fraîche.

Sticky toffee
♥ plum pudding ♥

SERVES 4

Prepare as for Sticky Toffee Banana Pudding (above) but use about 8 plums, halved and stoned (pitted), instead of the bananas. Add a small handful of slivered (flaked) almonds to the mixture too, if liked.

Ⓥ Nectarine filo tarts Ⓥ

You can use peaches instead of
nectarines, if you prefer.

MAKES 4

6 sheets of filo pastry (paste)
¹/₆ × 250 g/9 oz block or tub of butter
or margarine
4 nectarines, halved, stoned (pitted) and
thinly sliced
2 tbsp sugar
¹/₂ tsp ground cinnamon

1 Preheat the oven to 200°C/400°F/
gas 6/fan oven 180°C.

2 Put one sheet of pastry on a work
surface and smear with a little of the
butter or margarine. Add another
sheet of pastry on top. Continue to
smear and layer the sheets.

3 Using a saucer as a guide, cut out
four rounds from the stack of filo.

4 Smear a baking (cookie) sheet with
a little of the butter or margarine. Put
the rounds on the sheet and smear
with any remaining butter or
margarine.

5 Arrange the nectarine slices in a
starburst pattern on the pastry
rounds. Sprinkle with the sugar and
cinnamon.

6 Bake in the oven for about
15–20 minutes until golden.

7 Serve warm.

Ⓥ Apple filo tarts Ⓥ

MAKES 4

Prepare as for Nectarine Filo Tarts
(above) but use sharp, green eating
(dessert) apples instead of the
nectarines. Sprinkle with mixed
(apple-pie) spice instead of the
cinnamon.

Ⓥ Doughnut bites Ⓥ

This is a great way of using a loaf that
has been reduced in price because it
is near its sell-by date!

SERVES 4–6

For the sauce:
4 tbsp red jam (conserve)
1 tbsp lemon juice
2 tbsp sugar
5 tbsp water
For the bites:
1 small white uncut loaf
1 mug of apple juice
2 eggs, beaten
Oil, for deep-frying
4 tbsp caster (superfine) sugar
¹/₂ tsp ground cinnamon

1 Make the sauce. Put all the
ingredients in a saucepan and heat
over a moderate heat, stirring, until
the sugar has dissolved. Let it bubble
for 2 minutes, then remove from the
heat.

2 Cut the crusts off the bread, then
cut the loaf into large cubes.

3 Dip first in apple juice, then in
beaten egg, to coat completely.

4 Heat about 2.5 cm/1 in of oil in a
large saucepan or deep frying pan
(skillet) until a piece of the crust
from the loaf browns in 30 seconds.
Deep-fry the bread cubes for about
3 minutes until crisp and golden
brown, turning occasionally if
necessary. Drain on kitchen paper
(paper towels).

5 Mix the sugar and cinnamon
together in a bowl. Add the bread
cubes and turn them over in the
mixture to coat. Pile on to plates.

6 Reheat the sauce briefly, and trickle
it over. Serve straight away.

Pineapple upside-down
Ⓥ pudding Ⓥ

Reserve the unused juice, if liked, to serve with the pudding.

SERVES 4–6

*½ × 250 g/9 oz block or tub of butter
or margarine
2 tbsp golden (light corn) syrup
1 × 225 g/8 oz/small can of
pineapple rings
4 glacé (candied) cherries, halved
A few 'leaves', cut from
a piece of angelica,
or green jelly diamond cake decorations
8 tbsp sugar, preferably caster
(superfine)
¾ mug of self-raising (self-rising) flour
1 tsp baking powder
2 eggs*

1 Preheat the oven to 190°C/375°F/ gas 5/fan oven 170°C.

2 Grease the sides and then the base of a 20 cm/8 in flan dish (pie pan) or similar ovenproof dish with 1 tbsp of the butter or margarine, spreading it thickly on the base.

3 Add the syrup and spread it over the base.

4 Lay the pineapple rings in the base. Put the cherries, cut sides up, in the centres of the rings and around the fruit, and arrange the angelica leaves or jelly diamonds around.

5 Put the remaining butter or margarine, the sugar, flour, baking powder and eggs in a large bowl and beat until smooth with a wooden spoon, hand blender or balloon whisk.

6 Spread over the pineapple.

7 Bake in the oven for about 20 minutes until risen, golden and the centre springs back when lightly pressed.

8 Cool slightly, loosen the edge, then invert on to a serving dish and give a good shake to release the pudding.

9 Serve warm or cold.

Pear and mincemeat
parcels

The number of parcels depends on the number of pear halves in the can, which tends to vary. Any remaining mincemeat will keep in the cupboard for ages. If you haven't a pastry brush to spread the butter or margarine, you can use your fingers, but take care that the fat isn't too hot!

MAKES ABOUT 6

*About 6 sheets of filo pastry (paste)
¼ × 250 g/9 oz block or tub of butter
or margarine, melted
1 × 410 g/14½ oz/large can of pear
halves, drained, reserving the juice
1 × 450 g/1 lb jar of mincemeat*

1 Preheat the oven to 200°C/400°F/ gas 6/fan oven 180°C. For each parcel, smear a filo pastry sheet with a little melted butter or margarine. Fold in half to form a square and smear again.

2 Place a pear half in the centre and add a spoonful of mincemeat. Draw the filling up over the fruit and pinch the ends together to form a pouch.

3 Grease a baking (cookie) sheet with a little of the butter or margarine. Put the parcel on the sheet and smear with a little more butter or margarine. Repeat with the remaining pear halves.

4 Bake in the oven for about 15 minutes until golden brown.

5 Serve hot or cold with a little of the reserved juice spooned over.

Bread and butter ⓥ pudding ⓥ

You'll get the best result if you can leave the mixture to stand for 30 minutes before baking. You can use mixed dried fruit or raisins instead of sultanas, if you prefer.

SERVES 4

4–6 slices of white bread
Butter or margarine
4 tbsp sugar
4 tbsp sultanas (golden raisins)
2 mugs of milk
2 eggs
A few drops of vanilla essence (extract)

1 Preheat the oven to 180°C/350°F/ gas 4/fan oven 160°C.

2 Spread the bread with butter or margarine. Cut each slice into four triangles.

3 Line a medium-sized ovenproof dish with half the bread. Sprinkle with half the sugar and most of the fruit.

4 Top with the remaining bread triangles, arranged attractively on top. Scatter the remaining fruit over.

5 Beat the milk and eggs together with a fork and add a few drops of vanilla essence. Pour over the bread and sprinkle with the remaining sugar.

6 Bake in the oven for about 1 hour until golden and set.

Bread and butter pudding ⓥ with jam ⓥ

SERVES 4

4–6 thin slices of white bread
Butter or margarine
3 tbsp raspberry jam (conserve)
4 tbsp sugar
2 mugs of milk
2 eggs
A few drops of almond essence (extract)

1 Preheat the oven to 180°C/350°F/ gas 4/fan oven 160°C.

2 Spread the bread with butter or margarine and jam. Cut each slice into four triangles.

3 Line a medium-sized ovenproof dish with half the bread. Sprinkle with half the sugar.

4 Finish with the remaining bread triangles, arranged attractively on top.

5 Beat the milk and eggs together with a fork and add a few drops of almond essence. Pour over the bread and sprinkle with the remaining sugar.

6 Bake in the oven for about 1 hour until golden and set.

Cherry and orange
ⓥ cobbler ⓥ

Economy-range pie filling and fruit scones are ideal (and cheap!) for this recipe. If you don't want to use the oven, you can heat the fruits in a saucepan and divide between four pudding bowls. At the same time, grill the buttered scones until golden, then put one on top of each dessert.

SERVES 4

*1 × 400 g/14 oz/large can of
cherry pie filling
1 × 300 g/11 oz/medium can of broken
mandarin orange segments, drained
2 bought fruit scones (biscuits)
A good knob of butter or margarine
4 tsp sugar*

1 Mix the pie filling with the mandarin oranges in an ovenproof dish.

2 Split the scones in half and spread with the butter or margarine. Sprinkle each with sugar.

3 Arrange on top of the fruit and bake in a preheated oven at 190°C/375°F/gas 5/fan oven 170°C for about 15 minutes until hot through and the tops of the scones are turning golden.

ⓥ Sweet pancakes ⓥ

MAKES ABOUT 4

For the pancakes:
*8 tbsp plain (all-purpose) flour
A pinch of salt
1 tbsp sugar
1 egg
½ mug of milk
or milk and water mixed
Oil, for cooking*
For the filling:
*Knobs of butter or margarine
Sugar or golden (light corn) syrup
Wedges of lemon or bottled lemon juice*

1 Mix the flour, salt and sugar in a bowl.

2 Make a hollow in the centre and add the egg and half the milk. Beat with a whisk or wooden spoon until thick and smooth. Stir in the remaining milk.

3 Heat a little oil in a frying pan (skillet) and pour off the excess into a small bowl to use for the next pancake. When very hot, pour in just enough batter to coat the base of the pan when tipped and swirled gently. Cook until set and the base of the pancake is golden brown.

4 Toss or flip over with a fish slice or knife. Cook the other side. Slide out on to a plate and keep warm wrapped in foil while cooking the remainder.

5 Spread the pancakes with a little butter or margarine. Sprinkle with sugar or trickle with syrup. Squeeze a little lemon juice over, roll up and serve.

Pancakes with chocolate
Ⓥ and nut sauce Ⓥ

MAKES ABOUT 4

1 small block of plain (semi-sweet)
chocolate, about 50 g/2 oz
A good knob of butter or margarine
2 tbsp chopped walnut pieces
1 quantity of sweet pancakes
(see page 395)
Single (light) cream (optional)

1 Break up the chocolate and put it in
a small bowl with the butter or
margarine. Heat a small pan with
some water in it. Stand the bowl over
the hot water and stir until melted.
Stir in the nuts. Turn down the heat
as low as possible and leave while
making the pancakes.

2 Cook the pancakes (see page 395).
Roll them up and place on plates.
Spoon the chocolate nut sauce over
and serve with cream, if liked.

Feeling Thirsty ... Drinks

Here are some great drinks that don't cost a fortune, to get a party going. Some contain booze, some don't, and I've included some comfort drinks for when study gets just too much but you need to keep a clear head.

There are also the serious cocktails in this chapter for when you're pushing the boat out – after all, if you're going to be sophisticated, you've got to know how to do it properly! – and when the inevitable arises, turn to pages 433–4 for quick hangover cures.

Alcoholic party punches

These are great to get the party in full swing – a collection of lively drinks for a variety of tastes.

Stretched mull

This tastes just as alcoholic as Glühwein but is much cheaper to make and no one will know it's half grape juice!

MAKES 12 GLASSES

1 bottle of red wine
1 litre carton of red grape juice drink
1 orange, sliced
1 lemon, sliced
1 clove
½ cinnamon stick
½ tsp ground ginger

1 Put all the ingredients in a saucepan and heat gently, stirring until almost boiling.

2 Ladle into mugs or thick glasses and serve.

Minted cider cup

SERVES 6–8

½ mug of granulated sugar
Boiling water
1 large sprig of fresh mint
3 tbsp lemon juice
Ice cubes
5 cm/2 in piece of cucumber, cut into very thin slices
1 litre of dry cider

1 Measure the sugar in the mug. Top up with boiling water and stir until dissolved. Add the mint sprig and leave until cold. Pour into a large bowl.

2 Remove the mint and stir in the lemon juice and cider.

3 Put ice cubes and slices of cucumber into tall glasses. Pour the cider mixture over the ice. Serve.

Glühwein

MAKES 6 GLASSES

1 bottle of red wine
½ orange, sliced
½ lemon, sliced
1 clove
5 cm/2 in piece of cinnamon stick
2 tbsp granulated sugar

1 Put all the ingredients in a saucepan and heat gently, stirring until hot. Don't allow it to boil or the alcohol will evaporate!

2 Ladle into small mugs or thick glasses and serve.

Peach and ginger sizzler

SERVES 6

1⅓ mugs of Archers peach liqueur
1 lemon, halved and sliced
1 fresh peach, thinly sliced
Ice cubes
4 mugs of ginger ale, chilled

1 Put the liqueur in a jug with the lemon and peach. Chill.

2 Fill tall glasses with ice cubes. Stir the ginger ale into the jug, then pour over the ice cubes and serve.

Pimms

SERVES 6

5 cm/2 in piece of cucumber,
thinly sliced
A handful of fresh borage or mint leaves
1 lemon, halved and sliced
½ bottle of Pimms No. 1 Cup
Ice cubes
Lemonade

1 Put the cucumber, borage or mint and lemon in a large jug and add the Pimms. Chill until ready to serve.

2 Top up the jug with lemonade to taste, stir and serve over ice in tall glasses.

Planters' punch

SERVES 6–8

1 mug of dark rum
4 tbsp grenadine syrup
1½ mugs of pure orange juice
1⅓ mugs of pure pineapple juice
Juice of 1 lime
I orange, sliced
1 lemon sliced
Ice cubes

Mix all the ingredients except the ice cubes together in a large jug. Chill until ready to serve, then pour over the ice.

Sangria

MAKES 6–8 GLASSES

1 mug of water
3 tbsp caster (superfine) sugar
1 bottle of red wine
2 tbsp lemon juice
1 orange, sliced
1 lemon, sliced
1 mug of lemonade, chilled

1 Mix all the ingredients except the lemonade in a large jug. Chill until ready to serve.

2 Add the lemonade, stir and serve immediately.

Black velvet

For those with a sweeter tooth, choose Mackeson or other milk stout rather than Guinness.

SERVES 8

2 bottles of Guinness, chilled
1 bottle of sparkling wine, chilled

1 Pour the Guinness into eight tall glasses.

2 Top with sparkling wine and serve.

Non-alcoholic party punches and punch bases

These are for those times when you want a fun drink without the alcohol.

Blackcurrant and orange mull

MAKES 6 GLASSES

2 oranges
½ mug of blackcurrant cordial, undiluted
5 cm/2 in piece of cinnamon stick
1 litre carton of apple juice

1 Cut all the rind off the oranges and place in a saucepan. Squeeze the juice and pour through a fine sieve (strainer) into the pan.

2 Add the remaining ingredients. Heat gently, stirring until very hot but not boiling.

3 Remove the orange rind and cinnamon stick and serve in small mugs or thick glasses.

Caribbean pineapple pleasure

SERVES 6–8

1 × 250 g/9 oz/medium can of crushed pineapple
1 mug of apple juice
1 mug of pure orange juice
1 mug of canned coconut milk
2 tbsp lemon juice
Ice cubes
1 mug of sparkling mineral water

1 Mix the pineapple, apple juice, orange juice, coconut and lemon juice together and chill.

2 Fill tumblers with ice cubes. Mix the mineral water into the juices and pour over the ice.

Quick tropical sparkler

SERVES 10–12

4 mugs of tropical fruit juice drink
½ mug of lime juice cordial
4 tbsp lemon juice
1 litre bottle of sparkling bitter lemon
Ice cubes

1 Mix the tropical juice drink with the lime juice cordial and lemon juice. Chill.

2 When ready to serve, add the bitter lemon. Pour over ice cubes in tall glasses.

Iced lemon tea

It's worth making a big jug of this and keeping it in the fridge.

MAKES 4 GLASSES

2 tea bags
1 mug of boiling water
1 small lemon, sliced
Sugar, to taste

1 Put the tea bags in a jug or other container. Pour on the boiling water and stir and mash the bags for 1 minute until most of the flavour is extracted.

2 Remove the tea bags and add the lemon. Add 3 mugs of cold water and sweeten to taste with sugar. Chill until ready to serve.

Iced coffee

SERVES 1

2 tsp instant coffee granules or powder
5 tbsp boiling water
Ice-cold milk
Sugar, to taste

1 Put the coffee in a tall glass or mug. If using a glass, keep the spoon in it while you add the water. Add the boiling water and stir until dissolved.

2 Top up with ice-cold milk, stirring well. Sweeten to taste and serve.

Red bull dozer

MAKES 2 GLASSES

1 can of Red Bull
2 tbsp blackcurrant cordial
2 tsp lemon juice
Ice cubes
Lemonade

1 Mix half the Red Bull with half the blackcurrant and lemon juice in each of two tall glasses.

2 Add ice cubes, then gently pour in the lemonade so it doesn't quite blend – it will be lighter at the top than the base. Serve with straws.

Serious cocktails for serious drinkers

Here are the traditional favourites for when you really want to push the boat out! I'm not suggesting for one minute you should spend all your money on hard liquor but, for a special occasion, these are the business (and if you buy supermarket own brands of spirits, you can make them more cheaply).

Daiquiri

SERVES 4

Juice of 3 limes
1 tbsp icing (confectioners') sugar
⅔ mug of white rum
Cracked ice

1 Mix the lime juice and sugar together until dissolved.

2 Pour into four cocktail glasses.

3 Stir in the rum and fill the glasses with cracked ice. Serve straight away.

Banana daiquiri

SERVES 4

1 ripe banana, broken into pieces
1⅓ mugs of white rum
2 tbsp banana or orange liqueur
Juice of 2 limes
1 tbsp caster (superfine) sugar
Cracked ice

1 Put the banana in a jug with all the ingredients except the ice. Purée with a hand blender until smooth and thick.

2 Fill four tumblers with cracked ice and pour in the cocktail. Serve at once.

Pineapple daiquiri

SERVES 4

1 × 250 ml/9 oz/medium can of
crushed pineapple
Juice of 2 limes
⅔ mug of white rum
1 tbsp brandy
Crushed ice

1 Put the pineapple in a jug with the remaining ingredients. Purée with a hand blender until almost smooth but still with some 'bits'.

2 Pour over lots of crushed ice in four cocktail glasses and serve.

Strawberry daiquiri

SERVES 4

8–10 ripe strawberries, hulled
Juice of 2 limes
⅔ mug of white rum
2 tbsp icing (confectioners') sugar
1 tbsp orange liqueur
Crushed ice

1 Put all the ingredients except the ice in a jug. Purée with a hand blender until smooth.

2 Fill four cocktail glasses with crushed ice and pour the cocktail over. Serve straight away.

Brandy sour

SERVES 6

⅔ mug of brandy
Juice of 3 lemons
Ice cubes
Sparkling mineral water
1 lemon, sliced, to decorate

1 Put the brandy and lemon juice in a shaker (or any container with a sealable lid) full of ice. Shake well, then pour into tall glasses.

2 Top up with sparkling water to taste, stir and serve.

Champagne cocktail

SERVES 6

6 small sugar cubes
12 dashes of Angostura bitters
1 bottle of Champagne, chilled

1 Put a sugar cube in the base of each champagne glass. Add 2 drops of bitters to each.

2 Top up with Champagne but do not stir.

Margarita

SERVES 2

Juice of 2 limes
Sea salt
6 tbsp tequila
2 tbsp orange liqueur
2 tsp caster (superfine) sugar
Crushed ice

1 Dip the rim of two cocktail glasses in the lime juice, then in sea salt, to give a frosted rim.

2 Whisk the remaining lime juice with the tequila, orange liqueur and sugar (or put in a cocktail shaker).

3 Fill the cocktail glasses with crushed ice and pour the cocktail over. Serve straight away.

Martini

SERVES 2

6 tbsp gin
6 tbsp dry vermouth
2 green olives
or 2 thin shavings of lemon peel

Mix the gin and vermouth together in cocktail glasses and add an olive or shaving of lemon peel to each.

Gibson

SERVES 2

Prepare as for Martini (above) but add a white pearl cocktail onion to each glass instead of the olive or lemon peel.

Rusty nail

SERVES 2

Cracked ice
⅔ mug of whisky
3 tbsp Drambuie
Ice cubes

1 Put lots of cracked ice in a cocktail shaker or jug.

2 Add the alcohol and shake or stir well.

3 Fill two tall narrow tumblers with ice cubes. Strain the cocktail over and serve.

Whisky sour

SERVES 2

½ mug of whisky
2 tbsp pure orange juice
2 tbsp lemon juice
1 tbsp caster (superfine) sugar
2 maraschino cherries

1 Mix all the ingredients except the cherries together.

2 Pour into cocktail glasses and add a maraschino cherry to each.

Sidecar

They say if you can make a good one
of these, you're a great barman!

SERVES 2

¼ mug of brandy
4 tbsp Cointreau
1 large lemon
Cracked ice

1 Mix the brandy with the Cointreau.
2 Pare off two strips of lemon peel
and reserve. Cut the fruit in half,
squeeze the juice and pour through a
sieve (strainer) into the alcohol.
3 Fill two tall narrow tumblers with
cracked ice. Add a strip of lemon peel
to each. Pour in the alcohol and
lemon mixture, stir with a swizzle
stick and serve.

Tequila sunrise

SERVES 2

Crushed ice
1½ mugs of pure orange juice
⅓ mug of tequila
2 tbsp grenadine syrup

1 Fill two tumblers with crushed ice.
Add the orange juice, then the
tequila. Stir well.
2 Hold the spoon over the top of the
drink and gently pour the grenadine
over. It should float. Serve straight
away.

Soothers for swots

Treat yourself to one of these when the going gets tough and you're
still slaving over that assignment at 1 am!

Brazilian bedtime mocha

If you love really sweet things, add
1 tbsp of sugar with the coffee.

SERVES 1

4 squares of plain (semi-sweet)
chocolate, chopped
¼ mug of strong black coffee
Scant ¾ mug of milk

1 Put the chocolate and coffee in a
saucepan and warm over a moderate
heat, stirring all the time until the
chocolate melts.
2 Whisk in the milk and continue to
heat, whisking all the time, until
almost boiling and frothy.
3 Pour into a mug and serve.

Butterscotch malted milk

SERVES 1

2 tsp light brown sugar or clear honey
A knob of butter or margarine
Scant 1 mug of milk
2 tbsp malted milk drink granules

1 Put the sugar or honey and butter
or margarine in a saucepan. Heat
over a low heat, stirring, until
bubbling and the sugar has melted, if
using.
2 Add the milk and granules and
heat, whisking with a balloon whisk
or fork, until almost boiling. Pour
back into the mug and serve.

Chocolate caramel velvet

SERVES 2-4

1 chocolate caramel bar, chopped
1 tbsp light brown sugar
2½ mugs of milk
¼ mug of double (heavy) cream, chilled

1 Put the chopped bar in a saucepan with the sugar and milk.

2 Cook over a gentle heat, stirring all the time, until the bar and sugar have melted. Bring almost to the boil, when bubbling gently round the edges.

3 Pour into mugs and carefully pour a little chilled double cream over the surface of each. Drink through the cream.

Hot chocolate mallow

SERVES 1

1 mug of milk
3 tsp drinking (sweetened) chocolate powder
2 marshmallows

1 Put the milk and chocolate in a saucepan and heat, whisking with a balloon whisk or fork, until frothy and almost boiling.

2 Pour back into the mug and float the marshmallows on top.

Hot lemon and lime

SERVES 1

1 mug of sparkling lemonade
2 tsp lime juice cordial
1 slice of orange or lime (optional)

1 Put all the ingredients in a saucepan and heat until almost boiling.

2 Pour into a mug and serve.

Minted hot choccie drink

Peppermint essence is great to have in the cupboard – when you've got a cold, put a few drops on a tissue to clear your sinuses (it's much cheaper than the proprietary medications you can buy from the chemist).

SERVES 1

1 mug of milk
3 heaped tsp drinking (sweetened) chocolate powder
A few drops of peppermint essence (extract)
1 mint candy stick (optional)

1 Put the milk in a saucepan with the chocolate powder.

2 Whisk with a balloon whisk, hand blender or fork over a moderate heat until piping hot and frothy.

3 Add the peppermint essence a drop at a time to suit your own taste. Pour into a mug and serve with a mint candy stick, for stirring, if you like.

Hot milk soother

If you are not keen on black treacle (or you don't think you'll make this very often) use golden syrup instead.

SERVES 1

2 tsp black treacle (molasses)
1 mug of milk
A pinch of ground cinnamon
1 tbsp double (heavy) cream

1 Put the treacle, milk and cinnamon in a saucepan. Heat, whisking with a fork, hand blender or balloon whisk until almost boiling.

2 Pour into a mug. Hold a teaspoon, rounded side up, over the surface of the milk and gently pour the cream over the spoon so it floats on top of the milk. Serve straight away.

Raspberry reward

If you are making this for one, store the remaining raspberries in a covered container in the fridge and eat them with yoghurt for breakfast (or for another warming drink).

SERVES 2

2 tbsp blackcurrant cordial
1 × 200 g/7 oz/small can of raspberries
Boiling water

1 Divide the blackcurrant cordial and raspberries and juice between two glasses.

2 Top up with boiling water, stir and serve with spoons to eat the fruit.

CﾘﾘKiNG FﾘR tHERaPY ... BaKiNG

When you're cheesed off with studying, or that vital essay simply isn't happening, you need to take a break and do something relaxing, and there is nothing more therapeutic than baking a batch of biscuits (cookies) or cakes. This section contains simple recipes for all your favourites and I've even included a couple of quick breads. If you don't have a wire cooling rack, use a grill (broiler) rack – but make sure it's clean.

ⓥ Carrot cake ⓥ

If you don't have a loaf tin, you can use a deep baking dish that holds 5 mugs of water.

MAKES 1 CAKE

2 large carrots, peeled
2 mugs of self-raising (self-rising) flour
2 tsp baking powder
1 tsp mixed (apple-pie) spice
½ mug of sugar, preferably light brown
½ × 250 g/9 oz block or tub of butter or margarine, plus extra for greasing
1 egg, beaten

1 Preheat the oven to 180°C/350°F/gas 4/fan oven 160°C.

2 Grease a 900 g/2 lb loaf tin (pan). Cut a piece of non-stick baking parchment the same size as the base and put in the bottom of the tin.

3 Grate the carrots into a large bowl.

4 Add the flour, baking powder and spice.

5 Put the sugar and butter or margarine in a saucepan and heat, stirring, until the fat melts.

6 Stir into the dry ingredients and mix in the beaten egg completely.

7 Turn into the tin and bake in the oven for about 40 minutes until risen and golden and a skewer inserted in the centre comes out clean.

8 Leave to cool in the tin for 10 minutes, then turn out, remove the paper and leave to cool.

ⓥ Frosted carrot cake ⓥ

MAKES 1 CAKE

Prepare as for Carrot Cake (left). Once cooked, make some lemon icing (frosting). Put ¼ × 250 g/9 oz block or tub of butter or margarine in a bowl. Using a fork, mash in 1 mug of icing (confectioners') sugar (sift it, to remove any lumps, if possible), and the grated zest and juice of a lemon or 2 tbsp of bottled lemon juice. Spread this over the top of the cooled cake and leave to set.

Carrot and walnut ⓥ cake ⓥ

MAKES 1 CAKE

Prepare as for Carrot Cake (left), but add ¼ mug of chopped walnut pieces to the dry ingredients (Step 3).

Carrot and orange
Ⓥ cake Ⓥ

MAKES 1 CAKE

Prepare as for Carrot Cake (see page 406) but add the grated zest of half an orange to the mixture. Once cooked, make some orange icing (frosting). Put ¼ × 250 g/9 oz block or tub of butter or margarine in a bowl. Using a fork, mash in a mug of icing (confectioners') sugar and the grated zest and juice of half an orange. Spread this over the top of the cooled cake and leave to set.

Extra-crunchy
Ⓥ flapjacks Ⓥ

MAKES 8

⅓ × 250 g/9 oz block or tub of butter
or margarine, plus extra for greasing
2 tbsp sugar, preferably light brown
2 tbsp golden (light corn) syrup
1½ mugs of muesli-type breakfast cereal
⅓ mug of plain (all-purpose) flour

1 Preheat the oven to 190°C/375°F/ gas 5/fan oven 170°C.

2 Melt the butter, sugar and syrup in a saucepan.

3 Stir in the remaining ingredients until well mixed.

4 Grease a 18 cm/7 in square baking tin (pan), add the mixture and press down well.

5 Bake in the oven for about 12 minutes or until golden.

6 Cool slightly, then mark into 18 fingers. Leave until completely cold before removing from the tin.

7 Store in an airtight container.

Ⓥ Traditional flapjacks Ⓥ

MAKES 8

Make exactly like Extra-crunchy Flapjacks (left) but use ordinary porridge oats instead of the crunchy oat cereal. Add 1 tsp of mixed (apple-pie) spice or cinnamon, if liked.

Ⓥ Shortbread wedges Ⓥ

MAKES 8

1½ mugs of plain (all-purpose) flour
A pinch of salt
2 tbsp cornflour (cornstarch)
⅓ mug of caster (superfine) sugar
½ × 250 g/9 oz block or tub of butter
or margarine

1 Preheat the oven to 150°C/300°F/ gas 2/fan oven 135°C.

2 Mix the flour, salt and cornflour into a bowl.

3 Add ¼ mug of the sugar and all the butter or margarine and mash with a fork until the mixture resembles breadcrumbs.

4 Press into an 18 cm/7 in round shallow baking tin (pan) or dish. Alternatively, squeeze the mixture together into a ball of dough and press it out to a similar-sized round on a baking (cookie) sheet. Prick all over with a fork and mark into eight equal wedges. Chill for 1 hour.

5 Bake in the oven for about 1 hour until a very pale golden brown.

6 Sprinkle with the reserved caster sugar. Leave to cool in the tin, then cut into wedges before serving.

ⓥ Vanilla cookies ⓥ

Make the dough, then leave it while you try to do some more work for a couple of hours – then go back to the kitchen to bake a batch.

Make the full quantity of mixture and store it in the fridge. You can then cook a batch of delicious fresh cookies whenever you like.

MAKES ABOUT 60

1¾ mugs of plain (all-purpose) flour
¼ mug of cornflour (cornstarch)
1 tsp baking powder
½ × 250 g/9 oz block or tub of butter or margarine
½ mug of caster (superfine) sugar
1 tsp vanilla essence (extract)
1 egg, beaten

1 Mix the flour, cornflour and baking powder thoroughly together.

2 Add the butter or margarine and work in with a fork until the mixture is crumbly.

3 Stir in the sugar, vanilla and egg to form a dough.

4 Draw together with your hands and shape into a long, fat sausage. Wrap in foil and chill for a few hours to firm it up. The mixture will keep for up to 10 days in the fridge.

5 To bake, preheat the oven to 190°C/375°F/gas 5/fan oven 170°C. Cut thin slices off the roll and lay a little apart on a greased baking (cookie) sheet.

6 Bake in the oven for about 12 minutes until a pale golden brown.

7 Cool slightly, then transfer to a wire rack to cool. Store in an airtight container.

ⓥ Almond cookies ⓥ

MAKES ABOUT 60

Prepare as for Vanilla Cookies (left), but use almond essence (extract) instead of vanilla and add 4 tbsp of chopped almonds, or mixed nuts, which are cheaper, to the mixture.

ⓥ Fork cookies ⓥ

A butter-flavoured margarine, such as Clover, gives the best flavour.

MAKES ABOUT 20

Oil, for greasing
¼ × 250 g/9 oz tub of soft margarine
4 tbsp caster (superfine) sugar
1 tsp vanilla essence (extract)
1 mug of self-raising (self-rising) flour
Glacé (candied) cherries, halved, to decorate

1 Preheat the oven to 190°C/375°F/gas 5/fan oven 170°C. Grease two baking (cookie) sheets.

2 Put all the ingredients except the cherries in a bowl and mix with a fork until the mixture forms a dough.

3 Shape the dough into walnut-sized balls and place on the baking sheets.

4 Flatten with a fork dipped in cold water. Press half a cherry in the top of each.

5 Bake on separate shelves in the oven for about 15 minutes until pale golden brown, swapping their positions halfway through cooking.

6 Loosen with a fish slice and transfer to a wire rack to cool. Store in an airtight container.

ⓥ Oaties ⓥ

If you've only got one baking sheet,
bake these in two batches.

MAKES ABOUT 20

Scant ½ × 250 g/9 oz block or tub of
butter or margarine
8 tbsp sugar
1 tbsp golden (light corn) syrup
1 mug of self-raising (self-rising) flour
1 mug of porridge oats
½ tsp bicarbonate of soda

1 Preheat the oven to 180°C/350°F/
gas 4/fan oven 160°C. Grease two
baking (cookie) sheets with a little of
the butter or margarine.

2 Melt the butter or margarine with
the sugar and syrup in a saucepan.

3 Stir in the flour, oats and
bicarbonate of soda.

4 When thoroughly mixed, shape the
mixture into small balls and place,
well apart, on the baking sheets.

5 Bake in the oven for about
15 minutes until golden. Cool for
5 minutes, then loosen with a fish
slice and transfer to a wire rack to
cool. Store in an airtight container.

ⓥ Sunflower-seed oaties ⓥ

MAKES ABOUT 20

Make as for Oaties (above) but add
4 tbsp of sunflower seeds to the
mixture before shaping into balls.

ⓥ Chocolate chip oaties ⓥ

MAKES ABOUT 20

Make as for Oaties (above) but add
½ packet of chocolate chips to the
mixture before shaping it into balls.

ⓥ Cherry oaties ⓥ

MAKES ABOUT 20

Make as for Oaties (left) but add
½ small tub of glacé (candied)
cherries, chopped, to the mixture
before shaping into balls.

ⓥ Snickers cookies ⓥ

MAKES ABOUT 20

¼ × 250 g/9 oz block or tub of butter or
soft margarine
4 tbsp sugar
1 egg, beaten
1½ mugs of plain (all-purpose) flour
2 Snickers bars, finely chopped
Oil, for greasing

1 Preheat the oven to 190°C/375°F/
gas 5/fan oven 170°C.

2 Melt the butter or margarine in a
saucepan. Stir in the sugar and leave
to cool slightly.

3 Add the egg, flour and chocolate
bars and mix to form a lumpy dough.

4 Shape into about 20 small flat
rounds about 4 cm/1½ in in diameter.
Place on a greased baking (cookie)
sheet. Bake in the oven for about
15–20 minutes until golden.

5 Cool slightly, then loosen with a
fish slice and transfer to a wire rack
to cool completely. Store in an
airtight container.

Ⓥ Jam oaties Ⓥ

MAKES 15

1 quantity of Oaties mix (see page 409)
Oil, for greasing
3 tbsp raspberry jam (conserve)
4 tbsp porridge oats, for sprinkling

1 Preheat the oven to 180°C/350°F/gas 4/fan oven 160°C.

2 Make up the oat mixture and press it into a greased 28 × 18 cm/11 × 7 in shallow baking tin (pan) or similar-sized ovenproof dish.

3 Spread with the jam, then sprinkle with the extra oats.

4 Bake in the oven for about 25 minutes until golden.

5 Cool for 10 minutes, then cut into fingers and cool on a wire rack.

Ⓥ Chocolate oaties Ⓥ

MAKES 15

Prepare as for Jam Oaties (above) but spread with chocolate spread instead of jam (conserve).

Ⓥ Peanut oaties Ⓥ

MAKES 15

Prepare as for Jam Oaties (above) but spread with peanut butter instead of the jam (conserve). For the topping, mix 2 tbsp of chopped roasted peanuts with 2 tbsp of porridge oats and sprinkle on top.

Ⓥ Peanut honey bites Ⓥ

Use any cheap biscuits for this recipe.

MAKES 12

⅓ × 250 g/9 oz block of butter
or hard margarine
3 tbsp clear honey
1 × 200 g/7 oz/small packet of
plain biscuits (cookies)
3 tbsp peanut butter
A good handful of roasted peanuts,
finely chopped

1 Melt the butter or margarine with the honey in a saucepan. Bring to the boil and remove from the heat.

2 Tip the biscuits into a plastic bag and crush with a rolling pin or clean bottle.

3 Stir into the saucepan with the remaining ingredients and mix well.

4 Oil an 18 cm/7 in square baking tin (pan) or similar-sized ovenproof dish. Press the mixture into the container and chill until firm.

5 Cut into squares and store in an airtight container.

Banana and cinnamon
ⓥ muffins ⓥ

This is a delicious way to use up really ripe, blackening bananas that you don't want to eat.

MAKES ABOUT 8

2 small ripe bananas (or 1 large)
3 tbsp sugar, preferably light brown
½ tsp ground cinnamon
3 tbsp sunflower oil
1 tsp baking powder
1 egg
1½ mugs of self-raising (self-rising) flour
3–5 tbsp milk
2 tbsp raisins
Butter or margarine, to serve

1 Preheat the oven to 190°C/375°F/ gas 5/fan oven 170°C. Line eight sections of a tartlet tin (patty pan) with paper cake cases (cupcake papers). If you don't have one, stand stacks of three cases inside each other at intervals on a baking (cookie) sheet.

2 Peel the bananas and put in a bowl with the sugar. Blend them with a hand blender or mash thoroughly with a fork.

3 Using the blender or a balloon whisk, blend in the cinnamon, oil, baking powder and egg.

4 Add the flour and blend again.

5 Mix in enough of the milk to form a thick batter and stir in the raisins.

6 Spoon the mixture into the paper cases, almost to the top.

7 Bake in the oven for about 20 minutes until risen and golden and the centres spring back when lightly pressed.

8 Cool on a wire rack. Eat plain or pull apart and spread with butter or margarine.

Double chocolate
ⓥ muffins ⓥ

MAKES ABOUT 12

1½ mugs of self-raising (self-rising) flour
3 tbsp cocoa (unsweetened chocolate) powder
2 tsp baking powder
4 tbsp caster (superfine) sugar
1 egg
1 mug of milk
6 tbsp sunflower oil
½ packet of chocolate chips

1 Preheat the oven to 190°C/ 375°F/ gas 5/fan oven 170°C. Line the 12 sections of a tartlet tin (patty pan) with paper cake cases (cupcake papers). If you haven't got one, stand stacks of three cases inside each at intervals on a baking (cookie) sheet.

2 Mix the flour, cocoa and baking powder in a bowl. Stir in the sugar.

3 Whisk the egg, milk and oil together in a small bowl until well blended.

4 Pour into the flour mixture and mix with a wooden spoon or the balloon whisk until smooth.

5 Stir in the chocolate chips.

6 Spoon the mixture into the cake cases, almost to the top.

7 Bake in the oven for about 20 minutes until risen and the centres spring back when lightly pressed. Cool on a wire rack.

Chocolate walnut
Ⓥ brownies Ⓥ

MAKES 12

Oil, for greasing
½ mug of plain (all-purpose) flour
¼ tsp baking powder
½ × 100 g/4 oz packet of walnut pieces,
finely chopped
¼ × 250 g/9 oz block or tub of butter
or margarine
10 squares of plain (semi-sweet) cooking
chocolate, broken into pieces
¾ mug of sugar, preferably dark brown
2 eggs, beaten
½ tsp vanilla essence (extract)

1 Grease a 28 × 18 cm/11 × 7 in
shallow baking tin (pan) or any
shallow ovenproof dish of similar size.

2 Preheat the oven to 180°C/350°F/
gas 4/fan oven 160°C.

3 Mix together the flour, baking
powder and nuts. Melt the butter or
margarine with the chocolate and
sugar.

4 Cool slightly, then beat in the eggs
and vanilla essence. Pour into the
flour mixture and mix well.

5 Turn into the prepared tin or dish
and bake in the oven for 35 minutes
until risen and the centre springs
back when lightly pressed.

6 Leave to cool in the container, then
cut into squares and lift out with the
help of a fish slice.

7 Store in an airtight container.

Date and walnut
Ⓥ bars Ⓥ

Use the leftover milk for Condensed
Milk Toast (see page 436).

MAKES 16

Oil, for greasing
⅓ × 350 g/12 oz/large can of sweetened
condensed milk
½ mug of plain (all-purpose) flour
½ tsp baking powder
A pinch of salt
⅔ mug of chopped stoned (pitted)
cooking dates
4 tbsp chopped walnut pieces
A pinch of grated nutmeg

1 Grease an 18 cm × 28 cm/7 × 11 in
shallow baking tin (pan) or similar-
sized shallow, ovenproof dish. Preheat
the oven to 190°C/375°F/gas 5/fan
oven 170°C.

2 Mix all the ingredients together in a
bowl.

3 Tip the mixture into the prepared
container and spread out.

4 Bake in the oven for about
30 minutes until golden brown.

5 Mark into fingers while still hot,
then leave to cool.

6 Remove with a fish slice and store
in an airtight container.

Serious sustenance chocolate Ⓥ crunchy bars Ⓥ

MAKES 12–16

Oil, for greasing
³/₄ × 250 g/9 oz block of butter
or hard margarine
4 tbsp sugar, preferably light brown
2 tbsp golden (light corn) syrup
3 tbsp cocoa (unsweetened chocolate)
powder
3 mugs of oat crunch cereal
6 tbsp raisins
1 × 200 g/7 oz bar of plain (semi-sweet)
cooking chocolate

1 Oil an 18 cm × 28 cm/7 in × 11 in shallow baking tin (pan) or similar-sized ovenproof dish.

2 Melt the butter or margarine, sugar, syrup and cocoa together in a saucepan.

3 Stir in the cereal and raisins and press into the prepared container.

4 Break up the chocolate and place in a bowl in a pan of hot water to melt or put it in the microwave and cook on Medium (50 per cent power) for 3–4 minutes, stirring once or twice and checking every 30 seconds until melted.

5 Spread the chocolate over the cereal mixture, right to the corners.

6 Chill until firm, then cut into fingers, remove and store in an airtight container.

Ⓥ Chewy apricot bars Ⓥ

Ring the changes with other dried fruits like pears or peaches – or even figs or prunes.

MAKES 15

1 × 170 g/6 oz/small can of
evaporated milk
4 tsp clear or thick honey
3 tbsp apple juice
¹/₄ × 250 g/9 oz block of butter
or hard margarine
4 tbsp sugar, preferably light brown
³/₄ mug of sultanas (golden raisins)
1¹/₃ mugs of dried apricots, chopped
1 mug of desiccated (shredded) coconut
2 mugs of porridge oats
Oil, for greasing

1 Heat the milk with the honey, apple juice, butter or margarine and sugar in a saucepan until just melted. Remove from the heat.

2 Stir in all the remaining ingredients and mix thoroughly.

3 Oil a 28 × 18 cm/11 × 7 in shallow baking tin (pan) or similar-sized ovenproof dish. Press the mixture firmly into the container.

4 Chill to firm, then cut into bars. Store in an airtight container in the fridge.

No-bake cherry and nut ⓥ fingers ⓥ

MAKES 12

Oil, for greasing
¹/₄ × 250 g/9 oz block of butter
or hard margarine
3 tbsp golden (light corn) syrup
4 tbsp sugar, preferably caster
(superfine)
1 mug of porridge oats
³/₄ small tub of glacé (candied) cherries,
finely chopped
¹/₂ × 100 g/4 oz packet of chopped
mixed nuts

1 Lightly oil an 18 cm/7 in shallow, square baking tin (pan) or similar-sized dish.

2 Put the butter or margarine, syrup and sugar in a saucepan and cook over a fairly low heat, stirring, until melted. Remove from the heat.

3 Stir in the remaining ingredients.

4 Press into the prepared container, leave to cool, then chill until firm. Cut into fingers.

No-bake cherry and ⓥ chocolate fingers ⓥ

MAKES 12

Prepare exactly as for No-bake Cherry and Nut Fingers (above) but use 10 squares of plain (semi-sweet) cooking chocolate, chopped, instead of the nuts.

ⓥ Chocolate biscuit bars ⓥ

This no-bake cake is always popular. You can buy broken biscuits very cheaply in supermarkets. For added chocolate flavour, break up a 200 g/7 oz bar of plain cooking chocolate, put it in a bowl and melt it over a pan of hot water. Alternatively, melt it in the microwave for about 3–4 minutes on Medium (50 per cent power), stirring once or twice and checking every 30 seconds. Spread the chocolate over the cold cake and chill until firm before cutting into fingers.

MAKES 15

¹/₂ × 250 g/9 oz block of butter
or hard margarine
1 tbsp sugar, preferably caster
(superfine)
1 tbsp golden (light corn) syrup
2 tbsp cocoa (unsweetened chocolate)
powder
2 mugs of broken plain biscuits
(cookies), roughly crushed
4 tbsp sultanas (golden raisins)
or raisins

1 Grease a 28 × 18 cm/11 × 7 in shallow baking tin (pan) or similar-sized ovenproof dish with a little of the butter or margarine.

2 Put the fat, sugar, syrup and cocoa in a saucepan. Cook over a moderate heat, stirring, until the fat melts and the mixture is well blended. Do not boil. Remove from the heat.

3 Add the crushed biscuits and the fruit and mix with a wooden spoon until thoroughly blended.

4 Tip the mixture into the prepared container and spread out evenly. Press down well with the back of a spoon. Leave until cool, then chill until firm. Cut into fingers. Store any remainder in an airtight container.

Chocolate bran flake Ⓥ cakes Ⓥ

You can make these with cornflakes or rice crispies, but I prefer the texture of bran flakes.

MAKES 12

$^1/_4$ × 250 g/9 oz block of butter
or hard margarine
3 tbsp golden (light corn) syrup
4 tbsp sugar, preferably light brown
2 tbsp cocoa (unsweetened chocolate)
powder
A few drops of vanilla essence (extract)
2 mugs of bran flakes

1 Put everything except the bran flakes in a saucepan and heat gently, stirring, until melted.

2 Stir in the bran flakes until thoroughly coated.

3 Spoon the mixture into paper cake cases (cupcake papers) and chill until firm.

Chocolate muesli Ⓥ cakes Ⓥ

MAKES 12

Prepare exactly as for Chocolate Bran Flake Cakes (above) but use muesli instead of bran flakes.

Ⓥ Strawberry mallows Ⓥ

MAKES 12

$^1/_4$ × 250 g/9 oz block or tub of butter
or margarine
3 tbsp strawberry jam (conserve)
$^1/_2$ × 100 g/4 oz packet of marshmallows,
preferably pink
2 mugs of rice crispies

1 Put the butter or margarine, jam and marshmallows in a saucepan. Cook over a fairly low heat, stirring until melted. Remove from the heat.

2 Stir in the puffed rice cereal and spoon into paper cake cases (cupcake cases). Chill until firm.

Banana and sultana Ⓥ flapjacks Ⓥ

MAKES 16

$^1/_3$ × 250 g/9 oz block or tub of butter
or margarine
$^1/_2$ mug of sugar, preferably light brown
1 tbsp golden (light corn) syrup
or clear honey
1 large ripe banana, peeled
and mashed
A good handful of sultanas
(golden raisins)
$2^1/_2$ mugs of porridge oats

1 Preheat the oven to 180°C/350°F/ gas 4/fan oven 160°C.

2 Put the butter or margarine, sugar and syrup or honey in a bowl and mix thoroughly with a wooden spoon until well blended.

3 Stir in the remaining ingredients.

4 Grease a 28 × 18 cm/11 × 7 in shallow baking tin (pan) or similar-sized ovenproof dish. Press the mixture into the tin.

5 Bake in the oven for 30 minutes until golden. Cool, then mark into fingers.

Quick baking-powder ⓥ bread ⓥ

So you've run out of bread – again. Don't worry, this doesn't take long and, if you eat it fresh, it's great!

MAKES 1 LOAF

2 mugs of plain (all-purpose) flour
2 tsp baking powder
½ tsp salt
¼ × 250 g/9 oz block or tub of butter or margarine, plus a little for greasing
About ½ mug of milk

1 Preheat the oven to 220°C/425°F/ gas 7/fan oven 200°C. Mix the flour thoroughly with the baking powder and salt.

2 Add the butter or margarine and mash with a fork until the mixture is crumbly.

3 Using a knife, stir in the milk, adding a little more if necessary, to form a soft but not sticky dough.

4 Shape into a small round loaf and put on a greased baking (cookie) sheet. Bake in the oven for about 25 minutes until golden and risen and the base sounds hollow when tapped.

5 Cool on a wire rack, then slice and serve.

ⓥ Yoghurt breads ⓥ

These breads freeze well if you don't want to eat them all at one go.

MAKES 6

1 mug of plain (all-purpose) flour
1 tsp baking powder
½ tsp salt
½ tsp sugar
4 tsp yoghurt
1 egg, beaten
Oil, for cooking

1 Mix the flour, baking powder, salt and sugar together in a bowl.

2 Stir in the yoghurt and enough of the egg to form a soft but not sticky dough (you may not need all of it).

3 Squeeze the dough together and knead it gently turning and pressing it until smooth.

4 Divide into six equal pieces and roll each into a ball, then flatten to rounds, about 13 cm/5 in.

5 Heat about 2.5 cm/1 in of oil in a frying pan (skillet). When hot but not smoking, add one of the rounds of dough. Turn down the heat to moderate and press down the dough with a fish slice into the oil until it starts to puff up. Turn it over and cook the other side for about 20 seconds until golden.

6 Drain on kitchen paper (paper towels) and keep warm, wrapped in kitchen paper or foil, while cooking the remainder.

Sauces ... to save You Money

My student daughter tells me that a lot of the weekly shop money is spent on ready-made cooking sauces for pasta, meat, chicken or vegetables. And that packet sauce mixes are not only expensive, but liable to go lumpy! Well, the recipes in this selection will all save you money and are so easy you can't go wrong. They are all enough for four servings. But if you're eating alone, simply store any leftovers in the fridge. They'll keep for at least a week, the uncooked ones even longer, in a clean, sealed container or screw-topped jar but are better used soon rather than later.

Quick pasta sauces

Cook any pasta you fancy according to the packet directions, then add one of the following quick and simple sauces for delicious, quick meals.

Almond and herb pesto

This is just as tasty as Pesto (see page 418) but you don't need a blender! You can add 1 crushed garlic clove or 1 tsp garlic purée to the mixture if you like.

SERVES 4

¼ × 250 g/9 oz block or tub of butter or margarine
½ × 100 g/4 oz/small packet of ground almonds
4 tsp grated Parmesan cheese
3 tbsp fresh chopped parsley
3 tbsp fresh chopped basil
Salt and pepper

1 Mash the butter or margarine with the almonds.

2 Work in the cheese and herbs and season well.

Anchovy sauce

SERVES 4

1 × 50 g/2 oz/small can of anchovies
½ mug of olive oil
1 garlic clove, peeled and crushed, or 1 tsp garlic purée (paste)
Pepper (preferably freshly ground black)

1 Drain the oil into the pan, then chop the anchovies with a sharp knife before adding to the pan.

2 Add the remaining ingredients and heat gently, stirring and pressing the anchovies against the side of the pan with a wooden spoon until they form a smooth paste. Season with pepper.

Creamy mushroom and white wine sauce

SERVES 4

A good knob of butter or margarine
1 large onion, peeled and chopped
12 button mushrooms, sliced
½ mug of white wine
½ mug of chicken or vegetable stock,
made with ½ stock cube
2 tsp cornflour (cornstarch)
1 tbsp water
1 small carton of single (light) cream
1 tsp dried parsley
Salt and pepper

1 Heat the butter or margarine in a saucepan. Add the onion and cook over a gentle heat, stirring, for 2–3 minutes until softened but not browned.

2 Add the mushrooms and cook, stirring, for 2 minutes.

3 Add the wine and stock. Bring to the boil, turn down the heat and when bubbling gently round the edges, part-cover and cook for 10 minutes until everything is soft.

4 Mix the cornflour with the water and stir into the pan. Cook, stirring, until thickened, then bubble gently for 1 minute. Stir in the cream and parsley and season with salt and pepper.

Pesto

You do need a hand blender for this. Bought pesto is fine – and I've used it in this book – but this is fantastic! Apart from adding it to pasta, try spreading it on slices of ciabatta or French bread and grill until melted, or use it as a stuffing for chicken breasts or fish.

SERVES 4–6

20 fresh basil leaves
1 large sprig of fresh parsley
4 tbsp pine nuts
1 large garlic clove, peeled and halved,
or 1 good tsp garlic purée (paste)
6 tbsp olive oil
2 tbsp grated Parmesan cheese
A pinch of salt
Pepper (preferably freshly ground black)
1 tbsp hot water

1 Put the herbs, nuts and garlic in a bowl and chop with a hand blender.

2 Gradually, add the oil in a thin trickle and keep blending to form a thick paste.

3 Add the cheese, salt and some pepper and blend again, adding the water.

4 Store in a screw-topped jar in the fridge.

Quick tomato sauce

SERVES 4

1 onion, peeled and finely chopped
1 garlic clove, peeled and crushed,
or 1 tsp garlic purée (paste)
1 tbsp sunflower or olive oil
1 × 400 g/14 oz/large can of
chopped tomatoes
1 tbsp tomato purée
½ tsp caster (superfine) sugar
Salt and pepper

1 Fry (sauté) the onion and garlic, if using, in a saucepan in the oil, for 2 minutes, stirring.

2 Add the tomatoes, tomato purée and sugar.

3 Bring to the boil over a high heat and boil rapidly for about 5 minutes until pulpy.

4 Season to taste.

Quick tomato sauce with fresh basil

SERVES 4

Prepare as for Quick Tomato Sauce (above) but omit the garlic and stir in 6–8 chopped fresh basil leaves before seasoning after cooking.

Piazza sauce

SERVES 4

2 tbsp olive oil
2 large garlic cloves, peeled and crushed,
or 2 good tsp garlic purée (paste)
2 mugs of passata (sieved tomatoes)
1 tsp dried oregano
1 tsp dried parsley
Salt and pepper

1 Heat the oil in a saucepan and fry (sauté) the garlic for 30 seconds.

2 Add the remaining ingredients and bring to the boil. Turn down the heat until bubbling gently around the edges and allow to bubble gently, stirring occasionally, for 15 minutes until rich and thick.

Sun-dried tomato and basil paste

Again, you don't need a blender for this one.

SERVES 4–6

1 × 200 g/7 oz/small jar of
sun-dried tomatoes in oil, drained,
reserving the oil
2–3 garlic cloves, peeled and crushed,
or 2–3 tsp garlic purée (paste)
4 tbsp olive oil
4 tbsp grated Parmesan cheese
8 chopped fresh basil leaves
½ tsp pepper

1 Chop the sun-dried tomatoes finely with a sharp knife, or put them in a bowl and keep snipping with scissors until they almost form a paste.

2 Mix in all the remaining ingredients, beating well.

Sun-dried tomato and cheese sauce

Traditionally this is made with Mascarpone cheese but this is cheaper (particularly if you use a supermarket own-brand cheese) and tastes just as good.

SERVES 4

2 sun-dried tomatoes in oil
1 × 200 g/7 oz carton of soft white cheese, such as Philadelphia
2 tbsp of the sun-dried tomato oil
1 small garlic clove, peeled and crushed, or ½ tsp garlic purée (paste)
1 tbsp tomato purée
1 tsp dried basil
½ tsp sugar
A good pinch of salt and pepper

1 Finely chop the tomatoes with a sharp knife or put them in a bowl and snip with scissors until they almost form a paste.

2 Using a fork, mash in the cheese, then the oil and then the remaining ingredients until well blended.

Sweetcorn and vegetable sauce

SERVES 4

1 × 300 g/11 oz/medium can of creamed sweetcorn (corn)
1 × 200 g/7 oz/small can of diced mixed vegetables, drained
A good handful of grated Cheddar cheese
½ tsp dried mixed herbs
4 tbsp milk
Salt and pepper

Mix all the ingredients except the salt and pepper in a saucepan and heat, stirring, until bubbling. Season to taste.

Quick curry sauces

Use any of these sauces to cook chicken, fish, beef, pork, lamb or vegetables. Remember, if using tougher meat, like stewing beef, you will need to simmer the curry for about 2 hours or cook it in the oven at 160°C/325°F/gas mark 3/fan oven 145°F. Tender meat, like chicken breast or pork stir-fry meat, and most vegetables will take only 20–30 minutes to cook, and fish only needs about 10 minutes. In most cases, it pays to heat a little oil in a pan and brown the meat or chicken on all sides before adding the curry sauce. You can add extra ingredients like sliced or chopped onion, peppers, aubergines or other vegetables at this stage too. Serve the curry on a bed of boiled rice.

Balti sauce

The sauce looks thin at first, but it should end up as a thick, rich sauce. If necessary, boil the curry rapidly for a few minutes at the end of cooking to evaporate excess liquid. If you have a hand blender, you can purée the cooked vegetables before adding the spices.

SERVES 4

2 tbsp sunflower oil
4 large tomatoes, chopped
1 green (bell) pepper, chopped
2 green chillies, seeded and chopped,
or ½ tsp dried chilli flakes
1 tsp garam masala
¼ tsp ground turmeric
¼ tsp ground cinnamon
1 tsp sugar, preferably light brown
½ tsp pepper
A good pinch of salt
1 mug of vegetable stock,
made with 1 stock cube

1 Heat the oil in a saucepan. Add the tomatoes, pepper and chillies or chilli flakes and fry (sauté) for 2 minutes.
2 Add the spices, sugar and salt and cook for 2 minutes.

3 Add the pepper and stock, bring to the boil and boil for 5 minutes.

Coconut oriental curry sauce

For a less authentic (but even cheaper) version, use 1 tsp of ground ginger instead of fresh.

SERVES 4

½ block of creamed coconut,
cut into chunks
2 mugs of boiling water
3 tbsp curry powder
1 tsp Chinese five-spice powder
2.5 cm/1 in piece of fresh root ginger,
peeled and grated
1 garlic clove, peeled and crushed,
or 1 tsp garlic purée (paste)
½ tsp salt

1 Put the coconut in a bowl. Add the boiling water and stir until the coconut melts.

2 Stir in the remaining ingredients and leave to cool. Use as a marinade before cooking.

Korma sauce

When simmering your pieces of vegetables, chicken or meat, the mixture may separate at first but will then become a rich, creamy sauce.

SERVES 4

1 tbsp sunflower oil
2 onions, peeled and grated
2.5 cm/1 in piece of fresh root ginger,
peeled and grated,
or 1 tsp ground ginger
1 green chilli, seeded and
very finely chopped
1 garlic clove, peeled and crushed,
or 1 tsp garlic purée (paste)
1 tsp ground turmeric
½ tsp ground cinnamon
1 tsp garam masala
½ block of creamed coconut, chopped
3 tbsp water
1 mug of plain yoghurt
Salt, to taste

1 Heat the oil in a saucepan. Add the onions, ginger, chilli and garlic and fry (sauté), stirring, for 2 minutes. Add the spices and fry for 1 minute. Turn down the heat.

2 Add the creamed coconut and water and heat gently, stirring, until melted. Stir in the yoghurt and add salt to taste.

Simple Chinese curry sauce

SERVES 4

2 onions, peeled
½ mug of water
3 tbsp sunflower oil
2 tbsp mild curry powder
1 tsp Chinese five-spice powder
1 tsp sugar
½ vegetable stock cube

1 Grate one of the onions in a small saucepan with 6 tbsp of the water. Bring to the boil and cook, stirring, for about 3 minutes until a soft paste is formed and the water has evaporated.

2 Halve and thinly slice the other onion. In a separate pan, heat the oil and fry (sauté) the sliced onion for 2 minutes until softened but not browned. Stir in the onion paste and the remaining ingredients, including the rest of the water, bring back to the boil, turn down the heat until gently bubbling round the edges and cook, making sure the stock cube has been dissolved, for about 5 minutes.

Pour-over curry sauce

Use this over hard-boiled eggs or plain grilled or fried chicken or pork. You can also use it to reheat leftover cooked chicken or vegetables. Simply simmer in the sauce for about 5 minutes until piping hot.

SERVES 4

1 × 295 g/10½ oz/medium can of
condensed celery or mushroom soup
6 tbsp water
2 tbsp tomato purée (paste)
1 garlic clove, peeled and crushed,
or 1 tsp garlic purée
1 tsp dried onion granules
1 tbsp curry paste
1 tsp garam masala
1 tsp ground turmeric
2 tbsp mango chutney
¼ block of creamed coconut,
cut into chunks
Salt and pepper

1 Put all the ingredients in a saucepan. Heat over a moderate heat, stirring, until the coconut is melted and the mixture is bubbling.

2 Thin with a little more water, if necessary. Season to taste.

Thai green curry sauce

SERVES 4

2 tbsp sunflower oil
2 tbsp Thai green curry paste
1 × 425 g/15 oz/large can of
coconut cream
2 tbsp Thai fish sauce
1 tbsp sugar, preferably light brown
2.5 cm/1 in piece of fresh root ginger,
peeled and grated,
or 1 tsp ground ginger
1 green chilli, seeded and finely chopped
3 kaffir lime leaves
or 1 piece of lemon zest
3 fresh basil leaves, chopped

1 Heat the oil in a saucepan and fry
(sauté) the green curry paste for
1 minute.

2 Add all the remaining ingredients,
bring to the boil, stirring, turn down
the heat until gently bubbling round
the edges and cook for 3 minutes.

3 Discard the lime leaves or lemon
zest before serving the finished dish.

Thai red curry sauce

If you like cooking Thai food, it's
worth buying a jar of lemon grass
purée, which will keep for ages
in the fridge.

SERVES 4

1 tbsp sunflower oil
1 onion, peeled, halved and thinly sliced
2 tbsp Thai red curry paste
1 × 425 g/15 oz/large can of
coconut cream
½ tsp salt
1 kaffir lime leaf
or 1 piece of lemon zest
1 stalk of lemon grass, chopped
1 tbsp Thai fish sauce
or ½ fish stock cube, crumbled
1 red (bell) pepper, cut into thin strips

1 Heat the oil in a saucepan. Add the
onion and fry (sauté) for 2 minutes
until softened but not browned. Stir
in the red curry paste and cook for
1 minute.

2 Add the rest of the ingredients.
Bring to the boil, stirring, turn down
the heat until gently bubbling round
the edges and simmer for 5 minutes.

3 Discard the leaves or zest before
serving the finished dish.

Special Thai curry sauce

SERVES 4

2 tbsp lemon or lime juice
2 tsp curry powder
¼ block of creamed coconut
¾ mug of water
3 tbsp peanut butter
1 tbsp wine or malt vinegar
1 small green chilli, seeded and
finely chopped
2 tsp clear honey
1 tbsp soy sauce
2 tsp cornflour (cornstarch)

1 Put all the ingredients except the
soy sauce and cornflour in a
saucepan and heat, stirring, until the
coconut melts.

2 Blend the cornflour with the soy
sauce and stir in. Bring to the boil
and simmer for 2 minutes, stirring.

Sauces for chicken

Use with chicken portions, skinless breasts, legs, thighs or diced meat. Simply dust the pieces all over with a little cornflour seasoned with a little salt and pepper and then brown them in a little hot oil on all sides, in a frying pan or flameproof casserole dish. Pour off any excess oil. Add the prepared sauce, bring to the boil, turn down the heat until gently bubbling round the edges and cook for 20–30 minutes until the chicken is completely cooked. Portions and bone-in thighs and legs take about 10 minutes longer than breasts or chunks.

Note that some chickens (frozen ones in particular) contain a lot of water. If you find the sauce is a bit thin when the chicken is cooked, blend 1–2 tsp of cornflour with 1 tbsp of water and stir into the sauce at the end, then let it bubble for an extra minute to thicken.

Goulash sauce

SERVES 4

1 tbsp olive oil
1 onion, peeled and finely chopped
1 garlic clove, peeled and crushed,
or 1 tsp garlic purée (paste)
1 tbsp paprika
1 green (bell) pepper, chopped
1 × 400 g/14 oz/large can of
chopped tomatoes
1 tbsp tomato purée
½ tsp sugar
Salt and pepper

1 Heat the oil in a saucepan and fry (sauté) the onion, garlic and pepper for 2 minutes, stirring. Stir in the paprika and cook for 1 minute.

2 Add the tomatoes, purée and sugar

3 Bring to the boil over a high heat and boil rapidly for about 5 minutes, stirring occasionally, until pulpy.

4 Season to taste.

Barbecue sauce

You can use cider or apple juice instead of wine.

SERVES 4

1 garlic clove, peeled and crushed,
or 1 tsp garlic purée (paste)
1 small onion, peeled and
finely chopped
2 tsp sunflower oil
4 tbsp tomato purée
1 mug of fruity dry white wine
2 tsp soy sauce
2 tbsp clear honey
2 tbsp vinegar
A few drops of Tabasco sauce
Salt and pepper

1 Put the garlic, onion and oil in a saucepan. Cook for 2 minutes over a high heat, stirring, until the onion is softened.

2 Add the remaining ingredients, bring to the boil, reduce the heat to fairly low and cook gently for about 20 minutes until thick, stirring frequently.

3 Taste and re-season, if necessary.

Piazzaiola sauce

SERVES 4–6

1 tbsp olive oil
2 onions, peeled and finely chopped
2 garlic cloves, peeled and crushed,
or 2 tsp garlic purée (paste)
1 green (bell) pepper, diced
6 button mushrooms, chopped
1 × 400 g/14 oz/large can of
chopped tomatoes
1 tbsp tomato purée
A few drops of Tabasco sauce
or a pinch of chilli powder
1 tsp dried oregano
Salt and pepper

1 Heat the oil in a saucepan. Add the onions, garlic and peppers and cook for 2 minutes, stirring.

2 Add the mushrooms and stir for 1 minute.

3 Add the tomatoes and tomato purée. Cook over a high heat until bubbling, then turn down the heat to fairly low and cook for 15 minutes until pulpy and the vegetables are tender. Season with Tabasco sauce or chilli powder and add the oregano and a little salt and pepper.

Provencal sauce

SERVES 4

1 tbsp olive oil
1 onion, peeled and finely chopped
2 garlic cloves, peeled and crushed,
or 2 tsp garlic purée (paste)
1 green (bell) pepper, chopped
1 × 400 g/14 oz/large can of
chopped tomatoes
1 tbsp tomato purée
½ tsp sugar
12 stoned (pitted) black or green
or stuffed olives, sliced
Salt and pepper

1 Heat the oil in a saucepan and fry (sauté) the onion, garlic and pepper for 2 minutes, stirring.

2 Add the tomatoes, purée, sugar and olives.

3 Bring to the boil over a high heat and boil rapidly for about 5 minutes, stirring occasionally, until pulpy.

4 Season to taste.

Sweet and sour sauce

For a chunky sauce, use a 225 g/8 oz/ small can of pineapple chunks in natural juice instead of the pineapple juice and add a 2.5 cm/1 in piece of finely chopped cucumber and a coarsely grated carrot. If you don't have pineapple juice, you can substitute apple juice or use all orange juice. It's very good with pork steaks or lean belly slices.

SERVES 4

2 tbsp cornflour (cornstarch)
2 tbsp water
2 tbsp soy sauce
3 tbsp tomato ketchup (catsup)
6 tbsp clear honey
4 tbsp wine or malt vinegar
4 tbsp pineapple juice
4 tbsp orange juice

1 Mix the cornflour with the water in a small saucepan with a wooden spoon or balloon whisk. Add all the remaining ingredients.

2 Bring to the boil over a high heat and cook for 1 minute until thickened and clear, stirring all the time.

Sauces for stir-fries

Simply cook the ingredients for your stir-fry in a tablespoon or two of oil, then add any of the suggested sauces below.

Use any vegetables you like – cut them into similar-sized pieces and cook the harder ones first. If you're using meat as well, cook it for 2–3 minutes before adding the vegetables (to make sure it's cooked through at the end).

Basic stir-fry flavouring

SERVES 1

1–2 tsp soy sauce
1 tbsp water
A pinch each of sugar and pepper

1 Sprinkle the ingredients over your cooked stir-fry, then toss and stir.
2 Taste and add more soy sauce and seasoning, if necessary.

Ginger stir-fry sauce

SERVES 4

2.5 cm/1 in piece of fresh root ginger
3 tbsp sherry or white wine
2 tbsp soy sauce
3 tbsp hot water

Peel the ginger and grate into a bowl. Mix together with all the other ingredients.

Honey, mustard and orange stir-fry sauce

You can add a pinch of chilli powder as well, if you like.

SERVES 4

1 tbsp clear honey
1 tbsp apple juice
2 tbsp orange juice
1 tsp lemon juice
1 tbsp soy sauce
2 tsp grainy mustard

Mix all the ingredients together.

Oriental chilli sauce

For a hotter sauce, add more chilli powder or a few drops of Tabasco sauce. This is also good as a dip with fried or grilled chicken, with tortilla chips – or even fish fingers!

SERVES 4

2 tsp cornflour (cornstarch)
5 tbsp water
2 spring onions (scallions), trimmed and finely chopped
2.5 cm/1 in piece of fresh root ginger, peeled and finely grated,
or 1 tsp ground ginger
1 garlic clove, peeled and crushed,
or 1 tsp garlic purée (paste)
4 tbsp apple juice or white wine
4 tsp sugar
2 tbsp tomato purée
½ tsp chilli powder
A good pinch of Chinese five-spice powder
Salt and pepper

1 Mix the cornflour with the water in a small saucepan with a wooden spoon or wire whisk.
2 Stir in all the remaining ingredients.
3 Bring to the boil over a high heat and cook for 1 minute, stirring.

Peking-style stir-fry sauce

SERVES 4

6 tbsp plum jam (conserve)
3 tbsp soy sauce
2 garlic cloves, peeled and crushed,
or 2 tsp garlic purée (paste)
2.5 cm/1 in piece of fresh root ginger,
peeled and finely grated,
or 1 tsp ground ginger
1 tbsp sunflower oil
1 tsp lemon juice
2 tbsp dry sherry or white wine

1 Whisk all the ingredients together.
2 Taste and add extra soy sauce, if liked.

Thai stir-fry sauce

SERVES 4

Finely grated zest and juice of 1 lime
1 tbsp sesame seeds
2 tsp Thai fish sauce
2 tbsp sunflower oil
2 tbsp apple juice
1 large garlic clove, peeled and crushed,
or 1 tsp garlic purée (paste)
2 tbsp roasted salted peanuts,
finely chopped
1 stalk of lemon grass, crushed
1 small green chilli, seeded and chopped
1 tbsp chopped fresh coriander (cilantro)

1 Put the sesame seeds in a frying pan (skillet) and fry, stirring, until golden. Tip into a bowl.
2 Stir in all the remaining ingredients.

White sauce and flavoured variations

I've given you the standard proportions for enough sauce for 2–4 people. If you make a sauce and don't use it all, you can keep it in the fridge for several days. Simply reheat it in a saucepan with an extra spoonful of milk, stirring it briskly all the time with a balloon whisk to remove lumps.

Basic white sauce

SERVES 2–4

3 tbsp plain (all-purpose) flour
1 mug of milk
A knob of butter or margarine
Salt and pepper

1 Put the flour in a small saucepan.
2 Using a balloon whisk and stirring all the time, gradually add the milk until the mixture is smooth.
3 Add the butter or margarine and a sprinkling of salt and pepper.

4 Cook over a fairly high heat, stirring with the whisk all the time, until the mixture is thick and bubbling. Continue to cook the sauce for 2 minutes. If necessary, thin with 2–3 tbsp more milk. Use as required.

Caper sauce

SERVES 2–4

1 Prepare as for Basic White Sauce (left) but add 2 tbsp of chopped capers before seasoning the sauce.
2 Serve with lamb or fish.

Cheese sauce

SERVES 2–4

1 Prepare as for Basic White Sauce (see page 427) but add a good handful of grated Cheddar cheese. For extra 'tang', add ½ tsp of made mustard too.
2 Serve with fish, chicken, pasta or vegetables.

Cucumber and dill sauce

SERVES 2–4

1 Prepare as for Basic White Sauce (see page 427) but add ¼ cucumber, finely chopped, and 1 tsp of dried dill (dill weed) to the sauce.
2 Serve with fish or chicken.

Green cress sauce

SERVES 2–4

1 Prepare as for Basic White Sauce (see page 427) but add 1 bunch of finely chopped watercress to the sauce and a pinch of cayenne.
2 Serve with fish or chicken.

Mushroom sauce

SERVES 2–4

1 Cook 4–5 finely chopped button mushrooms in 2 tbsp of water in a covered pan for 3 minutes.
2 Remove the lid and boil rapidly, if necessary, to evaporate any remaining liquid.
3 Stir into 1 quantity of cooked Basic White Sauce (see page 427) and add a squeeze of lemon juice, if liked.
4 Serve with chicken, fish, vegetables, pork or pasta.

Mustard sauce

SERVES 2–4

1 Prepare as for Basic White Sauce (see page 427) but stir in 2 tsp of made English mustard, 1 tbsp of sugar (preferably light brown) and a little malt vinegar, added a teaspoonful at a time until it's as sharp as you like.
2 Serve with ham steaks or oily fish, such as mackerel or salmon.

Onion sauce

SERVES 2–4

1 Peel and finely chop 2 onions.
2 Cook gently with 2 tbsp of water in a covered pan for 5 minutes until really soft.
3 Stir into 1 quantity of Basic White Sauce (see page 427) and re-season, if liked.
4 Serve with lamb, pork or chicken or vegetables.

Parsley sauce

SERVES 2–4

1 Prepare as for Basic White Sauce (see page 427) but add 2 tbsp of chopped fresh parsley to the sauce once cooked. Dried parsley won't do.
2 Serve with fish, chicken or vegetables.

Sauces for puddings

These sweet sauces are easy to make but a real treat.

Basic vanilla sauce

For a slightly thinner sauce, stir in an extra tablespoon or two of milk once cooked.

SERVES 4

3 tbsp cornflour (cornstarch)
1 mug of milk
¼ tsp vanilla essence (extract)
1 tbsp sugar

1 Mix the cornflour with a little of the milk in a saucepan with a wooden spoon or balloon whisk.

2 Stir in the remaining milk, the vanilla and sugar.

3 Bring to the boil over a high heat and cook, stirring, for 1 minute until thickened and smooth.

4 Serve with any hot puddings.

Cheat's custard

I usually use canned or carton custard, but if you haven't any (and don't have any custard powder), make this instead.

SERVES 4

Prepare as for Basic Vanilla Sauce (above) but add a few drops of yellow food colouring when mixing the milk and cornflour.

Peppermint custard

SERVES 4

Prepare as for Basic Vanilla Sauce (above) but add a few drops of peppermint essence (extract) and green food colouring and omit the vanilla. Serve it over Chocolate Walnut Brownies (see page 412).

Hot lemon sauce

SERVES 4–6

2 tbsp cornflour (cornstarch)
2 tbsp caster (superfine) sugar
1½ mugs of water
4 tbsp lemon juice

1 Blend the cornflour and sugar with a little of the water in a saucepan.

2 Add the remaining water and the lemon juice.

3 Bring to the boil over a high heat and cook for 2 minutes, stirring, until thickened and clear.

4 Serve hot with pancakes (see page 395) or fruit crumbles or pies (see pages 388–9).

Hot orange sauce

SERVES 4

1 Prepare as for Hot Lemon Sauce (above) but use pure orange juice instead of lemon juice.

2 Add a dash of lemon juice, if liked, to sharpen the taste.

3 Serve as for Hot Lemon Sauce.

Syrup sauce

SERVES 4

6 tbsp golden (light corn) syrup
2 tbsp lemon juice

1 Heat the syrup and lemon juice in a saucepan, stirring all the time, until hot but not boiling over a moderate heat.

2 Serve hot with rice pudding or Pineapple Upside-down Pudding (see page 393).

Velvet chocolate sauce

For a dark chocolate sauce, substitute cocoa powder for the drinking chocolate powder and add 1 tbsp of caster sugar, or more, to taste. For a slightly thinner sauce, stir in an extra tablespoon or two of milk once cooked.

SERVES 4

2 tbsp cornflour (cornstarch)
2 tbsp drinking (sweetened)
chocolate powder
1 mug of milk

1 Mix the cornflour and chocolate with a little of the milk in a saucepan with a wooden spoon.

2 Stir in the remaining milk.

3 Bring to the boil over a high heat and cook for 2 minutes, stirring all the time, until thickened and smooth.

Sauces for ice cream

You can make a simple block of ice cream into a full-blown dessert with a sauce and a sprinkling of nuts or grated chocolate.

Hot chocolate caramel sauce

For Caramel Sauce, make this with a Caramac bar and omit the chocolate powder.

SERVES 2–4

1 chocolate caramel bar
6 tbsp milk
1 tbsp butter or margarine
1 tbsp drinking (sweetened) chocolate powder

1 Cut the bar into pieces and place in a saucepan.

2 Add the remaining ingredients and heat gently, stirring all the time with a wooden spoon, until smooth and thickened.

3 Serve hot over ice cream.

Chocolate fudge sauce

SERVES 4

3 small fingers of chocolate fudge
A good knob of butter or margarine
3 tbsp milk

1 Break up the fingers of fudge and put them in a small saucepan with the butter or margarine and milk.

2 Heat, stirring, until blended and the bars have melted. Serve hot.

Instant chocolate sauce

You can make as much as you like!
Make sure you use drinking chocolate
powder with milk powder added – the
kind that makes an instant hot
chocolate drink. It's also good over
canned or fresh pears or bananas.

SERVES 1

*3 tbsp instant drinking (sweetened)
chocolate powder
Boiling water*

1 Put the instant chocolate powder in
a small jug or cup.

2 Using a wire whisk, whisk in
boiling water, 1 tsp at a time, to form
a smooth paste. Stop when you have a
thick, pouring consistency.

Mars bar dream

SERVES 4

*2 Mars bars
6 tbsp milk*

1 Break the Mars bars into pieces and
put in a saucepan with the milk.

2 Heat through, stirring all the time
with a wooden spoon, until melted
and thick.

Jam sauce

SERVES 4

*4 tbsp jam (conserve), any flavour
2 tbsp sugar
1 tbsp lemon juice
5 tbsp water*

1 Finely chop any pieces of fruit in
the jam.

2 Mix with all the ingredients in a
saucepan and cook over a moderate
heat, stirring all the time, until the
sugar has dissolved.

3 Continue to bubble gently for
2 minutes.

Pineapple and orange sauce

SERVES 4-6

*1 × 300 g/11 oz/medium can of crushed
pineapple, drained, reserving the juice
2 tsp cornflour (cornstarch)
½ mug of pure orange juice*

1 Put the crushed pineapple in a
saucepan. Mix the cornflour with a
little of the pineapple juice in a cup
and add to the pan with the
remaining pineapple juice and the
orange juice.

2 Bring to the boil over a high heat
and cook for 1 minute, stirring all the
time, until thickened and clear.

3 Serve hot.

Raspberry jelly sauce

SERVES 6

*1 tablet of raspberry-flavoured
jelly (jello)
¾ mug of water
1 tsp cornflour (cornstarch)*

1 Break up the jelly and put it in a
saucepan with most of the water.
Heat gently, stirring until dissolved.

2 Mix the cornflour with the
remaining water and stir into the
mixture. Bring to the boil, stirring
until slightly thickened and clear.
Serve hot.

Rainbow pineapple sauce

Add this to vanilla ice cream for Italian Cassata with a difference!

SERVES 4-6

1 × 300 g/11 oz/medium can of crushed pineapple
2 tbsp sugar
¼ small tub of glacé (candied) cherries, chopped
1 tbsp chopped angelica
1 tbsp currants
2 tsp cornflour (cornstarch)
4 tbsp water
1 tbsp lemon or lime juice

1 Put the pineapple in a saucepan and add the sugar, cherries, angelica and currants.

2 Mix the cornflour with the water in a cup, then add to the pan with the lemon or lime juice. Bring to the boil over a high heat, stirring all the time, and cook, stirring for 1 minute.

3 Serve hot over ice cream.

Raspberry sauce

SERVES 4

1 × 300 g/11 oz/medium can of raspberries
2 tsp cornflour (cornstarch)

1 Purée the raspberries and their juice with a hand blender or mash with a potato masher or fork.

2 For a smooth sauce, tip into a sieve (strainer) over a bowl and rub with a wooden spoon to press the fruit pulp through. Discard the seeds.

3 In a saucepan, mix a little of the raspberry purée with the cornflour until smooth using a wooden spoon. Stir in the remaining purée. Bring to the boil over a high heat and cook for 2 minutes, stirring all the time, until thickened and clear.

4 Serve hot or cold.

QUICK FIXES ... FROM HANGOVER CURES TO PARTY FOOD

Recognise these scenarios?

- You've got a hangover.
- You don't feel well and Mum isn't there to make you feel better.
- That essay deadline is imminent and you just can't formulate the sentences.
- You're having a party and you know you've got to have some nosh for when everyone starts looking for something to eat at 3 am.
- You want to cook a meal to impress someone, to celebrate a special occasion or to say 'sorry' for something (to a boyfriend/girlfriend/ your housemates or whoever).

Whatever your problem is, you'll find the solution here, the ideal recipe to cover the situation. This chapter contains a miscellaneous selection of ideas for all those times when you need inspiration.

Most of them are made from storecupboard standbys or things you have probably got in your fridge. It's a good idea to make sure, when you go shopping, that you pick up at least some of the extra ingredients, so that you'll always have them to hand, just in case ...

The morning after ...

A few ideas to help you feel better after a good night out.

ⓥ The vitamin reviver ⓥ

If you have a headache as well, dissolve a soluble painkiller in the drink or take one with it.

SERVES 1

1 glass of pure orange juice
1 tbsp lemon juice
1 tbsp clear honey
1 effervescent vitamin C tablet

1 Mix the fruit juices with the honey until the honey is dissolved.

2 Drop in the vitamin C tablet and stir until it is completely dissolved. Drink straight away.

The great British fry-up

The skill is to get everything into one frying pan. You don't need to cook masses. If it goes down well, you can always cook another lot because you'll be feeling so much better. And if it doesn't work, there's not point in wasting good food!

SERVES 1

2 tbsp sunflower oil
1 sausage
½ slice of bread
1 rasher (slice) of bacon, rinded
1 tomato, halved
1 egg
Tomato ketchup (catsup), brown table
sauce or Worcestershire sauce, to serve

1 Heat the oil in a fairly large frying pan (skillet). When hot but not smoking (see page 35), add the sausage and cook for about 2 minutes until browned on one side.

2 Turn the sausage over and add the bread, bacon and tomato halves. Cook for about 2 minutes until the bread, bacon and tomatoes are browned on one side, then turn them over.

3 Turn the sausage just a little, to cook the remaining pale part. Fry (sauté) everything for a further minute. Push the bread, bacon and tomato to one side of the pan as far from the heat as possible. Turn the sausage over so the last pale side is down.

4 Break the egg into the pan, or break it into a mug first, then slide it into the pan. Fry for 1–2 minutes until cooked to your liking, spooning any fat in the pan over the yolk as it cooks.

5 Transfer everything to a plate and eat with tomato ketchup, brown sauce or Worcestershire sauce.

Ⓥ The anti-sick cure Ⓥ

Ginger is a great cure for nausea. Buy the ginger beer when you buy the drinks for the party, but keep it hidden away for later emergencies.

SERVES 1

1 slice of bread
A very thin scraping of butter
or margarine
A tiny scraping of Marmite
or other yeast extract
1 glass of sparkling ginger beer

1 Toast the bread. Spread with the thinnest scraping of butter or margarine and Marmite. Cut into bite-sized squares.

2 Take a sip of ginger beer. Wait 30 seconds, then nibble a square of the toast. Repeat until you feel better, then polish off the rest!

Hot tomato Ⓥ pick-me-up Ⓥ

The Vitamin Reviver (see page 433) is also a great hangover cure, but here is a warm, soothing version.

SERVES 1

1 mug of tomato juice
1 tsp Marmite or other yeast extract
Worcestershire sauce

1 Put the tomato juice and Marmite in a pan and heat, stirring until the marmite dissolves.

2 When hot but not boiling, pour back into the mug and sprinkle with Worcestershire sauce.

Study sustenance

You're tired, fed-up, and know you've still got hours of work to do: that's when you need decadent comfort food that takes only a minute or two to make.

ⓥ Fairy bread ⓥ

Yes, this is an Aussie speciality, but it is very good (maybe it's all the e-numbers in the colourings that give you the added boost!). Two slices are usually enough to satisfy the cravings, but the quantities are up to you.

SERVES 1

Bread
Butter or margarine
Hundreds and thousands (also called Coloured strands or Sprinkles)

1 Spread the bread with butter or margarine.

2 Sprinkle liberally with a layer of Hundreds and thousands and press lightly into the bread with a knife to hold them in place.

3 Cut into quarters.

Chocolate spread and ⓥ banana sandwiches ⓥ

These really do help the brain to work – lots of carbs for sustained energy and plenty of chocolate – something we all need in a crisis!

SERVES 1

2 slices of bread
Butter or margarine
1 tbsp chocolate spread
1 banana, sliced

1 Spread the bread on one side with butter or margarine. Spread one slice with the chocolate spread, then add the sliced banana.

2 Sandwich together with the other slice of bread and cut in half.

ⓥ Indemnity dip ⓥ

These ingredients will provide all the sustenance you need.

SERVES 1

A few spoonfuls of thick plain yoghurt
2 tsp clear honey
1 small chocolate Flake bar, crumbled
1 eating (dessert) apple, quartered, cored and sliced
1 satsuma, peeled and segmented
A handful of dried apricots
A few pieces of crystallised (candied) ginger
2 digestive biscuits (graham crackers) or ginger nuts or 1 slice of ginger cake

1 Put the yoghurt in a small bowl and add enough of the honey to sweeten to taste. Stir in the Flake bar.

2 Put in the centre of a large plate. Arrange the fruits and biscuits around and enjoy dipping and munching to your heart's content.

ⓥ The wrap ⓥ

SERVES 1

1 flour tortilla
1 small carton of cottage cheese
1 carrot, peeled and grated
A handful of raisins
A handful of pine nuts
A pinch of ground ginger

1 Spread the tortilla with the cheese.

2 Top with grated carrot, then sprinkle with the raisins, pine nuts and ginger.

3 Fold in half, then fold again and eat.

ⓥ Nut reviver ⓥ

SERVES 1

A handful of whole almonds
Peanut butter
Clear honey

1 Put the three ingredients into separate little dishes on a tray. Find yourself a comfortable spot – the bed, the sofa or a floor full of cushions.

2 Take an almond, dip it in peanut butter to coat almost completely, then in the honey. Pop it into your mouth and let the peanut butter melt, then crunch the nut. Eat as many as you need to feel better!

ⓥ Condensed milk toast ⓥ

This is sticky, gooey and deliciously sinful!

MAKES UP TO 6 SLICES

Slices of bread
Butter or margarine
½ × 350 g/12 oz large can of sweetened condensed milk
Grated nutmeg (optional)

1 Toast the bread until well-browned.

2 Spread with butter or margarine, then condensed milk. Sprinkle with grated nutmeg, if liked, before cutting into quarters.

Late-night party munchies

It's okay providing a few crisps and nuts when you've got mates round to party – and we all know about putting out French bread, cheese, etc. to keep the booze mopped up. But when it comes to 3 am, everyone will be starving and, unless you have a take-away on the corner that stays open all night (which is a much more expensive option!), urgent action is required.

Here's how to be prepared. Earlier in the evening, put a load of sausages and/or frozen chicken nuggets in baking tins (pans) in the oven at 200°C/400°F/gas 6/fan oven 180°C and bake for about 30 minutes until golden, turning once if you remember. Drain off any excess fat when they've cooked. Lay out on plates cold frankfurters, breadsticks, tortilla chips, wedges of scotch egg, mini pork pies, loads of fingers of carrot and cucumber. Prepare lots of garlic bread (see page 439) and make a selection of dips. There are a few here to start you off and for more ideas, see pages 43–44. Then, when everyone's ready to start raiding the fridge, put it all out (it doesn't matter if the cooked nuggets and sausages have gone cold).

Simple thousand island dip

MAKES 1 SMALL POT

4 good tbsp mayonnaise
1 tbsp tomato ketchup (catsup)
¹/₂ tsp Worcestershire sauce
Pepper
A few drops of Tabasco sauce

Mix all the ingredients together with a spoon in a small bowl and use as required.

Ⓥ Piquant dip Ⓥ

MAKES 1 SMALL POT

6 stuffed green olives, finely chopped
1 spring onion (scallion), trimmed and finely chopped
5 tbsp mayonnaise
2 tbsp tomato ketchup (catsup)
A few drops of Tabasco sauce
Salt and pepper

Mix all the ingredients together in a small bowl and chill until ready to serve.

Ⓥ Aioli Ⓥ

MAKES 1 SMALL POT

6 tbsp mayonnaise
2 garlic cloves, peeled and crushed, or 2 tsp garlic purée (paste)
¹/₂ tsp lemon juice
A few drops of Tabasco sauce
Salt and pepper

Mix all the ingredients together in a small bowl and chill until ready to serve.

Ⓥ Curry dip Ⓥ

MAKES 1 SMALL POT

1 small carton of plain yoghurt
1 × 170 g/6 oz/small can of cream
2 tbsp mayonnaise
1 tbsp curry powder or paste

Mix all the ingredients together in a small bowl.

Ⓥ Marguerita bites Ⓥ

MAKES ABOUT 15 SQUARES

1 packet of pizza base mix
3 tbsp tomato purée (paste)
¹/₂ tsp dried oregano
4 ripe tomatoes, sliced
2 tbsp olive oil
Pepper
3 good handfuls of grated Mozzarella or Cheddar cheese
8 fresh basil leaves, torn
A few black olives

1 Make up the pizza base mix as directed on the packet. Preheat the oven to 220°C/425°F/gas 7/fan oven 200°C.

2 Using a rolling pin (or clean bottle), roll out the dough to as large a rectangle as possible and place on an oiled baking (cookie) sheet.

3 Spread with the tomato purée and sprinkle with the oregano.

4 Top with the tomato slices and trickle half the oil over the surface. Add plenty of pepper.

5 Bake in the oven for 10 minutes. Top with the cheese, trickle the remaining oil over and scatter the basil and olives over. Bake for a further 10 minutes or until golden round the edges and the cheese has melted and is bubbling. Serve hot.

Ham and mushroom pizza bites

MAKES ABOUT 15 SQUARES

Prepare as for Marguerita Bites (see page 437) but add 4 slices of chopped, cooked ham and 3–4 sliced mushrooms to the topping before adding the cheese.

Ham and pineapple pizza bites

MAKES ABOUT 15 SQUARES

Prepare as for Marguerita Bites (see page 437) but add a drained 225 g/ 8 oz/ small can of pineapple chunks and 2–3 slices of chopped, cooked ham before adding the cheese.

Pepper and sweetcorn Ⓥ bites Ⓥ

MAKES ABOUT 15 SQUARES

Prepare as for Marguerita Bites (see page 437) but add 1 (bell) pepper, sliced, and a 200 g/7 oz/small can of sweetcorn (corn), drained, before adding the cheese.

Anchovy and olive bites

MAKES ABOUT 15 SQUARES

Make as for Marguerita Bites (see page 437) but arrange a 50 g/2 oz/ small can of anchovies in a criss-cross pattern and scatter a few olives over the top of the cheese-covered pizza.

Ⓥ Quick nachos Ⓥ

SERVES ABOUT 8

1 large bag of tortilla chips
1 jar of chilli salsa sauce
4 good handfuls of grated Cheddar cheese

1 Spread the tortilla chips out in a large, shallow, flameproof dish.

2 Spread the sauce over the tortillas and sprinkle with the cheese.

3 Grill (broil) for about 3 minutes, turning the dish round as necessary, until all the cheese has melted.

4 Serve straight away.

Ⓥ Tortilla potato slab Ⓥ

I was given this at a friend's barbecue, as a nibble while the food was cooking – it was fantastic! It's also great served hot, for a main meal. If eating on your own, you can eat part of it hot, then have the rest cold over the next few days with salads or pickles. Ring the changes by using courgettes or large carrots, grated, instead of the potatoes.

MAKES ABOUT 40 SQUARES

2 good handfuls of grated Cheddar cheese
1 large onion, peeled and grated
3 medium potatoes, peeled and grated
1 mug of plain (all-purpose) flour
5 eggs
½ mug of sunflower oil
1 tsp ground cumin
1 tsp dried oregano
A good sprinkling each of salt and pepper

1 Preheat the oven to 190°C/375°F/ gas 5/fan oven 170°C.

2 Mix all the ingredients together in a bowl.

3 Grease an 18 cm × 28 cm/7 in × 11 in shallow baking tin (pan) or similar-sized ovenproof dish. Pour in the mixture and spread out evenly.

4 Bake for about 40 minutes until firm to the touch and golden brown.

5 Serve cut into pieces.

ⓥ Garlic bread ⓥ

Everyone loves it. Make up as many loaves as you need in advance, keep them wrapped in foil, then pop them in the oven just before you're ready to eat them. They're better than bought ones because they're much oozier!

SERVES 4-6

1 small baguette
¹/₄ × 250 g/9 oz block or tub of butter or soft margarine
1-2 garlic cloves, peeled and crushed, or 1-2 tsp garlic purée (paste)

1 Preheat the oven to 200°C/400°F/ gas 6/fan oven 180°C.

2 Cut the bread into 12 slices, not quite through the base crust.

3 Mash the butter or margarine with the garlic.

4 Spread between each slice and over the top.

5 Wrap in foil and bake in the oven for about 15 minutes until the crust feels crisp and the centre soft when squeezed.

Garlic and herb ⓥ baguette ⓥ

SERVES 4-6

Prepare as for Garlic Bread (left), but add 1 tsp dried mixed herbs and a handful of chopped fresh parsley to the mixture.

Treating yourself

So you don't feel well and you're missing your mum. Time for those little touches that make you feel better.

Fluffy convalescent's ⓥ omelette ⓥ

This is really tempting when you're beginning to feel better but aren't yet that hungry. It is so light it almost melts in the mouth. Make the hot chocolate while the omelette is cooking, then snuggle down in front of the telly in your dressing gown and slippers.

SERVES 1

2 eggs
2 tbsp water
Salt and pepper
A knob of butter or margarine
Bread and butter and a mug of hot chocolate, to serve

1 Separate the eggs.

2 Beat the yolks with a pinch of salt and pepper and the water.

3 Whisk the egg whites until stiff with a hand blender or balloon whisk, then stir gently into the yolk mixture.

4 Heat a knob of butter or margarine in an omelette pan over a moderate heat. Add the egg mixture.

5 Cook until the base of the omelette is golden brown. Meanwhile, preheat the grill (broiler).

6 Place the pan under the grill and cook until the omelette is risen and golden on top, 2-3 minutes.

7 Fold in half and slide on to a plate.

8 Serve with bread and butter and a mug of steaming hot chocolate.

Filled fluffy convalescent's 🔽 omelette 🔽

SERVES 1

Use any of the fillings suggested for omelettes on pages 146–47. Prepare as for Fluffy Convalescent's Omelette (see page 439). Either mix the filling gently into the egg mixture before cooking or spread over the browned omelette, then heat through under the grill (broiler).

Sweet fluffy convalescent's 🔽 omelette 🔽

SERVES 1

Prepare as for Fluffy Convalescent's Omelette (see page 439) but omit the salt and pepper and whisk 1 tbsp sugar into the whisked egg whites. When cooked, spread with a little jam (conserve) or honey, then fold and serve. Dust with a little sugar before serving.

🔽 Hot lemon and honey 🔽

This is excellent when you've got a really bad cold and you feel horrible. Make this up and retire to bed with a hot water bottle and a box of tissues.

SERVES 1

¼ mug of bottled lemon juice
Boiling water
1–2 tbsp clear honey
1–2 pain killers

1 Measure the lemon juice into a mug.

2 Top up with boiling water, then stir in honey to taste (it should be sweet yet sharp).

3 Sip while hot, then, when cooker, use to wash down the pain killers.

Boiled egg and 🔽 soldiers 🔽

If you're having hot milk, prepare it before you cook the egg. Heat it in a saucepan, watching it all the time, until just about to boil (before it rises up the pan). Alternatively, put the mug of milk in the microwave and cook on High (100 per cent power) for 1–1½ minutes until really hot, then stir once before drinking.

SERVES 1

1 egg
1 slice of bread
Butter or margarine
Marmite or other yeast extract (optional)
Pepper
1 mug of hot or cold milk

1 Put the egg in a small pan and add just enough water to cover. Cover with a lid and bring to the boil.

2 As soon as the water boils, time it for exactly 3½ minutes.

3 Meanwhile, toast the bread and add butter or margarine and Marmite, if liked. Cut the toast into four fingers.

4 Cut the top off the egg to expose the yolk, then dip in the soldiers and eat them first. Season the rest of the egg with pepper and eat with a spoon.

Chicken soup comforter

SERVES 1

*1 × 300 g/11 oz/medium can of
cream of chicken soup
1 tbsp single (light) cream
A pinch of dried parsley
1 soft bread roll
Lemon barley water*

1 Heat the soup in a saucepan until piping hot but not boiling. Alternatively, tip it into a bowl and heat in the microwave on High (100 per cent power) for 1–2 minutes until piping hot, stirring once or twice.

2 Pour into a soup bowl, if necessary. Add a spoonful of cream and a sprinkling of parsley.

3 Put it on a tray with a spoon, the bread roll on a plate and a glass of Lemon Barley and curl up in front of the TV or go back to bed!

Ⓥ Cheat's chocolate cake Ⓥ

You're not going to knock up a cake when you're feeling poorly so this is the next best thing.

SERVES 1

*4 digestive biscuits (graham crackers)
Chocolate spread
1 tbsp chopped walnut pieces
1 mug of tea or coffee*

1 Spread the digestives thickly with chocolate spread and stack on top of each other.

2 Sprinkle the top with the nuts and eat with a mug of tea or coffee.

Tomato soup Ⓥ appetite-tempter Ⓥ

Try this when you're on the road to recovery – when you're beginning to feel hungry!

SERVES 1

*1 × 300 g/11 oz/medium can of
cream of tomato soup
1 tomato, chopped
A handful of grated Cheddar cheese
A hunk of crusty bread
A can of cola*

1 Heat the soup with the tomato in a saucepan until piping hot but not boiling. Alternatively, put it in a bowl and cook in the microwave on High (100 per cent power) for 1–2 minutes until piping hot.

2 Tip it into a bowl if necessary and smother with the grated cheese.

3 Dunk the crusty bread in the soup, then eat the rest with a spoon and wash it down with a can of cola.

Posh nosh

Finally, there will be a few occasions when you will think it's actually worth while making a proper celebration dinner. Here are a few simple ideas for really great three-course menus that won't break the bank but will impress your guests!

Menu 1

ⓥ Pears in blue cheese ⓥ

Half a standard-sized, pre-wrapped wedge of cheese will be just the right amount.

SERVES 4

1 mug of crumbled Danish Blue cheese
4 tbsp mayonnaise
3 tbsp crème fraîche
1 tsp lemon juice
Salt and pepper
4 ripe pears
Lettuce leaves
1 tbsp milk
1 tsp dried chives
A little paprika, to garnish

1 Mash the cheese with 1 tbsp of the mayonnaise until fairly smooth.

2 Briskly stir in the remaining mayonnaise, the crème fraîche, lemon juice, salt and pepper to taste.

3 Peel, halve and core the pears. Lay them, rounded sides up, on beds of lettuce arranged on individual plates.

4 Thin the blue cheese mayonnaise with the milk and stir in the chives. Spoon the dressing over the pears and sprinkle with paprika. Chill until ready to serve.

Lamb steaks with mint jus and leek mash

SERVES 4

4 medium potatoes, peeled
2 large leeks
2 tbsp butter or margarine
4 lamb steaks
Salt and pepper
2 large carrots, peeled
2 courgettes (zucchini)
4 tsp cornflour (cornstarch)
2 tbsp bottled garden mint
1 tsp clear honey

1 Cut the potato into small, even-sized chunks. Place in a pan of cold, lightly salted water.

2 Trim the leeks, cut almost right through from the green end to the white and wash well under running water. Chop and add to the potatoes.

3 Pare the carrots and courgettes into thin strips with a potato peeler. Place in a colander over the potato pan. Bring to the boil, reduce the heat, part-cover and simmer for about 8 minutes until all the vegetables are tender.

4 Lift off the colander of carrots and courgettes, transfer them to a dish, cover with foil or a lid and keep warm in a very low oven.

5 Drain the potatoes and leeks in the colander over a bowl, reserving the cooking liquid. Tip them back in the saucepan.

6 Using a potato masher or fork, mash the potatoes and leeks with half the butter or margarine. Put the lid on the saucepan and keep warm in the oven.

7 Melt the remaining butter or margarine and smear over the lamb steaks on both sides. Season lightly.

8 Place on foil on the grill (broiler) rack and grill (broil) for 5–8 minutes on each side until cooked to your liking. Transfer to a plate and keep warm.

9 Tip the cooking juices on the foil into a small saucepan and scrape any sediment off the foil. Stir in the cornflour and garden mint. Measure 1½ mugs of the potato and leek cooking water into the pan and stir to blend completely. Add the honey. Bring to the boil, and cook for 1 minute, stirring all the time. Season to taste.

10 Spoon the leek mash in domes in the centre of four warm plates. Top each pile with a lamb steak. Spoon the mint jus over and put a small pile of carrot and courgette on top. Serve straight away.

Ⓥ Chocolate cups Ⓥ

This is a complete cheat but is so impressive, everyone will think you've slaved away for ages! It will stretch to fill six cases if you need it to.

SERVES 4

1 small carton of whipping cream
2 tbsp chocolate and hazelnut
(filbert) spread
1 tbsp brandy or any liqueur
4 ready-made chocolate cases
4 toasted hazelnuts, to decorate
2 kiwi fruit, peeled and sliced

1 Put the cream in a bowl and whip

with a hand blender or balloon whisk until standing in soft peaks.

2 Add the chocolate spread and brandy or liqueur and whisk gently again until blended.

3 Spoon into the chocolate cases and top each with a hazelnut. Chill until firm.

4 To serve, put a chocolate case on each plate and lay two or three slices of kiwi fruit to one side.

Menu 2
Ⓥ Italian egg salad Ⓥ

For this recipe you want Mozzarella cheeses that are about the size of a large egg.

SERVES 4

4 eggs
4 beefsteak tomatoes,
each cut into 6 slices
2 whole Mozzarella cheeses,
each cut into 6 slices
12 stoned (pitted) black olives
8 fresh basil leaves, torn
2 tbsp olive oil
1 tbsp red wine or balsamic vinegar
Pepper, preferably freshly ground black

1 Hard-boil (hard-cook) the eggs, then place immediately in a bowl of cold water to cool. Shell and slice the eggs.

2 Arrange the slices of tomato, egg and cheese overlapping each other attractively on four plates. Scatter the olives and basil over.

3 Trickle the oil and vinegar over the salads and sprinkle with pepper. Serve.

Shiraz beef with seeded roast potatoes

You can, of course use any other red wine and change the recipe name!

SERVES 4

700 g/1½ lb lean braising steak,
all fat removed, diced
2 tbsp plain (all-purpose) flour
Salt and pepper
2 rashers (slices) of streaky bacon,
rinded and diced
1 garlic clove, peeled and crushed,
or 1 tsp garlic purée (paste)
1 large onion, peeled, halved and
thinly sliced
12 button mushrooms, wiped
but left whole
1 mug of Shiraz red wine
1 mug of beef stock,
made with 1 stock cube
1 tbsp tomato purée
1 bay leaf
½ tsp dried mixed herbs
12–16 smallish potatoes, scrubbed
2 tbsp sunflower or olive oil
2 tbsp poppy or sesame seeds
1 tbsp chopped fresh parsley,
to garnish
A large head of broccoli, cut into florets

1 Preheat the oven to 160°C/325°F/ gas 3/fan oven 145°C.

2 Put the flour with a little salt and pepper in a plastic bag. Add the meat and shake well to coat. Place in a large flameproof casserole dish (Dutch oven) with all the remaining ingredients, except the potatoes, oil and seeds.

3 Bring to the boil, stirring gently. Cover with the lid and transfer to the oven.

4 While the meat is cooking, cut the potatoes in half. Place in a roasting tin (pan) and add the oil. Turn the potatoes over in the oil to coat completely, then sprinkle with the seeds and a little salt. When the meat has been in the oven for 1½ hours, put the potatoes on the shelf near the top of the oven. Cook everything for about 1 more hour until the meat is really tender.

5 Just before the casserole is ready, put a pan of water on to boil and add a pinch of salt. Cook the broccoli for 4–5 minutes until just tender but still bright green and with some 'bite'. Drain in a colander in the sink, then put back over the saucepan and cover with the lid to keep warm.

6 When the casserole is cooked, stir well, remove the bay leaf, taste and add more salt and pepper if necessary.

7 Sprinkle the casserole with the parsley and serve with the seeded potatoes and broccoli.

Bananas with Ⓥ hot lemon sauce Ⓥ

SERVES 4

4 tbsp butter or margarine
6 tbsp clear honey
2 tbsp lemon juice
1 large carton of Greek-style yoghurt
4 bananas
2 tbsp toasted flaked (slivered) almonds

1 Put the butter or margarine in a small saucepan with the honey and lemon juice. Bring to the boil and bubble for 2–3 minutes until slightly thickened.

2 Spoon the yoghurt into four glasses. Peel the bananas, slice and pile on top of the yoghurt. Spoon the sauce over and sprinkle with toasted almonds before serving.

Menu 3

Prawn cocktail

SERVES 4

4 tbsp mayonnaise
2 tbsp single (light) cream
1 tbsp tomato ketchup (catsup)
1 tsp Worcestershire sauce
A few drops of Tabasco sauce
Pepper
½ round lettuce, shredded
1 mug of frozen cooked peeled prawns
(shrimp), thawed and drained on
kitchen paper (paper towels)
Paprika, for dusting
4 slices of lemon, to garnish
Brown bread and butter, to serve

1 Mix the mayonnaise in a small bowl with the cream, ketchup, Worcestershire and Tabasco sauces and pepper to taste.

2 Put the lettuce into four wine goblets.

3 Top with the prawns, then the sauce.

4 Sprinkle the top with a dusting of paprika. Make a cut from the centre to one edge of each lemon slice and hang one over the rim of each glass.

5 Serve with brown bread and butter.

Chicken in red wine

The brandy is optional, but really makes a difference to the flavour. You can also use vodka, if you prefer.

SERVES 4

1 tbsp olive oil
A good knob of butter or margarine
4 chicken portions or breasts
2 rashers (slices) of rindless streaky
bacon, diced
1 large onion, peeled and
roughly chopped
3 tbsp plain (all-purpose) flour
12 button mushrooms
1½ mugs of red wine
½ mug of chicken stock,
made with ½ stock cube
Salt and pepper
1 tbsp brandy
1 bouquet garni sachet
1 tbsp chopped fresh parsley, to garnish
French bread and a Green Salad
(see page 45), to serve

1 Preheat the oven to 180°C/350°F/ gas 4/fan oven 160°C.

2 Heat the oil with the butter or margarine in a flameproof casserole (Dutch oven) over a fairly high heat. Brown the chicken portions on all sides and remove.

3 Add the bacon and onions and cook quickly, stirring, until lightly browned.

4 Stir the flour into the bacon mixture and cook for 1 minute, stirring. Remove from the heat and gradually stir in the wine and stock. Return to the heat and bring to the boil, stirring (don't worry if it is still slightly lumpy). Return the chicken to the casserole and add the mushrooms. Season with salt and pepper and add the brandy and bouquet garni sachet.

5 Cover and cook in the oven for 1¼ hours. When the chicken is cooked, stir gently, remove the bouquet garni sachet, taste and re-season, if necessary.

6 Sprinkle with chopped parsley and serve hot with French bread and a Green Salad.

Ⓥ Baked peach brûlée Ⓥ

SERVES 4

1 × 425 g/15 oz/large can of peach
slices, drained, reserving the juice
2 tsp cornflour (cornstarch)
1 tsp lemon juice
1 small carton of plain yoghurt
1 large egg
1/2 tsp ground cinnamon
3 tbsp sugar, preferably light brown

1 Preheat the oven to 180°C/350°F/
gas 4/fan oven 160°C.

2 Put the peaches in a shallow
ovenproof dish.

3 Using a balloon whisk, mix the
cornflour with a little of the reserved
juice in a saucepan. Stir in the
remaining peach juice and the lemon
juice. Bring to the boil, stirring until
thickened and clear. Allow to bubble
for 1 minute. Pour over the peaches.

4 Use the same whisk to blend the
yoghurt with the egg and cinnamon.
Pour over the peaches.

5 Bake towards the top of the oven
for about 20 minutes until the custard
is set.

6 Preheat the grill (broiler). Sprinkle
the top of the pudding liberally with
the sugar and place under the grill
until the sugar melts, bubbles and
turns a rich brown.

7 Serve warm.

Menu 4
Antipasto speciality

SERVES 4

8 thin slices of Milano salami
8 thin slices of Mortadella
1 small melon
2 tbsp olive oil
Freshly ground black pepper
1 lemon, cut into small wedges
Crusty bread, to serve

1 Arrange the meats attractively on
individual plates.

2 Halve the melon and remove the
seeds. Cut each half into six wedges.
Cut off the rind.

3 Arrange three wedges beside the
meats on each plate.

4 Scatter the olives over, drizzle with
olive oil and add some freshly ground
black pepper. Put a lemon wedge on
each plate and serve with French
bread.

Chicken and cranberry pouches

SERVES 4

1 tbsp sunflower oil
4 skinless chicken breasts
4 large sheets of filo pastry (paste)
1/4 × 250 g/9 oz block or tub of butter or
margarine, melted
Salt and pepper
1/2 tsp dried thyme
4 tbsp cranberry sauce
1 × 295 g/10 1/2 oz/medium can of
condensed cream of mushroom soup
16–20 new potatoes, scrubbed
1 1/2 mugs of mangetout (snow peas),
topped and tailed
Sprigs of fresh parsley, to garnish

1 Heat the oil in a frying pan (skillet) over a high heat. Add the chicken breasts and cook for 4 minutes until lightly browned underneath. Turn over and cook for a further 4 minutes until lightly browned on the other side. Remove from the pan with a fish slice and place on a plate to cool while preparing the pastry.

2 Preheat the oven to 190°C/375°F/ gas 5/fan oven 170°C.

3 Lay the sheets of pastry on a board and smear with some of the butter or margarine. Fold in half and smear again.

4 Put a cooled chicken breast in the centre of each piece of pastry. Sprinkle with salt and pepper and the thyme. Top each with 2 tsp of cranberry sauce, then add the mushroom soup.

5 Draw the pastry up over the filling and pinch together to form pouches. Smear a baking (cookie) sheet with a little of the remaining butter or margarine and arrange the pouches on it.

6 Smear the pouches all over with the remaining butter or margarine and bake in the oven for about 15 minutes or until golden brown and cooked through.

7 Cook the potatoes and mangetout in boiling water in separate pans with a pinch of salt added. Cook the potatoes for about 10 minutes, the mangetout for 3 minutes. Drain in a colander in the sink.

8 Use a fish slice to lift the pouches on to warm plates. Garnish each with a spoonful of the remaining cranberry sauce and a sprig of parsley and serve with the new potatoes and mangetout.

ⓥ Strawberry sparkle ⓥ

Serve with triangles of shortbread.

SERVES 4

1 × 225 g/8 oz/medium punnet of strawberries, hulled and sliced
4 tsp sugar
4 tsp lime or lemon juice
½ bottle of sparkling wine, chilled

1 Put the strawberries into four wine glasses.

2 Sprinkle with the sugar and add a squeeze of lime or lemon juice to each.

3 Chill for at least 30 minutes.

4 When ready to serve, top up with the sparkling wine and serve straight away.

INDEX